THE GUPTA POLITY

THE GUPTA POLITY

V. R. Ramachandra Dikshitar

MOTILAL BANARSIDASS PUBLISHERS
PRIVATE LIMITED • DELHI

First Edition: Madras, 1952
Reprint: Delhi, 1993

ISBN: 81-208-1024-4

Also available at:

MOTILAL BANARSIDASS

41 U.A. Bungalow Road, Jawahar Nagar, Delhi 110 007
120 Royapettah High Road, Mylapore, Madras 600 004
16 St. Mark's Road, Bangalore 560 001
Ashok Rajpath, Patna 800 004
Chowk, Varanasi 221 001

PRINTED IN INDIA

BY JAINENDRA PRAKASH JAIN AT SHRI JAINENDRA PRESS, A-45 NARAINA INDUSTRIAL AREA, PHASE I, NEW DELHI 110 028 AND PUBLISHED BY NARENDRA PRAKASH JAIN FOR MOTILAL BANARSIDASS PUBLISHERS PVT. LTD., BUNGALOW ROAD, JAWAHAR NAGAR, DELHI 110 007

CONTENTS

PREFACE

Ever since the publication of my *Mauryan Polity* by the University of Madras in 1932 I had been thinking of bringing out a book on Gupta Polity as a companion volume to it. But owing to my pre-occupation with the preparation of a comprehensive index for the major historical 'Purāṇas, the first volume of which was published by the Madras University last year, I could not complete my work on the Gupta Polity till very recently.

As will be seen from the book, the sources of information for a study of the subject are not, after all, many as compared with the sources for a study of the Mauryan administrative institutions. I have come to the irresistible conclusion that Kalidāsa, the prince among the Indian poets, was not a prótegé of the Gupta court, but lived in the 2nd century B.C. and so his prolific works cannot be taken to throw any light on the machinery of government and administration in the Gupta empire. One has therefore to depend mainly on the Kāmandakīya Nītisāra, the inscriptions and coins of the Gupta rulers besides the accounts of the Chinese pilgrim Fa-hién for a knowledge of the Gupta Polity.

One chapter is devoted to the examination of the extent of the Gupta empire. It is shown that it included not only considerable territories in the Deccan and South India but also colonies in the Far East. Two chapters are devoted to an account of the central administration. Another chapter is on the military organisation and another to provincial government.

The religious conditions in the Gupta empire are considered in a separate chapter. It is my firm conviction that the imperial Guptas were not really Vaiṣṇavas as they are usually taken to be but were Smārtas by religion worshipping different Gods like Śiva, Viṣṇu, Kārttikeya and Devī.

I am deeply indebted to the Vice-Chancellor and the Syndicate of the Madras University for publishing the work under the University Historical Series.

My thanks are due to Mr. V. Vriddhagirisan, M.A., M.Litt., for preparing the index.

UNIVERSITY BUILDINGS,
MADRAS–5
1st September, 1952.

V. R. R. DIKSHITAR.

CHAPTER I

SOURCES OF INFORMATION

Section I—Contemporary Literature

Among the contemporary literary records the Purāṇas occupy the foremost position. The bias with which this class of literature was looked upon by early Indologists, has been slowly given up and modern scholarship treats the Purāṇas as transmitting genuine historical tradition. A closer examination of the dynastic accounts set forth in the Purāṇas by scholars like Pargiter, Kirfel and Jayaswal has enabled them to arrive at the definite conclusion, that the Purāṇic accounts relating to the political history of the period are trustworthy material, which could be safely drawn upon. Though there are as many as eighteen major Purāṇas, still for our purpose the Vāyu, Brahmāṇḍa, Matsya, Viṣṇu, and Bhāgavata may be pressed into service. The theory[1] that the Bhaviṣya was the first Purāṇa to furnish an account of the dynasties of the Kali Age, and that the other Purāṇas like the Vāyu, Brahmāṇḍa and Matsya copied it, is not quite acceptable. We need not go into this question here. Suffice it to say that these Purāṇas treat of the dynasties that ruled in India over a long period covering several centuries before the Christian era and the first four centuries after. The accounts in the Vāyu and Brahmāṇḍa are almost similar, as also those in the Viṣṇu and Bhāgavata. The Matsya generally agrees with the older accounts of the Vāyu and Brahmāṇḍa.

We are at present concerned with the history of India in the early fourth century A.D. This was the period of the rise of the Imperial Guptas. It is reasonable to suppose

1. F. E. Pargiter: *The Purāṇa Text of the Dynasties of the Kali Age*—Introduction, p. XXVI (Oxford, 1912.)

that the version of these Purāṇas was compiled again in the reign of Samudra Gupta. For it reflects the political condition of India in the early fourth century A.D. and especially in the epoch of Samudra Gupta.[2]

Among the historical Purāṇas, the Matsya account stops with the fall of the Āndhras as an imperial power. It is particularly interesting to note that the dynastic accounts given in the Purāṇas are all concerned with the imperial line of kings. But the Vāyu and the Brahmāṇḍa deal with the successors of the Imperial Āndhras. They were the Vindhyaka or the Vākāṭaka line of kings. In this line, Vindhyaśakti and his son Pravīra are prominently mentioned. After Pravìra, began the great Gupta line of emperors. This was also the period, according to the Vāyu and Brahmāṇḍa, when the Nāgas who were ruling in Bihar declined. But the version as seen in the Viṣṇu Purāṇa shows that the Guptas rose to power even when the Nāgas were reigning.

नव नागा: तु भोक्ष्यन्ति पुरीं चम्पावतीम् नृपा: (Br. III, 74. 194)

This is a very significant statement. For this definitely places the Nava Nāgas as the contemporaries of the Guptas. This also indirectly helps us to picture the political map of India in the early fourth century A.D. Padmāvatī, Kāntipurī and Mathurā were the important cities of the Nava Nāgas. What is more significant is the information it furnishes about the Guptas. The Guptas are styled Magadha Guptas who are said to be in the enjoyment of the territory of Anugangā-prayāga. From this the late Jayaswal makes out that the Guptas, especially the predecessors of Samudra Gupta were ruling from Magadha and were the natives of Magadha. Having been dispossessed of Magadha they ruled from Allahabad and that not on the Jumna side but on the Ganges

2. *Ibid.*, Intro. XII; *contra* D. C. Ganguly, *I.H.Q.*, XXI 2, pp. 141-3.

side, *i.e.* on the side of Oudh and Benares.[3] Another plausible interpretation is that the early Guptas of Magadha extended their sway to the Anugangā-prayāga region during the reign of the Nava Nāgas who are identified with the Bhāraśivas.

The following is the account in the Vāyu and Brahmāṇḍa of the contemporary Guptas of this early period.

Nava Nāgās tu bhokṣyanti purīm Campāvatīm nṛpāḥ
Mathurām ca purīm ramyām Nāgā bhokṣyanti sapta vai
Anu-Gangā Prayāgām ca Sāketam Magadhāms tathā
etān janapadān sarvān bhokṣyante Sapta-vamsa-jāḥ
Naiṣadhān Yadukāms caiva Saiśitān Kūlatoyakān
etān janapadān sarvān bhokṣyante maṇidhānya-jān
Kośalāms ca Āndhra, Pauṇdrāms ca Tāmraliptān sa-sāgarān
Campām caiva purīm ramyām bhokṣyante Devarakṣitaḥ
Kalinga Mahiṣāś caiva Mahendra-nilayāś ca ye
etān janapadān sarvān pālayiṣyati vai Guhaḥ
Strīrāstrānbhojakāms caiva bhokṣyate Kanakāhvayah
Saurāṣṭr-Āvanty-Ābhirāś ca
Śūdrā Arbuda-Mālavāḥ
tulya-kālam bhaviṣyanti
sarve hi ete mahīkṣitaḥ ||
alpa-prāsāda hi anṛtā
mahā-krodhā hi adhārmikāḥ. |

The above texts shed a good deal of light on the empire of the Guptas and its extent. They also give us detailed information about the provinces of the empire and their extent. The texts further make a nice distinction between the territories that formed an integral part of the empire and those that were outside the direct jurisdiction of the empire. Those territories which were beyond the scope of direct imperial sway

3. K. P. Jayaswal: *History of India* 150-350 A.D., p. 123.

were, first, the Strīrāṣtra, Bhōjaka, Trairājya and Mūsika ruled over by the dynasty of Kanaka, secondly, the Ābhāras of Surāṣtra and Avanti, thirdly, the Sūras, fourthly, the Mālavas of the Arbuda and fifthly, Sindhu Chandrabhāga, and Kashmir. Thus we can infer that the Gupta empire under Samudra Gupta did not include the above states and cities. Among the five groups of states outside the provinces of the Gupta empire, the second, third and fourth, *viz.* the Ābhīras, Sūras and Mālavas, are characterised by the Bhāgavata Purāṇa as belonging to the category of the Vrātyadvija, meaning members of the twice-born castes who having fallen from their *svadharma* and become vrātyas were almost enjoying the status of the Śūdra caste. The fifth group of countries above mentioned is characterised as being occupied by what are known as the *Mleccha-śūdras.* This is the statement of the Viṣṇu Purāṇa (IV. 24.69). Jayaswal's interpretation is ingenious. The people in these countries were *Mlecchas* or aliens to India, but they had gained the status of Hindu Śūdras after their permanent settlement on the Indian soil.[4]

The Purānas again help us in locating the names of kings and the minor dynasties as well as in identifying places. For example, according to the Vāyu and Brahmāṇḍa, the first ruler of the Magadha Kula, considered to be a feudatory family (Vā: 99, 386: Br. III 74-198), was one Guha. The Visṇu Purāṇa gives a different form of the name, namely Guhan, or Guham. This family was ruling from Kalinga as testified to by the *Dāṭhā-vamśa* (ed. by B.C. Law 1925). The Purāṇas enable us to conclude that a name like Guha is not that of a dynasty but only a personal name. The same applies to another name Kanaka mentioned among the independent states outside the Gupta empire. This Kanaka, too, must be interpreted as the name of the ruler of a territory and it does not refer to a particular dynasty. The Purānas also

4. Jayaswal, *op. cit.*, pp. 124-5.

aid us in fixing up the period of the rise of some of the small states either as independent ones or within the empire. We shall examine these in detail in the chapter on the extent of the empire and also in the sequel. In the same way the identification of a place like Śaśikas is quite possible on the evidence of the Purāṇa texts. The locality of this place is furnished by the Viṣṇu Purāṇa.[5]

Thus the Purāṇas are an invaluable source for the early history of the Imperial Guptas. An account of Samudra Gupta's empire is furnished but it is not full. This leads us to infer that this section of the Purānic account was redacted during the reign of Samudra Gupta and not after the end of his rule. For instance, the Punjab is not included in his empire. The account stops with the death of King Rudrasena (Rudradeva) of the Vākāṭaka empire. The last incident of the Purāṇic account is the disappearance and death of Rudrasena. This must have occurred in the year 348-349 A.D. It is reasonable to suppose that the Purāṇas should have been recast about 350 A.D. and not later. By giving a fuller account of the contemporaries of Samudra Gupta in the first half of his reign, such as the history of the Nāgas and Vākātakas, of the Śakas in Sindh and the W. Punjab, the Purāṇas put us in definite possession of facts about the political India of the early half of the fourth century A.D.

Analysing the evidence of the Purāṇas, we find that the Guptas especially Candra Gupta I ruled over Prayāga (Allahabad), Sāketā (Ayodhyā) and Magadha. The non-inclusion of Sāketā in some texts of the Viṣṇu Purāṇa and the inclusion of Suhma of West Bengal in some *mss.* of the same Purāṇa need not deter us. For the matter of that, the Bhāgavata does not mention Magadha, while it speaks of the source of the Gangā and Prayāga. On this account we cannot

5. Wilson, p. 189 (London, 1840).

rule out that Magadha was not a part of the kingdom of the early Guptas. At best we have to collate all the available materials and come to some definite conclusion. It is reasonable to conclude that the Vāyu Purāṇa provides a basis to start with, and this we can accept without any reservation. Whenever we get material to supplement this information, we shall do so provided authentic evidence exists.

The Evidence of the Dharma Śāstras

Though the Gupta Age is considered to be the golden age of Hinduism, it is surprising to find a dearth of literary production in the age. The accredited authority of the *Mānava dharmaśāstra* and of the epic *Mahābhārata* is evident even from the inscriptions. But these two works are decidedly pre-Gupta. So also the *Yājñavalkya Smṛti*. To some extent the other authorities equally great, like Bṛhaspati, Parāśara and even Nārada seem to have composed their works prior to the Gupta epoch. The dates of these *Dharmaśāstras* are still vague and could not be established with any definiteness. A recent writer[6] who has studied the history of the *Dharmaśāstras* in a critical way thinks that the composition of these *Dharmaśāstras* should be assigned to the period between the first and the fifth centuries A.D. Parāśara quotes Manu in several places with approval and speaks of him in one place as one versed in all the śāstras. A certain Parāśara is quoted by Kauṭalya at six different places. We should not confound this ancient Parāśara who was an authority in polity with the author of the extant law-code.

If we proceed to examine the *Nārada smṛti* there again we find Nārada quoting *in extenso* Manu's opinions. On the other hand there is a correspondence between Nārada and the Agni Purāṇa, especially the Vyavahāra section of it. There is again similarity extending almost word for word between

6. P. V. Kane, *History of Dharmaśāstra*, Vol. I (1932).

Nārada and the *Kauṭalīya Arthaśāstra.*[7] This means that Nārada followed the Kauṭaliyan tradition so far as Vyavahāra was concerned. That Nārada is much later than the author of the *Yājñavalkya smṛti* is seen from the fact that Nārada mentions seven kinds of ordeals as against the five of Yājñavalkya and deals with them in fuller detail. In the *Mricchakaṭika* one meets with Nānaka in which sense the term *dināra* is used by Nārada. This and the fact of Nārada hedging the king with divinity have made Jayaswal assign Nārada to the epoch of the early Guptas. Nārada uses the term *dināra* in two senses as a jewel and as a coin. This may be cited as another argument to place him in the fourth century A.D.

If we turn again to Bṛhaspati the jurist there seems to be some reason to bring him also to the early Gupta epoch. There were two Bṛhaspatis or more. There was a Bṛhaspati who was the author of a treatise on polity. He was an ancient writer, accepted by Kauṭalya as an acknowledged authority on Politics. We are concerned here with the jurist Bṛhaspati. But unfortunately we have not yet discovered the complete work of this author. What we possess is an incomplete work collected and translated by Dr. Jolly in the well known series of the Sacred Books of the East (Vol. 33.) As is the case with other *smṛti kartas,* Bṛhaspati is indebted to Manu, for his views and opinions are largely quoted and referred to. This can be seen from the sections dealing with debt and interest on money lent. We saw Nārada mentioning seven kinds of ordeals. But Bṛhaspati goes a step farther and enumerates nine kinds. He also makes a distinction between civil and criminal justice. A wealth of information is given by Bṛhaspati on the procedure in a law suit. In several points of the procedure there is correspondence between Nārada and Bṛhaspati. In the definition of *dināra* both the jurists

7. cf. Dharmasthīya section in the Arthaśāstra.

agree. (Nā. Appendix 60 Jolly p. 232: Bṛ. X. 15.) Further, Bṛhaspati is quoted as an authority by Kātyāyana. Taking these things into consideration it is not possible to bring down the date of Bṛhaspati to the 6th or 7th century as Jolly wishes to make out (S.B.E. 33, p. 276). It is undoubted that Bṛhaspati was a contemporary, perhaps an younger contemporary of Nārada. As Mr. P. V. Kane puts it, we cannot place Bṛhaspati later than the fourth century A.D.

It was remarked above that Kātyāyana quotes Bṛhaspati with approval. But as for Kātyāyana, his position is uncertain, because we are not able to recover his complete work. That a certain Kātyāyana lived and that he was the author of a *Dharmaśāstra* is seen from the profuse quotations made by writers beginning with Viśvarūpa and ending with the author of the *Vīramitrodaya*. In dealing with the technique of *vyavahāra* Kātyāyana looks like a close student of Nārada and even Bṛhaspati. Of course in conformity with other writers, Kātyāyana shows his indebtedness to Manu. He was an accepted *Smṛti karta* in the hands of Viśvarūpa and Medhātithi. If we collate these pieces of evidence, inference is forced upon us that Kātyāyana should have flourished at a time when Nārada and Bṛhaspati should have become accredited authorities. It would be safe therefore if Kātyāyana is assigned to the end of the fifth century or at the commencement of the sixth century A.D.

Confining ourselves to the age of the Imperial Guptas, we do not find many jurists in this period. A critical study of the works on law makes it possible to assign to this period three or four *Smṛti kartas*. These are Vyāsa, Hārita, Pitāmaha and Pulastya. Vyāsa is perhaps the author of the extant *Vyāsasmṛti*. Examining in detail the portion dealing with the procedure in *vyavahāra*, Vyāsa seems to be a close student of the schools of Nārada, Bṛhaspati and Kātyāyana. The rules laid down agree more with these writers on law. In

Vyāsa the documents are broadly classified into three, and what are known as *laukika* documents are divided into eight classes. He refers to royal grants and their significance. Two verses of his, occur in some inscriptions whenever there is an occasion for a royal grant. In the matter of sureties he improves on Kātyāyana and possibly on Hārita. While these two refer only to five kinds of sureties, Vyāsa refers to seven. It seems reasonable to fix his date immediately after Kātyāyana.

To the same age, more or less, belongs another jurist Hārita. As has been already pointed out, he refers to five kinds of sureties. In his treatment of procedure in law and law suits, he seems to follow the beaten track and does not originate any new rule or doctrine. He lays, however, emphasis on the title for possession of property.

Pitāmaha was another jurist who figures in this age. In the definition of documents, he follows the lead given by Vyāsa. He agrees with Bṛhaspati in enumerating nine varieties of ordeals. Pitāmaha throws fresh light on the different stages of a suit, and on the king's final appellate authority. It is interesting that this law-giver refers to the eighteen *prakṛtis* and adds new information about the social life of the age. His views about litigation correspond to those of Bṛhaspati. He flourished after Vyāsa and perhaps in the fifth or sixth century A.D.

It is just possible that the law-giver Pulastya belonged to this period. He follows the rules and regulations of the Vṛiddhayājñavalkya. He is quoted by Viśvarūpa and in the *Mitākṣara*. The *Smṛticandrika* also quotes him. From these quotations one has to infer that Pulastya was an authority on law. He lived probably about the time of Pitāmaha.

There is testimony in the Gupta inscriptions to the profound influence exercised by the rules of the *Dharmaśās-*

tras. This is evident from an inscription attributed to Yaśodharman (532-33 A.D.) where he is designated as *samrāṭ* or a universal sovereign. The present age is condemned as one of unśāstraic conduct (*nindyācāraḥ*). Yaśodharman who possessed irreproachable character unlike his contemporaries deserved that title. (Fleet, *Gupta Inscriptions*, p. 147). In a later inscription again which relates to Mahārājā Dharasena II of Valabhi, among the ancestors of Dharasena mentioned is one Droṇasimha. It is said that this king ruled the land according to the laws and ordinances promulgated by Manu and other sages. This definitely shows the firm hold which the *Dharmaśāstras* of Manu and other law-givers had on the monarchs of the time (*Ibid., p.* 168). The same tendency is expressed in a still later inscription (No. 39) which is dated A.D. 766-7. Though this does not come exactly in our survey, these references lend strong support to the influence of the *Dharmaśāstras* on the character and conduct not only of the king but also of the administration.

The Evidence of the Arthaśāstra Treatises

We are not in a position to assign any Arthaśāstra work to this period. A study of the institutions as can be gathered from the inscriptions, which are our primary sources of information, reveals the irrefutable fact that the Kauṭalīya tradition was still strong. This is further corroborated by the view that the *Kāmandakīya Nītisāra* belongs to this age. Kāmandaka is frank and even blunt. He openly declares that he is summarising the *Arthaśāstra* of Kauṭalya whom he applauds as a great authority on polity. (ch. I. verses 2 to 8: ch. II. verse 6.) Is then the *Nītisāra* of Kāmandaka only a replica of the entire *Arthaśāstra* text? The answer is in the negative. For, if we turn to the *Kauṭalīya Arthaśāstra*, we have 180 chapters dealing with the science of Politics. In the *Kāmandakīya*, on the other hand, there are only thirty-six chapters. An examination of the subject-matter in both the treatises shows that the matter dealt with in four *adhikaraṇas* of the *Arthaśāstra* finds no place in the *Kāmandakīya*. These four books are *Adhyakṣa Pracāra* dealing with civil administration in general, *Dharmasthīyam* (civil law), *Kaṇṭakaśodhanam* (criminal law) and *Aupaniṣadikam* (secret means such as the efficacy of spells and charms). The first three books cover practically nearly half of the text of the *Arthaśāstra*. They deal with civil service and legal technicalities.

It is indeed a moot question why Kāmandaka who aimed at an epitome of the *Kauṭalīya Arthaśāstra* ignored these important topics which are very vital to any administration. One argument put forward is that this celebrated *Nīti* writer could not grasp and understand the original of Kauṭalya and in support of this it is contended that Kāmandaka cultivated the habit of literally versifying the aphorisms of Kauṭalya in an artificial manner, without understanding the point at issue, and that he gave prominence to court favourites, female attendants and others in the hierarchy of government, which was against the spirit of his master[8]. It is rather difficult to subscribe to this view. A writer who could understand the other parts of the texts may well be credited with ability to understand the whole. He states as a matter of fact that he presents a portion (*yat kiṃcit*). His writings do not show that he was an immature youth dabbling in politics. It seems reasonable to suppose that his object was to present to the public a work containing general maxims which will be popular and catch the imagination of people. The very fact that he has been quoted as an authority by subsequent writers points out that his work evoked respect from the public. Further it may be that he wanted his work to be a first class Nītisāra where a discussion of legal and administrative techni-

8. K. V. R. Aiyangar, *Some Aspects of Ancient Indian Polity*, pp 24-25 (Second Edition).

calities should have no place. No one can deny that the *Kāmandakīya* takes the first rank among the Nītisāras.

As for the other point of assigning a status to favourites, jesters and others of that nature, it may be that the *Kāmandakīya* reflects the spirit of the age. True the spirit of the Kauṭaliyan tradition pervades all through the *Nītisāra*. At the same time one or two departures may be due to the environment and circumstances of the age. To quote one or two instances. Both authors disagree regarding the doctrine of the *Maṇḍala*. It must be noted, as Jacobi admirably puts it, that Kāmandaka was not a biassed partisan of his *guru* or more accurately *Paramparāguru*. Kauṭalya would agree to the appointment of a court astrologer, though in principle he would condemn astrology and astrologers. Kāmandaka has a definite recommendation to appoint an astrologer to the king. Whatever that may be, the fact remains that Kāmandaka has presented what we may call an abridged edition (*saṃkṣiptagrantha*) of the *Kauṭalīya*, omitting certain portions, however important they may be to a student of Hindu administration. One notable difference between Kauṭalya and Kāmandaka is that while the former was a statesman, the latter's interest was purely academic.

What is more difficult is to fix up Kāmandaka's date. Dates ranging from the first to the sixth century A.D. have been assigned. The extant *Pañcatantra* could not be later than the sixth century A.D. It contains as many as fourteen quotations from Kāmandaka. Again, the reference to the *Kāmandakīya nīti* in the opening chapter of the *Daśakumāracarita* by Daṇḍin (circa 550 A.D.) is another positive proof that the *Nītisāra* had become popular before the middle of the sixth century A.D. Prof. Jacobi, who is an impartial critic, would place the *Nītisāra* at the earliest in the third century A. D. (*Ind. Ant.* 1918, p. 159). It will be more acceptable if the date is fixed about a hundred years later. Kāmandaka may be assigned to the close of the fourth century when the Gupta empire was firmly established and a Pandit like the author of the *Nītisāra* would have felt the need for a good manual on politics and he wrote one for the benefit of the Imperial Guptas. The very fact that the author drew all his material from the Arthaśāstra of Kauṭalya shows that the treatise was felt too detailed and too cumbersome for the ever-busy monarch to digest. So a handy volume on polity was most necessary and this task fell on the shoulders of Kāmandaka, the erudite Pandit of the time. This also demonstrates beyond doubt that the Gupta emperors followed faithfully the Kauṭalīyan tradition of government and methods of administration perhaps with some modifications and changes here and there. All the same, the spirit of Kauṭalya pervaded the Gupta atmosphere. In his introduction to the translation of the *Kāmandakīya Nītisāra,* M. N. Dutt writes: "From a report submitted by Dr. Frederich to the Batavian Society of Arts and Sciences on the Sanskrit literature of Bali, it appears that the most popular work in that island on polity is entitled *Kāmandakīya Nītisāra,* and all the Sanskrit books there extant are acknowledged to be the counterparts of purely Indian originals." Further researches in the Far East showed that the Hindus of the region were aware of the *Nītisāra* of Kāmandaka at a date anterior to the fourth century. It is well known that the people of Bali were familiar with a *Nītisāra* and a Kāmandaka, certainly imported from the shores of India into that island. Thus it can be seen that this is a work of the Gupta times.

This view is further strengthened by the fact that Abu Salih who made an abstract of this book calls the author of this book as Safar[9] which corresponds in Sanskrit to Śikhara. The Arab writer gives the name of this book as

9. Elliot and Dowson: *History of India,* Vol. I, pp. 110-11.

Instruction to Kings. We know that Śikhara was the Prime-minister of Candragupta II Vikramāditya. Kāmandaka was most probably the family title of Śikhara as Kauṭalya was that of the family of Viṣṇugupta. The Arab translation of this work was probably undertaken under the Abbasid Caliphs. K. P. Jayaswal is right in holding that it was a Gupta production (See *History of India* pp. 118-19 and also JBORS. XVIII, pp. 37-39). The late Ganapati Śastri who edited the *Kāmandakīya Nītisāra* in the Trivandrum Sanskrit Series also holds the view that it was an ancient work at least as ancient as the time of Bhavabhūti and Daṇḍin. Both Bhavabhūti and Daṇḍin knew this work and so to be popular during their time it should have been in existence before their period. (TSS. No. 14, pp. 5-6).

It is further held that the opening verse of the *Kāmandakīya Nītisāra* gives a clue to the time in which the author flourished, i.e., the reign of Candragupta II. He calls his patron as 'deva'. We have inscriptional evidence in Āmrakārdava that the pet name of the king was Deva. Hence Candragupta II is well-known as Devagupta which name occurs in some Vākāṭaka inscriptions (Fleet: *Gupta Inscriptions* p. 240), where Prabhāvati Guptā is described as a daughter of Devagupta. The identity of Candragupta II and Devagupta has been discussed. (See *IA*. 1912 p. 215; *JRAS* 1914 p. 325). We are to understand that the term Gupta is a surname and not a royal name. The Royal name was however in this case Deva and the opening verse of our *Nītisāra* mentions that name as can be seen clearly.

There are one or two internal evidences to show that the author of *Kāmandakīya Nitisāra* was none else than Śikhara, the Prime-minister of Candragupta II. In Section 1 verses 7 and 8 the author is explicit when he says that he is giving instruction to the king by his manual. In another verse Chapter 25, verse 71, he seems to defend the murder of a

Śaka by his sovereign by stratagem when he says: "Morality is not offended by a murder of an enemy through disguise". This was the Śakādhipati of the empire of the Śakas. He was also Shāhānushāhi, i.e. he was not only their emperor but also their religious leader. Śikharasvāmin was so powerful that he made his son Pṛthivīsena continue as *mantri* and *Mahābalādhikṛta* under Kumāragupta I. Thus we are inclined with Jayaswal to identify the author of the *Kāmandakīya Nītisāra* with Śikharasvāmin who was the *mantri* of Candragupta II Vikramāditya.

The Evidence of Kāvya-Nāṭaka.

The Gupta age is called generally the literary age of Hindu India. To strongly support it the voluminous and wonderful productions of Kālidāsa of revered memory are assigned to this period. Among others, two erroneous views are expressed in our text-books on ancient Indian history. One is that Aśoka was a Buddhist, which fallacy has been exposed in my book on the *Mauryan Polity*. The other is that Kālidāsa, the immortal poet, belonged to the Gupta age. To this view we do not subscribe as will be shown in the sequal.

Another blunder that is generally committed by students of the history of Hindu India is the pressing into service for the study of the Gupta life and governance, works like Daṇḍin's *Daśakumāracarita* and Bāṇa's reputed classics, the *Harṣa carita* and *Kādambari*.[9-a] At the earliest Danḍin can be placed circa 550 A.D. and Bāna circa A.D. 630. If we turn our attention to the chronology of the Guptas, we find the imperial line began to decline from about 500 A.D. The period between the decline of the imperial line and the rise of the later Gupta dynasty of Magadha may be put roughly as fifty years. According to accepted dates, the later

9-a. See for example, Saletore, *Life in Gupta Age*.

Gupta dynasty of Magadha flourished from circa 535 to 720 A.D. If we take these dates into account, then the great works of Daṇḍin and Bāṇa could not be taken as reflecting the age of the Guptas. By the Guptas we mean only the Imperial Guptas who alone have contributed to the glory of the age, while the later Guptas had nothing worthy of mention to their credit. If we thus remove these works and the equally well-known works of Kālidāsa, then the known literary output of the age is reduced to a great degree. There might have been literary productions of value which are probably lost. But judging from the extant works of the period, leaving alone for the present scientific treatises on astrology, Buddhist logic and philosophy which throw no light on the polity of the period, we meet with no works of value, either in the form of Kāvya or Nāṭaka. Even with regard to the literature extant, much uncertainty hangs around the question of the dates of their composition.

We shall take into consideration four works which may be roughly attributed to this period. There are the *Setubandhakāvya* or *Setukāvya*, *Kaumudi mahotsava*, *Devīcandra-guptam* and the *Mudrārākṣasa*. The *Setubandham* is a prākṛt poem dealing with the invasion of Lankā and the defeat of its king Rāvaṇa by Rāma. Daṇḍin testifies to its literary excellence. First of all the authorship is questioned. This is due to a statement made by the commentator of the Kāvya that Kālidāsa composed this work. Also the ambiguous colophon in the edition in the Kāvyamala Series which says *Śri Pravarasena viracite Kalidāsakṛte Daśamukha Vadhe mahākāvya*. This seems to suggest a joint authorship which is on the face of it absurd. The colophon in the Nirnayasagara edition of the Kāvya runs thus: *mahākavi Śri Pravarasena mahīpati viracitam Śatamukha vadhāya nāmakam setu-bandham!* Here is a definite statement that the work is by the king and poet Pravarasena. Then there is the authority of Ksemendra who in his *Aucityavicāra carca,* otherwise named *Aucityālankāra,* quotes from Kālidāsa, Mātṛgupta and Pravarasena. The two verses quoted by Kṣemendra occur in the *Setubandha* (I.2 & III.20). This confirms that the author of the *Setubandha* was Pravarasena only. In the *Harṣacarita* again the authorship of the Kāvya is attributed to Pravarasena. There has been a tendency in our literary tradition to father good works on a well-known author. In that confusion Kālidāsa has been dragged. For one thing, according to the view taken here, Kālidāsa was never in the Gupta age. Secondly, we have no other works of Kālidāsa written out fully in Prakrit. Thirdly, the tradition that Pravarasena was the author is unassailable. In these circumstances it is legitimate to conclude that Pravarasena was the author of the work.

The next question arises who was this Pravarasena. It has been rightly said that he was no other than the Vākāṭaka king Pravarasena. The internal evidence of the book bears no marks of historical value. It is simply a narrative of the events found in the *Rāmayaṇa* of Vālmīki, done in Prakṛsta-Prākrita in the words of Daṇḍin. The deities invoked in the opening verses are respectively Hari and Hara. This shows that the Vākāṭaka rulers followed the established religion of the land, Vaiṣṇavism and Śaivism and were not sectarian in their outlook. Beyond this, the Kāvya is not historically useful.

The Evidence of Kālidāsa

Among the literary sources of information for the period of the Guptas, Kālidāsa's works have been largely utilised, on the assumption that Kālidāsa lived in the epoch of the Guptas. This has been almost accepted by both the Indian and European scholars as an established fact. Ever since a critical study of the works of that immortal poet was undertaken, there has been a view that we should not be quite certain of the date for the poet, and that he could have lived in some century earlier than the period of the Guptas. It is regrettable that this viewpoint has not been thoroughly examined as it deserves to be investigated, but it has been completely overlooked. It is true that we have no certain materials or definite landmarks on which we can finally base our conclusions. Still a scientific historian should carefully examine the evidences available in an impartial manner, and arrive at conclusions as a result of deep deliberation. Here an attempt is made to sift the materials which we are able to get. About the life and character of the great poet of whom India can ever be proud, we know practically nothing. There are a number of legends hovering round this notable figure, and it would be idle to waste our time in tracing the career of that glorious poet. It is definite that very little is known about his life.

So we plunge ourselves into the valuable texts which the poet has so kindly bequeathed to us, and seek for internal evidences to find out his place in the tangled maze of ancient Indian chronology. These pieces of evidence will be taken into account in so far as they are corroborated and confirmed by what we may call external evidences. First of all, we must not be guided by the name Kālidāsa, though there is a magnetic touch in that name. Kālidāsa may be a name or may not be a name. The fact remains that there were a number of poets bearing that name. It is Rājaśekhara who informs us that he knew of at least three Kālidāsas before his time, who were renowned authors and masters of aesthetic language. Some of us are easily led away by a name; and there is a lurking tendency to attribute anything with the name Kālidāsa to one and the same person, without pausing a little to know how works of different centuries as revealed to us by the style and language of such works, could be fathered on one and the same writer. It has so happened to a large extent in the case of Kālidāsa.

We are here concerned with the Kālidāsa who was the inspiring author of the well-known works like the *Raghuvaṁśa* and the equally well-known dramas like *Mālavikāgnimitra, Śākuntala,* and the *Vikramorvaśīya* which are appropriately attributed to his pen. And there need be no hesitation in accepting this. We shall now examine some of these texts and find out whether they are of any help in settling the date of Kālidāsa, the author of the above mentioned works.[10]

Three theories hold the field to-day with regard to the date of Kālidāsa. One is that he was flourishing in the days of the Imperial Guptas[11] and especially under Candragupta II Vikramāditya. In support of this theory there is no tangible evidence. It is based on three assumptions which have turned out to be assertions. The first assumption is that Kālidāsa's name is associated with a certain Vikramāditya. And Candragupta II bore the title Vikramāditya and hence the poet should have lived during his reign. There was another Vikramāditya who came later. This was Yaśodharman who vanquished the Hūṇas and who commemorated his victory over these tribes by erecting a column at Mandasor about 533-34 A.D. Mandasor was the ancient name of Daśapūr or Dasor. Here was built a famous Sun temple which was completed in 437-38 A.D. Kālidāsa has occasion to refer to this Daśapura in his *Meghadūta* but he is silent about the temple of the Sun God in his description of the town which was to be free from licentiousness. According to inscriptional evidence during the rule of the early Guptas, it was a city of noble temples

10. I must acknowledge here the previous writers on the subject from whom I have largely and freely drawn. Among them may be mentioned G. R. Nandargikar. *The Raghuvaṁśa of Kālidāsa* (3rd edition, Poona, 1897); Keith, *A History of Sanskrit Literature* (Oxford, 1928): Kshetrachandra Chattopadhyaya. *The Date of Kālidāsa* (Allahabad University Studies, Vol. II pp. 79-170)- K. G. Sankara. *The Date of Kālidāsa* (Indian Historical Quarterly, Vol. I, pp. 309-316).

11. Keith: *A History of Sanskrit Literature*, Oxford, pp. 74-101.

including the Sun Temple. From this it transpires that Kālidāsa could not have been a contemporary of Yaśodharman Vikramāditya. The only other alternative is that he was a contemporary of Candragupta II Vikramāditya. But the internal evidence afforded by the mass of writings attributed to Kālidāsa, does not betray anywhere a resemblance between the conditions, political or social, or even religious of the Gupta times and the age of Kālidāsa. The usually worn out argument that the *digvijaya* of the *Raghuvaṁśa* reflects the campaigns and conquests launched by Samudra Gupta[12] has no legs to stand on. In the first place, it is irrelevant to treat the *digvijaya* as referring to any historical incident or incidents. We have no correspondence in the names of territories and countries subjugated and conquered. Samudra Gupta did not confront the Keralas nor did he cross the sea to defeat the Pārasīkas (Persians). Nor did the Gupta emperor march against Kāmarūpa which Raghu did. Secondly, if there is any historical truth to be discovered from his description of the N.W. Frontier Provinces and beyond, it may be somewhat appropriate to the time of Candragupta Maurya. The Pārasīka country described in the *Raghuvaṁśa* (IV. 60) shows the state of affairs in Persia before the Hūṇas crossed the river Vankṣu (Ornis) to India and when they were in the Ornis valley.

Thirdly, the abrupt ending of the *Raghuvaṁśa* with Agnivarṇa has to be accounted for.[12-a] There is nothing in the political condition in the Gupta period, especially after Candragupta II Vikramāditya, that conforms to that portrayed by Kālidāsa towards the end of the *Raghuvaṁśa.* Fourthly, is the tradition of nine jewels in the Gupta court in which Kālidāsa was a shining light. Of equal value are the traditions prevalent in the court of a

12. R. Basak: Parallels between Raghu and Samudra Gupta (Proceedings of The Second Oriental Conference. pp. 325-34).

12-a. XIX. 53 ff.

Vikramāditya of Ujjain or later on of Bhoja, King of Dhār. The *Bhoja Campu* is full of Kālidāsa. The fact was that one of the poets of these ages might have been designated Kālidāsa, and later Hindu tradition always associated that name with the immortal poet Kālidāsa irrespective of the age or territory. Any age may have a poet Kālidāsa by name. But the poet who composed the *Raghuvamśa, Mālavikāgnimitra* and *Śākuntala* could not have been one of the gems of Candragupta II Vikramāditya's court. Further, genuine historical tradition associates him as the chief poet of the royal court at Ujjain. If he had really lived in the reign of Candragupta II Vikramāditya he should have been a member of the royal court at Ayodhyā, which served as a capital of the great Gupta empire. So it is much more reasonable to find out the possibility of a royal court at Ujjain, preferably presided over by a certain Vikramāditya to fix up once for all the date of this immortal poet.

Fifthly, there is the association of an accidental name Kumāra in the *Kumārasambhava* with the birth of Kumāra Gupta. It is difficult to see any connection between the events in the reign of this king and those referred to in Kālidāsa's work. On the other hand, an entirely new picture is envisaged and presented by the poet. Sixthly, as if to buttress their arguments in favour of the theory, viz. Kālidāsa was an honoured member of the royal court of the Guptas, much is made of the mention of the expression *jāmitra* in the *Kumārasambhava* (VII. i.) Unfortunately the protagonists of this theory identify this term *jāmitra* with the Greek Diametron and argue that Kālidāsa lived when the ideas of Greek astronomy had become current and popular in India. A study of the passage in which *jāmitra* occurs would help us in our further enquiry. It is stated in the *Kumārasambhava* (VII. i) that Himavān was much concerned with the marriage of his daughter and he started the vow (*dīkṣa*) for the wedding of his daughter at that auspicious time when the moon was on the wane and when it was all *jāmitra guṇa.* According to ancient Hindu astronomical conception, *jāmitra* means simply the seventh zodiacal sign from the natal sign (*lagna*). Some derive the word from *jāyā* in the science of astrology. The *jāmitra* sign indicates the future good luck of one's wife (jāyāmitram?) (Apte: *Sanskrit-English Dictionary*). The zodiac is generally divided into twelve divisions, and in this division *jāmitra* is assigned the seventh place.

What does this show? It clearly bears out that Kālidāsa lived at a time when the division of the zodiac into twelve places was current in the Indian continent. This was an ancient Indian calculation accepted in popular belief. It has therefore nothing to do with Greek astronomy, the influence of which was seen later, as one could see from Āryabhaṭṭa's astronomical treatise or Varāhamihira's astrological work. The passage in question where the expression occurs simply records the anxiety of Himavān to start his *dīkṣa* at an auspicious hour in the interest of his daughter's happy wedded life. The Greek idea of *jāmitra* is conspicuously absent in Kālidāsa's works. This is in itself enough to show that Kālidāsa lived at a time when the Greek astronomical ideas had not yet penetrated the Indian horizon. Besides, Baudhāyana and Vālmīki in the *Rāmāyaṇa* are quite familiar with the Rāśis and reference to a lunar eclipse in the *Raghuvaṃśa* is not an astronomical fact but an optical phenomenon. (XIV. 40). [12-b]

While we are dealing with the astronomical and astrological data in Kālidāsa's writings, it is appropriate to point out another fact which really clinches the question on hand. In the *Baudhāyana sūtras* of the fifth century B.C. we have the following:

12-b. See also Dr. Kunhan Raja's article "Kālidāsa and Astronomy" in the *Journal of the U.P. History Society*, Vol. XV. pt. ii.

मेषवृषभौ घरो वसंत:। मीनमेषौ वा

(S. B. E. XIV. II. p. XLI. See also the *Ramāyaṇa* I. 18. 9 & 15; II. 15. 3; Mhb. sabhā, 35. 16-18).

The Greek astronomy itself is indebted to Babylonia. India's contact with Babylonia was certainly earlier than that of Greece.[13] Could not have then India borrowed from the ancient Babylonians? In astrology we have to distinguish between two months, one known as *amant* month and the other as *Purṇimant* month. The latter is entirely a conception of the North Indian tradition. The Gupta era follows faithfully this tradition of *Purṇimant* month. It is again followed by the era of 57 B.C. called the Mālava era or Vikrama era.

With these preliminary remarks let us examine Kālidāsa's references in this connection. According to the very second stanza in the *Meghadūta,* the journey of the Megha (cloud messenger) commences on the first day of Āṣāḍha (śukla). The counting of the month is from śukla Pratipada. T. J. Kedar says, "If the month began in those days with Vadya Pretipada, the journey started 25 days before Āṣāḍha śukla 11. If on the other hand, if the month commenced on śukla pratipada, the journey started ten days before the Āṣādha śukla 11. In the latter part of the *Meghadūta,* it is stated that the year's exile will end on the Kārtika śukla 11."[13-a]

This shows that four months had yet to elapse after the delivery of the message to the wife of Yakṣa. If the reading of the *Meghadūta* justifies us in concluding that the Megha must have reached Alaka on āsāḍha śukla 10 or 11, the calculation of four months is absolutely correct. Then he proceeds to arrange the time-table of the journey from Rāmagiri (Ramtek) to Alaka (sts. 20 to 63). The

13. *Nagpur University Journal,* No. 5, December 1939, pp. 1-22. Kālidās by T. J. Kedar.

13-a. E. Hultzsch: *Meghadūta,* (London, 1911), st. 109.

plan of the journey had been drawn in such a way that the cloud-messenger reached Alaka just four months before the termination of his exile.

A critical examination of the texts shows that the month of commencement was *śukla pratipada* which is technically known as *amanta* as against the *pūrṇimanta*. *Pūrṇimanta* means the month ending on Pūrṇima, the day of the full moon. Calculation on the *pūrṇimanta* basis began with 57 B.C. Prior to this date it was all on the basis of *amanta*, meaning the month ending on the new moon day. This is also confirmed by a passage from the *Mahābhārata* where the month came to a close on the amāvāsya day. The *pūrṇimanta* system of calculation was no new thing. (Virāta Parva ch. 52.) It was in vogue in Vedic times. Apparently with the ushering in of the neo-Kṛta yuga[13-b] by which name the Vikrama era was earlier known, the state wanted to revive the Vedic calendar, and hence the introduction of the *pūrṇimanta* system into the 57 B.C. era.

Between the fall in use of the Vedic calendar of the *pūrṇimanta* and its revival in B.C. 57 a long interval elapsed when the *amanta* system held the field. Perhaps Kālidāsa was the last to use this system of *amanta* as could be seen from the data furnished by the *Meghadūta*. From this, inference is irresistible that Kālidāsa wrote his work before B.C. 57. Dr. Fleet has shown on the authority of inscriptions like the Khoh copperplate grant of the year A.D. 528-29 that the arrangement of the fortnights of the months of the Gupta year was the northern *Pūrnimanta* system, which Kālidāsa, as we have seen, has not adopted.

In this connection it is worthwhile to point out another idea belonging to the domain of astronomical science which occurs in Kālidāsa's writings, being a departure from accepted

13-b. The Kṛta era by Prof. K. B. Vyas, *Proceedings of the Tenth Indian History Congress* (Bombay) pp. 151-59,

later authorities like Varāhamihira. Kālidāsa gives prominence to the Graha, Rāhu. Reference is made to this planet in two places in the *Raghuvamśa*. In the first reference Rāhu is called *suradviṭ* (II. 39). The verse is put in the mouth of the lion addressing king Dilīpa just as the nectar of the moon comes in the way of the planet Rāhu, the cow has come in his (lion's) way for him to drink its blood. In the second reference (XII. 28) Rāhu is definitely named as a Graha. Here it is said that just as the Graha crosses the moon, Virādha crossed Rāma's pathway. What is important to us is that Varāhamihira, for example, does not accept with approval the planets Rāhu and Ketu as having any influence on the nativity of persons. This is seen from the *Bṛhat samhitā* V-1. These evidences are enough to demonstrate that Kālidāsa lived long before Varāhamihira and also before the alleged influence of Greek ideas of astronomy on India.

Again, in the quest for arguments for the support of Kālidāsa being placed in the Gupta period, there is more of quibble than of straight evidence. One such argument depending on ambiguous words is the occurrence of Dingnāga and Nicula in the *Meghadūta* (st. 14). It has been pointed out that these terms stand for men of flesh and blood and contemporaries of Kālidāsa. It is further argued that while Dingnāga the Buddhiṣt logician was a critic of Kālidāsa, Nicula was his friend and well-wisher. As Dingnāga could not have lived earlier, Kālidāsa should be brought down. Into the vexed controversy of the date of Dingnāga we need not enter for the present, nor in the vain search for finding out who the Nicula was. We do not come across a Nicula in literature or tradition. It is futile to see in this stanza any reference to human beings. The stanza is simple and plain. It is the ingenuity of the commentator or the interpreter that places Kālidāsa in an awkward position and the sympathetic readers in an uncomfortable position. With some, Dingnāga becomes Nāgārjuna too. In the passage under reference only elephants and sticks are mentioned as objects for removing obstacles in the way during his sojourn to the north by the cloud messenger. The poet has happily put it and we are unhappily misreading it.

The above facts should make it plain that it is difficult to assign a place for Kālidāsa in the period of the Imperial Guptas. There are on the other hand positive evidences to indicate that Kālidāsa flourished long before the rise of the Guptas. The next question to consider is how long before the Guptas Kālidāsa flourished. In our investigation we reach another milestone which positively puts our author before Aśvaghosa, the celebrated author of the *Buddha carita.*[14] Both in manner and matter Aśvaghoṣa follows Kālidāsa. The latter has a peculiar way of using periphrastic perfect and future, which is seen in the *Buddha carita.* (By E. B. Cowell, Oxford, 1893)

प्रभ्रंशयां यो नहुषं चकार (Raghu, 13 36, also 9 61; 16 86)

यथावदेनं दिवि देवसंघा:

दिव्यै: विशेषै: महयां च चक्रु:। Bud. VI 58

Kālidāsa uses the root दृश् with the Dative instead of the Accusative. The *Buddhacarita* uses it likewise

प्रत्यभिज्ञानरत्नं च रामायादर्शयत् Rag XII, 64 etc.

आदाय धात्र्यंकगतं कुमारं

संदर्शयामास तपोधनाय ॥ Bud. I. 64

The term *saumya* finds again parallel

प्रीतास्मि ते सौम्य चिराय जीव Rag. 14 59

तत्सौम्य शोच्ये हि मनुष्यलोके। Bud. 1 81

14. See in this connection K. C. Chattopadhyaya on Kālidāsa & Aśvaghoṣa, *op. cit.* (Allahabad University Studies, Vol. II); G. R. Nandargikar: Notes on Kālidāsa, pp. 161-195.

Tap. governing a cognate object is another mark of the two poets.

यच्च तप्तं तपस्तस्य विपक्वं फलमद्य वः Kumāra VI. 16

सुखलान्यमुक्त्वापि तपांस्यतप्त Bud. II. 49

For the use of Dākṣiṇya with regard to women solely, see the following

तस्य दाक्षिण्यरूढेन नाम्ना मगधवंशजा Rag. 1 38

रूपस्यास्यानुरूपे दाक्षिण्ये नानुवर्तितुम् Bud. IV 69

Another peculiarity is the use of two negatives by both the authors.

नासौ न काम्यो न च वेद संयक् Rag. 6. 30

तन्नारतिर्मे न परापचार: Bud. 7 49

The use of the term शिवं in the sense of auspicious may be also marked.

राज्ञः शिवं सावरजस्य भूयात्। Rag. 14 50

प्रयामि चाद्यैव नृपास्तु ते शिवं Bud. IX 69

Every writer on the subject sees considerable similarity between the *Buddha carita* III. 13-24 and *Raghuvaṃśa* VII 5-12, 16-17 and *Kumārasambhava* VII 56-70. In Kālidāsa, just to have a look at the beauty of the bridegroom, women at their toilets leave them in a hurry and crowd the windows. Aśvaghoṣa on the other hand induces ladies still in their beds to forsake them to feast their eyes with the beauty of the prince passing by. In agreement and similarity the *Buddha carita* is closer to the *Kumārasambhava* than to the *Raghuvaṃśa.* The correspondence of the latter with *Saundarānanda* is striking and original. In this connection the third, sixth, tenth to twelfth verses of Canto 1 of the *Saundarānanda* are in agreement with the *Raghuvaṃśa* Canto 1, 26; II, 17, I.

50-52, 53, II. 8 etc. In the same way every canto may be examined and resemblances pointed out.[14-a]

If we pass on to the *Buddha carita*, there is much of correspondence between it and the *Kumārasambhava* to a large extent and to the *Raghuvaṁśa* to a smaller extent. Verse 11 of the *Buddha carita* reminds one of the sixth verse of Canto 1 of the *Kumārasambhava*. Instances of similarity may be supplied in the succeeding cantos of the *Buddha carita* and Kālidāsa's books, especially the *Kumārasambhava* and the *Raghuvaṁśa*. Thus we see not only verbal agreement but also agreement in ideas. Prof. Cowell[15] and Prof. Keith are exponents of the theory that Kālidāsa and not Aśvaghoṣa was the borrower. But the concluding verses of the *Saundarānanda* are helpful in deciding the indebtedness of Aśvaghoṣa to Kālidāsa.[16]

A critical study of these verses shows that Aśvaghoṣa was not a poet of eminence which undoubtedly Kālidāsa was. The subjects which interested Aśvaghosa were religion and philosophy. He was a monk first and then an author. He was plunged in metaphysics. He was out to preach salvation as the goal of life and the only means to attain it was to discard worldly pleasures. He wanted, one has to suppose, to produce a Kāvya, and he set before himself the famous Kāvyas of his time as his ideal. Hence the resemblances and similarities between his writings and those of the master Kāvya writer Kālidāsa. If these were the facts impressed by Aśvaghoṣa himself, should we hesitate even a minute to accept that he was borrowing and not giving? If he had borrowed, it was only from Kālidāsa. Hence we can safely conclude that Kālidāsa lived a century or two earlier than

14-a. For instance, compare *Raghuvaṁśa*. 1.28 with the *Saundarānanda* II. 22-23.

15. See Preface pp. X to XIV to his edition of *Buddhacharitam*.

16. See also K. S. Ramaswami Sastri, *Kālidāsa*, pp. 28-29.

Aśvaghosa whose date is probably the first or second century A.D.

The next theory that Kālidāsa lived in the days of Agnimitra the Śunga was adumbrated some time back and is given prominence again by the latest writers on Kālidāsa.[17] The main point in the discussion of this theory centres round the Bharatavākyam of the *Mālavikāgnimitra* of Kālidāsa. There is a distinct mention of the hero of the story in this *Bharatavākyam,* and it is Agnimitra. This evidences the fact that the *Mālavikāgnimitra* was written during the reign of Agnimitra who was the son and successor of Puṣyamitra Śunga. Going back to the Mauryas, the last ruler of that great dynasty was Bṛhadratha and Puṣyamitra was the *senāpati* or the commander-in-chief of that ruler. It appears that Agnimitra, the son of the *senāpati* was appointed Viceroy of Mālva, even when Puṣyamitra continued only as the *senāpati.* Puṣyamitra found Bṛhadratha imbecile and weak and got him murdered. By his valour and courage, he got himself crowned on the Pāṭaliputra throne. Agnimitra became crown-prince and continued to rule from Vidiśa (Bhilsa in the Gwalior State in Madhya Pradesh). Agnimitra's queen was Dharanī. When Pusyamitra made his preparations for the Aśvamedha sacrifice (this was perhaps the first of the two sacrifices credited to him) he still held the status of the *senāpati.* For, when he invited Agnimitra for the sacrifice, he styles himself as Senāpati Puṣyamitra. Vasumitra was the son of Agnimitra. The young Vasumitra was deputed by the grand-father to vanquish the Yavanas in the Punjab (Act V) before he commenced the sacrifice. This was not apparently liked by Agnimitra

17. Kunhan Raja, Annals of Oriental Research, University of Madras, 1941-2, VI. Pt. I. Notes on Kālidāsa; Indian Historical Quarterly, 1942, pp. 128-136; Journal of U.P. Historical Society, Vol. XV, Pt. II.

and his queen, and it led to some misunderstanding between them and Puṣyamitra. By the latter extending a personal invitation to Agnimitra, a reconciliation was effected.

In the meantime, Agnimitra who was a distinguished soldier of much valour had an engagement with the Rāja of Vidarbha who was a relation of a Mauryan minister and who did not countenance the Śunga usurpation. The circumstances that led to this expedition to the Vidarbha country (Berar) are seen from the *Mālavikāgnimitra*. Agnimitra sent a messenger to the king of the Vidarbhas asking him to immediately release Mādhavasena. The Vidarbha monarch sent back the reply that he could effect it on the condition that the Mauryan minister (*Maurya Saciva*) who had been imprisoned by the Śunga king was set free. This incensed much the Śunga king who considered himself as the overlord of all-India. He felt humbled when the Vidarbha king dictated terms on his orders. So he consulted his minister and resolved on war. The Śunga minister applauded the king that he took the right step as such a course had the approval of the science on politics (*Śāstra dṛṣṭam* Act I. 8). To venture a conjecture, the Śāstra referred to must be the *Arthaśāstra* of Kauṭalya which asks the conqueror to vanquish a recalcitrant king.

For some reason or other, the Śungas abandoned Pāṭaliputra the ancient capital and settled in Vidiśa itself. Vidiśa continued to be a flourishing capital under the Śungas, being centrally situated. According to the *Kaliyuga Rāja Vṛttānta* there were many beautiful damsels in the city of Vidiśa who took to illegal amusements and licentious enjoyment. There were dancers and the king himself who took to heavy drinking spent much of his time in the company of the prostitutes. This condition of affairs in the city prevailed in the reign of the last king among the Śungas, Devabūti or Devabhūti. Kālidāsa speaks in glowing terms of Vidiśa as Rājadhāni. Agnimitra's period of kingship was only eight years if we are to follow the chronology of the Purānas. Of the ten Śunga monarchs, the reigns of the fifth, sixth, seventh and eighth kings were equally of short duration. Perhaps under Bhagabhadra (also Bhagawat), Vidiśa was at the height of its glory and pre-eminence. This honour, it continued to enjoy until about 57 B.C. when historical circumstances necessitated Ujjain to become the capital and throw Vidiśa comparatively into shade.

Thus the description of Vidiśa (*Meghadūta* 23-24) as the capital and the mention of Agnimitra the hero in the Bharatavākya of the *Mālavikāgnimitra* are two definite landmarks which would lead any impartial critic to assign Kālidāsa to the Śunga period. In no other period of its subsequent history did Vidiśa flourish as the capital of an empire or kingdom. While this is true, yet there are other statements and facts which are found in the other works of Kālidāsa which warrant the conclusion that the poet flourished not in the reign of Agnimitra but in the last years of the Śunga period and perhaps survived the Śunga period to witness the emerging of a new power at neighbouring Ujjain. In the *Mālavikāgnimitra,* (Poona, 1918) he was chronicling the historical events which were still fresh in his memory. The name and achievements being of a far-reaching character had not yet faded from the public memory and these induced the poet to pay homage to the founders of the dynasty of which he continued to be the honoured poet-laureate. This leads us to the examination of the third theory which has gained momentum in recent years among Indian savants.

Not long ago all India celebrated the Vikramāditya day after a lapse of two thousand years. The tradition is strong that the Vikrama era of 57 B.C. is associated with this Vikramāditya who by his valiant deeds won the distinction of Śakāri and established his capital at Ujjain. Nothing tangible is known of this Vikramāditya. He has almost passed into the realm of tradition and legend. But still patient research has been able to cull out certain pieces of evidence to establish some historicity of authentic value.

Before we proceed to examine the alleged association of Kālidāsa with this Vikramāditya we shall show under what circumstances this king shot to glory in Ujjain, which has been celebrated as the City Beautiful by Kālidāsa with its lofty mountains, noble rivers and inspiring temples (*Meghadūta* 27-38). The Śungas were overthrown by the Kaṇvas about 72 B.C. Pāṭaliputra became once more the imperial capital. About this time the Śaka tribes of Seistan entered India from the north-west and settled in the Indus region. They gradually extended their power and advanced as far as Ujjain and occupied it too. Now comes handy the *Kālakācārya Kathā*, (Norman Brown, *The Story of Kālaka*, Washington, 1933, ch. I.) a Jain work of value, as an evidence. According to the legend, king Gardabhilla then ruling from Ujjain insulted the Jaina saint Kālakācārya who was his contemporary. Unable to brook the insult offered by the ruler, the saint left Ujjain and joined hands with the growing power of the Śakas to teach Gardabhilla a severe lesson. Entreated by Kālakācārya, the Śaka satraps advanced towards Ujjain and displaced the reigning king and proceeded to settle there. Gardabhilla's son was the glorious Vikramāditya. He collected an army and fought the new settlers in such a thoroughgoing manner that they fled for escape. Tradition avers that he pursued them in a revengeful spirit and completely exterminated the Śaka power in India. He earned the title of Śakāri and won the universal respect and esteem from all India for having vanquished the foreigner on the Indian soil. It gave the impression of the destruction of the Kali age and the ushering in of the Kṛta age.

In commemoration of this great achievement, a special era called Vikrama era was started by the Mālavas as this feat of importance was accomplished in the Mālava country.

Add to this the evidence of the *Kathāsaritsāgara.* According to the account given in this text, Vikrama's father was one Mahendrāditya. Mahendra is Indra and this name appears in the play of *Vikramorvaśīya* as many as fourteen times. After Mahendra, Vikrama was anointed. It is held by some that the *Vikramorvaśīya* glorifies the patron's name, the patron being Vikramāditya. That Vikrama was Mahendra's son is seen from *Kathā.* 18, i. 59-60.

(See Journal of the University of Bombay, I. Pt. VI, pp. 232-46).

Attention to this story is drawn to show that the Vikramāditya tradition persisted in this land and found expression in literary works. Sir William Jones believed in this tradition and assigned the commencement of the rule of Vikramāditya of Ujjain to 56 B.C. It was he who founded the Samvat era which Dr. Fleet equates with the Mālava era and which later on is mentioned in epigraphy as Vikrama era. Last but not the least is the evidence of the *Rāja Tarangini* of Kalhana which refers to two Vikramādityas who were rulers at Ujjain. The first is said to have installed one of his relatives Pratāpāditya on the throne of Kashmir.

S. C. Sarkar draws our attention to another account regarding Kālidāsa based on a Tibetan passage in an early 18th century cyclopædia. According to this version Kālidāsa was a contemporary of King Bhagabhadra of the Śunga dynasty ruling from Vidiśa, of Wima Kusala Kadphises, of King Svāti Śatavāhanā of Dakṣiṇātya and Aparānta, and that he married a daughter of Wima Kadphises by name Vasanti. In the literary sphere the poet is said to be a contemporary of Vararuci, the junior, Śanku, Bhavarṇa and Saptavarma. He was also a prior contemporary of

Nāgārjuna, of the Apabhrana poet and Tantric philosopher Saraha-pāda, Rāhula Bhadra, and of Indra-Dhruva who revised the *Aindra Vyākaraṇa.* Notwithstanding the unintelligible account furnished herein the chronological calculation of the period brings Kālidāsa to the first century B.C.[17-a]

That Kālidāsa lived in the last days of the Śunga rule is evident from his description of the social life of Vidiśa, especially of the last King Devabhūti who was leading an easy life in the company of dancing girls. This shows deterioration in the administration and in the morals of the people. This picture of Vidiśa could not be either true of Agnimitra's time or even Bhagabhadra's. It was surely of the time of Devabhūti. Kālidāsa who had identified himself with the Śungas, could not reconcile himself to their overthrow by the Kaṇvas. Perhaps he protested against the new regime and hence courted exile for a year if the *Meghadūta* has any historical significance at all. If we can conjecture aright he went away to Ujjain where he was welcomed by the rising Vikramāditya to his court of learned men. That is why the poet seems to bestow all his love to Ujjain which is being celebrated in a number of verses.

Another similarity between the end of Devabhūti's reign and Agnivarṇa's indicated in the last canto of the *Raghuvamśa,* is significant. This shows Kālidāsa was nearing the completion of the *Raghuvamśa* when Devabhūti was supplanted by the ambitious Kaṇvas. So the poet could not continue further his thoughts and preferred to end abruptly the career of Agnivarṇa which he was describing. If we study carefully the closing stanzas, the poet does not end in complete despair but he expects better days under a good ruler.

17-a. Journal of the Ganganath Jha Research Institute, August, 1944.

Again there is the significant omission of Kālidāsa to mention Pāṭalīputra or Ayodhyā which were the imperial capitals of the early Guptas. If he were in the court of Candragupta II he ought to have mentioned the glory and greatness of the ancient city in Magadha, especially as the *rājadhāni*.

One should seek justification for the name Vikrama era. If reference to the Vikrama samvat occurs for the first time in the ninth century in tradition and epigraphy, and if that is equated exactly with the era of 57 B.C. why should this be named Vikrama era? There should have been a real man of valour and courage (Vikrama) after whom only this appellation for the era was given. If it was Candragupta II Vikramāditya we have to postulate two eras for the Guptas. This is not warranted by historical facts. There is not even a hint that Candragupta II Vikramāditya started a new era. There must be some meaning, some significance attached to the naming of the era of 57 B.C. as Vikrama era. This is undoubtedly the Vikramāditya of Ujjain whose distinct achievement was the crushing victory over the unwanted Śaka hordes who began to spread beyond the Sindhu region. The era itself is dated in the Pūrṇimanta month which was not in vogue in the year preceding 57 B.C. And Kālidāsa shows his acquaintance with *amanta* month and not *pūrṇimanta*. Apparently Kālidāsa did not produce any classic after 57 B.C. except perhaps the *Vikramorvaśīya* which was possibly the last of his works. Luckily we have in Hāla Śātavāhana's *Saptaśati* (V. 64) a clear reference to the liberality and generosity of a Vikramāditya. Surely we must postulate a Vikramāditya before Hāla. What A. Cunningham wrote years ago,[17-b] of 57 B.C. as the era of Vikramāditya of Ujjain, no doubt holds good.

17-b. *Arch. Surv. of India*, X. p. 34.

There are other evidences which bear testimony to the fact that Kālidāsa could not have been a product of the Gupta age. In the *Śākuntalam* Kālidāsa refers to the law of inheritance and also the law governing the punishment for theft. Surely Kālidāsa was a follower of the Dharmśāstras in vogue in his time. According to the *Śākuntalam* VI Act a widow was not entitled to inherit the property of her deceased husband. This is the ruling of the authors of early Dharmaśāstras like Āpastamba and Baudhāyana, and also Manu.[18] But Bṛhaspati, Vyāsa, Śankha and Likita who may be said to belong to the Gupta period rule that the widow had the right to succeed to her husband's property. (**राजा- ननु गर्भः पित्र्यं रिक्थम् अर्हति** । Act VI). In the *Śākuntalam* again capital punishment[19] is recommended for theft (see also *Vikramorvaśi*). But in the days of Bṛhaspati, this was relaxed and a heavy fine was imposed for punishing a thief, though death in certain cases was still in vogue.

There is again the Bhītā medallion (C.H.I. I, Plate XXIX). This was found in the Śunga strata. The figure that is represented here is interesting. Here are a king and his charioteer seated on a chariot. They appear in the pose of hunting a deer seen below. We meet with a hermit in front of the chariot who calls halt at hunting the innocent animal. The scene is apparently near a hermitage where is represented a girl watering the plant in front. All this suggests the beautiful dramatic description of Duṣyanta in the first act of the *Śākuntala*.

Further in the *Raghuvamśa,* in his reference to the South Indian powers during his time, Kālidāsa mentions the ascendency of the Pāṇḍyan ruler. (IV 49-50.) He refers to Uragapura as the capital of the Pāṇḍyas. In the historical

18. In my opinion Manu should be placed much earlier than 2nd century A.D.

19. See the opening lines of Act VI.

period Uragapura or Uṛaiyūr continued to be the capital only of the Cōlas. The Pāṇḍyan usurpation of the Cōla capital should have been sometime in the Śangam period, which must be again before the days of the *Śilappadikāram* which we have placed in the second century A.D. Probably it was in the first century B.C. when a certain powerful Pāṇḍya had occupied Uṛaiyūr and established his hegemony over the entire Cōla kingdom also. Add to this the total silence of Kālidāsa about the Pallavas of Kāñci, who came to power sometime in the third century A.D. When Kālidāsa had mentioned the Pāṇḍyas and Kēralas, he would not have neglected such a powerful and influential dynasty like that of the Pallavas. Just as we have no direct evidence of any reference to the Guptas (even the great Samudra Gupta finds no mention), there is no reference to the Pallavas. All these point out that Kālidāsa was an early poet, earlier than at least the second century A.D.

The tradition embedded in the *Jyotirvidabharaṇa,* which is attributed to Kālidāsa but is certainly of later date, makes mention of the nine gems of poets, who adorned the court of Vikramāditya. The oft quoted stanza containing the nine names is

> धन्वन्तरिः क्षपणकाऽमरसिंहशङ्कु-
> वेतालभट्टघटकर्परकालिदासाः।
> ख्यातो वराहमिहिरो नृपतेः सभायां
> रत्नानि वै वररुचिर्नव विक्रमस्य ॥

There is no reason why they should not have been contemporaries. The one mistake committed by some of our orientalists is that there was only one Kālidāsa or one Vararuci or one Varāhamihira in the whole range of Sanskrit literature. There may be a number of Kālidāsas as we have shown above, a number of Vararucis and Varāhamihiras. We have for example not one Vikramāditya but half a dozen

Vikramādityas in the course of ten centuries from the first century B.C. to the eleventh century A.D. In the same way poets of different ages bore the same name which was only an accident. On this account we cannot rule out that Vararuci or Varāhamihira or for the matter of that any other poet could not have been contemporaries. Judged by this test, judicious criticism allows the existence and contemporaneity of the poets mentioned in the above verse in the court of Vikrama.

Speaking on the political conditions of India as described by Kālidāsa in the *Raghuvaṁśa,* there is nothing to indicate that the work reflects those in the great Gupta Empire. We shall not go into details but suffice it to point out one or two instances which warrant a condition of affairs centuries before the Gupta times. Let us take the mention of Aṅga. Kālidāsa refers to Anga as an independent kingdom with its ruler (VI. 27). The last we hear of Anga as a separate independent political unit is from the inscriptions of Khāravela of Kalinga (J.B.O.R.S. IV, p. 384). This gives the clue that Kālidāsa was living more or less close to the times of Khāravela. Kālidāsa again speaks of a ruler of Mathurā. This is again not true of the Gupta period. These and other similar references to Avanti, Anūpa and others go to prove that, if Kālidāsa's works mirror to some extent contemporary political conditions, it did not relate to the Gupta age but to an age nearer to that of Khāravela of Kalinga.

The inscription of Vatsabhaṭṭi in the temple of the Sun at Mandasor dated 473 A.D. is sometimes taken as a clue to assign Kālidāsa to the early Gupta epoch. This could not be. Vatsabhaṭṭi, who was one of those numerous poets who have faded into shade in the march of time wanted to put his verses in the form of a Kāvya, and in his ideas and expressions he follows the master Kāvya writer Kālidāsa. If Kālidāsa had lived just before his time, is it possible, one has to ask, in those days of no printing and press, for Vatsabhaṭṭi to get a full knowledge of Kālidāsa's writings and to imitate him? Common sense dictates that some two to three hundred years should have elapsed before Kālidāsa's works were available to the reading public. Judging by this test again Kālidāsa could have flourished only long before the Gupta era.

In the light of these evidences, we are on firm ground in concluding that Kālidāsa cannot belong to the Gupta period, and it would be unhistorical to cite his writings as a source of information for the age of the Imperial Guptas.

Other Works

The *Bhāva Śataka* which is now printed in the Kāvyamāla Series (Part IV, 1899, pp. 37-52) is a work composed during the reign of Gaṇapati Nāga and dedicated to him (see Jayaswal: *History of India*, pp. 38-39). The book contains a little over hundred verses, mainly devoted to sentiments. It is not a connected piece with one idea running through it. Each verse conveys one idea and is complete in itself. Several verses are in honour of Śiva and this shows that Gaṇapati Nāga was a follower of the Śaiva faith. Apart from its literary character, what interests the historian is the reference to Gajavatra-sur Nāgarāja wrongly printed as Gajavaktra-sur Nāgarāja. The late Jayaswal who examined the original manuscript in Mithilā discovered this significant correction and this Gajavatra-sur Nāgarāja has been, with reason, identified with Gaṇapati Nāgarāja. According to this text, this Gaṇapati was a man of profound learning ruling from Padmālayā, the well-known Padmāvatī. From the description of the family (vv. 98-100) it is clear that one Jālapa was his father and one Vidyādhara his grandfather Both these were not kings. Evidently Gaṇapati came to the throne of Padmāvatī from a collateral line. It is said in a verse (80) that Gaṇapati was a terror to all the Nāga leaders.

We are also enabled to read Gaṇapati's character. He was a great soldier and a man of excellent attainments. He was not given to sexual extremes. He is called the king of Dhārā (Western Mālva) and is said to belong to Tākavaṁśa. Perhaps he belonged to the Yādava community, which migrated from Tākkadeśa in the Punjab. Karpati was the *gotra* of Gaṇapati. This Gaṇapati was a contemporary of Samudra Gupta, his conqueror.

The *Kaumudīmahotsava* is a drama in five acts of much historical value (Ed. by Ramakrishna Kavi and S. K. Ramanatha Sastri in the Daksina Bharati Series, Madras). The second verse in the drama gives the certain clue that the author of this play was one Kiśorika though the editors would infer this name to be Vijjika. We are not actually concerned with the authorship of the drama for the present but with what fresh light it throws on the period of its composition. Dr. Jayaswal is positive that it is a composition of 340 A.D. and that it portrays the political picture of Magadha at the time. (*Annals of Bh. Research Institute,* Vol. XII, pp. 50-56).

The facts recorded in this drama are as follows: There was a king of Magadha, Sundaravarman by name. He had a number of queens but still he had no son to succeed him. When he was advancing in age, he adopted one Candasena as his son. He belonged to the Magadha *kula* and his wife's relations were the neighbouring Licchavis. It may be noted that these Licchavis were the hereditary enemies of the Magadha dynasty. They are designated as *mlecchas* in the drama. As ill-luck would have it, after the adoption of Candasena by Sundaravarman, a son was born to him. This son was named Kalyāṇavarman. The old king became more attached to his own son, Kalyāṇavarman, and this incensed the adopted Candasena. He rose in revolt against the aged adoptive father who defended Pāṭalīputra, the capital. In the course of the battle, the old man died and Candasena crowned himself on the throne.

This was not liked by the Prime Minister Mantra Gupta and the Commander of the forces, Kuñjaraka. These espoused the cause of Kalyāṇavarman. They took him away for safety to Pampa in the Kiṣkindha hills. He was there for a number of years. In the meanwhile the Prime Minister and the Commander were waiting for an opportunity to enthrone the boy-prince Kalyāṇavarman. The citizens of Magadha were also in his favour. Public opinion was against Candasena who was regarded as an usurper. It so happened that Candasena had to leave the capital to put down the rebellions of the frontier chiefs, which were really set up by the ex-minister and his colleagues. This was the time for bringing in Kalyāṇavarman. Secret emissaries were sent to bring him back to the capital. The Council met and deposed Candasena and approved of the coronation of Kalyānavarman. As if to strengthen his power, an alliance was made with the King of Mathurā, the Yādava Kīrtisena. This political alliance was cemented by a marriage alliance, Kalyāṇavarman marrying the daughter of Kīrtisena. In honour of the marriage celebration, the festival of the *Kaumudīmahotsava* was instituted. At this time a woman poet of Pāṭalīputra got ready a drama, which was put on the stage perhaps in the immediate presence of the king Kalyāṇavarman, being a biographical sketch of the king upto the time of his marriage. In the last act it is mentioned that Candasena was killed.

From this it has been claimed that Candasena whom the play characterises as a Kāraskara was no other than Candra Gupta I of the Gupta dynasty. Baudhāyana assigns to the Kāraskaras a low status in the social scale. They are mentioned along with the Āraṭṭas, perhaps the people of the Kāra valley. They were a Panjabi community at the foot of the Himalayas, like the Śalvas. A division of this community goes by the name Jārtikas, the early ancestors of the modern Jats. Possibly the Gupta Candragupta was an ancestor of the present-day Kakkor Jats. That Candragupta hailed from the Panjab is further confirmed by his coins wherein he is depicted in true Panjabi military dress. It is surmised that the family of Candasena migrated to Bihar during the Bhāraśiva period and acquired a fief from them.

Why the city council deposed him during his absence from the capital is explained in the drama. The new king became unpopular. The people showed hostility to him. The enraged king threw the leading citizens of the place into prison and played the role of a prison-warden. This cruel act combined with his being a member of a low community and also with his marriage with the enemical Licchavis, all these flared up the people and they disowned him. They wanted a Kṣatriya who could carry on the traditional path of administration. The Prākrit Canda is Sanskrit Candra. He added as a suffix his grand-father's name which was Gupta (Jayaswal, *History of India,* pp. 114-18).

After the liberation of the Ganges Valley by the Bhāraśivas, a new family of orthodox Kṣatriyas began to rule from Magadha. This royal family is mentioned as the Magadha *kula* in the *Kaumudīmahotsava.* Possibly it is the same family as the Kota-kula, which finds a distinct mention in the Allahabad Pillar Inscription of Samudra Gupta. The names of the kings of this family ended in Varman. To this family belonged Sundaravarman and Kalyāṇavarman. These had their capital at Pāṭalīputra, and their palace is named Sūrganga. (This occurs in the Khāravela inscription and also in the Mudrārākṣasa). Kalyāṇavarman was crowned in the Sūrganga palace. At this time it is important to note what the drama has to say. The unorthodox Candasena's regime is gone: the new regime of Varṇa-dharma is once more revived. The play is significant for the fact that for some centuries past, orthodoxy had been dethroned and the rules of *varṇa* and *āśrama* were not observed. The traditional system of government founded on *dharma* had become a thing of the past. In the elevation of Kalyāṇavarman to the Magadha throne, the authoress sees signs of a new age, a new social revival and above all a revival of orthodox Hinduism. Though Kalyānavarman's family ceased to reign, still the successors to the Magadha throne Samudragupta and Candragupta II did much to take Hindu India into the promised land of Dharma. They upheld Dharma and Brahmanism, served learning and learned men and promoted the cause of Hindu civilisation in every field of activity.

The historical events adumbrated by the drama seem to be a little supported by the Allahabad Pillar Inscription. (Fleet, *Gupta Ins.*, pp. 1-17). Here Samudragupta's first target of attack was Puṣpapura, which is another term for Pāṭalīputra. This clearly shows that at the commencement of his career, he had to fight once again for the throne which was once in the possession of his father Candragupta. The ruling family of Kalyāṇavarman was vanquished, that is, the Kōṭa kulaja king. Also Nāgasena had to be defeated. As has been surmised he was the son of Kīrtisena of Mathurā and therefore the brother-in-law of Kalyāṇavarman. This reconquest of Pāṭalīputra is itself a strong evidence to show that his father had been deprived of that capital. It is natural to infer that it is due to Kalyāṇavarman's *abhiseka.* The drama further shows that king Candragupta died in exile and in distress. Naturally when Samudragupta came to occupy the throne, he learnt a telling lesson from the acts of his predecessor and profited greatly by his mistakes. · Statesman as he was, he could read the temper of the public and adjusted his rule according to it. By his acts and deeds he won the love and esteem of his people and by celebrating Vedic sacrifices enjoined on a true Kṣatriya prince, he endeared himself to the orthodox public. So his successors continued that policy and thus the true foundations of the Gupta Empire were laid firm and stable.

In conclusion, the discovery of the *Kaumudīmahotsava* has thrown considerable light on the origin and rise of the Gupta dynasty and the historical data in it have solved many a riddle in the early Gupta history, which would otherwise stand unsolved. The materials in the play have enriched the Gupta history in several ways, which remained a puzzle to early Gupta historians.[19-a]

The *Devīcandraguptam* is a political drama attributed to Viśākhadatta, the reputed author of the *Mudrārakṣasa*. It is unfortunate that the drama has been lost to us. All that we have are the quotations made here and there by certain writers like Abhinava Gupta in the *Abhinavabhārati* (ch. XVIII), Bhoja in *Sṛṅgāraprakāśa* (ch. XII), Rāmachandra in *Nāṭyadarpana* (Gaekwad Oriental Series), and Sāgaranadin in *Nāṭakalakṣana Ratnakośa* (Ed. by Myles Dillon, London, 1937). The passages quoted by these authors are our primary authority for reconstructing the text of the *Devīcandraguptam*. Basing on these passages, several scholars have examined the historical data and come forward with their theories.[19-b]

As the subject-matter of the discovered passage of the *Devīcandraguptam* has been elaborately discussed by a host of scholars it is unnecessary for us to repeat everything that has been already said. We shall therefore confine ourselves to the important historical data furnished to us, by this source

19-a. Dr. M. Winternitz, however, does not accept this viewpoint. (*Dr. S. K. Aiyangar Commemoration Volume*, pp. 359-62).

19-b. (A. R. Sarasvati, *Indian Ant.*, July 1923, pp. 181-84). Sylvain Levi, *Journal Asiatique*, Oct.-Dec. 1923: Altekar, *J.B.O.R.S.* 1928 pp. 223-253 & 1929 pp. 134-141 V. V. Mirashi, *Ind. Ant.* 1933, pp. 201-5; Dasaratha Sarma, *Journal of Indian History*, 1935. pp. 30-34; K. P. Jayaswal, *J.B.O.R.S.* 1932, pp. 17-36; D. R. Bhandarkar, *Malaviya Commemoration Volume* pp. 189-211; V. Raghavan, *Journal of the Benares Hindu University*, 1936, pp. 23-54.

book for the history of the Guptas. The hero of the play is Kumāra Candragupta, the later Candragupta II Vikramāditya. The king as seen in the play was Rāmagupta and his queen was Dhruvadevī.

The *Nāṭyadarpaṇa* extract shows that Rāmagupta was the elder brother of Candragupta II and also an affectionate brother. The next important character in the play is the courtesan Mādhavasenā. The latter was an attendant on the queen in the harem. Prince Candragupta became her lover. Rāmagupta's enemy was a Śakapati. In the battle that took place between Rāmagupta and the Śaka chief, Rāmagupta was vanquished and he entered into an ignominious agreement with the enemy to hand over his queen Dhruvadevī to him. The queen felt desperate and despondent. Prince Candragupta bucked up, summoned all his courage to devise a plan to vanquish the Śaka chief and prevent the unholy treaty becoming true. It is said that Rāmagupta accepted such terms on the advice of his ministers (*Prakṛtis*) and not of his people as is made out by some. Candragupta's idea was to kill the enemy in his own camp. Several plans ran through his mind. One was to get the aid of a Vetāla, vampire by going to the cemetery at dead of night and by propitiating it (*Vetālasādhana*).

In the meantime Mādhavasena was presented by the queen with her own dress and ornaments. She was of course perturbed by the disquieting news of the Devī being given away to the enemy. Anxious to meet Candragupta she came to his camp along with the presents which she had received at the hands of Dhruvadevī. At this the prince abandoned his original plan and decided to disguise himself in the dress of Dhruvadevī, enter the Śaka's camp and overpower him. It was an act of *sāhasa* but Candragupta was ready to perform that *sāhasa* with success. So it was done, and Rāmagupta was informed that the Śaka chief had been killed. Before Candragupta actually did away with the despicable enemy, he had occasion to meet Dhruvadevī, when she should have opened her mind as to the shameful condition brought to her by her coward husband. This must have moved Candragupta to a considerable extent and strengthened his determination to kill the enemy at any cost.

After the murder of the enemy had been effected, Candragupta must have planned to get rid of his brother Rāmagupta who had proved imbecile and, a weakling. Some authorities aver that Candragupta himself killed his brother and ascended the throne. This enabled him also to marry his brother's widow Dhruvadevī. Whether the law-codes of the time allowed such marriages as legally valid is no matter for consideration either for the parties, or speculation by the modern scholar. Political exigencies of the time drove them to enter into a marriage alliance. And the public who had love and regard for Candragupta and who had been shocked by the humiliating peace effected by Rāmagupta which involved the honour and disgrace of the queen had to approve this wedlock as legal. The Sañjan copper-plate of Amoghavarsa I, (*Ep. Ind.*, XVIII, pp. 235 ff.) belittles Candragupta for this action. In the same strain a reference is made to him in the Saṅgali and Cambay Plates (*Ibid.*, VII, pp. 26 ff.) of the Rashtrakūṭa king Govinda IV.

The drama is a *prakaraṇa* and every *prakaraṇa* type of a drama has ten acts. After all the extracts so far discovered have nothing to refer to the later Acts of the play. But we have enough material to indicate that Candragupta after having vanquished the Śaka chief, was in a state of madness. It was not real madness but a feigned one, another act of *sāhasa* by the king. He wanted to carry out certain plans and to achieve them he had to pretend to be in a state of madness. A passage gives a glimpse of the cause which drove the prince to this condition. According to this there was some difficulty in getting admission to the palace for the prince. And this was effected by resorting to that device. So he entered the palace and perhaps the murder of the king and his marriage with Dhruvadevī are the subject-matter of the last Acts of the *Devīcandraguptam*.

A critical study of the outline of the story bears out that there was an elder brother of Candragupta II whose name was Rāmagupta. After Samudragupta, Rāmagupta got the throne by the right of primogeniture which was generally in vogue. He had to engage himself in a war with the Śaka satrap. This satrap was Rudrasimha, circa A.D. 388 according to some and Rudrasena II of the western Kṣatrapa dynasty (348-78 A.D.) according to others. The scene of battle was Ālipura in the Jālandhar Doab. According to Jayaswal it was Aliwal in the Kangra District in the Doab between the Beas and the Jhelum. One important point to note in this connection is that early students of Gupta history were not aware of the existence of a king named Rāmagupta. It was taken for granted that Candragupta II succeeded Samudragupta automatically. This drama shows beyond doubt that Samudragupta had an elder son Rāmagupta who succeeded to the Gupta throne and who had to fight the Śakas. He was not of the stern mettle as Samudragupta was. He had a humiliating defeat. But Prince Candragupta saved the honour of the queen and of the empire by killing the enemy, though by covert means, and thus re-established the Gupta empire on unshakable foundations. Rāmagupta's reign should have been a brief one and hence we do not find any records or coins of his period.

There is an intriguing problem in the Gupta history. And that is a find of Gupta coins bearing the name Kaca or Kacagupta. Scholars have been exercising their minds on who this Kacagupta was. The coins of Kaca bear close resemblance to the issues of Samudragupta. So one theory was

Kaca was another name of Samudragupta himself. A second was that they were the issues of a rival brother of Samudragupta and that this brother ruled for a brief time before Samudragupta. But the Allahabad Pillar Inscription rules out this possibility. For the father of Samudragupta said in the presence of his courtiers, 'Here is a noble man' and embracing him with shivers of joy addressed him 'Protect then this whole earth' (*Indian Antiquary,* 1913, p. 176). Therefore there was no interruption between the reigns of Candragupta I and Samudragupta. But that there was some interruption between the reigns of Samudragupta and his son Candragupta II is testified to us by the *Devīcandraguptam.* From this authority, the Kaca coins have been interpreted as the issues of Rāmagupta. Whether Kaca is a scriptal corruption for Rāma or not, we cannot say with any definiteness. But we do not see any reason why these coins should not be attributed to Ghaṭotkachagupta, the grandfather of Samudragupta. It may be that these coins were the models for Samudragupta to issue his own coins. It is not fair that this possibility should be ruled out once for all.

But as if to confirm this viewpoint there is the evidence of an Arabic story told in the *Mujmalu-t-Tawarikh,* (Elliot and Dowson, *Hist. of Ind.,* I, pp. 110-111) of about the eleventh or twelfth century A.D. This is the story of Rawwal and Barkamaris based almost on the plot of the *Devīcandraguptam.* Barkamaris (Vikrama) stands for Prince Candragupta and Rawwal for Rāmagupta. The Arabic version is interesting. Barkamaris had fixed up a lady for himself and coming to know that his elder brother wanted to marry her, he agreed and took to a life of a scholar. When Rawwal was defeated and his ministers sat mum the younger brother entered the enemy's camp in the queen's guise and did him to death with his dagger. This threw Barkamaris into great popularity and evoked at the same time the jealousy of his brother's ministers. So Barkamaris feigned madness and one day when the king and queen were chewing sugarcane, he reached there. The queen gave him a bit of the sugarcane and knife to cut the cane. With that knife Barkamaris cut Rawwal to death. If this story depicted a historical fact, it is no doubt that the Rawwal of the story was no other than Rāmagupta, the Gupta king.

This is not all. We have to examine carefully the other drama of Viśākhadatta the *Mudrārākṣasa,* confining ourselves for the present to the Bharatavākya of this drama. Here is a reference to Pārthiva Candragupta. When Viśākhadatta wrote the *Devīcandraguptam,* Candragupta was a Kumāra or prince. When he wrote his second play *Mudrārākṣasa,* Candragupta had already become a king. The Bharatavākya refers to Candragupta's exploit in rescuing Dhruvasvamini from the Śaka king. Just as Hari in his incarnation as Boar delivered the Earth from the deluge, Candragupta freed the queen from the clutches of the *mleccha.* For this brilliant feat Candragupta is compared by the poet to God Viṣṇu himself. On this evidence, as also on the evidence of the *Harṣa carita* (6th Uchvāsa) we can confidently conclude that Rāmagupta succeeded Samudragupta and reigned for one or two years and possibly the Kaca coins of the Gupta period are reminiscent of his reign, though this cannot be asserted.

The *Mudrārākṣasa* of Viśākhadatta is yet another source book of the Gupta epoch. The discovery of the *Devīcandraguptam* at least in fragments has settled once for all the date of Viśākhadatta. The early scholars like Wilson had to be under some illusion about the date of this work mistaking that the term *mleccha* connoted the Mussalman. When K. T. Telang published his edition of the *Mudrārākṣasa,* the evidences at his disposal could make out a case for the 7th century or a little earlier being assigned to the work. Much water has flown since, and we are on firm ground to say that

4

Viśākhadatta was a contemporary not only of Rāmagupta of the Gupta dynasty but also of Candragupta II Vikramāditya. If we read the Bharatavākya of the *Mudrārākṣasa*

> वाराहीमात्मयोनेस्तनुभवनविधावास्थितस्यानुरूपां
> यस्य प्राग्दन्तकोटिं प्रलयपरिगता शिश्रिये भूतधात्री ।
> म्लेच्छैरुद्विज्यमाना भुजयुगमधुना संश्रिता राजमूर्तेः
> स श्रीमद्बन्धुभृत्यश्चिरमवतु महीं पार्थिवश्चन्द्रगुप्तः ॥ (vii. 19)

where there is an unmistakable reference to Pārthiva Candragupta as the ruling prince of the time, it settles the problem to a great extent. That it should be Candragupta II only has been attested by the reference in the *Devīcandraguptam* which is indeed an invaluable testimony. In fact both the dramas, *Devīcandraguptam* and *Mudrārākṣasa,* if read together, give us a deep insight into the early history and career of Candragupta II when he was a crown prince and later when he became emperor.

Though the plot of the *Mudrārākṣasa* deals with the establishment of the Mauryan dynasty by Candragupta Maurya, largely through the untiring efforts of Cāṇakya, the eminent author of the *Arthaśāstra,* still our author seems to refer to contemporary events of establishing the Gupta dynasty which was a little shaken by the weak rule of Rāma Gupta and by the intrusion of Śaka chiefs. Whatever this may be, the fact remains that the drama is full of diplomacy and politics. Domestic virtues come in, if they come at all, casually. The whole spirit of the drama which reflects the age of the author is replete with sacrifice and a stern sense of duty. The importance of the minister in running the ship of administration is given the certain emphasis. To achieve political ends in the interest of the crown and country is the main theme, and in achieving them, the end justifies the means. Here we find elaborately the Kauṭalīyan idealism and imperialism well reflected and practised. After all, a statesman should be guided by the exigencies of political conditions but without much violation to the existing law of the land. Such acts were not immoral but may be put down amoral.

Far-reaching plans for the promotion of the welfare of the State are laid after a good deal of reflection and are accomplished with the determination of a hard politician. Politicians endowed with less intelligence and vision are won by persuasion and intrigue, and the smooth sailing of administrative affairs is effected. The value of diplomacy in ensuring political ends is much stressed upon. Thus the *Mudrārākṣasa.* (Ed. by M. R. Kale, Bombay 1927) is a political drama of the first magnitude and shows beyond doubt how the Kauṭalīyan diplomatic code and ethics played an important role in the running of the administrative machinery of the Gupta epoch. The Gupta emperors and their ministers followed truly the tradition set up by Kauṭalya, and it may be said without any fear of contradiction that the Gupta polity was a faithful model of the Mauryan polity in all its essentials. There may be a departure here or there due to the events which had taken place between the decline of the Mauryan empire and the rise and growth of the Gupta empire. As we shall see in the following pages, the differences are not too many, and the Gupta emperors tried to emulate the example of their erstwhile glorious predecessors, *viz.* the Mauryas. To this extent the *Mudrārākṣasa* is invaluable to a student of the Gupta polity.

The work also throws sidelights on the religion of the monarchs and the religious condition of the age in the drama. The play refers to the worship of Viṣṇu in the form of the Boar Incarnation, and archæological studies bear out the devotion of the Guptas to the Varāha *avatar* of Hari and the erection of a number of temples by them. At the same time the toleration of the age is reflected in the play. (*Ibid.*, Act IV). The position occupied by the Jaina Jīvasiddhi in the *Mudrā-*

rākṣasa (Act IV) is an evidence in point. The ministers of the State like Cāṇakya and Rākṣasa who were not Jains take Jīvasiddhi into confidence. In fact Jīvasiddhi is a tool in the hands of the pronounced politician, Cāṇakya. Again when Candanadāsa is prepared to sacrifice his life for the sake of his friend Rākṣasa, it is remarked that his conduct transcended the nobility of the Buddhist.

> बुद्धानामपि चेष्टितं सुचरितैः क्लिष्टं विशुद्धात्मना
> पूजार्होऽपि स यत्कृते तव गतो वध्यत्वमेषोऽस्मि सः ॥
>
> (Act VII, St. 5.)

This shows the regard which the enlightened public had for the Buddhists of the time. Be it noted that it is put in the mouth of Rākṣasa who was a Brahmana by caste. It was almost the time when Buddhism showed signs of decline. The compliment paid to Buddhism by a non-Buddhist author like Viśākhadatta deserves to be noted.

The value of the material contained in the drama cannot be over-estimated. It gives a list of the names of peoples and tribes at that time, i.e. in the period of Candragupta II These are the Śakas, Yavanas, Kirātas, Kambojas, Pārasikas, Bāhlikas, and these names find mention in the second Act. Other peoples are mentioned in the fifth Act and these are Khāśās, Māgadhas, Gāndhāras, Cinas, Himas and Kaulutas. The term Mleccha of course occurs and it generally stands for any foreigner outside the pale of Hinduism. This shows the distribution of peoples and tribes of India towards the end of the fourth century A.D.

The Evidence of the Chinese Pilgrims

Among the sources for the Gupta history, the most valuable is the record left by the Chinese pilgrim Fa-hien (Fa-hsien). To the Chinese India was the Holy Land and hence a stream of pilgrims continued to visit the country through the ages. Some of them were enterprising enough to note the social and political conditions of India during their visit, and these records are of inestimable value to the study of the history of several periods in the annals of India. Fa-hien was one such. He was a native of Wu-yang in the province of Shan-si. It is said he became a śramanera in his third year. He started from Chang'an in A.D. 399. After passing through several places he reached Khotan where he saw a car procession. After many days of travel, he advanced to the Indus region, crossing which he came to the territory of Udyāna. After fifteen years of wandering and travel, he returned back to China. It was the reign of Candragupta II Vikramāditya when Fa-hien visited India. The accounts which he has left form the most reliable source of information on the times of Candragupta II Vikramāditya. There are several details with regard to the administration and social life of the people of the time in his records, besides religious conditions. Not only did he visit India but also he went to Ceylon in A.D. 412 when Buddhadāsa was ruling there.

Fa-hien's work entitled *Fo-kuo-ki* (Record of Buddhist Kingdoms) is considered so important that it has been translated as many as four times into English and once into French. Beal, Legge and Giles are the English translators of the *Fo-kuo-ki.* (See *The Travels of Fa-hien*, Retranslated by H. A. Giles, Cambridge, 1923.) Beal himself gave us two versions, one before the translation of Giles and the other after that. The translation by James Legge, (*A Record of Buddhistic Kingdoms*, Oxford 1886) who has taken into account the labours of his predecessors is still more valuable. Though the main object of Fa-hien was the search for Buddhist books and legends, still he has noted certain particulars of Candragupta's administration. Fa-hien spent nearly three years in the capital Pāṭalīputra and it is natural that he was impressed with the splendour and magnificence of the capital, its palace and its amenities. Speaking of Madhya-deśa, or Central India, (Giles, *op. cit.*, pp. 20-23; also p. 47), the Chinese pilgrim notes the wealth and prosperity of the towns and their citizens, and the numerous charitable organisations including free hospitals maintained by the State for the poor and the helpless.

The pilgrim was a restless wanderer from one part of the country to another. When he was passing from the Indus region to Mathurā on the Jumna, separated by a distance of 500 miles, he noticed a number of Buddhist monasteries which housed thousands of Buddhist monks. In and around Mathurā he came across twenty such buildings occupied roughly by three thousand residents. This is a picture of the flourishing nature of Buddhism in the land of its birth. The same prosperity, says Fa-hien, attended Mālva, the territory that lay to the south of Mathurā. He pays a glowing tribute to the highly popular government, which, when compared with the Chinese system, was mild, temperate and sensible.

On the whole the Chinese pilgrim gives a vivid picture of the country and its good government. Though his observations are all through the coloured glass of Buddhism, still he certifies to the flourishing nature of the Buddhist faith side by side with Hinduism of which the ruling sovereign of the land was a follower. His patronage of a particular faith did no violence or injustice to other faiths to which also toleration was extended in an even-handed manner. According to his own account, Fa-hien did not feel anywhere that he was a foreigner to the Indian continent. He was not restricted by the regulations which are enforced in the twentieth century even by advanced nations in the matter of passports and nationalities. He felt at home and moved freely from one part of the country to another. And to this complacent nature of the Government and the people the Chinese pilgrim testifies in more than one place.

We have not considered the records of the other distinguished pilgrim Hiuen Tsang who travelled in India from A.D. 629 to 645. By his time the epoch of the Imperial Guptas had come to an end and therefore Hiuen Tsang's accounts do not materially serve as a source of information for the early Gupta period with which we are concerned in the present volume.

Records of I-'Tsing.

I-'Tsing, another Chinese pilgrim who travelled in India from 671-95, refers to a Mahārajā Śrī Gupta who erected a shrine for the use of Chinese pilgrims near Mṛgaśikhāvana, and it came to be known as the Temple of China. I-'Tsing noted the ruins of this temple and has left the record that it was built about 500 years before his time. It is not correct to credit this 500 years with any chronological exactness. It may be 500 years or less. Most important is the tradition he heard about the Temple of China. He tells us that he was told that the temple was founded by Śrī Gupta. This Śrī Gupta can be taken to be the founder of the Gupta dynasty. But there is no evidence to prove it. It may be noted in passing that Śrì is only an honorific still in use with us in India. It has been recently and officially recognised by the Madras Government. This tradition is significant in another respect also. It shows the reigning monarch of Hindu India was complaisant of foreigners, allowed them to settle and follow their mode of worship, aided them to erect shrines and looked to their comforts.[19-c]

Numismatic Evidence

Numismatics have been aptly regarded as a handmaid to the muse of history. Several gaps in the list of dynasties and also in the chronology of various monarchs have been

19-c. (Chavannes: *Mémoire sur les Religieux eminents* 1894. pp. 82 and 3; Allan: *Catalogue of coins of the Gupta dynasties*, p. XV.)

filled with the aid of coins. Luckily there are several coins of the Gupta period which are of great value for the study of the Gupta history. A systematic study of these coins has been made by J. Allan (*Catalogue of the Coins of the Gupta Dynasties,* London, 1914). The concensus of opinion is that Candragupta I did not issue coins himself but it was Samudragupta who struck coins in the name of his father and mother, more as commemorative medals than as coins. With this viewpoint one may agree considering the brief tenure of Candragupta I's reign and his numerous engagements in founding the dominion. The coins of Candragupta I betray that the foundations of the Gupta Empire had already been well laid, and Samudragupta only built upon the superstructure though it was shaken to some extent by Candravarman of Puṣkaraṇa. We shall see more of this in the next chapter.

Reference has already been made to the Kaca coins. The identity of Kaca has been a bone of contention among scholars. It is difficult to accept the suggestion of Fleet that Kaca may be a formal name of Samudragupta. The other suggestion that it was the original name of Samudragupta, and that the latter name was assumed after the glorious conquests made by him is equally unacceptable. Yet another assumption that the legend on the Kaca type—*Karmabhir uttamair*—equates with that on the Archer type does not convince us. The legend on the Archer type is *sucarita.* This may be synonymous with that on the Kaca type. But both *uttama karma* and *sucarita* need not be equivalents. In the light of these reasons, one has to dismiss the identification of Kaca with Samudragupta. We are rather inclined to attribute these coins of the Kaca type to Ghaṭotkaca, the grand-father of Samudragupta or to Rāmagupta, the elder son of Samudragupta.

It is true that Ghaṭotkaca was still the ruler of a small state and that he had not attained the status of a *mahārājā.* But nothing prevents an independent ruler from issuing his coins. Have we not coins of Gaṇapati Nāga, Acyuta and others who were independent rulers of small states? In the same way we have to treat Ghaṭotkaca's coins. He might have issued them himself.

The other alternative would be to treat them as memorial medals struck by Samudragupta. When the latter could strike coins in memory of his father, what prevented him from doing so in the case of his grand-father who must have been reputed for his superior deeds as the legends would have it? One would even read the legend as a reference to Vedic *karmas* and say Ghaṭotkaca was a devoted and devout student of Vedic religion, and he put it in practice. And this paved the way for the popularity and support of his son Candragupta I against the foreign Scythians. If this were accepted—we see no reason why we should not—the independence of Ghaṭotkaca is well nigh established. Be this as it may, the testimony of Gupta-Licchavi alliance cemented by the bond of marriage has been well brought to light by the coins of Candragupta I and the legends thereon. On the obverse the king holds a standard with a crescent-top and is offering a ring or bracelet to his queen. On the reverse a goddess seated on a lion is depicted. She is perhaps Durgā or Mahādevī. This shows that Candragupta I was a man of ambition and embarked on a career of military conquests. Generally the Indian tradition is to invoke the aid of Durgā on the eve of such military exploits. Thus we see in the *Mahābhārata*, (Virāṭaparva, viii. 7-26 ch.), a hymn of praise and prayer to Durgā by Arjuna-Pāṇḍava and others on the eve of his military expedition. The association of lion with the Devī is another symbolical representation of the king's prowess and determination to extirpate the enemy and to proclaim his overlordship.

Proceeding to examine the coins of Samudragupta, we meet with a variety of types and specimens. We shall deal with some of the important types attributed to this emperor. The Tiger type of coins is worthy of note. The king is depicted here in an *utthāna* pose, with his waist-cloth, turban and jewellery. He is in a state of action. He is represented as trampling on a tiger which is his game. As he is engaged in shooting the animal, it falls back and he fearlessly tramples on it. On the reverse of this type of coins, one meets with the figure of a goddess standing on a *makara* (a fish with an elephant head), identified with the river goddess Gangā. Next to the lion, the tiger is a ferocious animal symbolical of one's valour and heroism. This may point to the king's quickness of action and daring, without which he would not have brought the mission of his *dig-vijaya* to a successful end.

Next comes the lyrist type of coins. (Allan, *op. cit.*, Intro. P. LXXV). It is also named luteplayer type. This type is interesting in that it shows the king's skill in music and his patronage of fine arts of which music takes an important place. The Allahabad Inscription brings confirmation on this point, where it is said that music of the celestials like (Fleet, *op. cit.*, Ins. No. 1) Tumburu and Nārada was his favourite amusement. On the reverse we have goddess Lakshmi seated. It is generally taken that this type of coins may belong to a later period in his career. It may be so. The figure of Lakshmi shows that his conquests were over, and that Śrī or fortune was smiling before him in all exuberance and abundance. Now that the whole of the Indian continent acknowledged his suzerainty he finds time for amusement and this was in the shape of music. By playing sweet tunes on the viṇā, he not only patronised musical talents but girdled all round with the music of his heart. This was one of his *sucaritas* referred to in the legend of the coins of the Archer type. This indicates that Samudragupta was a man of artistic tastes and was not a believer in the military rule of the empire.

A third type of coin of Samudragupta may be termed the *Aśvamedha* type. (Allan, *op. cit.*, Intro. pp. LXXVI ff.). There are different specimens of this type. On the obverse a horse—which is of course the sacrificial animal—stands near the *yūpa* which is again a sacrificial post, perhaps tied to the *yūpa*. On the reverse there is the representation of the *palnī*, the wife of the sacrificer. In this case she must be Dattadevī, the chief queen of Samudragupta. One fundamental principle of any *yajña* is that the performer of a sacrifice should do it only in the immediate presence of his *dharmapatnī*. Therefore it is no wonder that the chief queen is given prominence in this type of coins.

Another fact that emerges from these coins is that Samudragupta performed the *Aśvamedha*, which is the birthright of *samrāṭs* and *ekarāṭs*. In other words, the *Aśvamedha yajña* is a political yāga enjoined only on Ksatriyas par excellence. According to the *Brāhmaṇas*, only a king who feels that he is superior to all other rulers can venture on such a sacrifice. The Vedic texts also warrant its performance by one who has had his *dig-vijaya* completed without any interruption. So Samudragupta who had established his suzerainty after vanquishing all the monarchs of Northern and Southern India proclaimed himself as an All-India ruler by engaging himself in the *Aśvamedha* sacrifice. It may be remembered that this sacrifice could be done only by a man of vast prowess and resources. The last monarch to do this, before the Guptas, was Puṣyamitra Śunga, (C.H.I. Vol. I p. 520). It was only given to a few to engage themselves in a sacrifice of this kind, and Samudragupta did it successfully. The fact that it does not find mention in the Allahabad Pillar Inscription shows that the king performed this at a late period of his reign. This also shows that Samudragupta had been accepted by public opinion as a Kṣatriya, for according to the scheme of *Varnadharma*, it is only the privilege of a Kṣatriya monarch to perform the *Aśvamedha* and the *Rājasūya,* both of them signifying unquestioned royal supremacy. The *Aśvamedha* type of coins were issued either to commemorate this great event, or for the purpose of distribution and gift to the *adhvaryu* and other priests who officiated in the yāga. In the inscriptions Samudragupta is said to have lavished presents in the shape of cows and gold in tens and thousands (*aneka go hiraṇya kōṭi pradā*). The *hiraṇya* of the epigraphs may refer to the gold coins of the monarch. These coins have therefore the appropriate legends *Māhārajādhirāja Apratívāryavīrya, and Aśvamedha parākrama.*

There are other coins of Samudragupta also. The common coins are the standard type. Vincent Smith calls them Spearman or Javelin type, because he identifies the object in the king's left hand as a spear or javelin. J. Allan who has examined them more closely does not find any such instrument and is inclined to club them as the standard type of coins. The *garuḍa* standard is prominent in the Gupta coins. Then we have the Archer type. Here the bow takes the place of the standard. Then is the Battle-axe type. In these specimens the king holds a battle-axe in his left hand. On some there is the sword. These coins bear the evidence that Samudragupta was in the early part of his reign devoted to warfare, and plunged himself heart and soul in the conquest of the earth and in winning a name in heaven, (*gāmjitvā divam jayati*). This seems to have been the motto underlying his *dig-vijaya.* He wanted to play the regular role of a Kṣatriya hero and he played it well.

A good number of coins have been discovered, all attributed to Candragupta II. (Allan, *op. cit.,* pp. 24 ff.). The commonest is the Archer type with different varieties. Among them may be distinguished what are known as the Throne coins which were peculiar to the northern parts of the empire and the lotus coins belonging to the central or eastern parts of the empire. There is considerable similarity between the Archer coins of Samudra Gupta and Candra Gupta II so far as the obverse side is concerned. In these coins the bow is prominently seen held by the king. The bow and arrow are indicative of king Candragupta II's war-mindedness. They show that he was anxious to maintain the integrity of the empire annexed by his father Samudragupta. (*Ibid.*, p. 33.)

There is another type of Candragupta II's coins known as the Conch type. There are not many specimens of this type. Here the king is seated on a conch with high back. On the reverse is the figure of goddess Śrī. The issue of this type probably belongs to the early part of his reign. The next important type is the *chattra* type, *chattra* meaning 'umbrella'. In Indian tradition the *chattra* is always a sign of royalty. It is a paraphernalia of the majesty of the king. Even today in temple processions when an idol is taken out, a huge umbrella is held aloft, being a symbol of divine power. It is perhaps associated with the concept of divinity attached to a king of real power and remarkable valour. By far the most important is the lion-slayer type of coins. It may be that the king tramples on a lion, combats with a lion or slays a lion. The lion is considered by the Hindus as the king of animals. A noble hero is referred to as the lion among men. We have numerous lion-fighter legends not only in India but also in ancient Babylon and Greece. In these coins the bow is invariably seen held by the king. J. Allan remarks on this that this is a deliberate representation of the king as ambidexterous. There are also coins in which the lion is represented as retreating instead of facing the king, when he shoots it.

Candragupta II has also introduced the Horseman type of coins which were continued by his successor Kumāragupta I. (*Ibid.*, pp. 69 ff.). On the obverse the king is seated on horseback either fully dressed, or wearing only a waistcloth.

A sword and sometimes a bow are held by him. On the reverse is the figure of goddess Śrī seated on a wicker stool. These coins are the evidence to bear out that Candragupta II as also Kumāragupta I were great cavalry soldiers, and their strength lay much in the cavalry arm of the Gupta army. The importance of horse as a war-animal was well recognised, and it is to be assumed that cavalry force played a significant role in the wars conducted by Candragupta II and his successor.

The silver coins of Candragupta II (*Ibid.*, pp. 49-51) were struck probably after the overthrow of the Western Kṣatrapas who were in possession of the western parts of the Gupta empire. Samudragupta was too much occupied in the central and southern parts of India and his arms could not reach the territories ruled over by the dynasty of Western Kṣatrapas. It was given to Candragupta II to round off the conquests so ably and magnificently effected by his father. By vanquishing these Kṣatrapas, Candragupta II extended the limits of his empire to the west. Surāṣṭra-Mālva lay at his feet. After this was effected, he seems to have struck silver coins and made them current in these regions. The Ksatrapas had their own coins with the *Caitya* on the reverse. The issues of Candragupta II were imitations of the old Kṣatrapa coins but he took care to remove the Śaka era and substitute the Gupta era. In the same way *Garuḍa* took the place of the *Caitya*.

Garuḍa the vehicle of Hari is well known as the characteristic emblem of the Guptas. It was their badge and is seen on their seals. While the gold coins of the Guptas bear the *Garuḍadhvaja*, the silver and copper coins bear the figure of *Garuḍa* itself. *Garuḍa* is represented standing with its wings spread out. This shows that the emperor who had *garuḍalāñcana* is bent upon expanding his empire. For it was *Garuḍa* who aided Hari in his conquests over the hard-hearted Asuras, and the adoption of *Garuḍa* on their coins and seals by the Guptas lends support to the view that they, besides supporting the Vaiṣṇava faith, believed in Garuḍa as the symbol of certain victory.

It may be noted in this connection that *Garuḍa* figured on the reverse type of issue of Kumāragupta (see, for instance, *Ibid.*, pp. 89 ff.). But in some of his coins we also find a representation of the peacock which was the riding *vāhana* of Kumāra, the war-god. Kumāra is considered the commander-in-chief of the celestials and just like Garuḍa, the peacock has its own importance in bringing success to his master in all the terrible wars in which he engaged himself. These representations of animals like the lion and tiger, garuḍa and peacock by the different sovereigns of the Gupta dynasty show that they were anxious to achieve success and celebrity by following the example of the gods and demigods of the country. In the famous Junagādh inscription of Skandagupta, the followers of the king are compared to *garuḍas*, and his enemies to nāgas or serpents, the traditional foes of the *garuḍas*.

Kumāragupta I's coins (*Ibid.*, pp. 61-113) are equally abundant and are of value to a student of Gupta history. He issued the familiar archer type, *aśvamedha* type, horseman type, lion-slayer type, tiger-slayer type, and also a number of silver coins. In these issues he copied the example of his illustrious predecessors. Some coins with the legend Pratāpa on the reverse were issued by Kumāragupta I, as also the elephant-rider type. Here the king rides on an elephant, an attendant seated behind holding an umbrella over him. On the reverse is seen the figure of Lakṣmī with a lotus flower in her hand. The last two varieties Pratāpa and elephant-rider type are new to the series of Gupta coins and suggest Kumāragupta's use of elephants as one of the units of his army. All these coins bear marks of his mighty prowess, valour and courage and mark him out as a doughty champion for not only sustaining the empire but also for adding fresh territories.

They also suggest his insatiable thirst for conquest and imperial sway. Though there are no records signifying specific engagements still the performance of the *Aśvamedha* shows that his achievements, of which we are not aware, entitled him to assume paramount sovereignty. In his reign silver coins became current for the first time in the central province of the Gupta empire. Add to this the silver-plated coins of Kumāragupta with a copper core. Perhaps they are a debased issue struck during financial crisis. (V. A. Smith : JRAS, 1893, pp. 137 ff.).

During the reign of Skandagupta, the Archer type, (*Ibid.*, pp. 114-5) of coins is mainly of gold. The king is seen with a bow and a *garuḍadhvaja.* Some coins bear the legend *Kramāditya* which is a title of Skandagupta. Possibly he issued the horseman type of coins also. A close examination of the find spots and contents of hoards of Skandagupta's silver coins enables us to determine the limits of his empire. (Allan: *op. cit.* page *c.*). The reverse types are three which are *garuḍa,* bull and altar. We are familiar with the *garuḍa* type. The Bull type which is new is found on coins of base metal. This was perhaps a local coin circulated in the regions round the Gulf of Cambay. The Bull type may point to the religious leanings of Skandagupta. The Altar type is pre-eminently seen among the silver coins of Skandagupta. There are signs of fire burning on them. The altar suggests sacrifice, which the king might have performed on an elaborate scale. But there is no record to support this view. In the latter half of his reign we find debased currency. Pure gold from 108 grains was reduced to 73 grains. This must be due certainly to the heavy pressure on the treasury by incessant wars which he had to wage with the Huns and also the Puṣyamitra tribe.

There are coins then of Prakāśāditya. (*Ibid.*, pp. 135-6). Vincent Smith thinks Puragupta was the proper name, and

Prakāśāditya the title. His coins present a new type. It is the combination of the horseman-type and the lion-slayer type. The coins represent Prakāśāditya on horseback, rending a lion with his sword. It must be said to his credit that though the decline of the empire had begun, still he was not suffering from dearth of money as could be seen by the reform of currency effected by him. His gold coins extant weigh 121 grains of pure gold, much more in value than those of the early sovereigns of the Gupta period. So fortune still smiled on him. Though we do not meet with the Archer-type of coins in this reign, still his successor unanimously used that type only.

The Evidence of Inscriptions

Dr. J. F. Fleet has done a great service to the cause of Indology by publishing his magnum opus—Inscriptions of the Early Gupta Kings and their successors (*Corpus Inscriptionum Indicarum,* Vol. III, 1888). In this one volume Dr. Fleet has brought together not only the inscriptions of the early Guptas but also the inscriptions of the later Gupta period. For example, we have two inscriptions of the rulers of Mālava (Nos. 17 and 18). Then there are records of a feudatory family—the Parivrājaka Mahārājas (Nos. 21 to 25). The importance and value of these records consist in the fact that notwithstanding the decline of the early Gupta dynasty, the Gupta dominion continued to exist as a power till A.D. 528. They are also noteworthy for the fact that they used the twelve-year cycle of Jupiter.

In this Corpus are published the inscriptions (Nos. 26 to 31) of another royal family, the Mahārājas of Ucchakalpa ranging from A. D. 493 to 533-34. The moot point about them is whether they were feudatories of the early kings of the Kālacuri dynasty. There is then the famous record of Yaśodharman dated A.D. 533-34 in the Mandasor inscriptions (Nos. 33-35)—the reputed Yaśodharman who vanquished Mihirakula, son of Toramāna who belonged to the Hūṇa clan.

In this volume again we have a set of records belonging to kings of Valabhi ranging from A.D. 426 to A.D. 766 (Nos. 38 and 39). The importance of these inscriptions lies in the fact that the Senāpati Bhaṭṭāraka of about 500 A.D., the founder of this dynasty, overthrew the Maitrakas, perhaps a branch of the Hūṇas in Kathiawad. Next we have records relating to the Rājas of Śarabhapura and of the kings of Kanauj, besides the Vākāṭaka Mahārājas, and some miscellaneous inscriptions. Mention must be made of the iron pillar inscription at Meharauli (No. 32) belonging to Emperor Candragupta. On palaeographical grounds it is considered to belong to a fairly early date and it is suggested that this Candra may be Candragupta I of the Gupta dynasty. Meharauli is, it is contended, a corruption of Mihirapuri, the city of the Mihiras, to which tribe Mihirakula belonged.

We are primarily concerned with the records of the early Guptas. These are the first sixteen inscriptions in the Corpus. Their dates range from C. 360 to 466. The direct line of the early Gupta dynasty may be said to end with Skandagupta. But there are two names Budhagupta and Bhānugupta with their respective dates A.D. 484 and 510. These are mentioned in Nos. 19 and 20 of the Corpus. There is again the evidence of the inscriptions of the Parivrājaka Mahārājas which go to prove that the Gupta sovereignty continued in power down to A.D. 528. These two kings Budhagupta and Bhānugupta were perhaps not the direct descendants of Emperor Skandagupta but nevertheless belonged to the early Gupta lineage. In its chronological setting Budhagupta is the immediate successor of Skandagupta. In his reign or towards the end of his reign Toramāna seems to have occupied Eastern Mālava which was a part of the Gupta empire. This upset Bhānugupta's ambitions to some extent. All the same, Bhānugupta carried on the administration after Toramāna or as his contemporary until Mihirakula, his son, overpowered the Gupta monarch. From this it is legitimate to infer that the early Gupta dynasty ended only in A.D. 528. On this basis the genealogy of the early Gupta kings may be arranged as follows:—

- Gupta (Mahārāja)
  - Ghaṭotkaca (Mahārāja)
    - Candragupta (Mahārājādhirāja) m. Kumāradevī of the Licchavi family
      - Samudragupta (Mahārājādhirāja)
        - Rāma Gupta
        - Candragupta II (Paramabhaṭṭāraka and Mahārājādhirāja) m. Dhruvadevī
          - Kumāragupta (Mahārājādhirāja)
            - Skandagupta
            - Pura Gupta
              - Budha Gupta
                - Bhānu Gupta (?)
                  - Prakāśāditya (?)
          - Govinda Gupta (governor of Vaiśāli)

The inscriptions are then our primary authority for a study of the polity of the Imperial Guptas. We will survey briefly the importance of each of these inscriptions. First comes the most valuable record of the Allahabad stone Pillar Inscription of Samudragupta. It speaks of Samudragupta as already dead and therefore it was engraved during the reign of Candragupta II. Its value consists not only in narrating the conquests of the Emperor Samudragupta but also the different independent dynasties of kings and their people about the middle of the fourth century A.D. There is however an inscription of Samudragupta's period in the Ēraṇ Stone No. 2 which is a record of the emperor's power and achievements.

We have copious materials from the administrative and political points of view for the period of Candragupta II. The Udayagiri Cave Inscription, the Mathurā Stone Inscription, the Sāñci Stone Inscription and the Gaḍhwā Stone Inscription (Nos. 3, 4, 5 and 7), shed light on the attitude of the State to religion. There is also a fund of information about Kumāragupta as could be gathered from the mute records of his time. The Gaḍhwā Stone Inscription, the Bilsaḍ Stone Pillar Inscription and the Mankuwār Stone Image Inscription (Nos. 8-11) which refer to the Mahārāja Kumāragupta are replete with information valuable to students of Gupta history.

Equally informative are the inscriptions of Skandagupta. The Bihār Stone Pillar Inscription in two parts, the Bhitarī Stone Pillar Inscription, the Jūnāgadh Rock Inscription again in two parts, the Kahāum Stone Pillar Inscription, and the Indore Copper-Plate Inscription are the records attributed to him (Nos. 12-16.) The provenance of the inscriptions and the reliable materials supplied by them on various aspects of administration show the greatness and power of the early Gupta emperors. They also make us believe that in details the Guptas followed the traditional polity which was in vogue in the time of the Mauryas.

Seals at Vaiśāli

A number of seals that were discovered at Vaiśāli (Muzaffarpur district, Bengal) belong to the early Gupta period. In this collection there is the seal of the Mahādevī

Dhruvasvāminī, the queen of Candragupta II. This particular seal informs us that the queen was the mother of the Mahārāja Govindagupta. He was apparently a younger brother of Kumāragupta. And Govindagupta was the Governor of Vaiśāli during the reign of his father Candragupta II. This collection of seals includes those of the officials in the contemporary court of Govindagupta. As has been suggested, the location of the office for making seals was at Vaiśāli itself. The seals range from those of Ghaṭotkacagupta to those of Govindagupta and their officials. It has been contended that in as much as the seals of Govindagupta and of his contemporary officials are found in that collection, the seal containing the name of Śrī Ghaṭotkacagupta may not refer to the Mahārāja Ghaṭotkaca, the successor of Gupta Mahārāja but an officer of Govindagupta's court. It is difficult to accept this proposition. On the face of it, it looks funny. We have not got any other name Ghaṭotkaca among the Gupta rulers or their officials. The honorific Śrī need not disturb us. When it can be applied to the first Gupta, it can be equally applied to his successor also. One has to agree that this name is identical with that of Mahārāja Ghatotkaca only. (Dr. Bloch: *Report of the Archaeological Survey of India*, 1903-4, p. 102; V. A. Smith, *Early History of India*, p. 296 *note* 2).

The variety and character of the clay seals from the excavations at Basrah, the supposed site of ancient Vaiśāli, are something valuable to a student of polity. We can get an inside knowledge of provincial and local administration. The seals belong to officers of different denominations, both high and low. What is most important are the titles furnished by these seals. In fact we get a list of administrative offices, both civil and military. These seals are very useful for the study of the history of the Gupta administration. (Ibid., pp. 107-120.)

CHAPTER II

EXTENT OF THE EMPIRE

INTRODUCTION

After the great Imperial Mauryas, the Śungas, the Kaṇvas and the Āndhras ruled over Magadha. But their empires never reached the extent to which the Imperial Guptas were able to stretch their arms. It was Candragupta I who founded the Gupta sovereignty on a sure and firm basis. He succeeded in enlarging his territories to a considerable extent. Conditions seem to have favoured Candragupta I in erecting the edifice of a dominion which grew into an empire of great magnitude under his son and successor Samudragupta. One of the factors that helped Candragupta to power and prestige was his connection by marriage alliance with the Licchavis. He married the Licchavi princess Kumāradevī. This is evidenced by the coins of Candragupta.[1] Here we find Candragupta and Kumāradevī standing side by side, and luckily for us the names are struck separately. While this is true of the obverse, the expression *Licchavaya* is found on the reverse. The use of this expression in the plural number[2] has set some scholars athinking that the Guptas were originally of the stock of the Licchavis when they were living in Northern Bihar. But at the time when Candragupta I contracted the marital alliance with Kumāradevī, the Licchavis were a powerful oligarchy in Nepal. This means that in building up a large dominion Candragupta I commanded the rich resources and materials supplied by the Licchavis. Assisted by those people, Candragupta carried his arms to the heart of Magadha and occupied the country, which, however, it is believed was only for a brief period.

1. J. Allan, *op. cit.*, Intr. p. XVIII.
2. Fleet, *op. cit.*, p. 16 *n.* 1.

The Gayā copper-plate of Samudragupta has a distinct reference to the brief rule of Candragupta I. This plate was unfortunately treated as a spurious one by the late J. F. Fleet.[3] But further study has shown that it must have been a genuine grant which was issued in 328-29 A.D. This was the ninth year of the Gupta era, and therefore the accession of Candragupta I to the Magadhan throne could be fixed with definiteness in 319-20 A.D. It is probable that Candragupta I was already aged when he acquired Magadha.

A glance at the contemporary history of the period shows that Magadha was then in the possession of the Kṣatriya dynasty of Kōṭa. The last member of the dynasty was one Sundaravarman. Since he had no issue for a long time he adopted Prince Candragupta of the Gupta family. But sometime after the adoption a son was born to Sundaravarman and he was called Kalyānavarman. So the possibility of Candragupta succeeding to the throne of Magadha became remote. Therefore Candragupta invaded the Magadhan kingdom with the help of the Licchāvis. In the course of the battle that took place Sundaravarman died and so Candragupta became king. Kalyāṇavarman was taken away from Magadha for safety. But Candragupta's rule was very much disliked by the people. When once he was away from Magadha to fight against the Savaras, he was ousted and Kalyāṇavarman was placed on the throne. It appears that Candragupta got back the Magadhan kingdom from Kalyānavarman some time after.[4]

It has been estimated not without reason that Candragupta became the master of all Gangetic valley upto modern Allahabad. His dominion therefore included Tirhut, South Bihar, Oudh and also some more districts adjoining these. If

3. *Ibid.*, pp. 254 ff.

4. Jayaswal. *History of India*, pp. 114-116.

we thus examine the limits and the extent of Candragupta I's dominion, it can be easily seen that the most fertile and consequently the most populous part of the territory came into his possession. The result was an increase in revenue to the State and this led to more and more prosperity of the people and royalty. This again enabled the far-sighted Samudragupta to launch on an all-India expedition and come out in flying colours. If Candragupta I had not prepared the ground, the ambitions of Samudragupta could not have been realised so easily and fully.

The great achievement of Candragupta I was the conquest of Magadha and the establishment of peace and order on the traditional lines of administration and governance. This successful termination of hostilities and the replanting of Hindu monarchy devoted to *dharma* on the traditional throne of Pāṭalīputra were events of outstanding importance to Indian nationalism. Hence it was marked by the foundation of a new era, which became popularly known as the Gupta era. The initial year of this era has been generally accepted by scholars as 319-20 A.D. Apparently this was the year of the coronation of Candragupta I on the Magadhan throne. It was also known to the Licchavis as the Gupta-Valabhi era since they had also a share in the building up of the new edifice which came to be known later as the Gupta empire.

The celebration of the establishment of the new Gupta domain was rudely shaken by one Candravarman of Puṣkaraṇa, hailing perhaps from the modern Rajputana. This is attested to by two inscriptions found on the iron pillar at Meharauli[5] and the other on the Susuniā rock in Bankura district (*Ep. Ind.*, Vol. XIII, p. 133. See also *Ep. Ind.*, Vol. XIV, pp. 367-71.) From these epigraphs we gather that Mahārājā Simhavarman was a great ruler of

5. *Corpus*, pp. 139-142.

Puṣkaraṇa about the commencement of the fourth century A.D. He was perhaps a Kṣhatriya and would not suffer Candragupta I, who was himself perhaps not of Kṣhatriya origin, to enlarge his boundaries and establish himself on the throne of Pāṭaliputra, which had been for centuries the capital of successive empires. By the time of the conquest of Magadha, Simhavarman was out of the picture and his son and successor Candravarman was sitting on the throne at Puṣkaraṇa. This Candravarman of much prowess and ability carried his successful arms throughout the length and breadth of North India. By this time Candragupta I who was already advanced in years was unable to resist the whirlwind campaign of a young and powerful ruler like Candravarman, or he was dead leaving his legacy to the young hero Samudragupta. Whatever this may be, Candravarman launched into a blitz-like campaign and asserted himself to be the master of all Northern India from Eastern Bengal to the Indus region. But the glory of Candravarman was only shortlived. For according to the Allahabad Pillar Inscription, Samudragupta easily defeated this Candravarman and brought the whole of Northern India under his sway.

Notwithstanding this, the princes of Chandravarman's family continued to rule as independent chiefs from Mandasor, the far-famed Daśapura of literature and epigraphy, even in the days of Candragupta II and Kumāragupta I. This is evident from the Mandasor inscription of the time of Naravarman and the Gangdhar stone inscription of Viśvavarman.[6] In the former we see that even after the conquest of Mālava by Candragupta II, one Naravarman, a brother of the late Candravarman, assumed the role of an independent chief with Mandasor as his capital. In the *Corpus*, on the other hand, we are told that Viśvavarman, the son of Naravarman, was carrying on an independent rule when Kumāragupta I was

6. *Ep. End.* Vol. XII, pp. 315-21 and *Corpus*, pp. 72-78.

ruling over the Gupta empire. Perhaps towards the latter part of the reign of Kumāragupta, the Mandasor chief acknowledged the over-lordship of the Gupta emperor. This was Bandhuvarman who was the successor of Viśvavarman.[6-a] This indicates beyond doubt that Candragupta I's domain did not pass on quietly to Samudragupta. In fact he had to recover his father's dominion by reconquest.

The Evidence of Inscriptions

The real founder of the Gupta empire was then Samudragupta. A contemporary record of inestimable value like the Allahabad Pillar Inscription so elaborately composed by Hariṣena has enabled us to get a clear grasp of the extent of the Gupta dominions in the reign of this king. Harisena's record could not be treated chronologically, though its contents are absolutely historical. They may be analysed for purposes of clarity under five heads—the campaigns in Āryāvarta, those in Dakṣiṇadeśa, those in the frontier kingdoms, those in the forest tracts, and lastly those in distant foreign countries. It is commonsense to believe that he directed his campaigns first against his own neighbours in northern India, particularly in the Gangetic plain. If we are to credit the epigraphic material with all the authenticity which it deserves, then l. 21 of the inscription definitely demonstrates that Samudragupta plunged into a deadly war with the kings of the Gangetic plain. He waged relentless war and killed most of the kings and annexed their territories to his kingdom. Nine kings of Āryavarta whom he slew in battles are mentioned, and these were Rudradeva, Matila, Nāgadatta, Candravarman, Gaṇapatināga, Nāgasena, Acyuta, Nandi, and Balavarman.[7] There were many others whose names are not mentioned, and who were vanquished.

6-a. *Corpus*, pp. 79 ff.
7. See *Corpus*, p. 7.

Rudradeva has been identified with Rudrasena Vākāṭaka on the authority of the Purāṇic data furnished by the *Vāyu* and the *Brahmāṇḍa*.[7-a] The scene of the battle between Samudragupta and Rudrasena was Eran and that was in 348-9 A.D. In the absence of other reliable materials this can be accepted. Having subdued the Vākātaka country, Samudragupta founded a temple in honour of Visṇu at Eran in commemoration of his victory (Jayaswal, *op. cit.,* pp. 140-1). Matila was possibly a ruler of the region of Bulandshahar in the North-West provinces. The suggestion is based on an ancient Terra-cotta seal found in this town with the name Matila. There are a conch and a serpent suggesting the nāga origin of Matila. (F. S. Growse, *Ind. Ant*. XVIII, p. 289). J. Allan does not seem to agree with this identification and he regards it as a private seal, (*op. cit.*, Intro. p. XXIII.) Nāgabhaṭṭa, it is suggested, belonged to one of the gubernatorial Nāga families. Perhaps he was the son of Maheśvara nāga.[8] Candravarman was the king of Puṣkaraṇa who over-ran all the Gangetic plain and wrested the Gupta dominion conquered by Candragupta I. Gaṇapatināga was the king ruling from Padmāvati, 25 miles north-east of Narwar in the dominion of the Mahārāja Sindia.[9] Fortunately there are coins which are attributed to him. These and the evidence of the *Bhāvaśataka* show that he was the most powerful of all the Nāga chiefs and wielded tremendous power. The Purāṇas also deal with the Padmāvatī Nāgas. Samudragupta broke the Nāga power by slaying this reputed soldier and king Gaṇapati.

Nāgasena was also a Nāga chief of much importance, perhaps next to Gaṇapati in power and influence.[10] This Nāgasena was the ruler of Mathurā if he were to be

7-a. Jayaswal, *op. cit.*, pp. 141-2.
8. *Corpus*, p. 283.
9. *Ibid.*, p. 148.
10. *Ibid.*, p. 133.

taken as the son of Kīrtisena. But he should not be confounded with Nāgasena of Padmāvatī referred to by Bāṇa in his *Harṣacarita* as Rapson thinks. Acyuta belonged to the region covered by Ahicchatra. Luckily we have coins of Acyuta found at Ahicchatra.[11] These are copper coins with the legend Acyuta on them. As the symbols on these coins bear striking resemblance to the Nāga coins at Padmāvatī, it is reasonable to assume that he was also a scion of a Nāga family. Nandi was again a chieftain of a Nāga family. Some scholars speak of an Acyuta Nandi connoting one and the same person. But the inscription suggests that they were two different persons. On the evidence of the announcement of the victory on the Kauśāmbi Pillar that the king killed in the course of a day three rulers, Jayaswal thinks of a Nāga confederacy led by Gaṇapati Nāga against Samudragupta at Kauśāmbi or Allahabad. But the inscription seems to warrant different battles with different rulers, and incorporation of their territories.[12]

The last-named king of Aryāvarta was Balavarman. R. D. Banerji suggests that he may be the king of Assam and grandson of Puṣyavarman who founded the dynasty of Bhāskaravarman. The genealogy of this dynasty as reconstructed from the Nidhampur copper-plates of Bhāskaravarman is found on p. 69 of Vol. XII, *Epigraphia Indica.*[13] If we follow the order in the inscriptions, a scion of the Kōṭa family was also captured. His name is not traceable. The Kōtas were ruling from north-eastern Rajputana. If we take into consideration all these conquests, it appears that almost all north-western and central India and eastern India as far as Assam were incorporated in the dominion of Samudragupta. All north-India except the Punjab and

11. Allan, *op. cit.*, Intro. p. XXII.
12 *History of India* pp. 133-4.
13 See also Gait: *History of Assam*, p. 28.

regions round about Delhi lay at the feet of the conquering monarch. After this first round of victory, Samudragupta took rest in the traditional Magadhan capital Pāṭalīputra. After having consolidated these newly conquered territories, Samudragupta set his mind towards the Dekhan and Southern India.

Conquest of the South

Samudragupta led his campaign against twelve kings of southern India. These were Mahendra of Kośala, Vyāghrarāja of Mahākāntāra, Mantarāja of Kerala, Mahendra of Piṣṭāpura, Svāmidatta of Giri-Koṭṭūra, Damana of Eraṇḍapalla, Viṣṇugopa of Kāñcī, Nīlarāja of Avamukta, Hastivarman of Vengi, Ugrasena of Pālakka, Kubera of Devarāṣtra and Dhanamjaya of Kusthalapura.[14] The conquering monarch passed through Chota Nagpur and overthrew Mahendra of South Kośala which was in the valley of the Mahānadī. Then he had to cross the forest tracts, the Mahākāntāra of the inscription which comprised Orissa and parts of the Central Provinces. The chief of these wild regions was Vyāghrarāja, literally the Tiger king. He was defeated and the forest tribes were subdued. Kerala or Kauralaka was perhaps the region that lay on the banks of the well-known Kolleru (Colair) lake which lay between the rivers Godāvari and Krishna. (See Kielhorn, *Ep. Ind.* VI, p. 3.) Its king was Mantarāja whom also Samudragupta vanquished. Then he met the ruler of Piṣṭapura, the modern Pithapuram in the Godāvari district. Piṣṭapura[15] was the capital city of ancient Kalinga and its ruler during the time of Samudragupta was one Mahendra. The next campaign was against Svāmidatta who was reigning from the hill Koṭṭūra. Koṭṭūra is in the Ganjam district and lies 12 miles south-east of Mahendragiri. Svāmidatta was apparently in charge of the hill fortresses of Mahendragiri and Koṭṭūra.

14. *Corpus*, p. 13.
15. *Ibid.*, p. 7. *n.* 2.

Samudragupta proceeded on his march and went towards Eraṇḍapalla. Fleet and Vincent Smith identified this with Erandol in the East Khandesh district of the Bombay Presidency. "Eraṇḍapalli is, perhaps, identical with Eraṇḍapalla whose chief Damana, we know, was captured by the Gupta king Samudragupta in or about the 4th century A.D."[16]

The ruler Damana who was the contemporary of Samudragupta was defeated. Next was Viṣṇugopa of Kāñcī. Kāñcī is the modern Kāñcīpuram in the Chingleput district of the Madras Presidency. It was the Pallava capital from the third century A.D. Thus the Gupta emperor extended his arms to the extreme south. It is not easy to identify Avamukta. In his ingenious way Jayaswal thinks it the country of Āva people who had their capital at Pithuṃḍa near the Godāvari. He bases this inference from the mention of Āva and Pīthuṃḍa in the Hāthīgumphā inscription (*Ep. Ind.*, XX, p. 79 1.11). If it were to be accepted, Nīlarāja belonged to the Godāvari region, whom Samudragupta vanquished. There is however no difficulty about Vengi. It lay on the way from Mahākāntāra to Kurāla, or more exactly on the way to Kāñcī. Situated between the Krishna and the Godāvari rivers Vengi was a place of strategical importance for a conqueror to approach the extreme south. Vincent Smith presumes that the ruler of this region was Hastivarman, a Pallava. It is rather difficult to accept this suggestion, but it is not impossible that Hastivarman was an ally of the Kāñcī ruler.

Another chief subjugated by the Gupta emperor was Ugrasena, who was the ruler of Pālakka.[17] It is considered to be a place of importance in the Nellore district (*Ep. Ind.*, VIII, p. 161). In the early grants the name Palakkaḍa appears. If this were the place of Ugra-

16. MER, 1912-13 pt. ii, para 63.
17. *Corpus*, p. 13.

sena, we have to locate it near about the Krishna (see also Smith, *Early History of India,* 4th ed. p. 301). Smith originally identified it with Palghat on the Malabar coast. But with the discovery of Pālakka in the Nellore District this has to be given up.

The same difficulty faces us regarding the identification of Devarāṣṭra. The early scholars sought to identify this with Mahārāṣṭra. Jouveau-Dubreuil locates it in the Kalingadeśa on the evidence of the copper-plate found in Kaśimkōṭa in the Vizagapatam district. If this were to be accepted, then Devarāṣṭra should be a place on the eastern coast. Then Kubēra was a neighbour of Svāmidatta and Mahendra of Pithapuram (see *Report on Epigraphy,* 1909, pp. 106-7). Lastly, comes Dhanañjaya of Kusthalapura. This remains yet unidentified. Notwithstanding these identifications still one prefers the old view of Vincent Smith that Devarāṣṭra was the modern Mahratta country and Eraṇḍapalla, Khandesh (See also Fleet *JRAS,* 1898, p. 369). We could not reconcile ourselves to the position that Samudragupta's activities were all confined to the eastern coast and that he returned back to his capital by the same route which he took in his south Indian expeditions If commonsense and reason dictate anything, it must be taken that his homeward journey should have been through the western parts of the Dekhan when he subdued on his return the kings of the Mahratta and Khandesh territories. This will then justify the concept of his *digvijaya. Digvijaya* refers to all the four quarters of the empire and not to a particular *dik* or a few *diks* only. He might or might not have gone to Malabar coast, but that he marched through the Mahārāṣṭra region must be accepted as fairly certain.

The campaigns on the south by Samudragupta must have been of the nature of a blitz. They were in the nature of a *digvijaya* where the kings, some of whom had more than the status of local rājas, were defeated after brief resistance. They surrendered and became willing tributaries and allies. It is generally believed that Samudragupta did not conquer these one by one, but perhaps defeated a confederacy of these or some of these in one and the same battle-field. The arguments advanced do not convince us. Nor is there any definite clue to a combination of these rulers. It is to be noted that Samudragupta went on marching subduing each and every ruler on his way. Be this as it may, the rich spoils not only enriched his treasury, but the quick conquests added considerable territories to the Gupta empire in the Dekhan and Southern India.

Frontier Kingdoms

Line 22 of the Allahabad Pillar Inscription throws welcome light on Samudragupta's relations with his frontier kingdoms. This part of Harisena's inscription helps us to define with accuracy the limits of the Gupta empire under Samudragupta. It must be remarked at the outset that these frontier kingdoms were not independent ones, but they sought voluntary submission to the mighty arms of the emperor and promised to pay the necessary annual tribute to him. To use the modern expression the relations of the frontier states to the empire were one of subordinate alliance. This will be examined in a later chapter *in extenso*. It is enough to point out here the various states which agreed on a voluntary basis to be tributaries of the empire.

On the east, these states were: (1) Samataṭa which consisted of the valley of the Brahmaputrā. Later on the emperor found the necessity for a natural outlet to the sea and make this a part of the province of Champā. (2) Kāmarūpa or the province of Assam and (3) Davāka which represents the territory bounded by the Khasi Hills on the north, Meghnā on the east, the Ganges on the south and Karatoya on the west. This kingdom also included Dacca and

Sunargaon (*J. & Proc. of A.S.B.* 1910, p. 144; D.C. Sircar, *Select Ins.*, p. 258 *n.* 1).

(4) Nepala. In this kingdom the ruler was a Licchavi prince by name Jayadeva I. The Licchavis had been bound as we have already seen, by matrimonial alliance to the Guptas, and it is natural that they consented voluntarily to be on terms of subordinate alliance with the Emperor.

(5) On the west, the kingdom of Kartṛpura is mentioned as a frontier state. Kartarpur in the Jalandhar district may be a survival of the Gupta Kartṛpura. C. F. Oldham finds in this a reference to Katuria Rāja of Kumaon, Garhwāl and Rohilkhand.[18] If this interpretation be correct the ancient kingdom of Kartṛpura comprised all regions in the lower ranges of the Western Himalayas. In other words the Eastern Punjab region represented the ancient frontier kingdom.

(6) To these may be added the Mleccha state covered by Kashmir and North-West India. According to 1.23 of the inscription this region was occupied by Daivaputra Shāhi Shāhānushāhi, with the Mleccha tribes like the Śakas and Muruṇḍas.[19] Both the *Bhāgavata Purāṇa* and the *Viṣṇu Purāṇa* refer to this state. Shāhānushāhi was the Kushan king. He was apparently under the suzerainty of the Sassanian power. His kingdom included Kashmir, Rawalpindi and Peshawar on the Indian side besides Afghanistan. This king realised the power of Samudragupta and appeared before him in person and tendered voluntary submission. In token of this he agreed to accept and circulate the imperial coins as currency in his territories, and offered his daughter (*kanyā*) in marriage to the emperor.[20]

Taking all these accounts into consideration, it is an unquestionable fact that the empire of Samudragupta

18. *J.R.A.S.*, 1898, pp. 198-9.
19. *Corpus*, p. 14.
20. Jayaswal, *History of India*, p. 145.

extended from the borders of Assam practically to Afghanistan. It is not a question of actually carrying arms to these places and conquering them by sword. It is on the other hand the voluntary recognition by these chiefs of the Gupta emperor as the paramount power. It was not a policy of aggression that built up this empire but perhaps the psychological fear impulse that led these frontier chiefs to rally round the standard of the imperial power.

Republican States. The Gupta empire comprised within its arms several republican states. L. 22 of the Allahabad Pillar Inscription refers to a number of such states. These in the order as given in the epigraph, are the Mālavas, Arjunāyanas, Yaudheyas, Mādrakas, Ābhīras, Prārjunas, Sanakānīkas, Kākas, and Kharparikas.[21] There were other smaller tribal constitutions which were too insignificant for mention by the court-panegyrist. This is evident from the expression *ādibhiḥ* in the inscription. We hear of Malloi, Kathaioi and other republican tribes during the Mauryan age, and the Buddhist works testify to a good number of them and give details about their governance. The Republics enjoyed real autonomy and continued to enjoy their own self-government little disturbed by the imperial power. But from the time of the Mauryas, their decline set in. They however struggled through the Śunga and Kaṇva periods to exist as autonomous states. But with the expansion of the Guptas and the consolidation of their imperial power, these small states were driven to the necessity of forming a part and parcel of the empire but still enjoying internal autonomy. They continued to maintain their status but had to acknowledge the paramountcy of the Imperial Guptas. The Mālavas had their capital in Karkōṭa-Nagara or simply Nagara in the present Jaipur State. The coins of these found here in abundance

21. *Corpus*, p. 14.

are the basic evidence. Their prosperity continued to the period of the Imperial Guptas.

The Arjunāyanas were the immediate neighbours of the Mālavas. Again it is numismatic evidence that enables us to fix up their territory. From their coins it transpires that they were in possession of regions that centered round modern Alwar and Agra.[22]

The Yaudheyas were next to the territory of the Arjunāyanas. Their region extended from Bharatpur down to the lower course of the Sutlej. They were in a flourishing state in the time of Rudradāman. North of the Yaudheya state, lay that of the Mādrakas. Mādradeśa has been recognised to be the fertile tracts between the Jhelum, the Ravi and the Bias. Smith thinks that their tribal capital was Sangala or Sākala. (*JRAS*, 1897, p. 30). It is noteworthy that the *Bhāgavata Purāṇa* which speaks of the Mālavas and Ābhīras and others, does not refer to the Mādrakas. Perhaps the Mādrakadeśa had ceased to be a free republican state when the *Bhāgavata* was last rewritten.

The Ābhīras seem to have been a powerful republican state. Both the *Bhāgavata* and the *Viṣṇu Purānas* help us to definitely fix up their location. The Purānic text definitely mentions *Surāṣṭra-Avantya-ābhīras*. This shows beyond doubt that the Ābhīras were in possession of the Surāṣṭra and Avanti provinces. The Prārjunas find mention in the *Arthaśāstra* of Kauṭalya. They belong to Narsingpur district in the Central Provinces. (D. C. Sircar: *Select Inscriptions*, p. 258 n. 1).

The Sanakānikas are said to have occupied Eastern Mālva.[23] This is evident from the fact that a Sanakānika Mahārāja erected a shrine in honour of Candragupta II in the Udayagiri rocks.

22. Jayaswal, *op. cit.*, p. 148.
23. *Ibid.*, p. 258 *n.* 1.

As for the Kākas the fact that the Sāñci hill was called the Kākanada shows that these tribes had their place somewhere round this region. There is at present a town Kākpur within 20 miles from Bhilsa (*JBORS* 18, 212 and 213; see also *List of Ins. of N. India,* by Kielhorn, Nos. 438 and 444).

There is no clue to identify the region of the Kharparikas. But it is reasonable to suppose that they were more or less the neighbours of the Kākas. All Kathiawar, Gujarat down to the Mālava territory were occupied by the above tribes.

From the above study it transpires that the limits of the empire as defined by Vincent Smith are not altogether correct. The empire's southern frontier did not stop with the Narmadā. Though Samudragupta had reinstated the kings of the south whom he had conquered, still they were within the empire on terms of subordinate alliance. Such is also the case with the republican states. They were not outside the pale of Samudragupta's empire but within the empire as tributary states. So the correct position of the empire would be from Assam to the end of the present N. W. Frontier and in the south upto Kāñcīpuram including a good slice of the present Bombay presidency. It was as big as that of Aśoka.

The Empire under Candragupta II.

Samudragupta was succeeded by Rāmagupta, his son and Candragupta II was the *yuvarāja.* This is seen from the *Nāṭyadarpaṇa* (Gaekwad Oriental Series). Rāmagupta did not live long to enjoy the fruits of his father's conquests. His reign was one of disturbance from the foreign Śakas. Taking advantage of the little disturbed condition after the accession of Rāmagupta, the Śaka king threw a challenge to the imperial authorities. Rāmagupta, in spite of his prompt action, could not stem the tide of the foreign hordes. On the other hand, if we are to believe the

Devīcandraguptam, he suffered a crushing defeat at their hands and had to yield to an ignominious treaty by which his queen Dhruvadevī was to be handed over to the Śaka chief. This was resented by the people and more especially by the crown prince who entered the camp of the Śakas in the guise of the queen and did away with the Śaka chief. This diplomatic action on the part of prince Candragupta had a far-reaching effect. It once for all crushed the expansion of the Śakas over the Indian sub-continent and gave Dhruvadevī peace of mind having been rescued from the great shame to which she was put by her weak husband. This further increased to a large extent the prestige of the young prince Candragupta and made the rest of the empire stand intact. In the meanwhile Rāmagupta's life had come to an end, and Candragupta II ascended the throne in all pomp and glory having earned the name of a soldier of mighty strength that exterminated the Śaka power (*JBORS,* XVIII. pp. 29ff.).

The extensive empire thus bequeathed to Candragupta II was further augmented and maintained vigorously. Only the south-west of India was left unconquered by his father. Candragupta II set himself to the task of completing the conquest of these portions, so that he might proudly style himself as an All-India *cakravartin*.

The place where the Śaka chief was humiliated by Candragupta II is still a matter of contention. Two suggestions have been made. One was that this took place at Balkh in the north-west India in the heart of the Kushan territory. The other is that it was in Mathurā which was still in the possession of the scions of the Kushans. This receives further confirmation from the fact that a record of Candragupta II is found at Mathurā. There is no record of any previous monarch of the Gupta line discovered so far at Mathurā. The discovery of the Mathurā record[23-a] shows that the first

23-a. Fleet, *Gupta Ins.*, pp. 25-8.

conquest of Candragupta II should have been effected at Mathurā and the Kushan power there dislodged. From the provenance of his coins, especially silver coins,[24] all through the Punjab and on the banks of the Chenab, it can be safely admitted that the N. W. Frontier was in the possession of Candragupta II unaffected by the disturbances of Rāmagupta's reign.

In narrating the story of Candragupta II's conquests the coins and epigraphs are our primary authority. Candragupta II enjoyed a long reign of nearly forty years and it is reasonable to assume that the first half of his rule was spent more in conquests and consolidation. His inscriptions bear testimony to the fact that the entire Mālva country was overrun and annexed. He carried his arms right upto the Arabian Sea through Mālva and Gujarat both of which succumbed to his powerful arms. The Udayagiri Cave inscription in the Bhilsa district of the Gwalior State is proof positive that all N. E. Mālva had come into the possession of Candragupta II before A.D. 401-2. Yet another inscription in the same place mentions one Vīrasena *alias* Sāba, as a minister of the Emperor Candragupta II, engaged in the excavation of the cave **कौत्सश्शाब इति ख्यातो वीरसेन: कुलाख्यया** (Fleet, *op. cit.*, pp. 35 and 36). The Sāñci Inscription dated 412-3 in Bhopal, Central India, in which a donation of Āmrakārddva (a feudatory of Candragupta II) is recorded brings further corroboration of the conquest of the Mālva country (*Corpus*, pp. 31 ff.). Line 7 of this inscription adds another appellation to Candragupta II namely Devarāja.[24-a]

At this time in Kathiawad the later Western Satraps, belonging to the Saka dynasty were still in power. They had

24. Allan, *op. cit.*, pp. 49-51.

24-a. **महाराजाधिराजश्रीचन्द्रगुप्तस्य देवराज इति**

Note: The Vākāṭaka grants call him Devagupta *Ep. Ind.*, IX pp. 267-7.

long established themselves as an independent power. With the grim determination to break this combined power of the Western Satraps, Candragupta II should have carried his arms and added the peninsula of Kathiawar to his empire. This is attested to by the find of a large number of silver coins in the peninsula belonging to Candragupta II. This extension of the empire to the shores of the Arabian Sea on the Kathiawad peninsula had a telling effect on the foreign trade of India. From these ports brisk trade was carried on with Europe and Africa. And this again increased the prosperity of the empire.

The only power that was still enjoying independence was the Vākāṭaka power in Central India and the Dekhan. Pravarasena I was a powerful king of the dynasty, carried on his *digvijaya* conquests and styled himself a *samrāṭ*. He is said to have performed four Aśvamedha sacrifices. His power and prestige were however eclipsed by the splendid achievements of the Gupta emperor Samudragupta. The latter does not seem to have interfered with the Vākāṭakas in the course of his campaigns. He perhaps thought it wise to let them alone. The later Vākāṭaka period more or less synchronises with the assumption of royalty by Candragupta II. The contemporary Vākāṭaka monarch was Rudrasena. Candragupta II also felt the strength of the Vākāṭakas and realised the value and importance of their alliance. This political alliance was cemented by the bond of marriage. Candragupta II gave his daughter, Prabhāvatigupta born to his queen Kuberanāgā to the Vākāṭaka king Rudrasena.[25] R. D. Banerji says that by this alliance Candra-

25. Dr. S. K. Aiyangar remarks: "It is fortunate that a grant of this very Prabhāvati Gupta, as regent of her son who had the princely name Divākarasēna, has become available to us. It is not yet published *in extenso*, but the account of it as given in the *Indian Antiquary* for 1912 by Professor K. B. Pathak leaves no doubt as to her identity. She describes herself as the daughter of Chandragupta II and Kubhēranāgā, and became the crowned queen of the Vākātaka Rudrasēna. Her son is described as Yuvarāja Divākarasēna." (Q.J.M.S. XV. p. 157.)

gupta II protected his left flank (*op. cit.*, p. 34; see also *Corpus*, p. 237; *Ep. Ind.*, XV, p. 41).

Yet another political marriage contracted by Candragupta II was with the Kadambas. This is evident from a definite hint in the Tālagunda Pillar inscription of Kākusthavarman. It transpires from this that the Gupta monarch married a Kadamba princess (see also Heras, Relations between Guptas, Kadambas and Vākāṭakas, *J.B.O.R.S.*, XII, pp. 455-63; G.M. Moraes: *The Kadambakula*, pp. 21-22).

Thus by a series of conquests and by inaugurating a policy of dynastic marriages with the contemporary powerful monarchs of his time, Candragupta II was able to raise the prestige of the Gupta empire. Under his formidable arms the empire extended from the Bay of Bengal to the Arabian Sea, besides the whole of Hindustan reaching the farthest limits of the north-west up to Balkh. Southern India should have continued to be on terms of subordinate alliance as in the days of Samudragupta.

The empire under Kumāragupta and his successors.

This vast empire passed on peacefully to Kumaragupta, son of Candragupta II. He ascended the throne about A.D. 413 and ruled until 455. During the comparatively long period of his reign, he was able to retain every inch of territory. He proclaimed himself as a paramount sovereign and celebrated the *Aśvamedha* sacrifice as an assertion of his paramountcy. Vincent Smith concludes from this that Kumāragupta should have added more territories to the empire, though no records of his wars or conquests are available to us. That the empire continued to progress from strength to strength is further attested by the wide distribution of the inscriptions of this emperor's reign and also of his coins.

It is generally assumed by historians of this period that with the death of Kumāragupta I the decline of the empire set in. But it must be said to the credit of Skandagupta that he was a fitting successor of Kumāragupta. In his reign notwithstanding certain disturbances which should have cost his treasury a good deal, the empire did not suffer any diminution. One such disturbance occurred towards the end of the reign of Kumāragupta himself when Skandagupta was yet the *yuvarāja.* This is what is known as the rising of the Puṣyamitras, a tribe unknown to epigraphy but known to the Purāṇas (Pargiter, *Dynasties of the Kali Age,* p. 73). If we are to credit this evidence with any veracity, then the Puṣyamitras were one among several tribal dynasties even before the rise of the Guptas to power. Fleet made the suggestion that they were a tribe on the Narmadā region.[26] Perhaps they were responsible for the fall of Kumāragupta's power in Mālva. We should not confuse this tribe with the Hūṇas who inhabited North-western India. There is no evidence that they broke through the Gupta territory. Another suggestion came from Hoernle who proceeded to identify the Puṣyamitras with the Maitraka tribes under Bhaṭārka who was the founder of the dynasty of the Valabhis (*J.R.A.S.*, 1909, p. 126). The suggestion of Dr. Fleet stands more to reason, and can be accepted. There is no reason to connect them with the foreign tribes. Nor their name Puṣyamitras warrants such an inference. It appears certain that they belonged to a branch of the ancient Puṣyamitra Śunga family and still retaining some amount of independent local sovereignty like the later Mauryas or later Guptas. Towards the close of Kumāragupta's rule, they might have felt they had an opportunity to extricate themselves from the imperial yoke and might have risen like the Kalingas in Aśoka's time. That they had miscalculated is seen from the results of such a rising.

26. *Indian Ant.*, XVIII, p. 228.

The sudden upheaval and the severity with which these tribesmen fought, temporarily affected the prestige of the imperial power. But the crown prince, the future emperor, was a man of extraordinary energy and foresight. He marched straight and put down the rising with great severity. That was the first and last we hear of the Puṣyamitras. Skandagupta dealt with them in such a manner that they were no more heard of in history. But much is made of this incident, a petty rising by a local tribe as tending to endanger the stability of the dynasty or its great empire whose edifice had stood unshaken for a century and a quarter. It was no extraordinary calamity to an imperial house like that of the Guptas, and it required no military genius to retrieve such a calamity. It taught a lesson to Skandagupta that he should not indulge in a life of luxury and peace but should ever be active and prepared to meet risings here and there.

The more serious disturbance was from the Hūṇas. In the last days of Kumāragupta's rule, the Hun hordes had already entered the north-west passes and were spreading themselves all over the Punjab and northern India. Skandagupta[27] coolly faced the situation. He taught the barbarians a severe lesson by defeating them fully and securing a decisive victory. This successful war which saved the country from the clutches of the devastating savage Hun hordes was an event of much importance and deserved commemoration. This took the shape of a pillar of victory. This column still stands at Bhitāri, in the Ghazipur district, to the east of Banares, an example of living past. This occasion was taken advantage of, and Skandagupta erected a statue of Hari in memory of his father, surmounting this pillar. But this statue is no more there.

27. *Corpus*, p. 56; Cunningham, *Arch. Surv.* I, p. XXX.

The arrest of the Huns from further aggression was something vital to the strength of the empire. Skandagupta had to summon all his energy and resources to stem the ever flowing tide of these savages. He made them succumb before his august presence. The panegyrist who compared the document on the Bhitāri stone pillar[28] compares Skandagupta to the ancient hero Kṛṣṇa. Just as Kṛṣṇa carried the news of his full success over Kamsa to his mother Devakī.[29] Skandagupta took the welcome tidings of his success against the enemies to his mother, who was still alive. This once more brought peace of mind to the royal family. This is evidenced by the term *śānti* in 1.3 of Kahāum Stone Pillar Inscription dated 460 A.D.

राज्ये शक्रोपमस्य क्षितिप-शतपते : स्कन्दगुप्तस्य शान्ते

(Fleet, *op. cit.* No. 15).

From the provenance of inscriptions, one in Junāgaḍh, the other at Kahāum in the Gorakhpur District, and the third at Bulandshahar District, we are to infer that the Gupta empire did not suffer even a temporary eclipse in its extent and limits but was in all its ancient glory and tranquillity. The three inscriptions bearing Nos. 14, 15 and 16 in the *Corpus* bear abundant testimony that the Gupta government continued in the western provinces, eastern provinces and the central provinces as well. By his sheer ability and success Skandagupta earned the title Vikramāditya.

The decline of the empire really set in towards the close of Skandagupta's rule. It is believed that he died in 467. Just at that time or a year before there was another eruption of the Hūnas strengthened by fresh recruits eager for plunder and devastation. Gangdhār was occupied by them, and at this news Skandagupta marched to the north-western Punjab to resist the barbarian incursion once again. He would have

28. *Ibid.*, p. 52.
29. *Ibid.*, p. 54.

succeeded if he had had assistance from headquarters. This was not forthcoming because of the rivalry of Puragupta, his own brother. We are not however in possession of authentic documents relating to this period. All that we have to guess is that Puragupta was ambitious and set himself up as a rival to the emperor. He was waiting for an opportunity to succeed to the throne. When the emperor was engaged with the Huns in the distant Punjab, Puragupta assumed the sovereignty of Magadha and the eastern provinces. As ill-luck would have it, Skandagupta had no son to succeed him. His brother Puragupta was the only heir. He was not a good soldier or a general. Skandagupta probably died in the course of his resistance to the foreign intruder. His death and the weakness of his successor paved the sure way for the Hūṇas to spread themselves over the interior of India and establish their rule. In this way the weak rule of Puragupta led to the fall of the empire in the western provinces and thereafter the Gupta rule became confined to the east.

Empire and Imperialism.

Different are the motives that impel the powers to build up an empire. An empire need not necessarily be an overseas development, though expansion overseas has been a notable feature of big powers through the ages. In ancient days Greece and Rome set out on large scale colonial expansion. At present the powers that be vie themselves with one another in the acquisition of expansion of their territorial areas. Ancient India was no exception.

In the epic period Rāma annexed South India and Ceylon. Yudhiṣṭhira who wanted to be styled a *Samrāṭ* was bent upon conquests of all directions and sent his brothers on a *dig-vijaya*. The conquest of all-India was made including several islands in the seas. This resulted in the performance of the *Rājasūya* sacrifice that could be done only by a monarch who was the head of a *sāmrājya*. In historical times leading Kṣatriya kings launched a similar campaign of conquest and proudly called themselves the sovereign of sovereigns. Samudragupta and Candragupta were emperors of intuitive genius, and were men of remarkable ability and prowess. Samudragupta carried on his campaign with vigour and energy and re-founded the Gupta empire. What had been left over, Candragupta II completed and consolidated on the bedrock of stability. In this work of building up an empire, these monarchs were permeated by what is known as the Hindu spirit. They were ambitious to emulate the epic heroes in their action, to wit, to make a *dig-vijaya* and perform a sacrifice to entitle each one of them to become the one emperor of all-India and even beyond.

Writing on the ideas of imperialism H. G. Wells says: 'a powerful and advanced nation was conceded the right to dominate a group of other less advanced nations or less politically developed nations or peoples whose nationality was still undeveloped, who were expected by the dominating nation to be grateful for its protection and dominance'. (*The Outline of History*, Vol. II, p. 620). Viewed in this light the use of the word empire has been narrowed in its scope and widely differs from the earlier concept. In former times the word empire carried with it a wider idea and connoted universal significance. In other words, the conception of common human welfare was the prevailing note of the ancient empires. The domination or dominating motive was subordinated to the healthier concept of welfare of the people or what we may call universal welfare. The ancient Hindu conception accepted this. Their ideal and day-to-day prayer was *sarve janā sukhino bhavantu* (Let all the people of the world live in peace and prosperity). The Hindu monarchs of the epic days and after were actuated by this ideal and protected the earth with this idea uppermost in their minds.

The Guptas were no exception to this. They built up an empire by conquest as befits a Kṣatriya conqueror. But this conquest was not necessarily by the sword. Often diplomatic means were employed to achieve this purpose. For, this conquest, they realised, was not an end in itself. It was only a means to the end. There was no exploitation of the less advanced states or peoples. To cite an instance, after his conquest of Vāli, Rāma did not appropriate his kingdom but got Sugrīva, his brother, installed on the throne.[29-a] Rāma gave entire enjoyment of *svarājya* to Sugrīva as he did later to Vibhīṣana, brother of Rāvaṇa of Lankā, after conquering him in battle. These kings recognised the suzerainty of the emperor. Under these conditions one notices close connection between the idea of the empire and the peace of the world.

To-day in the acquisition of an empire or rather a colonial empire, the dominant motive seems to be economic. This economic motive manifests itself in various ways. Some of them are said to be opportunities for settlement, trade and the exploitation of raw materials. The aspiring powers make no secret of this and use these colonies to their advantage and profit. In analysing the components of power, a recent writer has laid stress on three things, military power, economic power and prestige or reputation for power.[30] It has been justly observed that 'rarely prestige is alleged as a motive'.[30-a] Herein lies the difference between the motive behind the modern powers and ancient Indian powers. Prestige was almost the only motive of conquest and foundation of empire.

29-a. अभिषिक्तः स्वराज्ये च सुहृदः सम्प्रहर्षय

(Kiskindhā, 60. 17.)

30. In a document submitted to the International Studies Conference of 1937 by Dr. R. Gale Woolbert—(see *The Colonial Problem*, Oxford University Press, 1937).

30-a. *Ibid.*, p. 57.

Dig-vijaya and Dharma-vijaya

The concept of *digvijaya* has not been properly explained. It is akin to the *dharmavijaya* of Kauṭalya and Aśoka, and also of the *Mahābhārata.* The principle underlying this concept is that the independent states and areas were to continue their status unchanged. They were sovereign in the administration of their states. But they had to acknowledge the suzerainty of the emperor by paying the customary tributes and presents, invariably payable annually. The same principle was applied to the border states which were incorporated in the empire for purposes of defence only. These were suffered to maintain the *status quo* in internal administration but were considered as buffer states for preventing aggressive powers from invading the empire. Most of these states which were put on terms of subordinate alliance were in the empire but were not of the empire. They were not subject to the rules and laws governing the imperial policy.

The principle of *dharmavijaya* bears the same significance. We shall appreciate the end of war only if we take into consideration the other side of the picture. War is *dharmaic* or righteous, or is *adharmaic* or unrighteous. It is *dharmaic* if it is fought on the lines laid down in the *Dharmaśāstras* and *Dharmasūtras*. Here no slaughter of innocents is involved nor greed the motive for territorial acquisition. Without aiming at territorial acquisition, the ancient Hindus aimed at the expansion and consolidation of the empire. Technically speaking all the land belonged to the emperor. But practically everything of every state was enjoying *svarājya.* This aimed at the political unity of the empire not to speak of the administrative unity of which we hear so much to-day. Politically every state was a group within a group, and was left to itself in the sphere of internal administration. In the hour of peril and in the interests of defence, of honour and self-respect, all the groups acted like one individual. It was thus a voluntary union of states, or a loose confederation where the liberty of the individual was not sacrificed, though he was a unit in the group. This *dharmavijaya* is backed by religion, moral in character and spiritual in outlook. The moral basis lies in the discharge of one's own duty, and here the Kṣatriya becomes ennobled by discharging his *svadharma* which is, taking part in war, whether he wins or dies. Whether he won or died he became the recipient of heavenly felicity. The ancient Hindu state believed in the mandates of religion. Religious fervour goaded them on to do acts of chivalry and acts of sacrifice. Winning heaven was the end of the soldier's life. War, but righteous war, was the means to this end.

But if one takes to *adharma vijaya* contrary to the rules of war and is able to win, that conquest is not worth the name. There is no charm in the extension of territory or the acquisition of wealth at the cost of *dharma*. Such a conquest will not be of permanent duration (*Adhruva*). Any moment the clouds of storm would gather from the cruelly dealt peoples, and the imperial capital would prove to be a serious storm centre. There would be no room for peace or consolidation. The unrighteous conqueror should be ever vigilant and be in a state of preparedness for war. That conquest is again an impediment to heaven (*asvargya*). Such conquest destroys the king and also the state.

अधर्मयुक्तोविजयो ह्यध्रुवो ऽस्वर्ग्य एवच ।
पातयन्त्येव राजानं महीं च भरतर्षभ ॥

Śānti, 96.2.

Thus the ruling passion of all righteous monarchs was to avoid unrighteous warfare and to engage themselves in righteous warfare. One of the forms which this lawful warfare took was *digvijaya*. Before the *Rājasūya* sacrifice of Yudhiṣthira, his four brothers went in the direction of the four *diks* and conquered all the quarters of the country. If we examine the chapters dealing with *digvijaya* in the *sabhā parvan* of the *Mahābhārata,* we find that rarely there were actual engagements. Generally it was conquest by peace. When once the message was taken that a Pāṇḍava prince was there on a *digvijaya* tour, the local chieftain or ruler had only two options. One was to resist him in battle and the other to express willing subordination. In almost all cases the second thing happened.

This was the method of Samudragupta's conquest and that of his successors. If this were not so, he could not have overrun the whole of the Dekhan and South India in such a meteor-like speed. There was little resistance and willing acquiescence on the part of the subordinate rulers to the conquering monarch.

Gupta India—a nation state.

Judged by the modern test of what a nation is, Gupta India was a nation state. Notwithstanding the existence of diverse tribes speaking diverse languages in different parts of the empire, all-India accepted one common language, Sanskrit. All the official documents of this period are written in Sanskrit as the numerous epigraphs indicate very clearly. Again all India adopted one common religion. It was Hinduism, the glorification of Śiva or Viṣṇu as the case may be. Buddhism was on the decline while Jainism was more local than universal. The keen sense of toleration practised by the Gupta emperors gave no room for religious dissatisfaction or wars. After all the religions had for their background the fundamental tenets and ideals of the Hindu religion. Throughout the length and breadth of India, the Hindu spirit pervaded the atmosphere. The importance given to religion in the state had a beneficent influence on the soul of the people. This was something akin to the Roman spirit where importance was given to the gods, affecting wholesomely the soul of the Roman people.

Yet another factor that profoundly reacted on the masses was a sense of security and freedom. By insisting on the healthy concept of *svadharma,* and consequently avoiding competition leading to the survival of the fittest, the Gupta empire achieved what we cannot achieve even in the twentieth century. Through the institution of the caste economy and by the fixation of services and sanctions, the Gupta empire ensured the working of economic democracy with political freedom. Whether the individual was a member of the group or in the group, he knew his duties and discharged them to the best of his ability. He enjoyed individual freedom to seek his salvation by doing his duty to the society and state. By nationalising industries and through a network of guilds and merchant organisations, the state allowed every man to earn his bread. By apportioning function to every individual and every group of individuals the Gupta empire had no difficulty in solving the unemployment problem.

In the same way as we shall see later, the Gupta monarch, albeit an *ekarāt,* realised that in the welfare of his people lay his welfare. He carried the people with him in his administration. The Government of the country was run on democratic lines. The republican organisations, the village republics, the corporate organisations of the different conquered states were suffered to have their old institutions intact and contribute to the peace of the empire. The Gupta empire had not the elements of the unhealthy nationalism of the nineteenth century. The essential idea underlying this nationalism was the legitimate claim of every nation to complete sovereignty. We all know how this idea has reacted on the peace of the modern world. The Gupta India was not influenced by a narrow nationalism of this type but evolved a national spirit which led to a fundamental unity, political, religious and cultural. Like its great predecessor the Mauryan state, the Gupta state was another example of a culture-state where the material welfare of the people had its basis in morality.

It was the state that formulated measures which had their basis in *dharma*. This appeal to *dharma* is enough to rouse the Hindu to gird up his loins and engage himself in action, whether it be civil or military. The state was the symbol of the general welfare of humanity. It was out to promote arts and crafts and the literature of the country. The study of humanities was taken up with avidity, and patronage necessarily flowed from the state to encourage such studies. Harisena calls Samudragupta a *Kavirāja*.[31] Not only was the great conqueror of the Indian world a finished and resolute soldier, but he also possessed all the qualifications of a poet and musician. Being personally interested in arts and humanities, no wonder he instilled that spirit among the intelligentsia in his empire. By so doing with a breadth of comprehension and goodwill, he and his successors moulded the spirit of the people at large. People with one mind responded easily to his call, for they realised the humanitarian view which swayed the minds of the Gupta emperors.

At this stage a study of the legends on the coins of the Gupta kings enables us to reaffirm this principle of *digvijaya*. In the standard type of coins of Samudragupta one of the legends on the obverse is

Samaraśatavitatavijayo jitaṛipur ajito divam jayati.[32] (He who is the victor in a century of battles and who has not been conquered by anyone attains heavenly felicity). In the Archer-type of coins of the same king two distinct legends are seen on the obverse. One is

Apratiratho vijitya kṣitim sucaritair divam jayati. The other is

31. Fleet, *Corpus*, p. 8.
32. Allan, *op. cit.*, p. 1.

Aparatiratho vijitya kṣitim avanipatir divam jayati. The unequalled one had conquered the earth to conquer heaven by good deeds. According to the second legend, the unequalled one had conquered the earth and had become its lord. By this he wins heaven. *Sucarita*[33] may be the same as *uttamakarma* which occurs in the Kaca type of coins. It is generally understood that a conquering monarch after completing the sacrifice of arms prepares himself to the spiritual sacrifice which leads him to heaven.[34] It is said in the early Tamil work *Śilappadikāram* that the Cēra king Śenguṭṭuvan performed a religious sacrifice after his victories in north Iṇdia. In the case of the Gupta kings they engaged themselves in *Aśvamedha* sacrifices. To a Hindu the highest righteous deed consisted in the performance of *yajñas* or sacrifices. This is further evident from the legend on the Aśvamedha type of coins. It runs thus

Rājādhirājaḥ pṛthvīm avitvā

Divam jayatyaprativāryavīryaḥ—*Ibid.*, p. 21.

meaning 'the king of kings, of irresistible prowess having protected the earth, wins heaven.' According to this the conquests were over and the empire was well consolidated. He had been acknowledged as the king of kings. He now looked forward to heavenly bliss. Again if we turn to the coins of Kaca and Candragupta II Vikramāditya, the same legends noticed in the coins of Samudragupta face us. For example in a legend on the Chattra type of coins of Candragupta II is inscribed, Kṣitim avajitya sucaritair divam jayati Vikramādityah.—*Ibid.*, p. 35.

If we turn to the Lion-slayer type of coins we meet with three distinct legends. Among them one is

Narendracandraḥ prathita (Śriyā) divam

33. *Ibid.*, p. 6.
34. *Ibid.*, p. 7.

Jayatyajeyo bhuvi simhavikramaḥ.—*Ibid.*, p. 38.

(The moon among kings (the unconquered) of lion-prowess wins heaven). Passing on to the coins of Kumāragupta I the following legend occurs in them:

Vijitāvanir avanipatiḥ Kumāragupto divam jayati.

—*Ibid.*, p. 61.

(Kumāragupta who had conquered the earth and had become its lord, conquers heaven.) The legend on the Swordsman type is little different.

Gām avajitya sucaritaiḥ Kumāragupto divam jayati.

—*Ibid.*, p. 67.

Here again it is significant to note the word *Sucaritaiḥ*. It is just plausible that this term may be taken along with the term *avajitya* and may be interpreted also that in the conquest of the earth the Gupta emperors took to the ordained righteous path of conquest, free from *lobha* and *asura vijayas* which have been condemned in Nīti literature. The same legends are repeated in the legends of other coins of Kumāragupta. In one he is called Mahendra Simha. In another legend he is definitely known as Mahendra.

Guptakulavyomaśaśī Jayatyajeyo jitamahendraḥ.

—*Ibid.*, p. 70 & 73.

This testifies that Kumāragupta I who was the invincible Mahendra and the sparkling star of the Gupta line was victorious. In several legends of this king, *divam jayati* often occurs. Conquest and heaven seem to be tacked on. The *Māhābhārata* asks—what if you are killed in a war or come out victorious, both lead you on to heaven.

ते वयं स्वर्गमिच्छन्तः संग्रामे त्यक्तजीविताः।
जयन्तो वध्यमानाश्च प्राप्नुयाम च सद्गतिं॥

Śānti, 100.42.

It is not mere conquest that is envisaged in these texts. It is conquest combined with irresistible and invincible prowess that opens the gates of heaven freely and without any hindrance. The epithets *apratiratha* and *aprativārya* in the Eran inscription stand for the *vīrya* of the person. No one can establish his absolute sovereignty over the earth unless he is definitely a *vīra* and *śūra*. And that too, a *vīra* should not resort to crafty and wily methods of war. Only righteous war will throw open the portals of heaven. Devoid of *vīrya* one could not maintain his territorial possessions and protect them. Hence it has been ordained that once the suzerainty of a monarch is firmly founded on the bedrock of *vīrya* combined with *sucarita,* he becomes fit for performing sacrifices, and the sacrifices are the means to the end, namely a place in Heaven. After his conquests Rāma, son of Daśaratha, began his sacrifice of Aśvamedha, and Yudhiṣṭhira the *Rajasūya* after the *digvijaya* done by his four brothers in the four directions. Following this epic tradition Samudragupta completed his *digvijaya* successfully, and finding himself in the position of *Samrāṭ,* he ventured to perform the *Aśvamedha yajña*. In this he was followed by his successors. We have similar legends on the coins of Skandagupta also. In the Central issues, the following are met with.

Vijitāvanir avanipatir Jayati divam Skandagupto jayam

Vijitāvanir avanipatiḥ Śrī Skandagupto divam Jayati.

—Allan, *op. cit.,* p. 132.

The legend on a coin of Prakāśāditya reads

Vijitya vasudhām divam jayati.—*Ibid.,* p. 135.

From a reading of the legends on the coins of these various kings, we should not rush to the conclusion that every one of them conquered the earth. But on the other hand on their accession to the throne every one of them received formal acceptance of his suzerainty by the other rulers and allies in the empire. This formal recognition of the real sovereignty amounted to a reconquest of the whole earth, and hence the legend. On the evidence of coins we can definitely say that the Guptas held undisputed sovereignty practically over all-India until the days of Prakāśāditya. Afterwards the successors had not the nerve to exact subordination from the different parts of the empire. For as the *Mahābhārata* puts it, none but a *śūra* could conquer and maintain vast portions of a territory.

> शूरबाहुषु लोकोऽयं लम्बते पुत्रवत्सदा ।
> तस्मात्सर्वेषु लोकेषु शूरः संमानमर्हति ॥
> न हिशौर्यात्परं किंचित् त्रिषु लोकेषु विद्यते ।
> शूरः सर्वं पालयति सर्वं शूरेप्रतिष्ठितं ॥

Śānti, 99.17-18.

So long as the earth was hugged by the victorious arms of emperors like Samudragupta and Candragupta II, the peace and prosperity of the people were ensured. The subjects felt that everything was safe in the hands of their paramount sovereign. Once the hands of these *śūras* were removed and got substituted by neo-*śūras,* there was a tendency on the part of subordinate powers to regain their independence. This is what happened after Skandagupta and Prakāśāditya.

The Aśvamedha and Digvijaya.

If we carefully examine the texts of the Brāhmaṇa literature, especially the *Aitareya Brāhmaṇa* and the *Śatapatha Brāhmaṇa,* we find that it is more or less incumbent on a great monarch to perform one of the *yajñas,* the *Rājasūya, Vājapeya* and *Aśvamedha,* if not all of them (*Ait. Br.* VIII. 23). Kings of the epic and heroic ages spent a good deal on performing these sacrifices. Mention has already been made of the *Rājasūya* of the Pāṇḍava hero, Yudhiṣṭhira. The *Śatapatha Brāhmaṇa* refers to the *Aśvamedha* of Bharata, son of Duṣyanta and Pitugā, who celebrated sacrifices after their respective *digvijayas* (VIII. 22 & 23). Later on the *Śatapatha* gives a list of thirteen kings who had celebrated the Aśvamedha (XXII, 5.4). These are political sacrifices but sanctioned by religious custom. The *Rājasūya* is mainly connected with *abhiṣeka* or anointment. After the ceremony of anointing and before actually ascending the throne, there is a religious function which goes by the name of the *Vājapeya.*

By the commencement of the historical period these yajñas fell into desuetude, due to the fact that true Kṣatriya lines had become impure by mixed marriages and there was no tall monarch like the kings of the heroic age to indulge in such costly rites. Be it also noted that the *Vājapeya* was not the exclusive right of the Kṣatriya, a Brahmana could also perform it. The Vedic idea that it was a ceremony preceding the accession to the throne was given up. If it were not so, how can we account for Rāma performing many *Vājapeyas* in his lifetime (*Rāmā,* II, 45.22; VII, 99.9). So its political colour had been lost. Whatever that may be, the fact remains that the *Aśvamedha* died hard and several kings of the historical period came forward to revive and perform it. The *Aśvamedha* came in the march of time to be regarded as the symbol of one's overlordship or paramount rule. It became a custom with kings of prowess and valour to conquer the earth and perform the *Aśvamedha* or the horse-sacrifice. The writer in the C. H. I. has not properly understood the truth underlying this when he remarks that the *Aśvamedha* was 'at bottom the elaboration of a simple rite of sympathetic magic.' (I, pp. 141-2). The *Aśvamedha* is a public confession of the monarch that he was not merely a secular person in outlook, but this conquest of the earth had not any material considerations behind it. It was again a public proclamation to other chiefs and friendly monarchs that he was to be acknowledged by one and all as the suzerain lord. Thus it was religion on the one hand and prestige on the other that dominated the performance of the *Aśvamedha* by a monarch. By this he established his pre-eminence in the empire, or what an historian of ancient India would term *sāmrājya.*

The *Aśvamedha* was in fact a challenge thrown to the existing political powers. The horse of the conquering monarch was set free to wander wherever he would for a period of one year. If no political power captured him, it meant that political power acquiesced in the pre-eminence of the conquering king. If on the other hand the horse was seized by any chief, then that chief was regarded as an opponent. The conqueror sent out his army or himself led the expedition, put down the opponent with the might of his arm and recovered the animal. Then the sacrifice was performed and full suzerainty was claimed as a matter of right. We know of some details about this horse-sacrifice from the *Mālavikāgnimitra* of Kālidāsa where a reference is made to that of Puṣyamitra Śunga.[35] Thus the *Aśvamedha* was a corollary of the *digvijaya.* In fact the *digvijaya* was incomplete in itself. It was the horse-sacrifice that gave it a completeness. In other words, the *digvijaya* always preceded the horse-sacrifice. The latter lent a religious colour to the secular aspect of conquest. Thus the *digvijaya* was countenanced and sanctioned by religion and usage.

The colonies and the Guptas

The colonial activity of ancient India was confined more or less to Farther India and Insular India. The *Purāṇas* speak of nine divisions of the earth, and we have tried to identify them elsewhere (see *Some Aspects of Vāyu Purāṇa,* 1933, pp. 17 ff). These divisions are technically named *dvīpas* and the conclusion we have arrived at still holds good. Indradvīpa was Burma. The Kaśerudvīpa was the region about the Khaśia hills, hence Manipur and Assam in general.

35. See C.H.I. p. 520; also H. N. Sinha, *Sovereignty in Ancient Indian Polity,* Luzac, 1938, p. 260.

Tāmraparni has been uniformly accepted as ancient Ceylon. While Ceylon was Taprobana major, Sumatra was Taprobana minor. There was a Kumarīdvīpa round about the present Cape Comorin. Varuṇadvīpa stood for the territory which lay to the west of the Gandhara country. Nāgadvīpa refers to the Nicobar and other islands.[36] The *Vāyu Purāṇa* (Ch. 48) refers to some other *dvīpas,* evidently lying in S.E. Asia. The Angadvīpa may possibly refer to Campā. Then there is a reference to Malayadvīpa, Yavadvīpa and so on, referring to Borneo, Java and other islands. These colonies were founded one after another by adventurers from South India, in the pre-Vākāṭaka-Pallava period as well as in the Vākāṭaka-Pallava age. When the Guptas proclaimed their universal sovereignty these states were already organised and were affected largely by Hindu culture and ideals. The language and style of the Vākāṭaka and then of the Gupta inscriptions are largely seen in the early inscriptions of Campā (Cambodia) and other islands. With the foundation of the Gupta empire, the colonies transferred their allegiance to the Gupta emperors. Tāmralipti was the main port of communication with these island colonies. Fa-Hien tells us that Sumatra was a replica of Gupta India in its ideals and idealism. The cult of Visnu, and of other gods was prevalent in these colonies.

Apart from these we have the most reliable evidence of the Allahabad Pillar Inscription which runs as follows:

Saimhalakādibhisca sarvadvipavāsibhiḥ—l. 23. This indicates that the king of Ceylon and of all islands thereabout acknowledged the supremacy of the Gupta monarch. These colonies were included in the *prithvī* of Samudragupta which he is said to have united within his two arms,[37]

36. *Gerini. Ptolemy's Geography* pp. 378-83
37. *Corpus,* p. 8.

a typical epic expression. That the same relations were kept up in the period of his successors is also evident. King Bhadravarman who fought the Chinese (380-410 A.D.) was a contemporary of Candragupta II. His son Gangarāja visited India and went back to Campā to take up the reins of government once again.[38] There was also regular communication between Ceylon and the Gupta capital, besides diplomatic missions. Add to this the influence which art and architecture exerted on the colonies. The temples of Cambodia were built in the Gupta style of architecture. In Burma besides the Gupta script there was a discovery of a large number of Gupta terracottas.[39]

From the foregoing evidences one has to come to the conclusion that the relationship between the Motherland and the colonies was cordial. Both were knit together by the ties of friendship and allegiance. The contact resulted not only in the political unity of India but also in the cultural unity. The Indian India of the Guptas which included Farther India and Insular India was an integrated unit, and the colonies were its integral parts. The imperial policy followed by the Guptas was one dictated by Hindu religion and usage. It was not a military domination but a peaceful penetration. The Gupta emperors were not militarists in the modern sense of the word. The imperial rule was a rule based on *dharma,* dictated by a high sense of justice and a high code of international morality. It was in no way a challenging policy but a well accommodating policy of peace and goodwill.

38. R. C. Majumdar, Champā, pp. 25-29.
39. V. A. Smith: *Early History of India*, 4th ed. p. 297 *n*.

CHAPTER III

THE CENTRAL ADMINISTRATION

Section I.

THE CHARACTER OF GUPTA MONARCHY

Introductory

The vast empire of the Guptas was held in succession by great kings like Candragupta I, Samudragupta, Candragupta II Vikramāditya, Kumāragupta, Skandagupta and other kings for nearly two hundred years. We are concerned here with the Imperial Guptas only and not with the later Guptas of Mālva or Magadha. The disintegration of the empire set in even in the days of Skandagupta and the empire declined under his weak successors. Besides the literary evidence, we have copious material in the inscriptions which aid us to get at a correct picture of the polity in vogue during the fourth and fifth centuries of the Christian era. The *Kāmandakīya nītisāra* is one of the sources of information for this period. Though it cannot be counted as a first rate authority, still it is certain that it was a product of the age, on which it is reasonable to assume that the polity of the Guptas was based. It is too well known that Kāmandaka was a disciple of Kauṭalya, and it then stands to reason that the Kauṭalīyan tradition of governance and statecraft continued to be in vogue in the age of the Imperial Guptas also. It is true that there was some change in the designations of officers and officials. But all the same the same departments of Government continued to exist and function. The extant evidence indicates that the king was an important limb in the body politic. The State consisted of seven limbs including the king.[1] The other six were the ministers, kingdom, fortresses, treasury, army and allies. This seven limbed State formed one organic unit.[2] The end of this State was the realisation of the *trivarga* or the three objects of worldly existence. These are *dharma* or religious merit, *artha* or wealth and *kāma* or hedonism.[3] Proper realisation of every one of these objects leads to the fourth *Puruṣārtha* which is salvation or freedom from the bondage of this world. For securing this triple end, the king should discharge his duties justly and well. In other words he could not lose his restraint and could not be self-centred. This was the ideal which the Gupta monarchs placed before themselves as can be seen in the sequel.

Succession; hereditary.

The succession was hereditary. Son succeeded father. Candragupta I was succeeded by his son Samudragupta. He was followed by his sons Rāmagupta and Candragupta II Vikramāditya. Similarly Kumāragupta I, the eldest son of Candragupta II succeeded him, and after him, Skandagupta, his son ascended the throne. As Skandagupta died without a son, his brother Puragupta got crowned. It was a generally accepted custom that the eldest son of the family was to be crowned *Yuvarāja*.[4] He was installed emperor either after

[1] स्वाम्यमात्यश्च राष्ट्रं च दुर्गं कोशो बलं सुहृत् ।
एतावदुच्यते राज्यं सत्त्वबुद्धिव्यपाश्रयम् ॥ I. 18.
TRV. Edition.

[2] स्वाम्यमात्यश्च राष्ट्रं च दुर्गं कोशो बलं सुहृत् ।
परस्परोपकारीदं सप्ताङ्गं राज्यमुच्यते ॥ IV. 1.

[3] जितेन्द्रियस्य नृपतेर्नीतिमार्गानुसारिण : ।
भवन्ति ज्वलिता लक्ष्म्य : कीर्तयश्च नभ :स्पृश : ॥ I. 65.

[4] अविनीत कुमारं हि कुलमाशु विनश्यति ।
विनीतमौरसं पुत्रं यौवराज्येऽभिषेचयेत् ॥ VII. 5 & 6.

the death of the reigning king or after his abdication if it so happened. In accordance with this practice, Candragupta I hailed his son Samudragupta as *Yuvarāja*. The selection may be left to the king but the final approval rested with the court and the people. This is clear from the Allahabad Pillar inscription.

The opening lines of the inscription (ll. 7-8) present us with a vivid picture of the selection of *Yuvarāja* by Candragupta I. The inscription says that the Mahārāja embraced Samudragupta in the open court and with tears of love and affection exclaimed him worthy of the place of the crown prince which created envy and jealousy in his other sons. If we read this with the Mathurā Inscription (Fleet No. 4) where the epithet *tatparigṛhīta* occurs in lines 9-10, we are on sure ground that the *Yuvarāja* was always chosen by the king. The term *tatparigṛhīta* means 'accepted as his chosen successor', and in this particular case Samudragupta accepted Candragupta II as his successor. In these two cases we have to infer that though there were other sons, they were overlooked, and even the eldest son was overlooked. This could not have been due to the fact that the selected prince was a favourite of the reigning king, but he was by his character and ability fit to occupy that privileged position. In cases where the eldest son did not have the requisite qualification for shouldering the responsibilities of administering the empire, he was superseded. The kings naturally looked to the greater interest of the State than to that of the family.

But there was always the rule that the eldest son generally should succeed the father. Samudragupta nominated Candragupta II as his successor. But though he had another son and most probably the elder son in Rāmagupta, Samudragupta had by-passed Rāmagupta because he found him weak, vascillating and unheroic. When Rāmagupta ascended the throne he justified his father's impression by yielding to Śakapati on ignominious terms. This cowardly action of his brother aroused Candragupta II and he devised a clever plan to vanquish the Śakapati and in this he succeeded. The *Devī Candraguptam* which has already been mentioned says that he was instrumental in taking away the life of his weak elder brother. Then he himself ascended the throne especially since his father had already chosen him as his successor. The Sañjan plates confirm the statement of the *Devī Candraguptam.*[4-a] If we are to believe the literary and epigraphic evidence, the young Candragupta removed the thorn on his way and was crowned emperor. He married his brother's widow and adopted her as his queen.

If a king had more than one son, the younger ones were sent out as Governors of provinces or drafted to high imperial posts of responsibility.[5] The brothers of Kumāragupta I were appointed heads of provinces in the vast empire of the Guptas. The term *tatparigṛhīta* raises a first class constitutional issue. If Candragupta II had been chosen, as the inscriptions aver, why did Rāmagupta succeed Samudragupta? The point at issue was of constitutional importance. It is true that the father had chosen Candragupta II. But his choice alone did not legally satisfy the position. It had to be ratified by the full assembly by the ceremony of *Yuvarājya abhisecana.* Before he could effect this, it appears Samudragupta attained *vīrasvarga.* So when the eldest son Rāmagupta pressed his claim, public opinion turned in his favour. So he secured the throne. This indicates that the choice of the king should be ratified by the people and the court.

4-a. *Ep. Ind.,* XVIII. p. 26.

5. For instance, Govinda Gupta, a brother of Kumāragupta I and a son of Candragupta II, was appointed governor of Vaisāli if we are to believe the Basrah seals.

A Constitutional Monarchy

From the above analysis we see that the succession was generally hereditary and the monarchs were constitutional and took the public opinion with them. There was no trace of autocracy in their mode of conduct and administration. They respected the established laws of the land and acted in the interests of the subjects committed to their charge. They did not force their views and opinions on the unwilling public. A recent writer says that the powers of Gupta kings were absolute.[6] He also remarks that all land was virtually State property and the king could dispose of it in any manner he liked. We shall take up the question of State and its proprietorship of land in a subsequent chapter. Suffice it to say here that if by the term 'absolute', it is meant that the king exercised unlimited and unqualified powers in administration, it is very difficult to accept his statement. As the head of the administration he was entitled to certain privileges but it did not mean that he enjoyed privileges only and had no responsibilities. The Gupta ruler, like his Mauryan compatriot, was bound by a system of checks and balances. His acts were controlled by his council of ministers and others. He was in short not all in all. He was allowed to have his own way so far as it was legitimate and satisfied the letter and spirit of the law and usages of the land. Otherwise he was curbed and curbed strictly. Kāmandaka[7] emphasises in more than

6. R. N. Saletore *Life in the Gupta Age*, p. 233.

7. इयं हि लोकव्यतिरेकवर्त्तिनी
स्वभावतः पार्थिवता समुद्धता।
बलात् तदेनां विनयेन योजये-
न्नयस्य वृद्धो विनयः पुरस्सरः॥ I—67
परां विनीतः समुपेति सेव्यतां
महीपतीनां विनयो विभूषणम्।
प्रवृत्तदानो मृदुसञ्जरत्करः
करीव भद्रो विनयेन शोभते॥ I—68

one place that the first essential requisite for a king is self-restraint. The king should not only practise self-restraint but see that his officers and also his kith and kin restrained themselves. A king without self-control could not be a successful ruler. He should conquer his senses and place his mind under strict control. He should not let it travel in the vast wilderness of physical or bodily enjoyments. A king desirous of real prosperity for the kingdom and real happiness for himself should behave as one who has subdued his passions. A king should be cultured and be in touch with the learned elders and preceptors. He should be thoroughly learned in the maxims of polity and should put them into practice in his day-to-day administration. Then alone the world pays homage to him and his sovereignty gets really exalted.[8] Surely with such ideals placed before the Gupta monarch he could not be put down as an absolute monarch whose word was law.

Divine Nature

If once he had been consecrated to the exalted place of kingship, which meant presidentship over the destinies of millions of his subjects, he should be regarded by the public with a certain amount of veneration and awe. Such veneration was due to the place he occupied and not to the person or the individual king whoever he might be. So he is mentioned as Parama Bhaṭṭāraka and Parameśvara frequently in the inscriptions.[9] This is exactly the position taken by Nārada, the lawgiver when he says even a ruler not worthy of the position he occupies must be paid due reverence by his subjects. If the people of a State treat him not seriously but lightly, there will crop up troubles, external and internal, which would lead to dislocation of civil and military life.[10] This did not mean

8. See also IV. 43-48.
9. *Corpus*, pp. 17 and 161, 171, 183, 185, 186, 212. 217 etc.
10. *Kāma*. XVIII. 20-23.

that any king and every king was treated as a god from heaven on earth fit to be an object of worship. But kings who walked in the righteous path of administration were entitled to some consideration, and it is no wonder that such kings were looked upon with a certain amount of veneration. This has nothing to do with the divine theory of kings as promulgated in some of our law-books. A panegyrist may in his enthusiasm speak of him as an *acintya puruṣa* or *paramadaivata.* But neither the Gupta monarchs nor the discerning public treated these eulogies with any seriousness. There is not a single phrase in the inscriptions to point out that these kings regarded themselves as men born with divinity. It was a moral obligation on them to respect law.[11] In the same way people were morally bound to respect the administrator and final arbiter of law. Beyond this we do not see anything of divine nature in the Gupta monarchs.

King, not a Law-maker

One cannot dispute the fact that the Gupta king was a sovereign ruler. But the question that naturally arises is whether he was an absolute sovereign. Or in other words whether the Gupta monarch was exempt from all control. The answer is simple. He was sovereign to the extent he wielded supreme power. But the highest sovereign of the state was the common law of the land, formulated by the chosen representatives of the people, the sages and seers of ancient India. While our modern states make and unmake laws, through the device of a legislative machinery, things in ancient India were different. Hindu India clung to the traditional law, which was sacred and inviolable. No king or minister could touch it or meddle with it. The law was above the king. It should be promulgated as having absolute authority. It could not be modified unless it had

11. *Ibid.*, I. 17.

sanction behind the letter of the law. The king was not a law-maker. At the most he could administer the law, without in the least violating the spirit underlying it. If a king failed in his duty and acted in contravention, there was bound to be conflict between the king and the people.

That is why we do not see in the mass of the Gupta inscriptions anything that would amount to a proclamation or an ordinance which had the force of law. Even in making gifts of land or other gifts, the inscriptions cite the authority of Vyāsa as propounded in the *Mahābhārata*[12] and make out that any individual who infringed such grants would meet with punishment prescribed in the *śāstras* and would find final abode in hell. The spirit of the age was essentially religious, and the kings did such meritorious works (*karmabhir uttamaih*) so as not to alienate public sympathy with such limited powers. The king could not under any circumstances behave like an autocrat. The Edicts of Aśoka, the Mauryan emperor, had the term *śāsana* which has been taken as ordinance. Even that term does not occur in the epigraphs of the Imperial Guptas. From this it is clear that the Gupta monarchs set much store by law and executed it as the usages of the land demanded its application. Beyond this they did not bother.

Other Limitations

Not only was the Gupta monarch fettered by the law of the land which abrogated all sovereign authority into itself, but also he was bound by other checks and balances. One of them was the *mantri pariṣad* or simply *Pariṣad.* The Kauṭalyan tradition was apparently followed. It advised the king on matters of administrative importance. It appears that the king did not attend the meetings of the council. Whatever his proposals, they were placed before the council

12. *Corpus,* pp. 120, 124, 129, 134, 139.

which discussed the pros and cons of the various suggestions and came to a final decision. The decision was communicated to the king for further action if he deemed it necessary. Otherwise it would not have been possible for the Gupta monarchs to man the ship of the state peacefully and efficiently.

History shows that most of the emperors were engaged in battles and added territories to the empire. They could not have personally attended to the home policy as well as to the foreign policy. The real instrument of government lay in the hands of the council which took cognisance of the current drifts and advised the king to effect political reforms which would tend to make the state really a culture-state. Indeed the Gupta Empire had all the features of a culture-state. We must not fail to notice that it was a fact accomplished because of the dominating personality of the emperor. That is why the *nīti* texts insist on the people to show full regard to the emperor and evoke his sympathy and co-operation. It was something like the relation of the individual to the group. The individual was the king and the state was the group.

Yet another check was the *Sabhā* or assembly. The *Sabhā* was an organ of public opinion. Even for consecrating prince Samudragupta, Candragupta I had to summon his *Sabhā* and place his proposal before it for its final approval. The term *sabhyeṣūcchavasiteṣu*[13] in the Allahabad Pillar inscription in connection with the anointing of Samudragupta as crown prince is important. The constitutional position is well borne out as to the limitation of the power of the ruler. Generally the assembly acquiesced in the king's suggestion. For a king was expected to be ever reasonable in his suggestion. He took care to put forward proposals which would command the attention of the public. The *Sabhā* represented various interests in the land and its voice

13. *Kāma*, II. 7-8.

was held to be the echo of the public opinion. Thus a good portion of the sovereign authority of the state was shared between the *Parishad* and the *Sabhā* and there was left only little room for the king.

Section II.
EDUCATION AND DISCIPLINE

Kāmandaka has laid emphasis on the discipline of mind and body in the opening section of his treatise.[14] Personality is not worth its name if self-control is not practised by the monarch. And self-control is the result of a disciplined mind. This is effected by extensive reading and depth of knowledge. A king should get himself taught in four branches of learning. These are *Ānvīkṣiki* which deals with the knowledge of self, *Trayī* or the three Vedas (the Atharvan lore is not commended), *Vārtā* which deals with the study of economics and particularly wealth, and *daṇḍanīti* or a study of the principles of politics. It is said that these four branches[15] of study are essential for a prince if he were to aim at the realisation of different objects. If a prince were to sit in judgment and decide the destinies of millions of people who were his subjects, surely proficiency in these branches of learning must be the first and foremost requisite to the king to use his discretionary powers.

The Gupta monarchs were not kings who claimed divine right, nor the state was merely the territorial unit. The outlook was cosmopolitan in character. It was in part political democracy and in part ethical democracy. The state recognised differences in capacities between men but actually every individual counted in as much as he contributed to the common good of humanity as a whole. The *digvijaya* and the consequent consolidation of the states within the empire still

14. See the first section of the second sarga. The section itself is entitled 'Vidyāvibhāgaprakaraṇam'.

15. *Ibid.*, II. 1-6.

kept the door open to cultural frontier. If we only reflect for a moment on the prevalent conditions in the Gupta times, we have to conclude that the king enjoyed rational freedom combined with self-reverence or self-control[16] and not political liberty which did not take into sympathetic account of other factors which made up a state. And this is considered even today as the true essence of human culture.

Ānvikṣiki teaches the virtuous quality of impartiality. The Vedic lore makes the king acquainted with the general moral code of injunctions and interdictions. Trade and commerce and other economic pursuits are easily handled by a systematic study of the principles of Economics. The ruler need not be afraid of any dislocation in the civil life of the state. *Daṇḍanīti* enables him to administer justice in the rightful path. Only a king equipped with these could realise the *caturvarga—dharma, artha, kāma* and *mokṣa*.[17]

In addition to this the kings learnt the use of handling weapons. *Dhanurveda* was a course of study incumbent on a prince. In those days of frequent wars when kings were fired with ambitious projects of *digvijaya*, a prince's education was not complete if he had not mastered the science of archery and the use of different weapons of offence and defence. They were proficient in various arts and there is testimony that Samudragupta was an expert in the science of music. Kāmandaka remarks that a king who is not versed fully in *Daṇḍanīti* is a blind king though he has physical eyes to see.[18] The idea is that an uncultured person would easily fall into temptations and vices which would go a long way in marring a good administration. His vision would be clouded by worldly things and he could not look ahead. The fear was that an

16. *Ibid.*, II. 17.
17. See *ibid.*, II. St. 1-17.
18. *Ibid.*, XIV. 3.

exalted person of the status of a monarch would fall into the trap of *kāma*. *Kāma* is a general term which stands for evils arising from hunting, gambling, lust and drink.

These and similar other evils come under the category of *vyasanas* of a king.[19] The evils of *mṛga vyasana* are enumerated in detail and a king is advised not to indulge much in it. In case a king wishes to take to hunting as an exercise, he is then advised to construct a beautiful park in the outskirts of the town and engage himself in sports. Such a park should be located near the bed of a river or at the foot of a mountain with plenty of water and grass facilities. The park should abound in wild game such as elephants and tigers, and beautified with thick growth of bushes, creepers and trees. In this park a king would go ahunting but to go about the woods and forests like a professional hunter does not become a king.[20] Then the evils resulting from gambling are enumerated and the examples of Yudhiṣṭhira and Nala are quoted since they lost their wedded wives as a result of gambling. This monster of dice is said to cut at elementary human virtues of love and sympathy and engenders eternal hostilities. Hence it is ordained that an intelligent monarch should avoid this, even though a challenge is thrown out for a gambling match[21].

Then a list of untoward effects as a result of over indulgence with women is furnished. It is pointed out how women are the seed spots of jealousy, intolerance, anger, hostility, and rashness which all profoundly affect the nature of the administration in a kingdom. It leads to loss of health, loss of energy, and loss of friends. So moderate sexual enjoyment is alone commended.[22] The next

19. *Ibid.*, 1-56 XIII. 6; XIV. 61; XV. 8.
20. *Ibid.*, XV. 24-43.
21. *Ibid.*, 44-55.
22. *Ibid.*, 56-62.

vyasana of a king is said to be drink. Too much of intoxication leads to loss of memory and weakness and hinders the power of discrimination. To-day there is a move to abolish drink altogether. It may be pointed out that while hunting and gambling were totally prohibited, drink and women were allowed to a moderate extent. Drink was not considered such a serious evil, if it were to be within the bounds of moderation. Only too much indulgence was condemned.[23]

There are other evils which a king should avoid. These are due to *Krodha*. The *Gītā* says ***kāma eṣa krodha eṣa rajo-guṇa samudbhavah*** (III. 37).

Krodha or wrath on the part of a monarch will tell on the administration. Its evils are said to be threefold: harshness in speech, unjust and hasty punishments and violent seizure of property. A king who indulges in these cannot claim to be a success in his rule. It is bound to lead to violation of law and order. Hence a wise king should get rid of these *vyasanas* and follow the path of rectitude. Nothing pays in the long run like moral uprightness and good conduct. Therefore much insistence is made on discipline, and discipline if it were to be real, must be a consequential development of wide learning and culture.

It is not enough if a king avoided these evil propensities. If he were to attain fame as a sound statesman, he should cultivate the great virtue of *utthāna*.[24] Much emphasis has been laid by Kauṭalya on this special virtue in a king. His disciple Kāmandaka points out in several places the value and necessity of *utthāna* in a king. It means active exertion. Kāmandaka states that possessed of full exertion and energy, a king would be able to bring about prosperity in his kingdom. To the enthusiast who is full of manly action, nothing daunts

23. *Ibid.*, 63-65.
24. *Ibid.*, viii, 13; XIV. 5, 9,

him. Success attends him in all his endeavours.[25] It is termed *simhī vṛtti* or lion-like conduct. By the sheer weight of his energy united with activity, even a big foe would be humbled.[26]

It must be remembered that *vyasanas* are not peculiar to a monarch. Every limb of the state organism has its own *vyasanas* to reckon with. An intelligent king who should be acquainted with all the evils which pertain to the various members of the body-politic should exert himself in such a way that these evils would vanish in thin air, and that welfare and prosperity of his Government are assured.[27] The sum total of this discussion is that a king should not allow himself to become lazy, indolent, and lethargic. He should conquer these by his vigilance, activity and energy. Such a king ensures the progress of the state and happiness of his subjects. Such healthy restrictions on the actions and conduct of a reigning sovereign are wholesome and give no opportunity to him to degrade himself into a position of an absolute ruler.

If we now turn to inscriptions, we find that the Imperial Guptas placed before themselves certain ideals and tried as far as it lay in their power to translate them into actual practice. Tribute is paid to Samudragupta's wisdom, calmness, study of the Vedas, and his poetical talents, as also to his skill and prowess in arms.[28] Further on, it is said that Samudragupta was full of compassion and had a heart surcharged with love. His sympathy to the miserable, the poor, the helpless and the afflicted was marked. On most occasions he did not appropriate the wealth of the conquered but restored it back to them. He had a keen intellect and had

25. *Ibid.*, XIII. 11.
26. *Ibid.*, XII. 25.
27. *Ibid.*, 93-94.
28. *Corpus*, p. 6.

many noble deeds to his credit.[29] In the same strain the inscriptions of Candragupta II[30] and of Skandagupta[31] speak about them. These kings are likened to gods like Dhanada, Varuṇa, Indra and Antaka in their observance of religious rites and in their resplendent gifts. These Imperial Guptas took care to see that they built up 'the pale of religion' and identified themselves with the strict observance of religious practices. By their worthy and notable deeds they endeavoured their best to root out poverty and misery from the empire. In this way they endeared themselves to the people at large. Thus the constitutional form of monarchy is wri' large in their epigraphs fortunately preserved to us.

Titles of Kings and Queens.

In the Mauryan times we hear of titles like Rājan, Mahārāja and Kumāra applicable to kings and princes. But in the Gupta epoch we have several titles which show that these titles had in course of time multiplied. The early princes of the imperial line like Śrī Gupta were satisfied with the title of Mahārāja. But soon it becomes an official title applied to feudatories and not to paramount rulers. To distinguish the feudatories from themselves the Imperial Guptas adopted the title Mahārājādhirāja indicative of their imperial power and position.[31]

In the Udayagiri cave Inscription[32] of Candragupta II, he is entitled Paramabhaṭṭāraka and Mahārājadhirāja. The Gadhwā stone inscription[33] and some others of Candragupta II add a still more appellation—Paramabhāgavata. The latter title is also given to Kumāragupta as could be seen from the

29. *Ibid.*, 11. 25-27.
30. *Ibid.*, p. 26.
31. *Ibid.*, p. 59.
32. *Ibid.*, p. 25.
33. *Ibid.*, p. 38.

opening line of the Gadhwā stone inscription[34] of this king. Skandagupta[35] is also designated Mahārājādhirāja.

Paramabhaṭṭāraka means 'the most worshipful one'. It is a vain-glorious title. The monarch wants to exhibit to the world that he is such a pious and godly man who would revere virtue and spurn vice. He wishes to pander to the religious spirit of the age. The same is the case with other monarchs who bore such titles. It need not be considered entirely as a title of paramount sovereignty.

The queens of these kings were generally entitled Dēvīs. For example Kumāra dēvī was the name of the queen of Candragupta I. Dattadevī was the queen of Samudragupta. From the fact that the names and effigies of Candragupta I and Kumāra dēvī appear in their coins,[36] it is reasonable to assume that the queen held an equal status in the administration of the land. In the case of Samudragupta and Dattadēvī the images are seen only in the *Aśvamedha* type of coins and not in all coins. Though this may not be a positive proof that the queen had lost her position in the administration, still it is an evidence that without the legitimate partner in life, the king could not embark on sacrifices. The performance of a Vedic *yajña* always demands the presence of the *Patnī*. From the fact that their joint images are seen in the Aśvamedha type, this can be clearly inferred. In the case of coins of other rulers after Candragupta I and barring the Aśvamedha type of coins of Samudragupta, the effigy of the queen disappears yielding place to the figure of Lakshmī, *i.e.* the goddess of Fortune. To deduce from this that women were debarred from all responsible duties in administration is a theory that could not be fully proved.

34. *Ibid.* p. 41.
35. *Ibid.* p. 50.
36. Allan, *op. cit. pp.* 8-11.

But generally speaking the Indian tradition always treated the woman as the queen of the home, the custodian of household economy and the up-bringer of family[37]. And it is well-known that in ancient India the family was the unit of society and stood for all the fine virtues and graces which made for the progressive welfare of society at large. Hence if under pressure of circumstances a queen or princess came out to wield the responsibilities of administrative offices, it may be pointed out that politics for a woman was not the rule but an exception.

Personal safety of the king.

The monarch who occupied such an important place in the body-politic of the state, would be susceptible to danger from any quarter. History records of disloyal queens, recalcitrant princes and unfaithful servants. Even a sympathetic king could not please anybody and everybody. He could not violate rules or transgress principles even though the violator be his nearest and dearest. Hence extreme precaution was taken to protect the royal person from the envious, the jealous and the discontented. And the precaution was there even against poisoning due to snakes or other venomous birds and beasts. Hence it is prescribed[38] that a monarch should be careful regarding his conveyances, bed, seat, drink, eatables, garments, ornaments, in fact, about everything. He is advised to bathe in good water, decorate with antidotary gems and get his food examined before he actually sat at the table. Generally his food and drink were previously tasted

37. Manu.

पितृभिर्भ्रातृभिश्चैता: पतिभिर्देवरैस्तथा ।
पूज्या भूषयितव्याश्च बहुकल्याणमीप्सुभि: ॥
यत्र नार्यस्तु पूज्यन्ते रमन्ते तत्र देवता: ।
यत्रैतास्तु न पूज्यन्ते सर्वास्तत्राफला: क्रिया: ॥

(iii, 55-56).

38. See the *atmarakṣitaka prakaraṇam of Kāmandaki niti.*

by the taster. This is true of all ancient and mediaeval kings, Hindu or Muslim. Among the officials of the establishment of Sultan Alauddin Bahmani Sāheb there was the Chāshnīgir to use the Dakkhanī dialect. His duty was to watch over the kitchen of princes and taste every dish brought to the table as a security against poison[39]. Kāmandaka deals elaborately in a whole chapter (VII) about the sources of poisoning and antidotes to the same.

The monarch's life was so precious that he was advised to avoid sojourning in dense forests, narrow lanes and fairs and festivals which attracted miscellaneous crowds. He was to pass through the high ways preferably with honest attendants[40]. He should be careful about his harem, where he should appoint men and women who would look after the purity and cleanliness of the inner apartments. The servants of the harem should be above the tempting influences of Jaṭilas, muṇḍas, magicians and harlots,[41] lest they should corrupt and induce them to inflict injuries on the royal person. The king should avoid contacting people suffering from virulent types of malady, lest he should catch infection. After a rather lengthy discourse on the personal safety of the monarch, Kāmandaka concludes the chapter with the remark that the sages have laid down these elaborate instructions to the make-up of a perfect monarch[42]. The neglect of punctilious attention to the body of the king would adversely affect his health and consequently deprive him of the mental peace and balance, without which the ship of state cannot said on smooth waters. The make-up of a perfect monarchy consists in sound body and sound mind of the monarch. To preserve this, attention should be paid even to

39. See Major J. S. King. *The History of the Bahmani Dynasty* p. 7, esp. note.

40. *Kāma*,. VII. 35-45.

41. *Ibid.* VII. 46.

42. *Ibid.*, VII. 47-59.

minute details, however negligent it might seem to an ordinary person. Without understanding the real spirit underlying these precautions[43], it has been glibly said by some scholars that such things smack of despotism.

Duties of the king.

Monarchs of Hindu India in general and the Gupta monarchs in particular were anxious to win the name of righteous rulers. From a study of the mass of the inscriptions and literature of the period, it is perceptible that the Gupta sovereigns did not assert their sovereignty in the sense that they arrogated to themselves all the privileges due to a monarch to the detriment of their duties and responsibilities. Though they had many privileges, they did not abuse them. But being fully conscious of their responsibilities to the state and their subjects, they conducted themselves in such a way as to earn their gratitude[44]. They fully realised the ends and the means to achieve them. The realisation of the *trivarga* was the ideal and they persevered to keep this ideal before themselves. Legitimate enjoyment of material comforts by the people and their sovereign was the one idea running through the pages of the *Arthśāstra* and *Dharmaśāstra* texts. Towards this end, the Guptas endeavoured their best.

First, they had religious duties. The Guptas were most of them *parama bhāgavatas*. They were wedded to the cult of *bhakti* which developed very much in later times. In their time the Purāṇic Hinduism had come to stay. They felt that they were the true custodians of the established religion of the land.

43. इति स्म पूर्व मुनयो बभाषिरे
नृपस्य राज्यस्य च साधु रक्षणम् ।
तवेतदेवं परिपालयन् नया-
न्नरेश्वर : पालनकल्पतां व्रजेत् ॥ *(VII—59)*

44. Ibid. IV. 76.

hand of co-operation voluntarily in times
ate.[56]

y of the king was to protect the people from
sorts. Under this head come pestilence,
ire, vandalism by wild animals and so on.[57]
take precautionary measures by a well-planned
uch calamities. If once that happened prompt
d be taken to tide over the crisis. In other
e state was expected to do its duty by the
they might not be deprived of their minimum
, food and clothing. This alone ensures the
the masses and evokes their loyalty and support.
amine-stricken people, provision of easy and
edical facilities, care of sanitary arrangements,
easures for improvement of agricultural lands
n channels and canals, promotion of trade and
these and other similar measures should be taken
uler who is the symbol of the state, if he and his
ere to be ensured continuous prosperity.

nother duty of the king was to patronise arts, educa-
Ancient India happily transmitted the tradition of a
ate. A state was to be governed by laws and rules, and
uard the people from the menace of foreign enemies.
e essential duties. But they would be regarded as a
shed structure of a building. To complete the edifice,
hould be literate. Besides, fine arts are a test of any
ion. In this behalf the duties of the king were

त्यादि वृष्यान् सम्वृध्य प्रजानामभिवृद्धये ।
विनयच्छिद्रयमुत्कर्षं राजा शल्यं समुद्धरेत् ।। VI—13
यथा बीजाङ्कुरः सूक्ष्मः परिपुष्टोऽभिरक्षितः ।
काले फलाय भवति साधु तद्वियं प्रजा ।। VI—14

57. *Ibid.* XIV. 22: 61 ff.
58. *Ibid.* II. 16.

They founded a number of temples and endowed them richly with large gifts of land and money. Besides this, they kept a watchful eye on the conduct of their subjects. They were to follow the instructions laid in the *Dharmaśāstras* and act according to the theory and practice of law. The *Varṇāsrama* Dharma[45] was the basis of the Hindu social polity. Each caste was to pursue its occupation and not compete with other professions. In pursuing its duty, the members of the community were to see that they did not infringe the traditional code. The same is true of the *āśramas*. Otherwise dislocation of the society would set in and peace of the land would be disturbed.

From the *svadharma* which is the particular duty of each individual in every group, the *Kāmandakīya* enumerates the *sādhāraṇa dharma,* the duties common to all castes and groups[46]. These are non-injury, good speech, truthfulness, purity of mind and body, mercy and forbearance.[47] The king is to promote these righteous practices among his subjects. In other words people should avoid ill-will, dishonesty, falsehood, envy and jealousy which are the seeds of dissension among the various communities. To make the country safe from rancour and hatred, the king should promote good feeling among his subjects[48]. This is the way to preserve *dharma* or righteousness. The Gupta kings had abundant faith in religious merit, and to achieve this they made it their foremost duty to observe *dharma* themselves and endeavoured to preserve and promote *dharma* among their subjects.[49]

The next set of duties incumbent on the king was political and administrative. Protection of life

45. *Ibid.* II. 10.
46. Ibid. The fourth section entitled *Varnaśramavyavasthā. prakaranam.*
47. IV. 32.
48. Ibid III. 1-2.
49. Ibid. 1-14.

and property engaged his best attention. Kāmandaka definitely rules that this protection of his subjects will be possible only if good order is preserved in society.[50] So it is for the king to see to the preservation of social order. It is just possible that the country may seem to be in a flourishing condition even in troublesome times. But this condition of affairs should not be tolerated. The prosperity may not be real in the absence of a settled order. Preservation of order, the author of the *Nītisāra* says, is preferable to that seemingly prosperous condition. For it is asked what is the value of all prosperity at the expense of good order[51]. To ensure peaceful and healthy movements of peoples, the king should take upon himself the onerous task of preserving order. People who pay taxes and tributes to the state expect in return nothing more than peaceful enjoyment of their legitimate rights undisturbed. This disturbance may be local, national or from foreign enemies. The king was expected to take necessary steps to see that the people were not put to distress of any kind. It is more or less a contract between the state and its subjects, but this contract is voluntary in character. The king who was the symbol of the state was to see that things moved on smoothly and without any hitch. To ensure life and order, he should wield his *daṇḍa* neither sternly nor tenderfully but impartially[52]. What was aimed at was equitable distribution of rewards and punishments. He should give succour to the oppressed and the helpless.

It is said that to the subjects there are five sources of apprehension. These are royal officers, thieves, enemies of the kingdom, the king's favourites and the covetousness of the monarch himself.[53] If any of these sources gets

50. Ibid. 1-17.
51. Ibid. I, 11-12.
52. Ibid. II. 37; VI. 15.
53. *Ibid.* V. 81-82.

loosened, then
The king must
the people by le
ments. He must
not misuse or abus
to their will and ple
might indulge in to
tribute patronage acc
king should therefore
behaviour of his officer
by vigilant watch ke
subjection. So *daṇḍa*
figuratively means king.[54]

The above prescription
theorist but was a statesman
from those sources. Besides
the true king should have an
those who cause internal diss
king's duty was to examine tho
was being administered. Kāma

'Inflicting punishments heavie
terrifies his subjects; while dealin
held in contempt by them. Ther
impartially mete out chastisement
offences.'[55] More of this later on.
Nītisāra drives home is that cherished

54 दमो दण्ड इति प्रोक्तस्तस्माद् दण्डो
तस्य नीतिर्दण्डनीतिर्नयनान्नीतिरुच्यते ॥
55 उद्वेजयति तीक्ष्णेन मृदुना परिभूयते ।
तस्माद् यथार्हतो दण्डं नयेत् पक्षमनाश्रितः ।

onerous. The Gupta rulers were not behind other rulers in discharging their duties in this direction. Being themselves cultured, they took abiding interest in the advancement of arts, especially fine arts. They erected huge temples to different deities. In point of architecture and sculpture their work was superb. Most of the buildings that have survived to-day are religious edifices. Some of them are the shrines and monasteries at Sārnath, the Hindu temple at Muṇḍeśvari near Bhabua in the Arrah district, the temple at Bodh Gayā, the temple of Pārvatī at Nachina-Kuṭhāra in the Ajayagaḍh territory, the Śiva temple at Bhumara in the Nagod territory, the later Gupta temple at Deogadh in the Jhansi district, and the Gupta temple at Sāñchi in the Bhopal State.[59]

Earlier writers like Cunningham attributed the śikhara or spire as a feature of the Gupta buildings, which, besides, had distinctive decorative motifs peculiar to the epoch. E. B. Havell thinks that the Mahābodhi temple was erected in much earlier days, as early as the 1st century B.C.[60] This can be accepted. A recent writer would assign the temples at Nachina-Kuṭhāra, and at Muṇḍeśvari to the post-Gupta period. One characteristic feature of the sacred buildings of the early Gupta period was the flat-roof over the sanctum, if we are to take the earlier Pārvatī temple at Nachina-Kuṭhāra as a typical example. The temple at Bhumara does not lend assistance as there is no structure over its sanctum.

R. D. Banerji believes that the early Gupta structure contained no *śikhara,* but had a covered path of circumambulation, a small open porch in the centre of the facade, with little or no ornamentation on the exterior. From this he draws the conclusion that the early Gupta structures were more or less those preserved on the Malabar Coast and especially in the modern districts of North and South

59. R. D. Banerji *op. cit.* p. 132-9.
60. *Aryan Rule* p. 100.

Kanara. It is difficult to subscribe to this view on the ground that generally climatic conditions determined the structure of a shrine. The Malabar and West Coast are ordinarily exposed to heavy showers, and hence the structure was so manipulated that it caused no inconvenience to the worshippers circumambulating and that much damage was not inflicted in the case of a flat-roof in rain-fed countries. Besides, the early extant Gupta temples are in complete ruins, and to cite one example as the general plan of all shrines is to say the least unconvincing. Add to this the ornamental sculptures at the Maṇḍapa in Bhumara and the decorated gateway leading to it are the evidence to show the Gupta temples had ornamentation of some sort.

Again Dr. Banerji has taken for granted that the *śikhara* as a feature of Indian architecture, began in the 6th century A.D., and hence he thinks that the Gupta temple at Deogadh is a post-Gupta structure. This position cannot be maintained. The late Jayaswal has proved beyond doubt that the śikhara style of architecture goes to the Mauryan epoch, if not earlier. In the light of indisputable evidence, we have to treat the temple at Deogadh as a Gupta structure only. The śikhara style was a continuation of the old Indian architectural motif. The Caitya window is a predominant decorative motif in the temples of this period.

More important than all these, is the study of the plastic art of the Gupta period. In the story of Gupta art, three distinct schools may be distinguished, the Mathurā school, the Banares school and the Pātaliputra school. In the Mathurā school some features of the Kushana styles are noticeable. The artists of Mathurā fashioned products from the mottled red sandstone found in plenty at Karri. That some of the products were taken to distant places can be seen from the Buddhist image discovered at Mankuwar, belonging to the reign of Kumāragupta. It resembles the early Kushana

Buddhist image. From the same place of Mankuwar comes a Jaina image, again modelled on the early Kushana type.

That the sculpture of the Guptas was something striking and unique may be seen from other examples provided. Though Banares itself had a school of sculpture running to the post-Mauryan epoch, still the dominance of the Mathurā School throughout the early Gupta epoch is perfectly seen from the Mathurā images discovered in Banares. Yet Banares continued its old style of art and sculpture. In the Banares school the use of red paint is uncommon. The material used was the one from Chunar. The art of Banares was not stereotyped and conservative. That it was progressive is seen from the fact that the Kushana technique did not provoke the imagination of the Banares artists. Says Banerji: "The earliest images discovered at Sārnāth show the use of that particular form of *Ma* which type is used in the Karamdanda inscription of Kumāragupta I."

The influence of the Banares school spread to the capital of the Gupta Empire, Pāṭaliputra. This is seen from the images discovered at Nālanda, both in stone and in metal.[61] The Pāṭaliputra school did not use the Chunar sandstone but in technique it did not differ from the Banares school. On the other hand there is a fundamental unity in the art of the Gupta period. This is noticeable in the method of treatment of bas-reliefs, and the subjects introduced into them. A study of the images of the Gupta epoch indicates that the sculptors paid more attention to real naturalism and symmetry. Codrington remarks: 'Gupta art has been praised for its intellectuality. It would be better to treat it as the natural outcome of ancient Indian art, with its vivid appre-

61. Coomaraswami: *History of Fine Art in India and Indonesia* p. 85.

ciation of form and pattern, and its love of the quick beat and rhythm of living things and of their poise and balance in repose'.[62]

Music was another fine art which came largely under the patronage of the early Gupta monarchs as is evidenced by the coins of Samudragupta. The foregoing summary demonstrates how the Imperial Guptas were true patrons of culture. In the field of education, the Imperial Guptas felt it as their sacred duty to spread literacy all round. In the epoch of the Guptas, Sanskrit which already held sway definitely came to stay. Every inscription of importance has a literary flavour about it. The ministers and higher officials of the state were men of talents and were profound men of letters. The performance of Hariṣena the author of the Allahabad Pillar Inscription of Samudragupta is classical by itself. There is a vivid description of the wars and conquests, told compactly. Brevity is the soul of wit and this is evident in Hariṣena, He imitates the celebrated Kālidāsa, as does Vatsabhaṭṭi.

In the Gupta period the Sanskrit *Kāvya* reached its acme. It is also true of the *Sāhitya śāstra.* The Junāgadh rock inscription points to the wide knowledge of the science of poetics. It is markedly true that a great impetus was given to Sanskrit, and this would not have been possible if the kings had not taken up a serious responsibility to promote and patronise Sanskrit learning. Another remarkable fact about this is that in point of learning, religious or social bias did not stand in the way. Samudragupta who earned the title *Kavirāja* was apparently the author of several poems. He was a friend and patron of the Buddhist sage, Vasubhandhu who was also known to his father Candragupta I.[63]

62. Rothenstein—*Ancient India* p. 62.
63. Smith, *Early History of India*, pp. 346 ff.

They founded a number of temples and endowed them richly with large gifts of land and money. Besides this, they kept a watchful eye on the conduct of their subjects. They were to follow the instructions laid in the *Dharmaśāstras* and act according to the theory and practice of law. The *Varṇāsrama* Dharma[45] was the basis of the Hindu social polity. Each caste was to pursue its occupation and not compete with other professions. In pursuing its duty, the members of the community were to see that they did not infringe the traditional code. The same is true of the *āśramas*. Otherwise dislocation of the society would set in and peace of the land would be disturbed.

From the *svadharma* which is the particular duty of each individual in every group, the *Kāmandakīya* enumerates the *sādhāraṇa dharma,* the duties common to all castes and groups[46]. These are non-injury, good speech, truthfulness, purity of mind and body, mercy and forbearance.[47] The king is to promote these righteous practices among his subjects. In other words people should avoid ill-will, dishonesty, falsehood, envy and jealousy which are the seeds of dissension among the various communities. To make the country safe from rancour and hatred, the king should promote good feeling among his subjects[48]. This is the way to preserve *dharma* or righteousness. The Gupta kings had abundant faith in religious merit, and to achieve this they made it their foremost duty to observe *dharma* themselves and endeavoured to preserve and promote *dharma* among their subjects.[49]

The next set of duties incumbent on the king was political and administrative. Protection of life

45. *Ibid.* II. 10.
46. Ibid. The fourth section entitled *Varnaśramavyavasthā. prakaranam.*
47. IV. 32.
48. Ibid III. 1-2.
49. Ibid. 1-14.

and property engaged his best attention. Kāmandaka definitely rules that this protection of his subjects will be possible only if good order is preserved in society.[50] So it is for the king to see to the preservation of social order. It is just possible that the country may seem to be in a flourishing condition even in troublesome times. But this condition of affairs should not be tolerated. The prosperity may not be real in the absence of a settled order. Preservation of order, the author of the *Nītisāra* says, is preferable to that seemingly prosperous condition. For it is asked what is the value of all prosperity at the expense of good order[51]. To ensure peaceful and healthy movements of peoples, the king should take upon himself the onerous task of preserving order. People who pay taxes and tributes to the state expect in return nothing more than peaceful enjoyment of their legitimate rights undisturbed. This disturbance may be local, national or from foreign enemies. The king was expected to take necessary steps to see that the people were not put to distress of any kind. It is more or less a contract between the state and its subjects, but this contract is voluntary in character. The king who was the symbol of the state was to see that things moved on smoothly and without any hitch. To ensure life and order, he should wield his *daṇḍa* neither sternly nor tenderfully but impartially[52]. What was aimed at was equitable distribution of rewards and punishments. He should give succour to the oppressed and the helpless.

It is said that to the subjects there are five sources of apprehension. These are royal officers, thieves, enemies of the kingdom, the king's favourites and the covetousness of the monarch himself.[53] If any of these sources gets

50. Ibid. 1-17.
51. Ibid. I, 11-12.
52. Ibid. II. 37; VI. 15.
53 *Ibid.* V. 81-82.

loosened, then the normal life of the people gets disturbed. The king must first show himself that he is the father of the people by levying mild taxes and executing just punishments. He must take particular care that his favourites do not misuse or abuse their position and drive people to pander to their will and pleasure. This is true of royal officials who might indulge in too much extortion or corruption and distribute patronage according to their likes and dislikes. The king should therefore protect his subjects from the misbehaviour of his officers and favourites. The monarch should by vigilant watch keep the thieves and enemies under subjection. So *daṇḍa* which literally means punishment figuratively means king.[54]

The above prescription shows that the author was no mean theorist but was a statesman who was alive to dangers arising from those sources. Besides warding off sources of danger, the true king should have an eye on the breakers of law, and those who cause internal dissensions. This means that the king's duty was to examine thoroughly whether proper justice was being administered. Kāmandaka happily puts it thus:

'Inflicting punishments heavier than the offences, a king terrifies his subjects; while dealing out lighter ones, he is held in contempt by them. Therefore a monarch should impartially mete out chastisements proportionate to the offences.'[55] More of this later on. What the author of the *Nītisāra* drives home is that cherished by their ruler the peo-

[54] दमो दण्ड इति प्रोक्तस्तात्स्थ्याद् दण्डो महीपतिः ।
तस्य नीतिर्दण्डनीतिर्नयनान्नीतिरुच्यते ॥ II—15

[55] उद्वेजयति तीक्ष्णेन मृदुना परिभूयते ।
तस्माद् यथार्हतो दण्डं नयेत् पक्षमनाश्रितः ॥ VI—15

ple extended their hand of co-operation voluntarily in times of crisis to the state.[56]

Another duty of the king was to protect the people from calamities of all sorts. Under this head come pestilence, famine, floods, fire, vandalism by wild animals and so on.[57] The state should take precautionary measures by a well-planned policy to avert such calamities. If once that happened prompt measures should be taken to tide over the crisis. In other words a culture state was expected to do its duty by the people so that they might not be deprived of their minimum wants—shelter, food and clothing. This alone ensures the happiness of the masses and evokes their loyalty and support. Relief to famine-stricken people, provision of easy and accessible medical facilities, care of sanitary arrangements, abundant measures for improvement of agricultural lands by irrigation channels and canals, promotion of trade and commerce, these and other similar measures should be taken up by the ruler who is the symbol of the state, if he and his subjects were to be ensured continuous prosperity.

Yet another duty of the king was to patronise arts, education, etc.[58] Ancient India happily transmitted the tradition of a culture state. A state was to be governed by laws and rules, and was to guard the people from the menace of foreign enemies. These are essential duties. But they would be regarded as a half-finished structure of a building. To complete the edifice, people should be literate. Besides, fine arts are a test of any civilisation. In this behalf the duties of the king were

[56] इत्यादि दूष्यान् सम्बूष्य प्रजानामभिवृद्धये ।
विनयञ्छ्यिमुत्कर्षं राजा शल्यं समुद्धरेत् ॥ VI—13
यथा बीजाङ्कुर : सूक्ष्म : परिपुष्टोऽभिरक्षित : ।
काले फलाय भवति साधु तद्वियं प्रजा ॥ VI—14

57. *Ibid.* XIV. 22: 61 ff.
58. *Ibid.* II. 16.

onerous. The Gupta rulers were not behind other rulers in discharging their duties in this direction. Being themselves cultured, they took abiding interest in the advancement of arts, especially fine arts. They erected huge temples to different deities. In point of architecture and sculpture their work was superb. Most of the buildings that have survived to-day are religious edifices. Some of them are the shrines and monasteries at Sārnath, the Hindu temple at Muṇḍeśvari near Bhabua in the Arrah district, the temple at Bodh Gayā, the temple of Pārvatī at Nachina-Kuṭhāra in the Ajayagaḍh territory, the Śiva temple at Bhumara in the Nagod territory, the later Gupta temple at Deogadh in the Jhansi district, and the Gupta temple at Sāñchi in the Bhopal State.[59]

Earlier writers like Cunningham attributed the śikhara or spire as a feature of the Gupta buildings, which, besides, had distinctive decorative motifs peculiar to the epoch. E. B. Havell thinks that the Mahābodhi temple was erected in much earlier days, as early as the 1st century B.C.[60] This can be accepted. A recent writer would assign the temples at Nachina-Kuṭhāra, and at Muṇḍeśvari to the post-Gupta period. One characteristic feature of the sacred buildings of the early Gupta period was the flat-roof over the sanctum, if we are to take the earlier Pārvatī temple at Nachina-Kuṭhāra as a typical example. The temple at Bhumara does not lend assistance as there is no structure over its sanctum.

R. D. Banerji believes that the early Gupta structure contained no *śikhara,* but had a covered path of circumambulation, a small open porch in the centre of the facade, with little or no ornamentation on the exterior. From this he draws the conclusion that the early Gupta structures were more or less those preserved on the Malabar Coast and especially in the modern districts of North and South

59. R. D. Banerji *op. cit.* p. 132-9.
60. *Aryan Rule* p. 100.

Kanara. It is difficult to subscribe to this view on the ground that generally climatic conditions determined the structure of a shrine. The Malabar and West Coast are ordinarily exposed to heavy showers, and hence the structure was so manipulated that it caused no inconvenience to the worshippers circumambulating and that much damage was not inflicted in the case of a flat-roof in rain-fed countries. Besides, the early extant Gupta temples are in complete ruins, and to cite one example as the general plan of all shrines is to say the least unconvincing. Add to this the ornamental sculptures at the Maṇḍapa in Bhumara and the decorated gateway leading to it are the evidence to show the Gupta temples had ornamentation of some sort.

Again Dr. Banerji has taken for granted that the *śikhara* as a feature of Indian architecture, began in the 6th century A.D., and hence he thinks that the Gupta temple at Deogadh is a post-Gupta structure. This position cannot be maintained. The late Jayaswal has proved beyond doubt that the śikhara style of architecture goes to the Mauryan epoch, if not earlier. In the light of indisputable evidence, we have to treat the temple at Deogadh as a Gupta structure only. The śikhara style was a continuation of the old Indian architectural motif. The Caitya window is a predominant decorative motif in the temples of this period.

More important than all these, is the study of the plastic art of the Gupta period. In the story of Gupta art, three distinct schools may be distinguished, the Mathurā school, the Banares school and the Pātaliputra school. In the Mathurā school some features of the Kushana styles are noticeable. The artists of Mathurā fashioned products from the mottled red sandstone found in plenty at Karri. That some of the products were taken to distant places can be seen from the Buddhist image discovered at Mankuwar, belonging to the reign of Kumāragupta. It resembles the early Kushana

Buddhist image. From the same place of Mankuwar comes a Jaina image, again modelled on the early Kushana type.

That the sculpture of the Guptas was something striking and unique may be seen from other examples provided. Though Banares itself had a school of sculpture running to the post-Mauryan epoch, still the dominance of the Mathurā School throughout the early Gupta epoch is perfectly seen from the Mathurā images discovered in Banares. Yet Banares continued its old style of art and sculpture. In the Banares school the use of red paint is uncommon. The material used was the one from Chunar. The art of Banares was not stereotyped and conservative. That it was progressive is seen from the fact that the Kushana technique did not provoke the imagination of the Banares artists. Says Banerji: "The earliest images discovered at Sārnāth show the use of that particular form of *Ma* which type is used in the Karamdanda inscription of Kumāragupta I."

The influence of the Banares school spread to the capital of the Gupta Empire, Pāṭalīputra. This is seen from the images discovered at Nālanda, both in stone and in metal.[61] The Pāṭalīputra school did not use the Chunar sandstone but in technique it did not differ from the Banares school. On the other hand there is a fundamental unity in the art of the Gupta period. This is noticeable in the method of treatment of bas-reliefs, and the subjects introduced into them. A study of the images of the Gupta epoch indicates that the sculptors paid more attention to real naturalism and symmetry. Codrington remarks: 'Gupta art has been praised for its intellectuality. It would be better to treat it as the natural outcome of ancient Indian art, with its vivid appre-

61. Coomaraswami: *History of Fine Art in India and Indonesia* p. 85.

ciation of form and pattern, and its love of the quick beat and rhythm of living things and of their poise and balance in repose'.[62]

Music was another fine art which came largely under the patronage of the early Gupta monarchs as is evidenced by the coins of Samudragupta. The foregoing summary demonstrates how the Imperial Guptas were true patrons of culture. In the field of education, the Imperial Guptas felt it as their sacred duty to spread literacy all round. In the epoch of the Guptas, Sanskrit which already held sway definitely came to stay. Every inscription of importance has a literary flavour about it. The ministers and higher officials of the state were men of talents and were profound men of letters. The performance of Hariṣena the author of the Allahabad Pillar Inscription of Samudragupta is classical by itself. There is a vivid description of the wars and conquests, told compactly. Brevity is the soul of wit and this is evident in Hariṣena, He imitates the celebrated Kālidāsa, as does Vatsabhaṭṭi.

In the Gupta period the Sanskrit *Kāvya* reached its acme. It is also true of the *Sāhitya śāstra*. The Junāgadh rock inscription points to the wide knowledge of the science of poetics. It is markedly true that a great impetus was given to Sanskrit, and this would not have been possible if the kings had not taken up a serious responsibility to promote and patronise Sanskrit learning. Another remarkable fact about this is that in point of learning, religious or social bias did not stand in the way. Samudragupta who earned the title *Kavirāja* was apparently the author of several poems. He was a friend and patron of the Buddhist sage, Vasubhandhu who was also known to his father Candragupta I.[63]

62. Rothenstein—*Ancient India* p. 62.
63. Smith, *Early History of India*, pp. 346 ff.

Another serious and very responsible function which fell on the kings was to formulate a sound foreign policy. Every king of the period was not only a scholar-statesman but also a soldier-statesman. Imbued with the ideal of the *digvijaya,* the Imperial Guptas launched on a career of conquest to earn the honoured title of *Cakravartin.* Some wars were defensive in character and others offensive. All the same, it was the duty of the king and his advisers to see that a vigorous policy was pursued in matters of foreign relationship.

In the conduct of foreign policy, the Kauṭaliyan theory continued to be the ideal par excellence. Kāmandaka being a pupil of Kauṭalya envisaged the same principle of maṇḍala or a circle of sovereign states.[64] This circle was a vicious circle in the sense that it consisted of enemies, allies, and neutrals. The king was necessarily a member of the circle of states. Three stages are mentioned in this connection, *viz.* deterioration, stagnation and progress. A ruler belonging to any one of the states in the circle must endeavour to attain the last stage of progress. For this he has to go through the two stages of deterioration and stagnation. In other words that ruler who wants to dominate the circle of states should gather men and material, equip himself thoroughly, note carefully the vulnerable points of the enemy and then assert his right by invasion and conquest. Such a ruler is termed vijigīṣu,[65] literally the conquering king. So a wise king should be on the alert and pursue that form of policy which would be a check-up to the enemy, and the unlawful elements in the State itself[66].

The same principle applied to their dealings with republics and vassal states, which technically speaking were

64. There is a special section entitled *maṇḍalacarita Prabaraṇam* in the *Nītisāra.* This chapter explains the relations that existed between the various states. This forms the second section of the eighth Sarga.

65. *Kāma.* VIII. 14-16.

66. *Ibid.* X. 16-18, 43.

lying outside the imperial territorial limits. There was a nexus between the soldier and the diplomat. In the case of the Gupta monarchs both were rolled into one person. Guided by a diplomatic code, the king led the life of a hard soldier whenever he was in the field of battle. In other words, the Gupta king did his duty to the state as a soldier, did his duty to the subjects by making them enjoy arts of peace, did his duty to the society by the observance of religious and social conventions, and lastly did his duty to himself and his family by his good behaviour and righteous mode of conduct.

Privileges of the king.

The right ideal placed before every member of the Hindu community was the discharge of his *svadharma* and not bother about its consequences. It was the ideal preached by Lord Kṛṣṇa to the hero Arjuna in the historic battlefield of Kurukṣetra. The significant line—*Karmaṇyevādhikāraste mā phaleṣu kadācana II.* 47—is a sure indication that particularly a Kṣatriya of noble descent, has a message. 'Do your duty, without thinking even for a moment the fruits thereof'. The Gupta emperors who were devout followers of Hindu ideals, acted according to this precept and earned laurels. Having this before their minds, they never seem to have worried about their rights. Yet as befitting their dignity and status, they enjoyed certain privileges which were their due. Kāmandaka says well: 'It is difficult to attain the status of royalty. When once a person is exalted to that status, all persons pay homage to him. This dignity is compared to that of a Brāhmaṇa. But even the slightest transgression sullies his reputation.'[66-a] Here Kāmandaka drives home the simple truth that once the king abused his status, it would leave a permanent stain on his character. He should maintain his status with dignity and his claims to respect.

66-a. *Ibid.* Trans. XI. 38.

Without infringing the rules laid down in the *Arthaśāstra* texts he should establish his prowess and assert his sovereignty by acquiring territories and adding to the extent of the empire. Possessed of *prabāva* or regal prowess a king should lord over his subjects and inspire terror into the hearts of his enemies. *Prabhāva* means his *prabhu śakti*. The other *śaktis* of the king are *utsāha* and *mantra*. Combining in himself these three *śaktis* or powers, a towering personality like the king should dominate over the empire. Otherwise people would not walk in the path of rectitude, and enemies would await the opportunity to invade his territory[67].

Mere prowess and its substantiation would not be enough for a monarch unless he is backed with an unfailing treasury. It has been happily said that 'the foundations of royalty are laid in the treasures', a king could easily command. Otherwise he would not command respect either from his own subjects or fear from his foes[68]. The king was traditionally accepted as the owner of forests, mines, waste lands, besides the various taxes which were collected from the people in return for his services to them in the shape of protection of their life and property. In addition to this the Gupta monarchs amassed much wealth from their conquests and tributes paid to them. This made them financially sound, and enabled them to spend lavishly on sacred buildings, learning and by way of gifts to the deserving and worthy, and by way of endowments to religious associations like the Ārya Sanga.[69]

This further made them undertake productive works like irrigation tanks and canals, roads and hospitals. Society conferred on them titles, and honoured them by comparing them to Indra, the Lord of Heaven. Skandagupta, for instance,

67. *Ibid.* I. 1; VIII. 12-13.
68. *Ibid.* XIV. 33-34.
69. *Corpus.* p. 31.

is compared to Indra and applauded as the lord of a hundred kings[70]. Samudragupta is depicted as a god dwelling on earth[71]. From these examples one can easily imagine with what reverence and regard the subjects treated their emperors.

Another prerogative of the crown accepted by the common will of the people was his right to deal with the treasonous officers and subjects without the least delay. Whether individually or in a group, if the officers of a king took to treasonous acts, the monarch is advised to resort to under-hand measures to do away with them. This does not smack of absolutism as one would say. The exigencies of the society of the fourth and fifth centuries A.D. were such that unless prompt action was taken it would affect the king and his peaceful subjects.[72] Treachery to the state and its ruler was ever regarded in ancient India as a heinous offence. One has only to look into the laws of treason promulgated by Kauṭalya for the benefit of the Mauryan kings.[73] Such persons who resorted to treason were thorns which prevented the normal working of the state. The aim of the state was peaceful and righteous rule. To attain this end, the king should resort to lawful means. But if people committed offences, secret or open, the law of the land permitted the king to take steps to quell them as he deemed fit.

Even a minute search among the inscriptions and the literature of the period does not throw much light on the various prerogatives exercised and enjoyed by the Gupta monarchs. All that we see is an insistence on works of religious merit and service to the people. So it is just to conclude that the Gupta emperors placed duties above rights, and enjoyed such privileges which came to them as the custodians of the empire.

70. *Ibid.* p. 67.
71. *Ibid.* p. 8.
72. *Kāma.* VI. 9-13.
73. See the author's *Mauryan Polity* p. 122.

CHAPTER IV

The Central Administration (Contd.)

Section I.

THE COUNCIL AND THE ASSEMBLY.

The *Kāmandaki* has an interesting chapter on *mantrà-vikalpa prakaraṇam* which sheds some light on the nature and procedure of the Council in the Gupta times. The *Arthaśāstra's* technical term for the Council was *Mantri-pariṣad*. Kauṭalya's disciple Kāmandaka designates it *Mantri-maṇḍalam.*[1] Excepting the change in the designation of the Royal Council, the composition of the cabinet and the qualifications of the councillors practically remained the same as we shall see in the sequel. It is equally interesting to see that in the Gupta inscriptions we meet with the term *Pariṣad,* which from the circumstances it figures in the texts, (*Corpus,* p. 44, l. 9) has been taken to stand for the cabinet by retaining the ancient name.

In the Bilsad stone inscription of Kumāragupta I dated A.D. 415-16 it is said that the *Pariṣad* honoured one Dhruvaśarman.[2] Unfortunately there is a lacunae just before the expression *Parishad* and we are not able to read the full text. But Dhruvaśarman's pious deeds are furnished such as a gateway and a lofty pillar erected by him in the temple of Mahāsena. An almshouse is also credited to his munificence. Himself a man of pious disposition who had accomplished works of merit, the council placed apparently on record his excellent and selfless services to the cause of

1 द्वादशेति मनुः प्राह षोडशेति बृहस्पतिः ।
उशना विंशतिरिति मन्त्रिणां मन्त्रिमण्डलम् ॥ XII. 48

2. Fleet, *op. cit.*, 10. 1. 9.

religion. Or it may also be that the honour done to Dhruvaśarman was by a *vidvat pariṣad* which was a society of learned and influential men. The honour need not be an official one but may be construed to have been conferred by the public. It is noteworthy that in Kālidāsa's extant works mention is made of *mantri pariṣad* and this evidences the fact that Kālidāsa was not a contemporary of the Guptas.[3] Apparently the term *mantri pariṣad* persisted to the beginning of the Christian era, while the nomenclature in the Gupta times became changed to *mantri maṇḍala.*

It is a pity that the term *Pariṣad* occurs only once in the inscriptions of the Guptas and it is extremely doubtful whether it stands for the Royal Council. It is therefore reasonable to assume that the Council was known by the expression *mantri-maṇḍalam* as furnished to us by the *Kāmandakīya.*

The Composition of the Council.

Even in its composition the Council was slightly different from that of the *Kauṭaliya.* The *Arthaśāstra* enjoins the king to counsel with three or four ministers[4]. But Kāmandaka recites the recommendation of Manu, Bṛhaspati and Uśanas and others. He is not definite in his recommendation of the number of members to form the cabinet, for many good and deserving men as are available, could be admitted to the cabinet. But for particular consultations,[5] Kāmandaka should not be taken as advocating an unlimited number of members to the cabinet. He should have been aware of the fact that the greater the number, the less would be the output. He who stood for absolute secrecy as we shall

3 कञ्चुकी—देव एवममात्यपरिषदे विज्ञापयामि
..............मन्त्रिपरिषदोऽप्येवमेव दर्शनम्
Mālavikāgnimitra, V Act.

4. I. 15.

5. *Kāma.* XII. 48. ff.

see soon, could not at the same breath recommend an unwieldy number for the royal council. His recommendation therefore amounts to this viz. that the experts in the different affairs of the state should be drafted to the Council,[6] as the above would lead to good counsel, and decisive action. Among the councillors themselves there was the *mantri mukhya*. We see this officer mentioned in the *Mudrārākṣasa* of Viśākadatta (Act II.). This means that there was a Prime Minister, who perhaps presided over the Cabinet meeting. Oftentimes the king was present and it is reasonable to suppose that he was the ex-officio President. In his absence, the *Mantri mukhya* presided over the deliberations of the Cabinet and duly reported to the king, decisions arrived at by the Council.

Qualification of the Councillors.

A study of the section dealing with *amātya sampat* in the *Kāmandakīya* bears out that the choice of ministers was by no means an easy task. Persons with good family traditions and who were pure, heroic, learned, loyal, versed in politics, were to be selected. They should have satisfied other tests also. A native of the soil, with an excellent character, a detecting skill, combined with intelligence and enthusiasm, he who would rise to the occasion, be firm, of friendly disposition, he who would stand the vagaries of the season, would be truthful, of attractive personality, diplomatic, wise, of sound physique and one who would overreach the foes is fit to be a councillor. He should keep the decision of the council secret till the thing was accomplished.[7] It may be noted that the *Purohita* was also a member of the Cabinet.[8]

निरुन्धाना: सतां मार्गं भक्षयन्ति महीपतिम् ।
दुष्टात्मानस्तु सचिवास्तस्मात् सुसचिवो भवेत् ॥ IV. 12

7. IV. 24-30.
8. *Ibid.*, 31 ff.

Particular care was bestowed on the choice of a minister. High qualifications and conduct decided the selection,[9] because *mantra* or council is of two kinds, *durmantra* and *kalyāṇamantra*. *Durmantra* leads a king to unhappiness and envelops the state with all its repercussions. So to accomplish any project or plan with success, the *saciva* should be an *āpta*[10] (devoted to the interest of the country) and *vipaścita* (a man with vision). If for any reason, a minister was considered to advance his own interests at the expense of the State, that minister should be got rid of. In tendering advice, the minister should take into account the actions taken by their fore-runners in the office, and proceed on righteous lines. The idea was that to attain the end, unscrupulous means should not be resorted to[11].

The author of the *Nītisāra* discusses the importance of *mantra śakti* and indicates how it is superior to the other two *śaktis*—*prabhu* and *utsāha*.[12] It is pointed out how Bṛhaspati, the Deva *purohita*, overcame by sheer *mantra śakti*, Śukrācārya, the *purohita* of the Asuras, though he was full of *prabhu* and *utsāha śaktis*. Mere show of prowess would ultimately lead to repentance and ruin. On the other hand a man of great wisdom and merit would be able to accomplish even the impossible. Sometimes even a well calculated policy

9. *Ibid.*, XII. 25.

10 मन्त्रयेतेह कार्याणि सहाप्तेन विपश्चिता।
आप्तं मूर्खमनाप्तं च मन्त्रिणं परिवर्जयेत्॥ XII. 4.

11 मार्गं सन्मार्गगतिभिः सिद्धये सिद्धकर्मभिः।
पूर्वैराचरितं सद्भिः शास्त्रीयं न परित्यजेत्॥ XII. 5.

12 प्रभावोत्साहशक्तिभ्यां मन्त्रशक्तिः प्रशस्यते।
प्रभावोत्साहवान् काव्यो जितो देवपुरोधसा॥ XII. 7.
(असुरान् मोहयामास शुक्ररूपी बृहस्पतिः।
बृहस्पतिं तथा शुक्रः शशापानुपमद्युतिः॥)

would end in failure. But this needs no regret. It is not possible to fight against Fate. But on this account one should not be wanting in his exertions. The pros and cons of a problem that faced the administration must be thoroughly discussed by the Council. The aim of the councillors should be first and foremost to succeed in their efforts. Proper steps should be taken to bring about the success of their undertaking. So much depends on the ability of a councillor.[13]

Duties of the Cabinet.

The seed of the Council (*mantrabījam*) is the seed of a king.[14] So it should be carefully preserved. When once the seed of the Council is destroyed, the king with all his subjects gets ruined.[15] So it is enjoined on the councillors to keep strict secrecy with regard to the discussions and decisions of the Council, whatever they might be. Kâmandaka says "Guptiranuttama".[16] In other words the maintenance of such strict secrecy leads to the welfare of the kingdom. If it were divulged prematurely it is bound to attract the attention of the undesirable elements in the state who would endeavour to wreck the scheme or the plan as the case may be. To ensure absolute secrecy it is ordained that a Council should not sit over a long period. A prolonged session would open the way to the leakage of secrets. The first important duty of the Council is to dispose of a certain scheme in a sitting or two.[16-a] The pertinent duties of the Council are set forth briefly in a śloka: viz. to study the various aspects of an intricate subject, to arrive at a correct decision on a known subject, to eradicate the doubts in a subject of doubtful nature, and to get to know

13. *Ibid.,* XII. 7-31.
14. *Ar. Sās.* I. 15.
15. *Kāma.* XII. 33.
16. *Ibid.*
16-a. *Ibid.,* 35.

fully the implications of a subject which is only partially known[17].

They are equally applicable to a War Council. In that case they would be to study the time, place and circumstances of an undertaking, to come to a decision, after clarifying the doubtful aspects which an invasion would present, and to finally decide after examining the full implications of the plan. We do not know whether there was a separate war cabinet. Perhaps there was one. But the members of the royal Council mostly constituted it. Therefore the duties were as much of the royal Council as of the War Council. In other words, Kāmandaka stresses the paramount importance of the work of the Council. It has to go into the root of the subject or subjects on hand, discuss them threadbare, and ultimately take a decision which would be carried through by the Government. In the discussion there should be no generating of heat or pouring of cold water on one another's suggestions. Every member should be allowed to have his full say in the matter. After patiently listening to all the views expressed, the wise man should aim at an unanimity of opinion which should be in strict accordance with the rules of polity. An action is right when it has won the approval of the learned and the good. The assumption was that the learned and the good would not launch on a project which would result in a defeated purpose. In the interest of the state, a king should not override the decision of the Council and find himself in a rut afterwards. (*Ibid.*)[18]. Finding that the councillors are unanimous in the decision, their minds unflinched by any misgiving, and finding their decision is approved by the men

[17] अविज्ञातस्य विज्ञानं विज्ञातस्य विनिश्चयः।
अर्थद्वैधस्य सन्देहच्छेदनं शेषदर्शनम्। XII. 30.

[18] यत्र मन्त्रिमनस्साम्यं यत्र चेतो न शङ्कते।
यत्र सन्तो न निन्दन्ति तत्र परीयाच्चिकीर्षितम्॥ XII. 39.

of equity and good conscience, that should be adopted unhesitatingly by a king. In certain cases, if a king felt that the whole question should be reconsidered by the Council, he could submit it for reconsideration and get its verdict.[19]

In formulating a theory of a five-fold aspect of *mantra* or Council, Kāmandaka simply follows his master Kauṭalya.[20] First is the preliminary part of beginning an undertaking. This is in other words to find out what amount of support would be forthcoming once a plan was mooted. Secondly, the means to the end. This is how to tackle the problem and pool the resources which would be manpower and wealth and consider the best use to which they might be put. Thirdly, the proper appropriation of the means according to place and time. Place and time (*deśa* and *kāla*)[21] played a commendable role in the politics of the ancient Hindu state. Much attention was devoted to them in the decision of a policy. A certain undertaking would bear fruit in a specified area, and at a specific time. The natural resources which are important to the success of any undertaking should be available only at a certain place and at a certain period. Hence the Council should take into account these factors of *deśa* and *kāla*.

Fourthly, the Council should anticipate the difficulties which would beset the path of accomplishment. Difficulties of men, material and also of seasons were considered paramount. Ways and means should be devised to overcome such difficulties if they were to be faced. The Council should take a whole range view of the things planned to carry through without much hindrance.

19. *Ibid.* XII. 40.
20. *Ibid.*, XII. 36.
21. इति चेति च सम्पश्यन् काले देशे सहायवान् ।
विशुद्धपार्श्वसंसिद्धः समाक्रामेन्न-चापलात् ॥
Ibid., XII. 55.

Fifthly, is *siddhi* or final success. This is the final part of the deliberation. This is the actual accomplishment of the work undertaken. Once a project is taken up, the council should see that it is executed properly. Again when a decision to embark on a certain project is taken, it must be put through without further delay. Prompt steps should be taken by direction. As far as possible care should be bestowed to see that such works are productive works, permanent and enduring.[22] In the light of these texts we have to conclude that the Gupta Council set up some high standards in the planning and executing of works in general. They were also careful to see that the administration did not suffer in the least, and aimed at good and efficient government of the empire.

There was also another procedure. The Council was a composite body. Hence a committee of the Council was sometimes invoked, and experts in a particular subject were members of that committee for consultation. The king was also present and put his case before the committee. After taking the opinion of the cabinet committee severally and jointly, he finally acted on the advice proffered by the wise men. This is another instance where the king submerged his personal opinion in preference to the opinion of the cabinet.[23] He never did things off-hand and on his own initiative. He was largely guided by the expert opinion and acted accordingly. Having once for all decided upon a certain course of action, the state should not allow the opportunity to

22. सहाया: साधनोपाया विभागो देशकालयो:।
विपत्तेश्च प्रतीकार: सिद्धि: पञ्चाङ्ग इष्यते॥
Ibid., XII. 36.

23. धृतेऽपि मन्त्रे मन्त्रज्ञै: स्वयं भूयो विचारयेत्।
तथा वर्तेत मन्त्रज्ञो यथा स्वार्थं न पीडयेत्॥
Ibid., XII. 40.

slip away. With the advantages of time and place in his favour, the king should authorise his government to put into execution the accepted plan and projects.[24] From these facts it emerges that the king even in emergency summoned the cabinet and consulted it. It also appears that there was nothing like the majority view. Unanimity was always aimed at in taking any decision.

The Council Chamber.

The royal council held its meetings in a special chamber. As the secrecy of the council proceedings was of far-reaching importance, necessary precautions were taken to house the Council in a place which was not easily accessible not only to human beings but also to birds and beasts. Have we not read in Kauṭalya's *Arthaśāstra* that birds and beasts could disclose the proceedings of the Council?[25] Kāmandaka accepts this position and points to other sources through which the Council business might leak out. The members themselves in a fit of inebriation or anger may burst out. They may inadvertently talk during sleep and speak out to their confidants in an unwary mood. Hence the members chosen should be free from such defects and should be resolute and sworn to strict secrecy. All ways and means should be resorted to, so that the proceedings do not become public until the object is realised. It is therefore recommended that a cabinet meeting should be held in a room in the uppermost storey of the king's palace. If the nature of the business is of the utmost administrative importance, for which no publicity of any sort can be given, it is advised to hold it in a place in the region of the forest—a place which contains no pillars, no windows and no nook and corner.[26] It has been realised that even pillars might resound

24. *Ibid.* 50-55.

25. Bk. I. ch. 15, also *Kāma*, XII. 47.

26. निस्तम्भे निर्गवाक्षे च निष्कुड्यान्तरसंश्रये ।
प्रासादाग्रे ह्यरण्ये वा मन्त्रयेदविभावितः ॥

the talks of the Council, while through the windows there was a possibility of the conversation being overheard. Sometimes inquisitive eavesdroppers might be concealed in nooks and corners and overhear the proceedings. So it is further suggested that the meeting should be held in such a place where there are no loopholes or outlets of any sort. The ideal place was thus a secluded spot, unapproachable to any one. With such precautions the meeting always commenced.

The Purohita.

Whether the *Purohita* was a member of the ministry or not, need not be disputed because he finds a place in the section on the *mantri sampat*.[27] He occupied a place of honour in the Council, which privilege he was enjoying from the Vedic times. The Vedic conception was that the *Purohita* was the guardian of the realm and the king was the Father of the people. This is outlined in the *Vasordhāra* doctrine and explained by a representation of the figure of a *cakravartin* at Amarāvati.[28] The representation shows the emperor summoned by his seven treasures raising his right arm to the clouds, from which a shower of coins is falling. The idea is that by performing sacrifices and patronising the same, the king causes seasonal rains to fall which results in the augmentation of wealth and welfare to the state. Kauṭalya assigned a veritable place to the *Purohita* in the Mauryan polity and the same position was held in the Gupta period also.

Kāmandaka says that the *Purohita* should be learned in the *Trayī* (the three Vedas) and *Daṇḍanīti* (Science of Politics). He should be versed in the Atharvan lore and

27. *Ar. Śās*, Bk. I. ch. 10.

28. Reproduced as Frontispiece in Ananda K. Coomaraswami's book *Spiritual Authority and Temporal Power in the Indian Theory of Government.*

should do the daily propitiatory ceremonies for the welfare of the state.[29] In the Council he exerted his moral influence. Whenever a decision was taken, it was the *Purohita* who was to certify whether such a decision fell in within the bounds of the śāstra injunctions. He should set his seal of approval before it was actually adopted by the Council. He was apparently the *buddhi saciva* as can be seen from the śloka (39) of the seventh *prakaraṇam*. It is further reasonable to suppose that the *Rājaguru* of whom so much is said in the opening pages of the *Nītisāra* was the *Rāja Purohita* also.[30] From him the monarch learnt *vinaya* and *śama,* in other words humility combined with self-control. The ruler was made to feel in his early training by the Guru that self-assertion was always suicidal.[31]

Ministers hereditary

One point to be noted in this connection is that the office of the councillors, sometimes designated as *amātya* and sometimes *mantri* was generally hereditary. This is attested to by the inscriptions and seals discovered. Though there was the selection of ministers and though there was also the change of portfolio in some cases, yet preference was given to the sons of ministers to occupy the office of the councillor, provided they had all the requisite qualifications expected of a minister. Heredity played an important part in the selection of officers and the belief was that it brought the tradition of learning and genius with it. A case of hereditary succession

29. त्रय्यां च दण्डनीत्यां च कुशलः स्यात् पुरोहितः।
अथर्वविहितं नित्यं कुर्याच्छान्तिकपौष्टिकम्॥
Kāma. IV. 31.
30. Ch. I. Prakaraṇam 2.
31. सुनिपुणमुपसेव्य सद्गुरुं शुचिरनुवृत्तिपरो विभूतये।
भवति हि विनयोपसंहितो नृपतिपवाय शमाय च क्षमः॥
Kāma. I. 70.

can be seen from the Karamdāṇḍa inscription dated 446-7 A.D.[32] This record shows that the Kumāramātya Śikharasvāmin, a Brahmana of the Aśvā-vāji gotra was the *mantrin* of Candragupta II. His son Kumārāmātya Pṛthivīsena became in his turn *mantrin* of the emperor Kumāragupta. We further see that this Pṛthivīsena was appointed the Commander-in-Chief (*mahābalādhikṛta*). This throws interesting light on two things. The minister was generally a member of the Brahmana community, proficient in higher learning. The second point is that even Brahmanas held the high place of commanders of the army.

The inscriptions record another case of a hereditary minister. A seal from Vaiśāli has it that the Amātya Hastabala was the son of Amātya Bhadrika.[33] Yet another record, the Udayagiri Cave Inscription[34] has reference to a hereditary minister. During the reign of Candragupta II again Vīrasena alias Śaba of Pāṭalīputra is shown as the hereditary minister (*anvaya prāpta saciva*). Śaba, the minister, was appointed further as the *Sandhivigraha* (minister of peace and war). From the terms *saciva, mantrin, sandhivigraha*, we are to infer that there was no one minister but a body of ministers in the government of Candragupta II and Kumāragupta. What applied to the period of these emperors, was also applicable to the period of the other kings of the Gupta dynasty.

Conclusion.

From the above study it has to be concluded that the Royal Council was not merely an advisory body assisting the king whenever he required its assistance but an important administrative organisation in the body-politic. The king always believed that without its assistance the administrative

32. *Ep. Ind.*, X pp. 70-72.
33. *Ar. Rep. of the Ar. Survey of India*, 1913-14, p. 134. No. 210.
34. Fleet, *op. cit.*, p. 35.

wheel would not move in the right direction. He had also implicit confidence in its advice because the prevailing opinion of the time was that nothing would go wrong if the counsel had been tendered by the highly intelligent and selfless ministers. These men manned the ship of state and enjoyed the full confidence of the king and the public. Even in emergencies the king summoned them and acted according to their advice. Thus it was a constitutional monarchy where the king oftentimes subordinated his will to the will of the cabinet and ruled in conformity with the decisions reached by the body.

The Assembly

It is really unfortunate that we do not have many details regarding the composition or work of the Assembly. We have a noteworthy expression *sabhā* in the *praśasti* of the Allahabad Pillar Inscription.[35] The *sabhā* undoubtedly stood for the assembly. It is generally taken that the *sabhā* was made up of ministers and feudatories. This seems to be unacceptable. The *sabhā* was a popular assembly wherein sat the representatives of the people, citizens of the capital and of the rural parts. It might have also included royal officials who might have been ex-officio members of the Assembly. This organisation must have been similar to the *Paura-Jānapada* organisation of which mention is made in the Mauryan period. (*Kāma* XVIII, 51). It is unreasonable to hold that these representative institutions had died out of existence. But there is not much evidence to assert that they continued to function as they did in the earlier epochs.

Fleet who edited the inscription with much care has not attached much significance to the term *sabhā* occurring in line 7. He simply translated it as the attendants of the court. He was not able to find out the constitutional importance of that term.

35. Fleet: *Corpus* p. 6. 17.

(Smith, *Early History* pp. 350). In later times when Harṣa was chosen king, it was the *sabhā* which offered the throne to him. Thus the *sabhā* was a factor reckoned with in the constitution of the Guptas. (P. V. Kane, *Kātyāyana* v. 55, 60, etc.) The *sabhā* might consist of courtiers also but it did not mean the attendants of the court only. The *sabhā* was then a representative body which had the primary function of approving the newly selected prince as suitable for the throne. It represented the public opinion. The constitutional position was that a reigning king might nominate his successor but he could not force it on the people. It was upto the assembly to accept the nomination as valid. It did so in the case of Samudragupta's accession which gratified the king, his father. It is Kātyāyana who speaks elaborately about the qualifications and duties of the members of the *sabhā*. (*Ibid.*, vv. 71-81).

Section II

Kumārāmātyas and Uparikas

Among the higher officials belonging to the Imperial Secretariat figure a class of officers who are designated *Kumārāmātyas*. Literally the term means princes as *amātyas,* and not as princes' ministers as had been rendered. But a study of the inscriptions and seals does not betray either of the two literal meanings attempted. It is therefore to be treated as a technical official title which has nothing to do with *Kumāra* or *Amātya*. R. D. Banerji who has bestowed some thought on this question, has rightly come to the conclusion that there were different classifications in the rank of *Kumārāmātyas.*[36] We shall re-examine these inscriptions and seals and see what light they throw on this mysterious office of the *Kumārāmātya*.

Among the different classifications of these Kumārāmātyas first come the highest officers of the state, the chief ministers.

36. *The Age of the Imperial Guptas,* pp. 71 ff.

Hariṣenā the minister of Samudragupta, Śikharaśvāmin, the minister of Candragupta II, and Pṛthivīsena, the minister of Kumāragupta were all *Kumārāmātyas.* They belonged to the Brāhmaṇa community and were not therefore princes of the blood royal.[37]

The second class of *Kumārāmātyas* is furnished by the Damodarpur copper-plate inscriptions where a district officer is named a *Kumārāmātya.* This was in the reign of Kumāragupta. To the district of Koṭivarṣa, in the province of Puṇḍravardhana, one Vetravarman was appointed and he was a *Kumārāmātya.*[38] We further hear of a governor who was in charge of the Suvvunga Viṣaya in Eastern Bengal and who was a *Kumārāmātya.* Wnat is of special interest in this case is that his descendants who had become independent of the empire continued to use the seal of the office of the *Kumārāmātya* upto the eighth century A.D.[39] Another example where a *Kumārāmātya* was in charge of a *viṣaya* was in Tīra. The legend runs: *Tīra-Kumārāmāty-ādhikaraṇasya.*[40] These seals were in lieu of signatures which are generally affixed to documents. This is borne out by seal No. 29 where the seal of the office of a *Kumārāmātya* is affixed to the same lump of clay bearing the seal of the Guild of merchants and bankers.[41] This is evidently a contract between the *Viṣayapati Kumārāmātya* and the guild.

Spooner discovered certain seals and one of them has the following legend: *Veśālī-nāma-Kuṇḍē-Kumārāmātya-adhikaraṇasya.*[42] The expression *nāma-Kuṇḍe* was puzzling to R. D. Banerji who left it therefore untranslated. Here is

37. *Ep. Ind.*, X pp. 71-2. See also *A New History of the Indian people* Vol. VI *Vākaṭaka-Gupta Age.* pp. 281-82. 1946 (Lahore).

38. *Ep. Ind.*, XV pp. 132-3.

39. *Ibid.*, pp. 304, 306.

40. *An. Rp. Arch. Sury* No. 22. 1903-4.

41. ṣresṭhi—sārtthavāha—kulika—nigama (*Ibid.*, p. 110.)

42. *An. Rep. Ar. Ṣ.I.* 1913-14 p. 134. No. 200.

also seen the figure of Lakṣmī with elephants. The translation is easy. The term *nāma* is used in the sense of (*Prasiddhi*) meaning (famous). *Kuṇḍa* stands for *sthala* or territory. The whole thing means the famous place or territory occupied by Vaiśāli. In other words the *Kumārāmātya* under reference was in charge of the well-known place Vaiśāli. It shows Vaiśāli was a noble city.

In addition to this there was the term *Mahā Kumārāmātya,* which must be a higher title than the ordinary *Kumārāmātya.* But we do not meet with the title *Mahā Kumārāmātya* in the Gupta inscriptions or seals. But it is seen from line 33 of the Bhagalpur grant of Nārāyaṇapāla.[43] It clearly shows how the title was in vogue for sometime in different parts of the country. Proceeding to examine the seals of the period J. Bloch discovered three specimens of seals of ordinary *Kumārāmātyas.* Here on these seals we find a figure of Lakṣmī standing in a lotus pond with two dwarfs on either side each of the latter holding some objects resembling money bags. The legend on these seals has been read as *Kumārāmātyādhikaraṇasya.* Dr. Vogel rendered it 'the (seal) of the office of the *Kumārāmātya*'.[44] Another class of *Kumārāmātyas* is distinguished from a find of seals which read *Yuvarāja pādīya-Kumārāmātyādhikaraṇasya*— translated as 'the (seal) of the office of the *Kumārāmātya* equal in rank to a prince'. In the legend *pādīya* is significant. R. D. Banerji would equate *pāda* with *kalpa*, and would interpret it as 'equal to'. But it seems better rendering to take it as 'attached to'. We would therefore translate it as *Kumārāmātyas* connected with the office of *Yuvarāja.* This would prove that there were certain *Kumārāmātyas* attached to the department of the *Yuvarāja.* The interpretation of *Kumārāmātyas* as belonging to the rank equal to *Yuvarājas*

43. *Ind. Ant. Vol.* XV. p. 306.

44. *An. Rep. of Ar. S. India,* 1903-4 p. 107 Note. 1.

cannot be tenable, as would be shown in the sequel. As many as twelve seals of this class of *Kumārāmātyas* have been discovered. On these seals the figure of Lakṣmī is seen with elephants, attended by two dwarfs who seem to be pouring out coins from pots in their hands. This is evidently a Gajalakṣhmi figure.[45]

There are again seals which have legends as follows: *Śrī Yuvarāja-bhaṭṭāraka-pādīya-Kumārāmātya-ādhikaraṇasya,* translated as 'the (seal) of the office of *Kumārāmātya,* equal in rank to the illustrious heir-apparent'. It would be proper to render it as the seal of the office of *Kumārāmātya* attached to the heir-apparent. *Bhaṭṭāraka* is an important title which is generally applied to the ruler or the emperor. In the case of the *Yuvarāja* who has been selected to the throne to succeed the reigning king, it is legitimate to use the title *Bhaṭṭāraka.* This class of seals betrays clearly that the Crown Prince was distinguished from other princes of the royal family. While the Crown Prince was entitled *Yuvarāja Bhaṭṭāraka,* ordinary princes were merely *Yuvarājas* and did not have the appellation *Bhaṭṭāraka* attached to their names. This further makes it clear that each prince had his own office and *Kumārāmātyas* of different ranks were attached to him. In the seals belonging to this class, we again note the figure of Lakṣmī with an elephant on each side but no attendants are seen.[46] This must be definitely the figure of Gajalakṣmī.

Again among the Vaiśāli seals, there is one specimen where the legend runs as follows: *Śrī Paramabhaṭṭāraka-pādīya-Kumārāmātyadhikaraṇasya* translated as 'the (seal) of the office of the *Kumārāmātya* equal in rank to His Majesty (the Emperor).[47] It would be more correct to render it as the seal of the office of *Kumārāmātya* attached to His Majesty'.

45. *Ibid.,* p. 107. No. 6.
46. *Ibid.,* p. 108. No. 8.
47. *Ibid.*

Here the expression *Paramabhaṭṭāraka* refers to the emperor. It is unthinkable that *Kumārāmātyas* should be ranked in office, power and prestige with the ruler of the empire. Hence is our contention to render *pādīya* as 'attached to'. But it is reasonable to assume that some *Kumārāmātyas* were attached to the king, placed in charge of some special business and made directly responsible to the king only. In the same way we have to treat the *Kumārāmātyas* attached to the heir-apparent and other princes of the blood-royal. Otherwise the term could not convey the proper meaning. And it would be difficult to assign any place to these officials either in the Central or Provincial Governments.

This view receives further strength from another seal discovered at Vaiśali. The legend on it runs *Śrī Yuvarāja bhaṭṭāraka-pādīya balādhikaraṇasya.*[48] It is not, as is supposed, that this commander of the army was equal in rank to the heir-apparent. It was the army commander who was attached to the office of the *Yuvarāja* the heir-apparent. The *Yuvarāja* had as much responsibility as the king to lead the forces to the battle-field, and cases where Gupta princes had taken the field in some of their expeditions are not uncommon. There was a contingent in charge of the *Yuvarāja* and its commander is mentioned in the seal under review[49]. This legend clinches the other question of *Kumārāmātyas* being not equal in rank but officials attached to the offices of the king, Crown Prince or ordinary princes respectively. An able minister like Śikharasvāmin could be in charge of the two offices—minister and *Kumārāmātya.* Or the minister took the portfolio of *Kumārāmātya* as the circumstances of the situation dictated. Hence he got both the appellations.

From an examination of the various seals it is to be concluded that there were different grades of *Kumārāmātya*

48. *Ibid.,* No. 12.
49. *Ibid.*

officials. It is further likely that when the services of some *Kumārāmātyas* attached to the royal office or the offices of the princes were not required, they could have been sent as Provincial or District officials according to their ability and capacity. Whatever it is, they were important officials attached to the Central government.

No attempt has been made so far to study the figures which are found on the seals of the various classes of *Kumārāmātyas*. The figure of Lakṣmī represents the Goddess of Wealth and is considered to be the emblem of imperial offices. *Gajas* or elephants on either side show plenty in the circulation of wealth. The dwarfs represent probably Kubera who is said to be diminutive in form and is believed to guard the divine treasure. All this is reminiscent of the Vedic *Vasōrdhāra* doctrine of which a representation of the sculpture in Amarāvatī has been already shown. The dwarfs hold in their hands circular pots and seem to pour out coins. The association of the ideas of Lakṣmī, elephants and dwarfs pouring out coins points to the wealth of the Gupta monarchs and incidentally that the office of the *Kumārāmātya* in the Central Government was concerned with royal treasury. They were officials perhaps in charge of the king's treasure and the personal property of the Crown Prince and other ordinary princes. In short these *Kumārāmātyas* were treasury officials and were engaged in promoting wealth and circulating riches for the welfare not only of the king and princes but also of the state in general.

Uparikas

In any Government the executive business must be divided among several departments and the head of each department should have sufficient experience not only in that department but in all departments as a whole. As John Stuart Mill put it, while the classification of functionaries should correspond to that of subjects, there should not be several departments independent of one another, involving the superintendence of different departments of the same natural whole. This is what has happened in the India of the Guptas. In the Bihar stone pillar inscription of Skandagupta,[50] the term *Uparika* occurs. It appears to have been a title of the higher officer of the Government. Dr. Fleet took it as a technical official title but could not describe the exact function of this official. The same expression *Uparika* occurs in the Karitalai Copper-plate Inscription of the Mahārāja Jayantha,[51] as also in the Khoh Copper-plate Inscription of the same Mahārāja.[52]

In both the places, it is said that the *Dūtaka* was the *Uparika, Dīkṣita, Gṛhapati,* and *Sthapati-Samrāj.* His name is Sarvadatta. In the inscription of Skandagupta, there is a lacunae, but immediately after the word *Uparika,* the expression *Kumārāmātya* occurs. The term *Uparika* occurs in later inscriptions also. What interests us here is that the *Uparika* was also the *Dūtaka. Dūtaka* is occasionally used as *Dūta.* But the *Dūtaka* may be different in status from the *Dūta.* The duty of a *Dūtaka* seems to have been to communicate the king's sanction and order to local officials and the *Dūta* carried perhaps the information.

The expressions in other records as *ājñā svayam*[53] or *sva mukha ājñā* do point out that the grantor directly ordered it by his own mouth. In those cases the *Dūtaka* is not mentioned. But there were then two kinds of grants. One by the grantor's own mouth and the other which emanated from the Department of Communications and which was duly sent to local officials for further action. And this department was that of the *Uparika. Uparika* was then the designation of one of the ministers of the cabinet. Prof. K. V. Rangaswami Ayyangar

50. Fleet. *op. cit.*, p. 50. 1.27.
51. *Ibid.*, p. 119.
52. *Ibid.*, p. 123.
53. *Ibid.*, pp. 115, 194, 199, etc.

would suggest with a question mark that he was the President of the Council of Ministers[54]. Whether the *Uparika* was occupying such a high status, we cannot definitely say. But one may not be far wrong in assuming that he was one of the ministers, perhaps in charge of Communications or Information to use modern terms. He was consequently a resident of the Imperial Capital, and an imperial officer.

Sometimes the same officer was expected to discharge the functions of more than one department. The *Dūtaka* was *Uparika* to cite an instance. In some cases he was also *Sthapati-Samrāj*.[55] The latter, Fleet suggests may be the Superintendent of the harem. Whatever this may be, there were different departments which were, to all intents and purposes, not independent of each other. The same official was in charge of more than one branch of the Executive business.

As if to confirm our position of an *Uparika* being a minister, evidence comes from an unexpected quarter. In commenting on the *Yājñavalkya smṛti*,[56] Viśvarūpācārya who most probably lived in the eighth century quotes the text of Bṛhaspati on *sacivas*. In his quotation from Bṛhaspati who should be the author of the well-known *Smṛti* which is unfortunately lost to us, Viśvarūpācārya mentions *Uparika* as a *saciva*. Be it noted that the quotation is from Bṛhaspati. The *Bṛhaspati smṛti* reads thus:

अविकार्योऽविकलेन्द्रियः प्रतापवान् सुभगः
सुमुखो ऽकृपणो ऽप्रमादी दक्षो दाक्षिण्य-
चारित्ररक्षणार्थमधिकरणसन्दिग्धविवेक-
कुतुपरिकः स्याद् ।

Thus we have in a nutshell the qualifications and functions of the *Uparika*. Steady in mind and body, dignified, of a commanding personality, courteous, generous, active and diligent

54. *Bṛhaspati smṛti* (Gaekwad Orient. Series Vol. LXXXV Intro. p. 84).
55. *Corpus*, pp. 115, 194, 199, etc.
56. I. 307

must be the *Uparika*. It is not expressly stated what his duties were. His office was mainly interested in protecting *Dākṣiṇya caritram*. We are unable to know the exact purport of this term which seems to be a technical one. *Caritra*, according to Kauṭalya, is one head of law, which deals with customs and precedents.[57] Even if we take *Caritra* in this light, the difficulty arises about *Dākṣiṇya* which might even relate to sacrificial fees. That this officer might have to do something with sacrifices can be inferred from the terms *Dīkṣita, Gṛhapati* and *Guru* in the inscriptions.

Perhaps one of his functions was to preserve the healthy conventions of society, by removing the difficulties which arose then and there. If on the other hand, we may stretch our imagination further, we may treat *caritra* as documents and *dākṣiṇya*, confidential—*dākṣiṇyam* generally taken to be delicate matters. In that case it would be fitting that *Uparika* played the role of *Dūtaka* who was closely associated in communicating the wish of the grantor to the local officials. Whenever doubts arose in the exact execution of such documents, the *Uparika* came to the aid of the *Dūtaka* or played the role of *Dūtaka* himself if we are to be guided by epigraphic testimony[58].

Whatever might have been the functions of the *Uparika* he figures as one of the *sacivas* in the list of Bṛhaspati who may be taken as an authority for the Gupta period.[59]

57. See the author's *Mauryan Polity*, p. 160.

58. Dr. Ch. Chhabra has drawn attention to this passage. and translated the words commencing with dākṣiṇya....vivekakrt, capable of administering justice in legal disputes in order to maintain 'impartiality and morality'. In other words, the *Uparika* is made to correspond to a magistrate (*D. R. Bhandarkar Comm. Volume* pp. 231-33). The interpretation seems to be unacceptable.

59. A recent writer has ingeniously connected *Uparika* with *Oparikara* and has argued that the term obviously originated from the tax *uparikara*. Therefore he concludes that that official was held responsible for the collection and administration of that tax. The writer has imagined that there was one official for collecting every tax of the empire. This confusion of combining similarity of names is born of pure imagination. The fact is that *Uparika* has nothing to do with *Oparikara* (R. N. Saletore *Life in the Gupta Age* p. 260.)

As in the case of *Kumārāmātyas,* there were also different classes of *Uparikas*. The five Damodarpur copper-plate inscriptions,[60] throw further light on the status and functions of the *Uparikas*. Proceeding to examine the five plates in detail we find Uparika Cīrātadatta as the Head of the Puṇḍravardhana *bhukti,* and who was responsible to the Emperor. He had also power to appoint the *Viṣayapati*. In the first plate it is seen that Kumārāmātya Vetravarman was appointed to be in charge of Koṭivarṣa *Viṣaya* by Uparika Cīrātadatta. This was in the time of Kumāragupta I.

Plate No. 2[61] which belongs to the same period mentions the transactions relating to the grant of a plot of land. Here again the same *Uparika* and the same *Viṣaya* occur. The third plate however belongs to the reign of Budhagupta. Here the translation refers to the *bhukti* government of Puṇḍravardhana which was by the way a part of modern North Bengal. The Head of the government of the *bhukti* was *Uparika* Mahārāja Brahmadatta who was responsible to the Emperor. In the fourth plate which also refers to the reign of Budhagupta, the governor of the *bhukti* of Puṇḍravardhana was under Uparika Mahārāja Jayadatta. In this plate the Koṭivarṣa *viṣaya* was under Āyuktaka Śandaka (or Gaṇḍaka). We notice it is no more a *Kumārāmātya* administering that *Viṣaya*.

Still more informing is plate No. 5,[62] which is dated 533-34 A.D., perhaps the time of Bhānugupta. The same *viṣaya* and *bhukti* are the place of action. The administration of Koṭivarṣa *viṣaya* was under one Svayambhudeva, and of Puṇḍravardhana under the Uparika-Mahārāja Rājaputradeva Bhaṭṭāraka. These titles at once point out that this *Uparika* was the son of the emperor himself.

60. Ed. by Radhagovind Basak *Ep. Ind.* XV. pp. 113 ff.
61. *Ep. Ind.*, XV, p. 114.
62. *Ibid.*, p. 115.

From a study of these records it transpires that the *Uparikas* who were imperial officials were sometimes appointed at the pleasure of His Majesty as heads of provinces when their services were absolutely necessary. At least it was so in the case of the province of Puṇḍravardhana under different emperors.

Purapāloparika may be the President of the City Council. If the word missing before Pura is *sura,* then it may be *Surapāloparika* meaning Superintendent of Temples and religious foundations.[63] These records further show that sometimes feudatories of the empire were drafted to the office of the *Uparika* and sometimes even the princes, sons of the reigning king were taken to it. The term *Mahārāja* added to the word *Uparika* evidences the fact that a feudatory was appointed as *Uparika* first and then a provincial chief. The fifth plate undoubtedly is a proof to indicate that princes of the blood royal were also appointed to responsible posts like that of an *Uparika* and the head of a province.

Two seals of the *Uparika* of Tīrabhukti or Tirhut were discovered at Vaiśāli. They contain the legend *Tīrabhukti-Uparikādhikaraṇasya.*[64] Thus the seals belonged to the office of the *Uparika* of *Tīrabhukti.* From these seals one has to conclude that the *Uparika* under review was the executive head of Tīrabhukti province, adjacent to modern Northern Bihar. The newly discovered copper-plate from Tippera being the Gunaighar grant of Vainyagupta in the Gupta era 188 gives two of the titles of the *Dūtaka* and are of some interest.[65] These are *Pañcādhikaraṇo-parika-pāṭyuparika* and *Purapālō-parika.* These have been interpreted 'President of the Board of five (district) court judges' and 'President of the City governors'. Really speaking the context warrants three titles.

63. *I. H. Q.* Vol. VI. p. 50.
64. *An. Rp. Arch-Sur.* 1903-4. No. 20.
65. *I. H. Q.* Vol. VI. p. 45.

Pañcadhikarṇo-parika is a separate one and means the *Uparika* who presided over the *Pañcādhikaraṇa,* probably the office dealing with law and constituting five members something like the High Court of Justice. The *Pāṭyuparika* may be the Accountant-General or the *Uparika* in charge of accounts and audit.

The above survey betrays the fact that there was frequent transfer of officers, even of rank. Whenever circumstances demanded their service in a particular locality, the emperor appointed them personally to carry out the administrative duties. This need not be taken that the *Uparikas* were only provincial officials. On the other hand they were imperial officials who were drafted to the responsible post of provincial officers sometime or other. In later times we hear of *Bṛhad-Uparika* translated as Privy Councillor[66] and *Daṇḍoparika* (Prefect of Police). But we are not concerned with these in our present enquiry.

Section iii

Revenue and Finance

The success of any government rests on sound finance and the Gupta government was no exception. Hence the treasury department has been considered always in Hindu India as one of the limbs of the state, and so it was in the Guptan India. The *Kāmandaka-nīti* says that it is sound government where the sources of revenue are abundant, and items of disbursement are limited.[67] The treasury should be replete with precious metals like gold and also with pearls

66. *Ep. Ind.* XII. p. 43.

67. मुक्ताकनकरत्नाढ्यः पितृपैतामहोचितः।
धर्मार्जितो व्ययसहः कोशः कोशज्ञसम्मतः॥ *Kāma,* IV, 61
धर्महेतोस्तथार्थाय भृत्यानां भरणाय च।
आपदर्थं च संरक्ष्यः कोशः कोशवता सदा॥ *Ibid.,* IV. 62

and jewels of value. But such immense wealth should have been got by lawful means and not by immoral ones. The treasury should not get exhausted in spite of heavy calls on it. It should be under the control and charge of financial experts.

The treasury was regarded as the barometer of the administration.[68] Controlling the business of Government is indeed distinct from actually doing the business. For the latter a replenished treasury is essential. There are different items of expenditure incurred by the state but the important ones are grouped under three categories. One item of disbursement was for religious purposes. The second, was pay and salaries for the employees of the state from the menials to the ministers. The third was to be spent in times of danger and distress, and therefore in providing means to avert them.[69] No government can go on without money being spent on what are considered the essential expenses which a state has to incur. Besides the traditional sources of revenue, the Guptas added much to their treasury with the wealth earned during their *digvijaya* campaigns. Tributes and spoils were got as a result of their conquests.

Later on Kāmandaka proceeds to discuss the importance of wealth to the empire. He remarks that it is a trite saying that the foundations of royalty are laid in the treasury of the kingdom. That king who possesses a solvent treasure evokes the respect and goodwill of his subjects. For the end of the state which is the achievement of the *trivarga* or *dharma, artha* and *kāma* cannot be achieved without the chief means which is the treasury.[70] Even the enemies think twice before they resolve to launch on an

68. *Ibid.* XIV. 33 ff.
69. *Ibid.* IV. 62.
70. सेतुबन्धो वणिक्कर्म प्रजामित्रपरिग्रह : ।
धर्मकामार्थसिद्धिश्च कोशावेतत प्रवर्तते ।। *Ibid.*, XIV. 32

expedition on a solvent monarch. Taking these statements together, one can easily understand how the ancient states attached special importance to the solvency of a treasury, and how they took active and serious steps to increase their wealth and thus to place both society and government on stable foundations.

Sources of Revenue

Different kinds of land tax formed the primary source of revenue in the Mauryan epoch. In the same way the Guptas depended primarily on land tax.[71] As there were different kinds of lands, it was not possible to fix a uniform rate on all the lands in the empire. Hence we find a number of taxes on land. In the Mauryan empire, there were two specific taxes on land—*sīta* or the produce of the Crown lands and *bhāga* or share of revenue from privately owned lands.[72] In the Gupta epoch the designations have changed. The term *sīta* is not found in the inscriptions. This does not mean that there were no crown lands under the Guptas. Again in the inscriptions of the Gupta period occur terms like *bhāga* and *bhāgabhoga*. The latter term is used for instance in the Karitalai copper-plate inscription[73] of the Mahārāja Jayantha in the sense of royalties. In a still later inscription of Silāditya VII the term *bhoga-bhāga* occurs as a fiscal term.[74] Both the terms *bhāga* and *bhoga* are used in the epigraphs of the Gupta period.[75]

71. *Ibid.*, IV. 49-52.

72. See the author's *Mauryan Polity* p. 142.

73. *Corpus*, p. 120.

74. *Ibid.* p. 189.

75. The *Arthaśāstra* refers to this term in connection with private owners of lands. Tenants who occupied lands from these held them on the condition of *bhāgabhoga*. Ganapati Sastri explains this term as referring to some agreement of paying a specific share of the produce. For instance in the light of this text and commentary one has to take it that *bhāga bhoga* stood for some stipulated share of the produce to the state. See also I.H.Q. Vol. V. No. 2 p. 277.

If we turn to the Gupta inscriptions we meet with several documents which record the bestowing of plots of land by means of grants. No stretch of imagination is required to show that most of the lands thus given belonged to the state, and naturally the revenue accruing from such lands filled up the coffers of the state. That the revenue was received both in cash and kind is evident from inscriptions. For instance, the Eran stone inscription of Samudragupta refers to money (*hiraṇya*) and grain in the treasury of that emperor.[76] In support of payment of grain as dues, we have the evidence of Fa Hien who relates the conditions and life in the reign of Candragupta II. He says 'only those who cultivate the royal land have to pay (a portion of) the gain from it'.[77] We have here a specific reference to the royal land and also the custom of paying dues to the treasury in kind.

In the effecting of sales of land we meet with three stages. The first was to send an application (*vijñāpyam*). The second stage was the verification of the relevant records by those in charge of them. The last was the inspection and proper separation of boundary limits. While all this elaborate procedure may point to state ownership, still all lands were not owned by the crown. An examination of the title deeds which are inscribed on copper-plates and which are registered at the Headquarters or the District office is proof positive to indicate private ownership of land.[78] From these one has to conclude there were crown lands, private lands and communal lands managed by village communities.

प्रक्रयावक्रयाधिभागभोगनिसृष्टोपभोक्तार:

(Bk. III. 9) Commn.

उपलब्धस्य फलस्यैतावान् भागो देय इति संविदा भोक्तार:।

76. Fleet, *op. cit.*, p. 20.
77. *A Record of Bud. kingdoms*, pp. 42-43.
78. Jayaswal: *Hindu Polity* p. 174.

The land revenue system of the Guptas is indeed a complicated one. Two terms which are frequently used in connection with lands deserve some notice. These are *uparikara* and *udranga*. The term *uparikara* has been interpreted in different ways. Fleet suggested that it was 'a tax levied on cultivators who have no proprietary rights in the soil'.[79] Dr. Ghoshal would interpret it as rent paid by the 'temporary tenants' as against the *udranga* which is revenue imposed upon the permanent tenants.[80] In reviewing Ghoshal's book Dr. Barnett rendered *uparikara* as equivalent to the Tamil expression *mēlvāram,* and therefore the *uparikara* tax meant the crown's share of produce.[81] *Mēlvāram* is opposite to *kuḍivāram* as it obtains in South India. *Kuḍivāram* is occupancy right. By this right a ryot is entitled to certain share of the produce. *Mēlvāram* is the landholder's right. *Mēlvārattār* are proprietors or owners ol the land. They are entitled to a proportion of the produce as owners of lands. The landholder may be the state or may be a private individual. There were crown lands apart from lands owned by private individuals. If they were crown lands the *mēlvāram* went to the crown. If they were privately owned lands, the *Mēlvāram* went to these private proprietors. Hence *mēlvāram* cannot be solely restricted to crown's share of the produce. In the case of crown lands, it was certainly the crown's share.

As regards *udranga,* Fleet could not offer any satisfactory explanation beyond quoting Dr. Buhler's tentative suggestion that it was 'the share of the produce collected usually for the king'.[82] Though these terms *uparikara* and *udranga* largely occur in the inscriptions of the Gupta period and even later,

79. *Op. cit.*, p. 98 *n*.

80. *Contributions to the History of the Hindu Revenue system* pp. 191-210.

81. *JRAS* 1931 p. 165.

82. *Ind. Ant.* XII, p. 189, *n*. Fleet, *Corpus*. pp. 97-98 *n*.

it is not possible to define exactly what these terms connote. It is undoubtedly clear that both stand for charges imposed by the state on the produce of the land and to venture beyond this seems to be audacious. The attempted explanations are far from satisfactory and cannot be therefore generally accepted. It must be noted that on the same land are levied both taxes *uparikara* and *udranga*. It does not stand to reason that one and the same land was both under the permanent and temporary tenants at the same time. Another source of income from land seems to have come from the sale of the land. This is evident from the Faridpur plate No. 1. Here it is stated that "the feet of the Emperor receives the sixth part of the price according to the law".[83] Though the Faridpur plate belongs on palaeographical grounds to the sixth century, it records evidently a Gupta practice in vogue.

It cannot be said with any degree of definiteness what exactly was the share of the produce that was collected by the state from the land. But it is reasonable to assume that the traditional 1/6 of the produce was continued in the Gupta age. The inscriptions give an insight of the kinds of land, their measurement, their assessment and conditions of sale. We gather that there were three kinds of land *samudāyabāhya*, *aprahata* and *khila kṣetra*.[84] Firstly, *Samudāyabāhya* means lands outside the jurisdiction of the village community. There were communal holdings of land and the state received a fixed annual revenue for such lands through the organisation of the village community. Or from the term *agrahārika*,[85] it is not far wrong to say that the official of the government, namely *agrahārika*[86] collected the sums due from the village and transferred them to the central revenue. Lands given as

83. *Ind. Ant.* Vol. XXXIX (1910) *Three copper-plate Grants from East Bengal* by F. E. Pargiter, p. 197.

84. *Damodarpur copper-plate Inscriptions Ep. Ind.* Vol. XV. p. 143.

85. Fleet, *op. cit.*, pp. 51, 52.

86. *Ibid.*, p. 257.

pious grants and as gifts to Brahmana families were outside the pale of the *Samudāya* or communal holdings of lands. They were of course treated as rent-free lands.

Secondly, the type of *aprahata* lands comes under the category of lands that could be cultivated provided proper steps were taken. They are perhaps what we to-day call '*puñjai*' lands in South India. Here wet crops would not be raised but the soil is capable of producing vegetable and fruit products. For this, no elaborate irrigation facilities are necessary. With careful husbanding of the resources of the soil, a large part of the land could be brought under cultivation for producing vegetables and even fruits, or plants for fuel.

The third type of land is *khila*. This may be the vast tracts of land which are unappropriated waste.[87] Perhaps these lands come under the category of uncultivable tracts of territory. They might be useful perhaps for the pasturage and other similar purposes. With the *vāstu* type of land we need not dwell at length, as it is well known that type of land was particularly suited for building sites where houses and other buildings could be put up.[88] Lands which were sold, were disposed of at two *dināras* for each *kulyavāpa*. Pargiter translated *kulyavāpa* as the land usually sown with a *kulya* of seed.[89] But it appears to have some connection with *kuli* still in vogue in South India. According to South Indian calculation, one hundred *kulis* make one *mā*, and three *mās* constitute one acre of land. The normal price of one *kulyavāpa* is two or three *dināras* (a Gupta gold coin).

In the Damodarpur copper-plates, the unit of land measurement is furnished as 8 x 9 reeds.[90] It is said that

87. *Ep. Ind.*, XV, pp. 137, 140 & 144.
88. *Ibid.*, p. 144.
89. *Ind. Ant.*, XXXIX, p. 214.
90. (*Ep. Ind.*, XV, p. 137). (See also Ghoshal, *Hindu Revenue Systems* p. 199 *n.*

a reed consisted of a certain number of cubits, and Pargiter is said to aptly compare it with the *kāṇi* the common land measure in East Bengal. The inscription reads *aṣṭaka navaka navaka nalābhyām*. There is no difficulty about other expressions except *nala*. In *Silpa* works and other treatises where units of measurement are given, no such term *nala* occurs. But the *Brahmāṇḍa Purāṇa*[91] deals with a number of measurements. Verse (100) says:

Caturhasto Dhanurdaṇḍo nālikā yugamevaca

In defining the units of measurement a *daṇḍa,* also called *Dhanus*, is said to be of four *hastas* or cubits or two *nālikas*. In the *Arthaśāstra* we find:

4 *aratnis* = 1 *daṇḍa,* 1 *Dhanus,* 1 *nālika* and 1 *Pauruṣa.*
Again 192 *angulas* = 1 *daṇḍa.*

The measure *daṇḍa* is said to be used in measuring such lands as are gifted to Brahmanas. In the division of time also the expression *nālika* figures but this is not to our present purpose.[92] *Nala* and *Nālika* are one and the same. *Nālika* is twice the *hasta,* i.e., 2 cubits or one yard. Two such *nālikas* make one *daṇḍa*. And *daṇḍa*, according to the Kauṭalya is generally associated with the measurement of *brahmadeya* land. So the meaning 'reed' is not appropriate as it is brittle, and also not countenanced by texts.[93]

Other sources of Revenue

It is well known that the Vākāṭakas were the contemporaries of the Guptas, and their inscriptions supplement the information that is gathered from the records of the Guptas. If we analyse the inscriptions in Fleet's *Corpus,* and also the *Epigraphia Indica* (XV. No. 4), we come across a large

91. II. 7. 100.
92. Bk. II ch. 20.
93. Dr. V. Raghavan drew my attention to this interpretation.

number of items of revenue from which the Brahmanas who had been recipients of land grants were exempted. In other words these were sources of revenue to the State. They have been examined by Ghoshal.[94]

(1) *abhaṭacchatra prāveśya*—literally 'not to be entered by the king's regular troops or by the king's umbrella-bearers'. The frequent term met with in similar inscriptions is *acāṭabhaṭa prāveśya*[95] meaning 'not to be entered by the irregular or regular troops'. All this means that it may be obligatory on the villages to pay some contribution of money or supplies to the royal troops and officials when they halted at or passed through such places. It was a sort of forced contribution to the State, not sanctioned by law but by convention and usage.

(2) *apāramparagobalīvardda.*—It is significant to compare this with the expression *apāramparabalivaddha gahanam* in the grant of the Pallava king Śivaskanda varman.[96] This would indicate the obligation on the part of the local people to furnish cattle in relays for transport. Fleet's interpretation is not satisfactory. When the bulls were tired after a long distance, they were to be replaced by a fresh set of bulls. This must also have been a customary obligation of the villages to the state.

(3) *apuṣpakṣīrasandoha.*—This again relates to an obligation of the villages to supply flowers and milk to the royal officials in their tours perhaps in the rural parts. One can understand the supply of milk. But one cannot see why the officials on tour wanted flowers also. Perhaps it was an ancient custom.

94. *op. cit.*, pp. 193 ff.
95. Fleet, *op. cit.*, p. 98.
96. *Ep. Ind.*, I. p. 6.

(4) *acārāsana carmāngāra.*—This shows that the State enjoyed the right of the pasturage, hides and charcoal. This is not impossible as the State in ancient India had its own Department of Industries and ran industrial establishments on a large scale. There must have been some arrangement by which the rural parts furnished the raw material and fuel at a stipulated rate. The *Arthaśāstra* and the Aśokan inscriptions refer to a superintendent of pasture.[97] The suggestion of Ghoshal is not convincing.

(5) *alavaṇa klinna kreṇīkhānaka.*—This points to the right of the State for salt mines. Fleet translates it as 'the mines for the purchase of salt in a moist state'. It may be said without any fear of contradiction that salt industry was the monopoly of the State, and salt mines belonged of right to the State, unless it specifically exempted certain mines of its own accord. The Poona plates of the Vākāṭaka Queen Prabhāvatigupta contain instead of *lavaṇa,* the term *kinva.* This shows that the purchase of fermenting drugs was taxed by the State.

(6) *a* (*paśu*) *medhya.*—It is difficult to explain this term. Whether *paśu* is the correct reading we cannot say. If it were so, it must refer to the heavy fine prescribed by Kauṭalya for killing cows and calves in his *Sūnādhykṣa* chapter.[98]

(7) *Sanidhi sopanidhi.*—The State's right to treasures hidden as well also to deposits is clearly stated here. According to Kauṭalya treasure finds, land and ocean mines were the property of the State.[99] Apparently the Gupta State also claimed such privileges. These were good sources of income to the government.

97. Bk. II. 33. Rock. Edict. XII also Hultzch, *Corpus,* p. 126.
98. *Ep. Ind.*, XV. p. 42; *Ar. Śās.* Bk. II. 26.
99. Bk. II. 12.

(8) *sarva viṣṭi parihāra-parihṛṣita*—This is forced labour. Under the category of income in the *Arthaśāstra, viṣṭi* is mentioned.[100] This indicates the Gupta State also resorted to forced labour for military purposes and perhaps on certain other occasions. At the end of the long list of dues we find *kliptopaklipta.* This goes to prove that certain dues among them were fixed payments while others were only unfixed or customary payments.

We have to add to this list *cora-varjam* or *caura-varjam* or again Coradaṇḍa-varjam or Cora-Drohaka varjam.[101] This is evidently a police tax. We see some connection to this in the expression *Cororajju* which is taken to be one of the receipts of the State in the *Arthaśāstra.* Then mention is made of the *Cororajju,* the police official who was responsible for watching the movements of the robbers and bringing them to book. His jurisdiction lay possibly beyond the village limits including the pasture land.[102] This shows that the State maintained the peace of the rural parts by a net work of police for which the local people were to pay some fixed fee to the Government. Evidently this was another source of income to the Gupta State.

There were also taxes collected from guilds of merchants and artisan classes. There were organised associations of bankers, traders, and merchants as could be seen from a number of seals of the Gupta period.[103] Being wealthy classes in the state, they paid good sums of money in the shape of a number of taxes. The income from the mint must have been considerable. The Gupta monarchs had an elaborate currency system. Gold and silver coins were struck and circulated widely. For all business transactions including the purchase

100. *Nārada* refers to it V, II. 25-43.
101. Fleet, *op. cit.*, No. 21, 23, 27.
102 *Ibid* II. 34.
103. For instance see *An. Rep. Arch. Sur.* 1903-4 p. 110. No. 29.

and sale of land or endowing for charitable establishments, the coins were the medium of exchange, though very small transactions were effected by means of cowries as mentioned by Fa Hien. We also know in extreme financial distress the State reduced the weight and fineness of coins as could be clearly seen from the later issues of the coins of Skandagupta.[104] Whether the debased coins were prevalent in one part of the Empire or the other, the fact remains that debased coins were issued. The mint was thus an unfailing source of income to the State.

If we believe the statement of Fa Hien, it is highly probable that the Gupta State pursued a policy of prohibition. The Chinese traveller writes that throughout the country the people do not kill any living creature, nor drink intoxicating liquors. He further records, 'In the markets there are no butchers' shops and no dealers in intoxicating drink'.[105] If this is a correct estimate, then we have to conclude that the Gupta Government lost heavily from the otherwise large income from these two departments which are mentioned in the *Kauṭalīya*. In the latter there was a superintendent over slaughter houses. There was also an excise officer in charge of the sale of liquors. In this way the Gupta Government had advanced far ahead of the times.

These and other sources of income which are not mentioned in the inscriptions must have swelled the revenues of the Gupta State, and they alone were responsible for the stability of the empire for two hundred years and more. The above examination of land grants to the Brahmanas who were the custodians of education and of other public and religious services in the State shows the anxiety of the Government to promote the well-being of that community by not merely granting lands, but also by granting immunities from taxes

104. V. A. Smith, *Early History of India*, IV edn. p. 328.
105. *Legge's* trans. p. 43.

otherwise due to the State. The grants were also made according to a plan and with a specific purpose. In this connection different systems are mentioned.

(1) *Bhumicchidra Dharma* refers to lands fit to be ploughed on the basis of Yādavaprakāśa's *Vaijayanti* (*Vaisyādhyāya*, verse 18; Fleet *op. cit.*, No. 31). According to the inscription there was the rule for *bhumiccitra* (*nyāya*). Such lands were granted hereditarily and could not be reappropriated by the Government.

(2) The term *akṣayanīvi* is found in the Bihar stone pillar inscription of Skandagupta[106] and in the Sāñchi stone Inscription.[107] In the Dhanaidaha copper-plate grant of Kumāragupta I, *nīvīdharma* means that the grant of the land was not permanent. It was perhaps granted for life and was retransferable.[108] Both *akṣayanīvi* and *nīvidharma* can be treated as synonymous terms. Line 8 of the inscription contains *nīvi Dharmakṣayam ālabhya.*—The land which was given away as a grant and was in possession of two Brahmanas was taken back and assigned to Varāhasvāmi, a Sāma Vedi Brahmana after reversing the process known as *nīvi Dharma* which is translated as destroying the permanency of the grant.[109]

In addition to this we find another type of grant called *aprada dharma,* also *apradā nīvidharma*. In a copper-plate grant of Mahārājādhirāja dated A.D. 433-34 it is said that the local authorities permitted one Kulaputraka Amṛtadeva to dedicate five *kulyavāpas* of *khila* land together with the *vāstu* land to the deity Śvetavarāha according to the *aprada dharma* for use for all time. This indicates that this dedication was not subject to alienation or even transfer.[110] More or less the

106. Fleet, *op. cit.*, p. 50. 1. 26.
107. *Ibid.*, 261 1. 3.
108. *JASB* (1909) V. No. 11. p. 461.
109. *Ibid.* p. 460.
110. *Ep. Ind.* XV. p. 144.

same conditions occur in a Damodarpur grant of Mahārājādhirāja Budhagupta. Here is seen the grant of *aprada* land of eleven *kulyavāpas* for two deities to Nagaraśreṣṭin Rithupāla who applied for more lands offering to pay for them. These were to be preserved by the administrating agents.[111] These were in other words perpetual endowments.

Other sources of income

We have been so far considering the sources of revenue to the state. By conquest and other methods of taxation the Gupta government had been able to collect a good sum which swelled their treasury. In addition, the Gupta State took up some industries and worked them through the departments of the State. Further, according to the authority of the *Mānava Dharmaśāstra* mining like treasure-trove belonged to the State and the public. We mean if the public discovered a mine of treasure-trove it was reported to the government and it is said the government levied a tax which amounted to as much as 50%.[112] The State again took upon itself the duty of protecting the land and its people. This is testified to us by the text of the same *Mānava Dharmaśāstra* quoted above. This must not confound the issue that the State was the proprietor of all lands. On the other hand the public ownership of the land was accepted and the State was entitled to the customary 1/6th share of the produce, generally of the cultivated lands. Kātyāyana says that the king was called *Svāmin* simply because he presided over the welfare of the people for which he was paid 1/6th of the share. Mitramiśra who has commented upon this explicitly says that as master, the king receives only 1/6th of the produce.

111. *Ibid.* pp. 140-41.

112. निधीनां तु पुराणानां धातूनामेव च क्षितौ।
अर्धभाग्रक्षणाद्राजा भूमेरधिपतिर्हि स:॥ Manu VIII. 40.

भूस्वामी तु स्मृतो राजा नान्यद्रव्यस्य सर्वदा।
तत्फलस्य हि षड्भागं प्राप्नुयान्नान्यथैव तु॥
भूतानां तन्निवासित्वात् स्वामित्वं तेन कीर्त्तितम्॥
तत्क्रियाबलिषड्भागं शुभाशुभनिमित्तजम् इति।

If one examines the Gupta title deeds which were inscribed on copper-plates and which were registered at the office of the District Registrar, one is clear that not only private ownership of lands was recognised but also that the State received in this case only 1/6th share. It is explicit from the term *Dharma-ṣaḍ-bhāga*[113] that the crown was entitled to only 1/6th share.

Money crops like cotton and jute are not new discoveries by modern geographers. These were known in Gupta India also. Commercial and other crops were preserved as much as possible in the land itself. These and others added to the sources of the state income in the Gupta times.

Public expenditure

Various functions of the state demanded a heavy toll from the State treasury. The Gupta monarchs realised[113-a] that the whole body-politic depended upon economics. It was their ambition to maintain an economic equilibrium in their government. As economic prosperity much depended upon the well-being of the mercantile classes particular attention was bestowed upon them. The relationship between them and the State was cordial. The contribution by these classes was a factor to be reckoned with. Therefore the State attempted its best to encourage trade and commerce. For effecting religious and social purposes and even realising political ambitions, the State was

113. (Quoted in the *Indian Antiquary* XXXIX, p. 195).

113-a. वार्तां प्रजा साधयति वार्ता वै लोकसंश्रया॥

—(*Kāmandaka* XIV. 27)

well laid on economic foundations. There was the civil list which consisted of pay and pension of not only the establishment of the royal household but also of other officials including the menial services employed by the State. A good part of this sum was taken up by the Defence Department. The soldiers, leaders of military corporations, and the animals required for war purposes were all maintained by the State.

We shall not go here into the details of expenditure incurred over the religious establishment or the royal household or even works of public utility like construction of sluices or repair of irrigation works or even maintenance of Trunk Roads[114]; but suffice it to say that the Gupta government ensured every man and beast not only general health but also inculcated morals in them.

One great item of expenditure for these monarchs was the grant of lands to *śrōtriyas* and ascetics who also served as teachers imparting instruction and training in scientific and technical arts. The Gupta State realised the value of education[115] and set apart lands for that specific purpose. These grants were either in the nature of life grants or hereditary grants. That is, the sons and successors of such donees enjoyed the produce generally tax-free given to them by the State. This comes perhaps under the social functions of the State and can be termed as public poor relief. Indirectly the donees of such grants spread education and culture far and wide in the land. For that was the service expected of them by the donors.

114. कृषिर्वणिक्पथो दुर्गं सेतुः कुञ्जरबन्धनम्।
खन्याकरो वनादानं शून्यानां च निवेशनम्॥ V. 77
अष्टवर्गमिमं साधु स्वस्थवृत्तं विवर्धयेत्।
जीवनार्थमिहाजीव्यैः कारयेत् करणान्वितैः॥ V. 78

115. See the section *Vidyāvṛddhavinaya samyogaprakaraṇam* especially sl. 68.

Departmental accounts

It cannot be doubted for a moment that in such a great empire like that of the Guptas, accounts were kept in an orderly manner. The accounts were maintained as during the days of their predecessors the Mauryas and were submitted periodically for audit and approval. This is made clear to us by the term *Paṭyuparika.* This may be translated broadly as corresponding to the modern Accountant-General It also implies that there was an Accounts Department where records were kept for inspection and audit. The records dealt with various kinds of grants. The Accountant-General who presided over the accounts department was responsible to the Council of ministers for his acts. We do not know the rules governing leave, transfers and pay of the different establishments including the Accounts officials. But from the fact that the Accountant-General is mentioned and from the fact that the Gupta government took the precaution of taxing the profit and not the capital, it is evident that there was an elaborate Department of Accounts in the Gupta times.

Speaking generally about the stability of the Gupta financial administration it can be asserted without any fear of contradiction that the Gupta monarchs had always an eye to build a state on sound economic considerations. They wanted that agriculture should be improved and protected at any cost. Agriculture was deemed as one important industry on which depended millions of people. In fact it was one of the declarations on the occasion of their coronation by the ancient Indian monarchs. If the *Mahābhārata* which is often quoted in the Gupta inscriptions is a test, the Gupta monarchs controlled public women, gamblers and theatricals who were all regarded as inimical to the State. The State gave no freedom of movement or peace of mind either to beggars or thieves who robbed the public. It also discouraged the practice of money being lent at high rates of interest. The State prevented import of luxuries and export of necessaries. It tried to nationalise several important industries while it encouraged ordinarily private industries.

Section iv

Administration of Justice

The early Hindu conception of polity went by the well-known expression of *Prajā Viṣṇu,* meaning that the people and not the king were sovereign. In other words, the monarch of the kingdom had no power to legislate for the people. It was the people's law that was administered by the king. The people's law consisted of the law-codes composed by sages and seers for the benefit of the community and also of the king. The latter appointed certain judges and delegated his authority to them to administer justice. Of course the king was the highest appellate authority. In case a certain party or parties felt that proper justice was not done to them, it was open to them to prefer an appeal to the ruler who with his Council went into the case and delivered the judgment which was final. So the law of the land established by convention, custom and usages was the subject which was interpreted ordinarily by the judges and in special cases by the king, and the decision was arrived at. This promiscuous weapon was in the hands of the people and was accepted by all classes as sacred in character.

In Gupta times though the *Mānava Dharmaśāstra* and the great epic *Mahābhārata* continued to be authoritative, still a number of law-givers flourished and promulgated laws according to the established usages of the time. In this galaxy of law-givers, mention may be made of three important *smṛti kartas* who flourished in the Gupta epoch. These were Bṛhaspati, Nārada and Kātyāyana.[116] These three law-givers did not evolve a new set of laws but improved on the

116. *Kātyāyana smṛti* ed. by P. V. Kane (1933).

existing laws, especially those of Manu.[117] These three acknowledged their indebtedness to the greatest law-giver Manu and freely drew from him. At the same time they took cognisance of the current notions and beliefs and changed a few rules and regulations in accordance with the existing conditions. In this way these three could be said to have advanced on the views of the original law-giver and this shows that law was not stagnant but was progressive. They also improved to a considerable extent the regulations laid down by the Arthaśāstra writers like Kauṭalya. But it was distinctly understood that equity played a significant role as a basis of law. This generally was put into application when the *smṛti* or the positive law cannot adequately provide equity of justice. We should not, however, confound this equity in Hindu law with that in the Roman law. The equity as realised in Hindu law was to broadly interpret the positive law of the *smṛti* and supplement it, if it was found necessary.[118]

Heads of Law

What Kauṭalya wrote of the four heads of law, is mentioned by Nārada. These are *Dharma, Vyavahāra, Caritra* and *Rājaśāsana*.[119] *Dharma* is to speak out the truth, *vyavahāra* is to have basis on evidence, *caritra* is to rest on customs and precedents, and *rājaśāsana* is the king's proclamation or edict. These are to be dealt with in the descending order of importance. In this category the king's edict occupies the last place. *Dharma* rooted in *satya* or truth occupies the first

117. See Bṛhaspati, Sec. 29, concluding verse; I. 113.

118. See Bṛhaspati IX. 8: Yājñāvalkya, an early *smṛti* writer cites this also II. 21.

119. धर्मश्च व्यवाहरश्च चरित्रं राजशासनम् ।
चतुष्पाद्व्यवहारोऽयमुत्तर: पूर्वबाधक: ॥
J. Jolly, (*Nārada* I; 10).

place.[120] But the royal edict could not go against the true letter and spirit of the positive law of the land.

Eighteen topics of the Law

Nārada cites categorically eighteen titles of the law. These are:—

1. *Ṛṇādānam* (relating to loans)
2. *Upanidhi* (Deposits)
3. *Sambhūyōtthānam* (Co-operative enterprises)
4. *Dattasyapunarādānam* (Resumption of presents and gifts)
5. *Asusrūṣābhyupetya* (Breach of contracts)
6. *Vetanasyānapākarma* (Non-payment of wages, etc.)
7. *Asvāmivikraya* (Irregular sale of property)
8. *Vikrīyāsampradānam* (recession of sales)
9. *Krītvānusaya* (pre-emption)
10. *Samayasyanānapākarma* (agreements of service, etc.)
11. *Kṣetravivāda* (Land disputes)
12. *Strīpuruṣyoḥ Sambandha* (Relations of sexes)
13. *Dāyabhāga* (inheritance and succession)
14. *Sāhasam* (Highway robbery)
15. *Vākpāruṣyam* (defamation)
16. *Daṇḍapāruṣyam* (assault)
17. *Dyūtam* (gambling)
18. *Prakīrṇakam* (miscellaneous).[120-a]

The above eighteen topics of law comprehend still more several titles of law. They constitute the main topics of which

120. तत्र सत्ये स्थितो धर्मो व्यवहारस्तु साक्षिषु ।
चरित्रं पुस्तकरणे राजाज्ञायां तु शासनम् ॥

(*Ibid*., I. 11.) See also Gaekwad Oriental Series LXXXV, Bṛhaspati, IX, 1-7.

120-a. *Ibid., I.* 16-19. See also Manu-Smṛti VIII. 3-7. for a slightly different version. I have also examined the Trivandrum edition of *Nāradiya Manu Saṃhita* (Tri. Sans. Series. 1929). See also Bṛhaspati Secs. 10-29. For details See *Kātyāyana* pp. 58-110.

there were many sub-titles of legal disputes, which Nārada himself has recognised, as also the celebrated author of the *Mānava Dharma śāstra.* There were then several cases which came within the purview of both civil and criminal jurisdiction. The sub-heads of law are mentioned by Nārada expressly as 132.[121] Bṛhaspati also enumerates eighteen titles of law. In fine in the Gupta period, as can be seen from Bṛhaspati and Nārada, the heads of legal disputes increased, and this leads to the conclusion that the judicial machinery had become more and more complicated.

The regulations of Nārada, Kātyāyana and Bṛhaspati, if critically studied, show much advance since the time of the *Kauṭalīya Arthaśāstra.* Kauṭalya refers to separate civil and criminal courts of law and it is reasonable that such distinct courts continued to exist in the age of the Guptas and dispensed justice which fell legitimately under their respective jurisdiction.

The court of law went by the name *Sabhā.* The presiding judge of the court was known *Prāḍvivāka.* This was perhaps the chief court of justice. There were other courts to which Bṛhaspati alludes. They were the courts of Āraṇyas (foresters), of Sainikas (army) and of merchants. Again there were the *Kula, Śreṇi* and *Gaṇa* courts.[122] Each dealt with its own guild and group organisation. These local courts had no power of jurisdiction over criminal cases like *Sāhasa.* While this system ensured local autonomy to develop uncurbed, the High Court dealt with bigger cases and especially criminal cases.

There is yet another classification of the courts in the *Bṛhaspati* code. These are *Pratiṣṭita, Apratiṣṭita, Mudrita,* and *Śāsita.*[123] If the court was definitely fixed in a certain city

121. *Ibid.* 20.
122. *Bṛhaspati*: *I.* 65-70, 73-74, 93-4.
123. *Ibid.*, I. 57-58.

or township, it was *Pratiṣṭita.* But if the court was not fixed in a certain locality and if it was held in some place, according as cases presented themselves, it was *apratiṣtita.* This was in the nature of temporary courts held by judges appointed for the purpose. If the *Smṛti Candrika* can be accepted as the evidence, the courts of *Āraṇyakas* and *Sainikas* come under this category. *Mudrita* was the court where the *Prāḍvivāka* or the judge appointed by the king presided. The other court *Śāsita* was perhaps the appellate court where the monarch presided, heard cases of appeal and delivered judgment. The term *Mudrita* suggests that the *Prāḍvivāka* had charge of the royal seal which validated the proceedings of the court. While the *Pratiṣṭita* and the *Apratiṣṭita* courts dealt with minor cases and inflicted *vākd-aṇḍa* and *dhikdaṇḍa,* the *Mudrita* and *Śāsita* could pass a sentence or a decree for money and inflict higher amercement. If the local courts known as popular courts could not give the proper decision satisfactory to a plaintiff, the latter had the option of taking up his case before the higher tribunal *Mudrita* and *Śāsita.* In other words, the whole judicial administration was in a way officialised. For, Kātyāyana definitely rules that only qualified men who were versed in Vedic Dharma and had self-control could be judges in rural courts. They could not arrogate the royal functions unless duly authorised. If they proceeded unauthorised, they were liable to be punished.

It is interesting to see that Bṛhaspati differentiates between the *Niyuktakas* and *Sabhyas.*[124] This is probably a reference to inferior judges and superior judges. The rural and district judges whose jurisdiction was limited formed the inferior judges as against the judges of the High Court of judicature. The *Sabhā* was the highest tribunal. Thus according to the laws of Bṛhaspati the whole empire

124. See *Ibid.,* I. 108.

contained a net work of courts, one linked up with another. This led to the uniformity of the administration of justice in the land. The award of corporal and capital punishment rested with the *Sabhā*.[125]

We should not confound this *Sabhā* with the Court-Sabhā. The *Sabhā* then was the law-court and not the Assembly. In the law-court sat judges and sometimes the king to administer justice. These judges were invariably of the Brahmana community who always took care to balance and to counterpoise "the estate of sword" and "the estate of wealth" in the words of Dr. Jayaswal.[126] It is important to note that even the king was afraid of the judge's decision and carefully examined it before he gave his judgment. In fact Nārada states explicitly that the ruler of the land always followed the opinion of the Chief Justice. (प्राड्विवाकमते स्थित) It may be remembered that the Prāḍvivāka or the Chief Justice was the President of the Supreme Court or the High Court in the Capital. With him sat the members of the Jury who watched the procedure and interpreted the law and advised the Judge. The Judge acted according to their advice. According to Nārada the Chief Justice was one who was well versed in the 18 titles of the law and all its sub-divisions. He should also be well acquainted with different branches of Science and patiently hear the case and then pass the sentence.[127]

Arbitration

One method by which justice was rendered was by arbitration. Cases where crimes were involved did not come under the purview of this court. The law-giver Nārada[128]

125. Seven, five, or three were the members of the *Sabhā*. (Br. I. 63).
126. *Hindu Polity* second edn. p. 331.
127. *Nārada* 1. 8-11, SBE. Vol. 33.
128. कुलानि श्रेणयश्चैव गणाश्चाधिकृतो नृपः।
प्रतिष्ठा व्यवहाराणां गुर्वेभ्यस्तूत्तरोत्तरम् ॥ (I. 7)
See also *Kātyāyana* 2.

believes in the system of arbitration and says that whenever disputes arose among merchants, artisans or similar persons, and whenever disputes arose among the agriculturists or weavers, experts in that profession were to be chosen and they had to arbitrate in such cases. Resort to arbitration tribunal has its own effect and cases coming before this court have had the benefit of experts examining and settling differences among them. This had also another beneficial effect, namely, that it checked the increase of litigation.

Law-Suits

Law-suits arose from different causes but Nārada has ruled that it might proceed from one of three causes. It may be due to (1) sex, (2) anger, (3) or ambition.[129] Hatred of one another or selfish motive was often the origin of law-suits. In other words, when the practice of *svadharma* was questioned it gave rise to unnecessary complication with the consequence that law-suit was launched. But it is ruled that neither the king nor his officials should be instrumental to launch a law-suit. When once a suit was filed then the pros and cons of that suit should be examined by a wise judge and sentence be passed binding both the plaintiff and the defendant. The plaint may be true or may not be true. It was the accused *i.e.*, the defendant who had to answer to the satisfaction of the court.[130] Nārada proceeds further and considers the plaint defective (1) if the subject is entirely different, (2) if it is not intelligible, (3) if there is no proper statement with regard to the claim, (4) if it is deficient in decorum, (5) if the writing is illegible, (6) if the subject is being stated again, and (7) if the plaint is damaged.[131]

129. S.B.E. 33. I. 26.
130. *Ibid.* 27 and 28.
131. *Ibid.*, II. 8.

The next stage was to issue summons. If the man wanted, absconded himself arrest might be effected. But Nārada rules that a person about to marry, a sickly one, a person engaged in *Yajña,* a calamitous one, an official in the king's service, cowherds who were engaged in tending cattle, peasants in the act of cultivation, artisans engaged in their own professions, minors, persons engaged in charity, men fulfilling a vow and others should be exempted from arrest.[132] Now it is the turn of the defendant to suitably reply to the plaint and not to evade the issue. He should prove his assertion.[133] Then were the witnesses who were examined though Nārada would dispense with them in some cases.[134] In such cases documentary evidence was let in and they were decided. According to Viṣṇu the witnesses were those who belonged to a noble family, possessed high educational qualifications or wealth, were skilled in law, were honest, and who had sons. In fact Viṣṇu recommends that only competent witnesses should be deposed. What is more important is that documentary evidence should not militate against local customs and general rules prevalent in that part of the land. In his legal procedure Nārada explains and discusses the false evidence which could be distinguished from the right one.[135]

Ordeal

Another mode of examining the evidence was by means of ordeal (*divya*). This does not appear to have been current in the Vedic times. But the growth in the interpretation of the law is indicated by the evolution of the institution of ordeal. Generally applied to criminal cases the ordeal was of different kinds.[136] It was by water, by fire or even by poison.

132. *Ibid., I.* 52-54. See also Banerjee, ***Public Administration in Ancient India.***

133. *Ibid.*, II. 31.

134. *Ibid.*, Trv. Edn. I. 147.

135. *Ibid.*, I. 177.

136. *Kātyāyana* vv. 441-ff,

Hieun Tsang witnessed an ordeal by water.[137] Though this evidence is not pertinent to our review it shows the persistence of the custom for a long time. But it must be noted that this method of ordeal was resorted to only on special occasions when the court could not come to any judgment on the evidence presented to it. In no way was it misused.[138] A copy of the judgment delivered was given to the party which won the case.[139] According to the law-giver Nārada the punishment may be either bodily punishment or fines.[140] In extreme cases the penalty of death was inflicted. The king, says Fa Hien, "in his administration uses no corporal punishments; criminals are merely fined according to the gravity of their offences. Even for a second attempt at rebellion the punishment is only the loss of the right hand".[141] A retrial of the case was ordered only when witnesses had not been examined in a previous case, or when the suit had been judged by the unauthorised.[142]

Conclusion.

Though there are many details pertaining to the administration of justice buried in the texts of the law-givers of the Gupta times we cannot examine all of them here. But we have taken the important characteristics of that administration and have dealt only with them. This itself indicates the responsibility with which the judges of this time viewed each and every case and pronounced judgment impartially. We also notice that by this time the customary law has grown and the law formulated by interpretation has also

137. See Beal. *Buddhist Records.* Bk. II. p. 54.

138. See also Manu VIII, 114.

139. Nārada, *Legal procedure,* 243.

140. Jolly, *Op. cit.,* Appendices vv. 53-54.

141. See Giles' account p. 21: Beal, *Buddhist Records of Western World,* Bk. I: Ch. 16.

142. Quotation from Nārada (Jolly. II, 114), See also Bṛhaspati, VIII. especially 1-4. Here Bṛhaspati mentions nine kinds of ordeal.

been on the increase. The judges of this period did not merely look upon the sacred law as the law of the land but attached equal importance to the customs prevalent in various localities of the country. One striking feature of the administration of justice is seen in the independent character of the judges who made the *Sabhā*. It is significant to note in this connection that the separation of the Judiciary from the Executive which is being tried today was already in vogue in Hindu India and more so in Gupta India.

CHAPTER V

MILITARY ORGANISATION

Section I

Introductory

After the great Mauryas, the Gupta monarchs established a vast empire covering a large portion of North India. Candragupta I, the first imperial ruler of the dynasty ruled only over a comparatively small area round Pāṭalīputra but it was given to Samudragupta to make a *digvijaya* and expand the small kingdom into an empire of considerable dimensions. Candragupta II Vikramāditya added some more territories to his heritage and consolidated the Gupta empire.

The empire must have been realised by the vigorous pursuit of a plan and policy which kings like Samudragupta and Candragupta II inherited from earlier generations. The diplomatic code of Kauṭalya was well understood in the Gupta period. The injunctions laid down in the *Rāja dharma* section of the *Mahābhārata* and the *Mānavadharma Śāstra* exercised considerable influence on the Gupta kings. With the changing conditions of the age some of the Kauṭalīyan dictates were not quite suitable and Candragupta Vikramāditya wanted one of his ministers Śikharasvāmin (Safar of the later Muslim historian) to prepare a Manual on politics and administration which he thought would be useful to himself and his successors. The Manual that was consequently prepared was the *Kāmandakīya Nītiśara* now in vogue.[1] A major portion of the book relates to the military organisation wherein the author deals with war, peace, treaties, army,

1. also edited in the *Trivandrum Sanskrit Series* No. XIV (1912).

ambassadors, spies etc. In the treatment of the military organisation under the Guptas we are largely following that work.

Foreign Affairs

The *Maṇḍala* theory of Kauṭalya and various other authors is elaborated by Kāmandaka. One theory is that a *Maṇḍala* consists of the *Ari,* the *Mitram,* the *Arermitram,* the *Mitrāmitram* and the *Arimitrāmitram.*[2] These are said to be the five sovereigns, who are supposed to be in front of the *Vijigīṣu,* or the conquering monarch. There is the *maṇḍala* of ten and twelve kings. The *maṇḍala* of twelve kings consists of five *prakṛtis* each and the twelve cardinal sovereigns together with their respective *prakṛtis* constitute the *Prakṛti maṇḍala* which consists of seventy-two elements. Here *prakṛti* means a circle of different sovereigns who have to be taken into consideration in case a war is declared. The *prakṛti maṇḍala* is mentioned not only by Kauṭalya and Manu but also by Kāmandaka.[3] Kāmandaka proceeds to mention a *maṇḍala* of eighteen sovereigns who have for each an ally and an enemy. This means 54 sovereigns are involved in a *maṇḍala* and Viśālākṣa a political writer, makes mention of this. Kāmandaka also refers to it.[4]

The various theories which were not only current in his time and which were once current regarding the *maṇḍala* have been put forth by Kāmandaka but the chief four monarchs of a maṇḍala are composed of the *vijigīṣu* (i.e. a conquering king) the *Ari* (enemy) the *Madhyama* (mediator) and the *Udāsīna* (neutral). But the *maṇḍala* which consists of twelve kings seems to be accepted and approved by the author of the *Kāmandakīya Nītisara.*[5] But in the next

2. VIII. 16.

3. Section VIII. stanza 25. I have followed the translation in this chapter.

4. *Ibid.* Stanza 28.

5. *Ibid.* 22 & 41.

stanza Kāmandaka speaks of him as a real politician who knows a tree having four roots.[6] A tree euphemistically stands here for the maṇḍala while the four roots are the Vijigīṣu, Ari, Madhyama and Udāsīna. The part played by Udāsīna is something remarkable and something akin to the prevalent International Law. He is a powerful common ally. His service must be used by both the ruler and the enemy. But the ruler of the earth should be sure of his position before he sets out for march. The ally of the enemy should first be paralysed if the conquest were to be a success. In other words, a conquering monarch should win over to his side not only the *Udāsīna* but also the ally of his enemy. In case the *Madhyama* desires for conquest the *Vijigīṣu* together with his enemy either should show a united front or submit to make peace with him.[7] If one then understands the true concept of a *maṇḍala* one must conclude that it is interspersed with hostile and friendly monarchs. Each one wants to outgrow the other, the result being a state of war due to distrust and fear.

A conquering monarch should try to use all the means at his disposal to win over the various chiefs, friendly or inimical. Standing in the path of justice a monarch should bring about the purification of a *maṇḍala.* This purification means the purification of the ally, the enemy and the Udāsīna.[8]

The Vijigīṣu

By far the most important and chief component of a Maṇḍala is the Vijigīṣu or the conquering monarch. In front of him and behind him are an enemy and an ally. He may

6. *Ibid.* 42.

अष्टशाखं चतुर्मूलं षष्टिपत्रं द्वये स्थितम्।
षट्पुष्पं त्रिफलं वृक्षं यो जानाति स नीतिवित्॥

7. *Ibid.* Stanzas 45-55.
8. *Ibid.* Stanzas 86 and 87.

oppose the enemy or join with the enemy and oppose the Madhyama. But the business of the *Vijigīṣu* is not only to befriend his ally but also the ally of his enemy. He must cultivate the alliance not only of foreign monarchs but also of local governors and foresters who are the props and the pillars of the kingdom. In extirpating his enemy the *Vijigīṣu*[9] should take care not to assail him, which would give the slightest chance of awakening another enemy. If he is really intelligent the *Vijigīṣu* would shudder before he gives reason for the whole *maṇḍala* to agitate and he should cherish the *prakṛtis* so that they would be ever loyal to him and prove to be scrupulously honest. He should take care not to be wrathful towards his opponents, some of whom may be innocent.

No doubt Kāmandaka refers to conquest of the earth as the legitimate duty of a monarch. But before launching on an expedition it is advised that a conquering monarch should take into account the time, place and circumstances of that expedition. In this regard a strong plea is made by the author of the *Kāmandakīya Nītisāra* for consultation with the chief War Ministers, and for action, as far as possible in consonance with their views and opinions.[10] The importance of the Council is elaborately dealt with and it is said that the power of a good Council is superior to the king's powers, energy and dignity. A true king could not disregard that Council which acts according to rules contained in the Śāstras. It is said that an act which is mutually deliberated upon by learned and sincere friends could never fail to bear fruit. If one would listen to the advice tendered, he need not repent afterwards. Mere valour would be insufficient to secure success in any undertaking.

9. *Ibid.* 30-35.
10. See cha. 11.

The advantages of Time and Place would not lead one to grief and disappointment.[11] Hence, a wise *vijigīṣu* should critically review his position as well as the position of the enemy by studying the pros and cons of both weakness and strength and then only embark on an expedition.[12] It is said to be an incumbent duty on the *vijigīṣu* to acquire things which could not be acquired otherwise and protect the things already acquired. This means the *vijigīṣu* should take counsel and whatever is wholesome, sincere, and prolific, of sources of prosperity should be executed with zeal and enthusiasm. Following the advice and the instruction as narrated in the *Kāmandakīya* the Gupta monarchs commencing with Candragupta II Vikramāditya consolidated the kingdom.

Diplomatic Agents

In the expansion of a great empire like that of the Guptas the use of diplomatic agents like the *Dūtas* or ambassadors or *cāraṇas* or spies should have been very considerable. A man of ability and one approved by the cabinet as ambassador went to the court of the foreign king and announced without fear or favour the determination of his monarch to set out on a military march. Kāmandaka distinguishes three kinds of ambassadors who should be conversant with the rules and communications of the enemy's state. In this he is advised to befriend not only the *antapālas* and also the foresters who would be of immense service in his undertaking.[13] An ambassador should not mind or be afraid of the enemy's strength but should take courage and deliver his master's message word for word even in the face of danger to life. He should study the ins and outs of the

11. ch 10. 39-40.
12. *Ibid.* St. 43-44.
13. *Ibid.* 13.5.

enemy's territory, the loyalty or otherwise of his people, the discontent or otherwise of his subjects and praise the enemy as if he was his own master. He should further acquaint himself with the movements of parties in the kingdom and study whether the seeds of dissension could be sown. He should wander about *tīrthas, āśramas* and temples and note secretly the views and opinions expressed by the public about the king and keep in touch with his own master.[14] He should be patient and put up with insults and avoid the influence of lust on all occasions.[15] These duties of the ambassador are dealt with *in extenso* in the *Kāmandakīya Nītisāra.*[16] Though the term *Dūta* stands for ambassadors not only in the *Nītisāra,* but also in all literature, yet the term in the inscriptions of the Guptas seems to stand for a scribe and his functions seem to be more civil than military in character. Sometimes the term *Dūta* and sometimes *Dūtaka* occur in inscriptions but do not connote anything relating to the ambassadorial system in vogue at that time.

Closely connected with the ambassadorial system is the spy system current in those days. "A person skilled in the interpretation of internal sentiments by conjecture and by external gestures, accurate memory, polite and soft of speech, agile in movements, capable of bearing with all sorts of privations and difficulties, ready-witted and expert in everything" is alone considered to be an intelligent spy.[17] These spies disguised themselves as ascetics, traders or artisans, roamed about the country and gathered public opinion from every nook and corner. Kauṭalya says that they were the

14. *Ibid.* 13. 14-15.
15. *Ibid.* 13.3.

निसृष्टार्थो मितार्थश्च तथा शासनहारकः।
सामर्थ्यात् पादतो हीनो दूतस्तु त्रिविधः स्मृतः॥

16. Whole of chap. 13.
17. 13. 26.

eyes of the king and Kāmandaka accepts it as an article of faith.[18] They probed into the secrets of the enemy and appraised their master with the news they got even if they were asleep. They were then a convenient instrument for a monarch to acquaint himself with the various movements in the enemies' territories. They mingled with the common people as one among them and studied their intentions and observations.[19] They were not like the Consuls of to-day established in all the capitals in foreign countries. But they wandered here and there without revealing who they were, but gathering whatever information they wanted. Much depended on their opinion for it practically clinched the issue before any decision was taken.

Peace and Treaties

Enough has been said that a conquering king should study carefully the *vyasanas* and remedy every one of them. He must even make friendship with his enemy if time and place required it. Women, intoxicating drinks, hunting, gambling, and Fate are said to be the *vyasanas* affecting a kingdom.[20] But a wise king must overcome them by means of expedients.

Though the author of the *Kāmandakīya Nītisara* is in favour of waging war with the enemy, still he is an eloquent advocate of peace.

He mentions sixteen kinds of peace which are as follows: Kapāla, Upahāra, Santāna, Sangata, Upanyāsa, Pratīkāra, Samyoga, Puruṣāntara, Adṛṣṭanara, Ādiṣṭa, Ātmāmisa, Upagraha, Parikraya, Ucchinna, Paradūṣana and Skandhopanēya.[21] When monarchs were of equal strength and resources the

18. 13. 28—31.
19. *Ibid.* 49.
20. 11-11.
21. 9. 2-4.

treaty concluded by them is Kapālasandhi but in the treaty where gifts are offered it is called Upahāra sandhi.[22] The gifts may be according to the commentator, the army and treasury of the vanquished monarch. Santāna sandhi is generally effected when the conquered king offers his daughter in marriage to the adversary.[23] Next comes the Sangata which simply means union and which may liberally mean that based on friendship. This kind of peace is superior for nothing is involved in this except that the parties agree to it.[24] Upanyāsa sandhi is that by which parties agree to fulfil their objects. This may be the acquirement of territories already resolved upon. This is in the form of a truce.[25] The object of Pratikārasandhi is to make peace by conferring benefits, perhaps mutually. "I shall do him good. He will also do so to me", is the underlying object of this peace.[26] It is rather difficult to define Samyoga sandhi. This may simply mean a firm alliance. This, in other words, shows the treaty effected when the advantages are equal to both parties. Again to distinguish it from Kapāla sandhi is difficult. The Puruṣāntara is another treaty where the conqueror dictates terms to his advantage. Generally, the conqueror wants the services of the best of the conquered troops. They should mingle with his troops and improve his interest.

Adṛṣṭanara is also known as Adṛṣṭapuruṣa sandhi. There is not much difference between this and the previous one. Adṛṣṭa sandhi is made when a strong adversary offers

22. *Ibid.* 5-6.
23. *Ibid.* 6.
24. *Ibid.* 7-10.
25. *Ibid.* 11-12.
26. *Ibid.* 13-14.

एकार्थां सम्यगुद्दिश्य यात्रां यत्र हि गच्छतः।
स संहतप्रयाणस्तु सन्धिः संयोग उच्यते॥
आवयोर्योधमुख्याभ्यां मदर्थः साध्यतामिति।
यस्मिन् पणः प्रक्रियते स सन्धिः पुरुषान्तरः॥

a part of his territory. According to S. W. Jones, Adṛṣṭa is a treaty where land is involved. The Ātmāmiṣa sandhi stands on a different footing being concluded between a king and his troops. This is perhaps in the nature of a compact between the monarch and his army. But Upagraha sandhi is that where the defeated king values his life more than anything else and that he is prepared to surrender anything for the sake of his life. Parikraya is purchasing peace by surrendering a part or whole of the treasury. Ucchina sandhi is one where the foe is deprived of the best lands of the state.[27] Paradūṣaṇa sandhi is concluded by the vanquished monarch by giving up the products of his whole kingdom. The last is Skandhopaneya sandhi which has given rise to different interpretations but indemnity is fundamental to this.[28]

If a conquering monarch resolves upon expedition it is only with the view to add to his wealth and more so to add territory to the kingdom. If he seeks the right time for action the enemy is vanquished. To avoid conflict, less powerful kings may offer him surrender of their arms and please him by means of booty and cession of territory. When they offer terms of peace a wise king accepts them. For it is not advisable to fight with a hero. It is advised therefore that as victory in war is doubtful, peace must be concluded even with one equal in every respect.[29] In that way the kingdom prospers.[30] The Gupta monarchs who followed the instructions given in the *Kāmandaka Nītisāra* would have been anxious to avoid wars as much as possible

27. *Ibid.* 16-18.
28. *Ibid.* 19-20.
29. *Ibid.* 60.
30. *Ibid.* 79.

सन्धिमिच्छेत् समेनापि सन्दिग्धो विजयो युधि।
न हि संशयितं कुर्यादित्युवाच बृहस्पतिः॥

but the fact remains that monarchs less powerful than they, have surrendered their territories to enable them to build up an empire. It appears that this thing was a *fait accompli* because they followed the principles of warfare generously by making peace even with equals but on the terms dictated by them. That is why Samudragupta was able to carve out an empire in so short a time.

Section II

Diplomatic Relations

Among the Imperial Guptas who built up and consolidated the empire mention must be made of Samudragupta who was able to build a huge empire and force his imperialism on the subjects of the conquered territories. If he was anything, Samudragupta was a great soldier and a brave fighter but a law-abiding citizen. He conquered Kashmir and Afghanistan which were practically Mleccha countries at that time and enlarged the Gupta empire. But he would not go beyond Afghanistan and make a show of his prowess, because the International law of the time as understood in Hindu India prevented him from marching towards the territories which were beyond the pale of Bhāratavarṣa which term signified only India proper. Though Samudragupta of the Gupta line was swayed by the ideas and ideals of Imperialism, yet he observed more the spirit of the law than adhering to the letter. When he set out for conquest Samudragupta, a powerful sovereign that he was, was full of ideas imperialistic in nature and which we find described in the *Sabhāparva* of the *Mahābhārata*.[31]

Politically the emperor effected the conquest of the frontier kingdoms which were mainly (1) Samataṭa

31. Chapter XIV Stanzas 9-12; See also XXXI 73-74.

(2) Davāka (3) Kāmarūpa (4) Nepāla and (5) Karttipura. These states were conquered in the sense that all their kings gave the emperor huge presents[32] in acknowledgment of his greatness. For political purposes these states became part of the empire. However, Samudragupta's Imperialism knew no bounds. He was not a friend of the republican forms of government. He crushed them and vanquished them and deprived them of all their independence. These republics which were old and which existed from the days of the *Aitareya Brāhmaṇa* and which had reached their acme in the time of the Buddha were crushed beyond recovery. Samudragupta endeavoured to destroy the republics of the Mālavas, Yaudheyas, etc. mentioned in line 22 of the Allahabad inscription and these were made part and parcel of the Gupta empire. These states which were deprived of their freedom promised to pay taxes to the Imperial treasury and to recognise Samudragupta as their emperor. Thus Samudragupta was not a believer in half-hearted, deteriorating and defunct republican units of government. He believed in a strong monarchy and he converted his people who were anxious to get freedom from the harassing Mleccha. The people of Bhāratavarṣa felt a thirst for reviving their glorious religion and literature. Luckily the hundred years of rule by the Bhāraśivas had paved the way for the Gupta Imperialism for which their subjects were avowedly ready.

The Guptas took up the thread of their predecessors namely, the Bhāraśivas and the Nāgas as seen from the Purāṇas and continued the policy in Farther India, namely the establishment of a Colonial empire. Indian geography as preserved in the Purāṇic tradition has often recognised that the whole world known then covered nine *dvīpas* of which Bhāratavarṣa or India was one. The identification of the other eight *dvīpas*

32. Allahabad Pillar Inscrp. line 22; Fleet op. cit. p. 8.

has varied according to the imagination of scholars interested in the subject. Though the identification which the late Jayaswal has attempted[33] can partly be accepted, yet there is no warrant for all his identifications. At least we do not agree with his identification of the Gāndhāra and Varuṇa dvipas with the Archipelago group. Whatever that might be, we can speak of a colonial system and colonial empire under the Guptas. In line 23 of the Allahabad Pillar inscription we have the evidence on the form of government prevalent in what we call Farther India. These far-off Indian colonies were in touch with the homeland; otherwise we cannot explain the extent to which the Gupta influence had exerted itself in these islands. The language of the inscriptions of this period in Campa, Funan, Java, and Sumatra is Sanskrit, while it was previously Prākṛit.[34] We may note that Bhadravarman who defeated the Chinese troops[35] was contemporaneous with Candragupta II. It transpires therefore that the father of this king and Samudragupta were contemporaries. We also know that the son of Bhadravarman had been in India before he actually took the reins of the government in his own territory Campa.

In Sumatra we have the evidence of Fa-hien[36] who visited it in the days of Candragupta II to show the decline of Buddhism and the rise and flourishing nature of Brahmanism.[37] In Funan on the other hand we find king Sudhavarman as a contemporary of Samudragupta. It is abundantly clear that king Sudhavarman made considerable changes in his administration so as to suit the new line of government which had been inspired under the aegis of the Guptas. An account of Farther India will be incomplete if we do not make mention of Western Java which was an

33. See *History of India*, pp. 154-5.
34. See Finot: IHQ. Vol. I. p. 599 ff.
35. *History of India*, pp. 156-57.
36. R. C. Majumdar: *Suvarnadvipa* Vol. II, pt ii pp. 25-29
37. J. Legge, *Fa-hien Travels*, p. 113.

important Hindu colony of the Guptas. The inscriptions of the 4th and 5th centuries A.D. in Western Java are clearly written in Sanskrit, and Sanskrit influence has been felt everywhere in the island. We further notice the Gupta sculptures chistled in the temples in Cambodia which are huge edifices and standing testimony to the prevalence of Gupta art and Gupta style throughout Cambodia.[38]

In Burma again there is much evidence of Gupta Art and its influence. Besides the script of the Gupta times, there are Gupta terracottas which are largely found throughout the length and breadth of Burma. This Gupta influence in Burma must have been even from the early years of the Gupta era.[39] Samudragupta whose aim was to bring about an unifying influence of his empire must have exerted his power not through arms but through the script. Commerce and art brought about the unity of Farther India with his empire. It is wrong to suppose that Samudragupta was the uncrowned expert in the art of war and hence he must have had the tendencies of a militarist. It is not true to say that the emperor was exercising his mind only on military considerations. If this were a fact, he could have achieved much more, but it is not a fact that he was a militarist. He pinned his faith on the law of the land but he showed to the world that he was made of sterner stuff. He could wield arms but if the people in the far-off colonies acknowledged his suzerainty, satisfaction was brought home to him.

To keep the colonial empire closely knit with the mother country Tāmralipti was improved as a mighty port carrying on active trade with all the *dvīpas* in what we now call the Bay of Bengal. This policy of bringing together the mother country and the colonies in closer touch had

38. Coomaraswami: *History of Indian and Indonesian Art*, pp. 157, 182-83.

39. *Ibid.* p. 169. See also V. A. Smith: *Early History of India*, p. 29.

far-reaching effects. One result of this policy was continued trade and that too a never-failing one which was carried on in merchant vessels. Besides we hear of the great influence wielded by *Kāmandaka Nītisāra* in the various parts of Farther India. This is an additional proof to show that the author of this *Nītisāra* was flourishing in the days of the Guptas. The fact that this *Nītisāra* was mentioned in the early days of king Candragupta II demonstrates that the colonies wanted to imbibe the art and culture of the Mother country. In the case of Farther India therefore it was not the mighty arms of a mighty hero that made these islands concur with the home country in their policy but the willing co-operation of the colonies themselves.[40]

Ceylon

Among the foreign powers which had relations with the Gupta emperors, especially Samudragupta, Ceylon may be mentioned. Whether they were in the nature of diplomatic ones viz., a foreign power calling at the court of the reigning emperor or not, sufficient light has not been thrown. We take it that for purposes of propagating their faith the Buddhists of Ceylon were anxious to have perpetual contact with India, especially Bodh Gaya. When Samudragupta was emperor of India, king Meghavarṇa who was reigning in Ceylon sent an embassy to India. This embassy consisted of two monks, one of them being his own brother. Meghavarṇa was no other than Śrī Meghavanna of the Buddhist books.[41] The embassy was to visit the monastery said to have been erected by Aśoka near the sacred tree of

40. See also Jayaswal: *History of India*, pp. 154-159.

41. It was the late Sylvain Levi who discovered the contemporaneity of Meghavarna and Samudragupta. According to the *Mahāvamsa* translated by W. Geiger the last king mentioned is Mahasēna who is said to have reigned from 325-352. But still there is another supplementary list of kings who were immediate successors of Mahāsēna. According to this calculation king Mēghavarṇa ruled for 27 years from 352-379 A.D.

the Buddha in Bodh Gayā. But due to religious or other causes it was not well received and scantily treated. The embassy returned to Ceylon and reported to their king all that had happened in India. The king of Ceylon resolved thereupon to present the emperor of India with gems and other valuables which were in the nature of a tribute. With them an embassy was sent to Samudragupta and incidentally permission was sought to erect a monastery on the sacred spot for the use largely of Ceylonese pilgrims.[42] Samudragupta received them with respect and honoured them as they came from a distant king who acknowledged his suzerainty. The aim of Meghavarṇa to erect a magnificent building with six halls and three storeys was accepted by the Indian emperor; and it was constructed according to plan. The whole edifice was encircled by a strong wall 30 to 40 feet high. The statue of the Buddha which was cast in gold and silver was enshrined in that building, which attracted a number of monks to it. Later in the 7th century when the Chinese traveller Hieun Tsang visited this great establishment he found a thousand monks who were members of the Mahāyāna sect occupying the premises. Pilgrims from Ceylon were hospitably treated.[43]

Another fact of great importance is that when Candragupta II Vikramāditya was ruling the empire, Fa-hien, another Chinese pilgrim visited India. According to him Tāmralipti which was a busy mart in those days was not only in active communication with the colonies in Farther India but also with Ceylon. It was the Chinese pilgrim who found a merchant vessel laden with articles of merchandise ready to start for Ceylon in the port of Tāmralipti. Thus we have the testimony of a distinguished Chinese pilgrim that

42. Geiger: *Mahāvaṃsa* Intro. p. 39.
43. Smith, *Early History of India*, pp. 303-4.

there was active trade communication with Ceylon, one of the important ports in India being Tāmralipti.

Śaka Chiefs

We have already noticed that Samudragupta did not carry arms beyond Afghanistan for reasons which are well-known. But portions of the N. W. Frontier were under the possession of the Kuṣāṇa kings, who were termed Mlecchas in our literature. Notwithstanding the efforts made by the emperors of India from time to time to ward off the hordes of Mlecchas, still their incursions into India for the sake of booty and territory were incessant. The Kuṣān empire did not die out completely and their successors who were known as Śakādhipatis or simply Śaka chiefs were giving trouble now and then in those parts which for the sake of convenience we call Western India. Besides in line twenty-three of the Allahabad Pillar inscription where the achievements of Samudragupta are recorded, mention is made of Sāhānusāhi who was the lord of the Mlecchas with whom the emperor of India had undoubtedly diplomatic relations. The Daivaputra-sāhi-Sāhānusāhi was probably a scion of the Kuṣān tribe which dominated India at the time of Kaniṣka. Whether the diplomatic relation which existed between the two kings was in the nature of a permanent embassy in both the capitals we cannot say definitely at present. But we can say safely that the modern system of appointing permanent Consuls in different capitals was not in vogue then. It may be asserted without any fear of contradiction that no permanent embassy of the Daiva-putra-sāhi-Sāhānusāhi was stationed in the capital of India or vice versa. The title Daivaputra should have been assumed after Kaniṣka, who was to all intents and purposes the Deva-putra Kaniṣka.[44]

44. C. H. I., I., p. 582.

Among the foreign powers which were prominent in the time of Candragupta II may be mentioned the Śaka Muruṇḍas. The Muruṇḍas have been taken to be foreigners, Scythian in origin. We do not know, whether this interpretation of making the Muruṇḍas a foreign power is justifiable. All that we know is that we have the high authority of Sten Konow who cites Muruṇḍa to be a Śaka word and means svāmi. The Muruṇḍas seem to have been an active tribe establishing themselves in various parts of Saurāṣṭra and Central India.[45] They seem once to have had preponderating influence even in the Ganges valley, as testified to us by Ptolemy.[46] In a Khoh inscription of Central India, what is curious is that a Muruṇḍa svāminī apparently a female is mentioned as a chief. They seem to have established foreign and diplomatic relations with the Gupta empire.[47]

China

It is not abundantly clear whether the Gupta empire had any diplomatic relations with the empire of China and sent an accredited embassy or embassies to that empire. But there was constant communication between the two countries and worthy Chinese pilgrims like Fa-hien visited the Gupta empire and found that changes in religion had been effected to such an extent that Buddhism showed signs of decline.

Besides, India exported to a large extent pearls and gems, diamonds and metals of value and many products which were not then available in China. Artistically and culturally, one country was indebted to the other and the little evidence we have indicates that the Chinese empire was more indebted to the Indian artists and to Indian government to gather and take away the manuscripts which were of value

45. According to the *Vāyu Purāṇa* they were a Mleccha tribe.
46 Ind. Ant. 1884 p. 377.
47. See Ray Chaudhuri: *Pol. Hist. of Anc. India.* p. 373. 3rd Edn.

to the Buddhist faith. Luckily for us there is an account of a South Indian embassy[48] to China about 500 A.D. preserved in the Chinese account of India. It is said that in the time of Seuen-woo of the dynasty of the later Wei A.D. 500-516 an ambassador was sent from South India with the presents of some fine horses, lions, elephants and other animals, diamonds and pearls, tortoise shell, metals of high value, muslins embroidered with gold and silver and also plants of various kinds. These were given away as gifts to the Chinese emperor who kept friendly relations with Southern India.

Later though not quite relevant to the subject, which takes notice of only the Imperial Guptas, a Buddhist mission was sent from China in the year A.D. 539 by Wu-ti or Hsiao Yen, the first Liang emperor of China, who was himself an ardent Buddhist. This mission had no political object in view and was sent to Magadha to collect the original Mahāyānist texts and at the same time to fix a scholar who would be able to translate into Chinese such texts for the benefit and use of Chinese Buddhists. At that time the ruler of Magadha was Jīvita I or perhaps Kumāragupta who readily consented to fulfil the object of the mission. It would appear that this cultural mission from China spent some years in India. One Paramārtha was placed at the disposal of the mission. He accompanied it to China and got several works translated. He seems to have died in China in 569 at the ripe age of seventy.[49]

South India

The Allahabad Pillar inscription of Samudragupta mentions his capture and liberation of a number of princes who were ruling over the different parts of the East coast of

48. K. A. N. Sastri: *Foreign Notices of S. India*, p. 83. See also V. R. R. Dikshitar, *Southern India and China*, p. 10.

49. Smith: *Early History of India*, p. 331.

the Deccan 'besides all other kings of Dakṣiṇāpatha'. Among the rulers specifically mentioned are Mahendra of Kośala, Vyāghrarāja of Mahākāntāra, Mantarāja of Kerala, Mahendragiri of Piṣṭhāpura, Svāmidatta of Koṭṭūru, Damana of Eraṇḍapalla, Viṣṇugopa of Kāñcī, Nīlarāja of Avamukta, Hastivarman of Vengi, Ugrasena of Pālakka, Kubera of Devarāṣṭra, and Dhanañjaya of Kusthalapura.[50] Time was when Kerala was identified with the Chera country, Koṭṭūra with Kothur (Coimbatore district), Pālakka with Palghat, Eraṇḍapalla with Erandol (Khandesh) District (Bombay), and Devarāṣṭra with Mahārāṣṭra and it was believed that Samudragupta's invasion covered practically the whole of South India. But recent opinion is that Eraṇḍapalla may be identified with Eraṇḍapalle (Ganjam District), Devarāṣṭra with the Yellamanchi taluk (Vizagapatam District), Koṭṭūra with Kothoor (Ganjam District), Pālakka with Pakkai (Nellore District), and Kerala with the Colair lake in the Godāvari district.[51]

If these identifications are accepted it may be taken that the area covered by Samudragupta's invasions of the south was confined to the east coast, and did not extend far beyond modern Nellore. But as said earlier this is still an open question. With regard to the treatment of the conquered rulers his policy was similar to the one followed by Alexander the Great with regard to Porus. All of them were liberated and allowed to rule over their respective kingdoms. It was enough that the rulers accepted the overlordship of Samudragupta. Probably it was to show his strength to the Deccan rulers that he invaded their country.

50. Fleet: *Op. cit.* p. 7.
51. K. P. Jayaswal: *History of India*, pp. 134-35.
Jouveau Dubreuil: *Ancient History of the Deccan*, pp. 60-61.

Section III

Ethics of War

It is abundantly clear that Kāmandaka belonged to the school of Kauṭalya. Kauṭalya divides conquest into three types: (1) *Dharmavijaya* (battle according to the rules of Dharma), (2) *Lobhavijaya* (battle through covetousness), (3) *Asura Vijaya* (battle involving Adharma). There is yet another classification in Kauṭalya, viz., Dharma Yuddha and Kūṭa Yuddha. While the first is war in open, the second is war by deceit and other undesirable means.[52] Students of history in modern days view this classification as unmoral and dub unnecessarily Kauṭalya as Machiavellian in politics. Because he has recommended the second alternative, which in the circumstances might not prove altogether unrighteous, he cannot be deemed as Machiavellian in his policy.

That such warfare is not altogether unrighteous is countenanced by the author of the *Kāmandakīya Nītisāra*. What he says is 'that the slaughter of the foes by deceitful measures is not detrimental to one's righteousness. The son of Droṇa with his sharp weapon slew the troops of the Pāṇḍavas, when they were unsuspectingly locked in the arms of sleep at night'.[53] In other words this recommendation of the *Kāmandakīya* is in line with that of Kauṭalya. To characterise him also as unmoral in politics has no meaning. The foes of a king should be conquered. Kauṭalya or Kāmandaka has never said that they should be beaten by unfair means. They first recommend the three well-trīed diplomatic means of Sāma, Dāna and Bhēda. If a conquering king could not effect reconciliation, then recourse was to be had to armed conflict.[54] When once war was launched upon they recommend that it should be carried on in the open and according

52. There is a section in chapter 19 of the *Kāmandakīya*.
53. *Ibid.* 19.71.
54. *Ibid.* ch. 18.63, 19.1.

to rules laid down in the *Dharma* and *Nīti Śāstras*. But with all his vigil if a king was not able to vanquish an enemy and the enemy resorted to different kinds of warfare and hid himself in different places, perhaps not accessible to the conqueror, then a conquering monarch could defeat him by unfair methods. So long as the foe was in the right path the conquering monarch could not do anything unrighteous and anything not warranted by the śāstras. But when once he found the enemy to be stubborn exerting himself in the wrong manner, such an enemy should be paid in his own coin and must be annihilated. The rules pertaining to the nocturnal attack should be observed closely by a conquering monarch. In unfair warfare when a foe was overtaken by calamities either internally or externally, or oppressed by want of food or pestilence, or even fatigued and distressed by long-winding marches over hill and dale, even then an accomplished general who was capable of leading a big army must overtake the enemy.

The use of forest tribes in warfare is mentioned pretty often in chapter 19 of the *Kāmandakīya Nītisāra*. This is nothing new and has been recommended by Kauṭalya. In the present case, however, Samudragupta had brought under his control a huge empire. In building up this mighty empire the Gupta monarchs not only vanquished the foresters as a class but there is evidence to show that the great monarch had made use of these forest troops in several of his wars. He is alone a clever leader in war, says the *Kāmandakīya,* who places the forest troops in the front and his own troops in the rear (19.38). This is said to accomplish the object, viz., bringing the enemy under control. It is natural that in a battle there would be a number of wounded soldiers and also weak soldiers. It is said that a true leader of any army should sympathise with them, comfort the wounded and encourage the weak.

Kāmandaka like his preceptor Kauṭalya is a Dharmic statesman who advocates the principles of righteousness in war but is one who does not deprecate unrighteous and unfair war, if the object of war is not to be defeated.[55] We have to take it that in the absence of other rules of warfare these were observed and not violated. We may add that non-combatants were left unmolested and were even respected. It may perhaps be remarked that Samudragupta[56] waged an unfair war in Āryāvarta or kingdoms in North India which he is said to have exterminated. Kings like Nāgasena, Acyuta, Nandin and others were put to the sword and their countries annexed. But in the case of the Dakṣiṇāpatha kingdoms he is said to have vanquished their rulers but they were liberated and reinstated. This kind of warfare which he waged against the emperors of the south may be said to be in the nature of *dharma yuddha* or righteous warfare.

That the kings of the forest countries were made his vassals is also evident from Samudragupta's inscription. According to the Khoh grant of the Mahārāja Saṃkṣobha[57] it can be seen that during the time of his ancestor, Hastin ruling the kingdom of Dahālā, as many as eighteen forest kingdoms are mentioned (*Āṭavi rājya*). It has not yet been satisfactorily identified what these forest kingdoms were, but it is reasonable to suppose that most of them lay in the Vindhya region.

Section IV

Army Organisation

Much change had not been effected in the organisation of the army since the Mauryan days. Our deep and close

55. Fleet, *op. cit.*, 18-66.
56. *Ibid.*, No. 1. 11. & 21.
57. *Ibid.* No. 25.

study of the *Kāmandakīya Nītisāra* proves beyond doubt that the four-fold divisions of chariot, infantry, cavalry and elephant corps continued to be the chief sections of the army of the Guptas. To these, however, were added two other forces, namely, (1) the power of Council (2) and a solvent treasury. Adding these to the traditional four-fold force the army of the Guptas constituted Shaḍanga-bala, an army of six divisions.[58] The work of elephants is highly praised and their duty seems to be 'to go in front in all marches, to first enter into forests and difficult tracts, to create roads and passages where there are none, to descend into and swim across watery expanses, to break through united ranks, to bring down walls and gates, and to effect retreat and pursuit promptly.'[59] It is the Indian conception that the strength of an army consists in its elephants, for they are responsible for slaying the troops of the enemy and it is said that success in an expedition would depend upon a number of brave animals well-equipped, caparisoned with iron works and led by able warriors. It is no wonder that the *Nāradasmṛti* waxes eloquent over the extra protection to be afforded not only to these animals but also to war materials.[60]

This does not mean that the other arms of the army were not made use of. While elephants were indispensable for the army, the Gupta monarchs paid equal attention to the horses. The number of horses was much more than that of elephants and these war horses were majestic steeds, which not only frightened the enemy but finished the enemy to the quick. The strength of the army consisted in its majestic and heroic horses. In those days, in the art of

58. एतन्मौलाविषड्भेदं चतुरङ्गं बलं विदु:।
षडङ्गं मन्त्रकोशाभ्यां पदात्यश्वरथद्विपै:॥ (19. 24)

59. Ch. *ibid.* 20. Stanzas i to iv.

60. P. 170.

warfare it was customary to divide the various detachments of the troops into different *vyūhas,* where all the forces could be put in service and this would decide the issue sooner or later but usually sooner (19.44). Any new *vyūha* would constitute the infantry, cavalry, chariots and elephants but different places would be assigned to different units. One might be in the centre, the other in the flanks and a third in the *kakṣas.* But fine horses, which were always considered to be noble animals, were stationed generally in the centre and were responsible for some of the fiercest accomplishments. (20.22).

Equally important were the various uses of chariots in a war. For a *vyūha* the chariots were sometimes posted in the *kakṣas* and sometimes in different places, but the efficiency of a battle rested with those heroic leaders who led the chariots here and there with bravery and skill. In case the chariots were not available, horses were substituted and posted in their places, but when these vehicles of war were made available, the leader of the army placed them along with the elephant at the interval of five, for according to the opinion of the Kāmandaka this arrangement had been generally accepted by all masters of war.

But the foot-soldiers formed the real pivot of the army.[61] (20.10 ff). It was on their advice that the roads were cleared and the camps were made. They were to supply fodder for the animals and food for the van. Generally, young men of noble families with great courage and prowess and with powers of enduring fatigue were selected to be foot-soldiers. In a *vyūha* their functions seem to have been many and were discharged loyally and faithfully to their good general. The infantry thought that the ground advantageous

61. Kāmandakīya: *Bhuta* and *Satrubalam* 19.5 & 8.

for its movement was that which was free from thorns, plants and trees, which was levelled, and which had ways for retreat.

But more powerful was the part of the Counsel. Much of victory in a war depended on counsel and hence it is recommended that a conquering monarch should meet his advisers in secret and act according to their joint advice.

An army generally consisted of the Kṣatriyas for according to rules of polity they were born and bred to fight for the defence of the kingdom and its subjects. Among the Kṣatriyas then, the best army consisted of Maula troops, full of energy and enthusiasm and loyalty. (19.12 ff). They were considered to be the best troops because they were long-standing and would stand a protracted siege or campaign. They would bear any loss and would not mind sacrificing their lives for the sake of the country. An intelligent king should make use of the Maulas only in cases of necessity.

There were two other kinds of troops which were temporarily taken into service. These were the mercenary troops and the troops of the enemy weaned over. But these troops could not be depended upon in case a campaign was protracted. Compared to the hereditary troops they were considered inferior in mettle. But in case of emergency a king usually depended for support on the strength of the Śreni and forest tribes. These were not used for the right kind of warfare and also were sparingly used. The foresters were usually rude in their behaviour and were easily irritated, especially when they entered the territory of another. An intelligent monarch should place them in the front of the army. When these troops fought and became exhausted and even showed signs of dissatisfaction, it was for a good general to notice these signs in them and let into service other troops. Lastly were the hereditary troops which always remained faithful and loyal to their monarch. (19.11-12).

Section V

War Office

Closely connected with the organisation of the army is the war office. There is no evidence on it either epigraphical or literary except the *Kāmandakīya Nītisāra* which indicates that there was a good and efficient war office which was under the control and management of the Gupta monarchs. The existence of the war office is strongly supported by the fact that the Gupta monarchs one after another built up a great empire and consolidated it. This could not have been done without a war office always on the vigil and without the exertions of the different limbs of the army which to all intents and purposes formed a formidable host being a match for the forces of several countries, including the forest ones.

Like the war office of the Mauryas that of the Guptas functioned very efficiently. No doubt we have no Arrian or Strabo to bring their evidence and confirm our remark. Whatever this may be, it was a fact of utmost importance that there was a leader for the foot-soldiers, a leader for cavalry, a leader for chariots and a leader for elephants. Already we have seen that each limb of this huge army had its own functions, to perform some of them being most onerous. We have already remarked that the Maula or hereditary army was the best so far as their fidelity or gratefulness was concerned. It is natural that with the hired soldiers, there would be no enthusiasm of any kind. Every department of the army above mentioned should have had its own rank and file well-knit together and well established. For example, the cavalry leader made arrangements for the feeding and equipment of horses under his charge. Some of those employed in his department attended to their cleaning and bathing while others attended to their dressing, caparisoning while yet others attended to the healing of their wounds by application of medicine. There was also an establishment of grooms who attended to the proper training and the modes of attack of the enemy. In this way every one of the four departments catered to the needs of that department and was responsible for the readiness for war.[62]

There were two departments of war under the able management of the war office, which we cannot lose sight of. One was the Commissariat which contained a number of miscellaneous things, mostly civil in character but quite essential for war purposes. For instance, there were cooks of different grades, animals not engaged in war, non-combatants like the *purohita,* sometimes the harem of the king, the medical establishment, etc., which constituted this vital department and without it no war could have been carried on successfully.[63]

Another department of the army which rarely finds mention both in literature and epigraphy is the department of admiralty. The Gupta monarchs ruled over a colonial empire. However peaceful and commercial the relations between the mother country and the colonies were, this could not have been effected but for big ports and huge men-of-war actively plying and maintaining communications between these foreign countries and the mother land. We know Tāmralipti figured as an important port in the Gupta times and contained huge vessels ready to start not only for the colonies of the Gupta empire but also for China and Ceylon. We have the testimony of Fa-hien, who supports the stand we have taken. The admiralty then should have played an important part in the military history of the Gupta empire. No doubt there were merchant vessels, which if necessary were converted into vehicles of war as had been done in the previous centuries. The Navy of the Guptas were a certainty and proved efficient for the defence of the country. We have no details of the

62. Ch. 20. Stanzas 32 & 33.
63. See Ch. 16 Stanzas 20, 23, 24.

working of this department but it may be taken that the naval leader of the times should have been an expert one and a skilled person.

Section VI

The War Council

By far the most important feature in the military history of this period is the existence of an organised War Council as could be inferred from the *Kāmandakīya Nītisāra*. This work on polity emphasises the importance of this war department. The power of the Council is said to be the most potent of all powers. With his choice Councillors, the monarch should hold consultation and take their advice to be final. The part played by spies as determining the action or inaction of a king was ever there.[64] But the most powerful factor determining an expedition or march against the enemy was the taking of a determined resolution by the Cabinet which was composed of twelve members according to Manu and sixteen members according to Bṛhaspati. A wise king would act upon the resolution of this Cabinet, for such action would not entail future regret but would ensure a series of successes.

The five parts of a *mantra*[65] should be carefully studied and weighed before coming to a final decision. The means to accomplish a desired end were to be discussed pros and cons and a decision had to be taken on it. A prudent monarch would see that his interests were not to be jeopardised and those of the foe were put in test. When once an undertaking was resolved upon, a conquering king must take quick action and work upon it rapidly. The secrecy of the Council should be scrupulously observed. "Following the

64. See the whole of ch. 12.

65. सहायाः साधनोपाया विभागो देशकालयोः ।
विपत्तेश्च प्रतीकारः सिद्धिः पञ्चाङ्ग इष्यते ॥ (12—36)

footsteps of the pious an intelligent king should carry out his project in proper season. Exerting in the right way and right time he enjoys the delicious fruits of his actions".[66] Such is the importance given to a Council or the War Cabinet in books on Polity and it is not even for a rash prince or arrogant monarch to disregard the salutary nature of the counsel given to him by his choice ministers. So what the śāstras insist upon is that a certain monarch who sought his own welfare would not find a place in the lap of sloth but would find a sure place in the lap of energy and exertion.

Section VII

Some Army Officials

That the war office was presided over by the *Mahābalādhikṛta* is evident from the Gupta inscription, No. 23 relating to Majhgawām copper-plate of Mahāraja Hastin. It is a military title perhaps answering to our army general who is the chief of the whole military establishment. There is another military title no less in importance, *Mahābalādhyakṣa*[67] occurring later, meaning more or less the same but perhaps a little different from *Mahābalādhikṛta*. It is very difficult to say whether *Mahābalādhikṛta or Mahābalādhyakṣa* was the supreme Commander-in-chief of the army under the Guptas. From the term *Adhyakṣa* appended to the word *Mahābala*, it is reasonable to suppose that he was the Superintendent of the army and his chief function was to superintend and control the army and see that its efficiency was not impaired in any manner. From the term *Adhikaraṇa* found in the title *Mahābalādhikṛta*[68] the inference has to

66. सतां मार्गेण मतिमान् काले कर्म समाचरेत्।
काले समाचरन् साधु रसवत् फलमश्नुते॥ (12--54)

67. See Gupta Inscriptions No. 39.

68. See also 1.2 of the Shahpur Stone Image Inscription of Adityasena: Fleet. No. 43.

be made that he was the officer who presided over the military establishments in general. It is not known definitely which term denoted exactly the office of the Commander-in-chief of the army. It seems to us that the term *Mahābalādhikṛta* connoted this high dignitary on the military staff of the Guptas.

If this were so, then the *Mahābalādhyakṣa* was a military officer second in command to *Mahābalādhikṛta*. The *Mahābalādhyakṣa*, however, was an officer who was superior to all *balādhyakṣas*. Therefore, it stands to reason that there were *balādhyakṣas* who were the various military officials perhaps in charge of the various units composing an army. The *balādhyakṣas* may possibly be compared to captains in charge of the divisions of the army. They were to send reports now and then to the *Mahābalādhyakṣa*, who was undoubtedly superior to them. Only in consultation with him they could effect any transformation in the unit.

The qualifications which were expected of a true general are furnished to us by the *Kāmandakīya Nītisāra* (*senāpati*). According to this high authority he alone could be the leader of an army 'who could know the mind of the army, who is of noble family, a native of the country, and who would act in conformity with the science of *Daṇḍanīti*, one possessed of the qualities of energy, heroism, forgiveness, patience, amiableness and richness, one endowed with power and manliness and who is depended upon by his followers for their support'. Besides it is said that he should have a number of friends, relations and cognates. He should be generous, large-hearted and popular. He should also be one who had not incurred anybody's ill-will and whose character was above suspicion. He should also be a profound scholar, acting in conformity with the precepts of the Council.

Further Kāmandaka adds that this man should be healthy, sound, courageous, capable of enduring and adapting himself to all seasons and climes, self-confident, expert in the knowledge of animals like horses and elephants, indefatigable in fighting, skilful, agile, one who could pitch upon the right place for camp and battlefield, who will be secretive and watchful, and fully acquainted with the movements of spies and scouts, who is pious, who is a clever administrator, who could read other's mind correctly, who knows all countries and their languages, who could decipher their writings and is possessed of excellent memory, who could easily lead nocturnal attacks, who could neither be frightened nor fatigued, who could withstand the alarm of an enemy, who could create dissension in the army of the enemy, who could undertake difficult operations, who could pacify his own troops in case there was alarm, who could study the disguises and pretences of spies and ambassadors, who could put forth his utmost exertion, who would not care for the consequences of his action, but would always care for the moral and material welfare of his kingdom, who could ford rivers and riverines, cross hills and dales and clear forests, and who possesses these and other qualifications could alone be a general and a true leader of the army.[69]

Still later in the Gupta inscriptions we meet with the title *Mahāsenāpati* with the title Mahārāja in inscription 58. The inscription is about the leader of the Yaudheya tribe. Already this military title has been noticed as equal in rank to *Mahārāja* and *Mahasāmanta.* This perhaps denotes one and the same person. The royal king acted also as Mahāsenāpati or the leader of forces in war. This may point out that the old conception of *Mahāsenāpati* continued with certain tribal chieftains. This need not mean that this term was current in the Gupta times and it denoted specifically a certain personage who was the commander-general of an army. It is better we leave it alone for it does not occur in the

69. Ch. 19. 27-43.

Gupta Inscriptions as such. We are therefore disposed to take *Mahābalādhikṛta* as the chief commander of forces, the military general who knew the pros and cons of not only his own army but also of that of his foes.

We meet with another military title given to a certain officer during the time of the Guptas. It is *Mahāsarvadaṇḍanāyaka.* We also meet with officers like *Sarvadaṇḍanāyakas* and therefore it can be easily imagined that the *Mahāsarvadaṇḍanāyaka* was the supreme commander and controller of *Sarvadaṇḍanāyakas,* who were only next in rank to him. The question that now presents itself is whether this category of officers belonged to the military staff under the Guptas. Though Dr. Fleet would make us believe that these are military titles, still it is an open question. The impression is that the *Daṇḍanīti* being understood as the science of punishment these officers were the Police officials who were the guardians of the country's law and order to a great extent. Therefore it may mean that these Police officials co-operated with the military department and helped the department by arresting this person or that for one offence or another. It is therefore legitimate to take that this class of *Sarvadaṇḍanāyakas* did the service of Police officials as in the present government of any country, namely, bringing the offenders to book. If they were not able to cope with the situation, then the military was called to aid.[70]

Another point to be considered in this connection relates to the duty of the *Mahādaṇḍanāyaka.* He was to be present in almost all the land transactions either when the lands were sold or given away as gifts.[71] Though there were other officers who were connected with this grant of land it had to

70. One of the seals in the excavations at Basarh terms the chief of police as Daṇḍapāsa. A.S.R., 1903-04, p. 108.

71. *Ep. Ind.* XV. C. P. See Gupta Inscriptions, p. 169 where we meet with the expression Cata-Bhata. It means simply Policemen and soldiers who were present in the land transactions.

get the approval and approbation of an officer like the Daṇḍanāyaka and this is evident from the transactions as seen in inscriptions of the Gupta times. We must therefore reckon with the civil duties assigned to functionaries like the *Sarvadaṇḍanāyaka* in the Gupta inscriptions. This is another evidence clinching the issue that after all these officers of the state would not be military officers in the real sense of the term though it is not surprising to a student of Indian history that the military officials had also similar duties to perform as is evident from the records of the East India Company in the British period of Indian history.[72]

This term may also be interpreted as connoting judicial staff. It has been suggested that *Mahādaṇḍanāyaka* may convey the meaning of a magistrate. This can only be a suggestion for it cannot be proved. But it has been pointed out that this term may connote a military title according to a certain inscriptional evidence, where *Daṇḍanāyaka* stands for *Camūpa, Camu* being an army and *Camūpa* being leader of an army. One is doubtful whether this application of the extended meaning of *Daṇḍanāyaka* being *Camūpa* can be applied in the case of the Gupta inscriptions. This is further supported by the Allahabad pillar inscription where the writer of the inscription, Hariṣena is said to be a *Mahādaṇḍanāyaka* and the son of Mahādaṇḍanāyaka Dhruvabhūti.[73] On page 16 of Fleet: *Gupta Inscriptions* we find 'the matter has been effected by the *Mahādaṇḍanāyaka*'. From this we have to infer that the term *Mahādaṇḍanāyaka* would not be a military title in the Gupta epoch as has been understood by some scholars.

In some inscriptions of the Guptas we find an interesting expression '*Sandhivigrahika*'. Synonyms of this title are found in many inscriptions.[74]

72. M. Rutnaswami: Some Influences that made the British Administration, pp. 181-182.
73. Fleet: *Gupta Inscriptions*, p. 16.
74. See *IA*. Vol. VII. p. 70.

However in the *Kāmandakīya nītisāra* the term *Nāyaka* occurs in the sense of a technical military title. This shows that the *Nāyaka* who was a military official in the olden days, especially during the time of the *Arthaśāstra* of Kauṭalya and the Epic *Mahābhārata* continued to do his duties even in the Gupta times. Kāmandaka makes mention of the *Senāpati* and differentiates him from the *Nāyaka*. From the text one has to gather that the *Nāyaka* had special duties to perform. It is said that a *Nāyaka* leads an army when it is on the march. And when he leads he should see that skilled men adept in warfare accompany him through thick and thin. These followers are known by the name *Pravīra puruṣa*. There is no doubt that this *Nāyaka* is an inferior official in rank to the *Senāpati*. Five kinds of military marches are mentioned and they are, (1) *Vigṛhya* (2) *Sandhāya* (3) *Sambhūya* (4) *Prasangata* (5) *Upekṣa* (11-2). In all these marches the *Nāyaka* took a leading part and looked to the comforts of his followers by providing them with the necessary food and other articles and ridding them of all the *vyasanas* that befell them on the march. He seems to have been also responsible for his formation of *Vyūha* in a march.[75]

There was a grade higher than that of *Sandhivigrahika* which is evident from the expression *Mahāsandhivigrahika*, occurring in lines 29 and 30 of the Khoh grant of Mahārāja Hastin.[76] This term means literally an officer in charge of peace and war and *Mahāsandhivigrahika* may be the chief officer for peace and war. Among other titles conferred on Hariṣena, the author of the Allahabad pillar inscription of Samudragupta, occurs *Sandhivigrahika*.[77] He is also, as we have already seen, a *Mahādaṇḍanāyaka*. He could not have therefore been a regular military officer, but he enjoyed the

75. 19 Chapter. 45-53.
76. Fleet: *Op. cit.* No. 22.
77. *Ibid.*, p. 16.

status of a high military official, for he was such an adept in counsel, that he would never be deflected from his just duty and would always preach the path of virtue to his monarch. There were a number of *sandhivigrahikas* who were prominent in times of wars. It appears that they advised the *Mahāsandhivigrahika* individually and jointly and the *Mahāsandhivigrahika* decided either to continue the war or to effect a treaty. Thus on his shoulders fell the responsible duty of continuing an armed contest or making terms acceptable to both. Anyway he was a prominent military official though he was not war-minded. His counsel was always salutary and wholesome. Undoubtedly the monarch benefited much by his considered advice.

We have to reckon with the other military officials of the Gupta period. One officer went by the name of *Raṇa-bhāṇḍāraka.*[78] Any army, in fact any department must be successful only if it has large funds. In Hindu India, we know even in Mauryan times there was a separate Finance Minister for war purposes. It was much more true of the Gupta times when a huge empire was made by sheer conquest. Rightly the *Kāmandakīya* speaks of an army as *ṣaḍaṅga-balam* which included the indispensable department of Finance. It has been definitely advised that only when the Treasury was solvent, a king could think of conquering an enemy or enemies, for mere physical strength would not convey the victory but it is always a solvent treasury that is to a large extent responsible for securing success in a battle. So a wise king,—the Guptas are no exceptions—would study his finances before he would embark on a military expedition. The official who was in charge of the War Finances was called *Raṇa-bhāṇḍāraka* and it was he who was responsible for the satisfaction or otherwise of the whole military establishment. Among the excavations at Basarh there is an

78. *Excavations at Basarh,* No. 13, pp. 108 Arch. Report 1903-4.

interesting seal which reads as follows: '*Srīraṇa bhāṇḍāgāra adhi karaṇasya.*'[79] In other words he was the key so to say to the whole department, for on treasury and treasury alone the soldiers and army officers depended.

Generally a victory was celebrated by erecting a column on the battlefield (*Raṇa stambha*). The Mandasor pillar which contains the inscription of Yaśodharman may be cited as an actual instance of the planting of columns of victory in war. So the practice of erecting war memorials is not peculiar to the present day, but was known in the past as testified to us by inscriptions.[80]

We meet again with another officer of war, perhaps a commandant of elephants entitled *Pīlupati.* This occurs in the Gunaighar inscription of Vainya Gupta.[81] What is still more interesting is that mention is made of *Mahāpīlupati* who was evidently in charge of *Pīlupatis.* It may be taken that he was the chief officer of the elephantry and the responsibility pertaining to the elephant force of the kingdom lay with him. Then the spurious Nālanda copper-plate of Samudragupta makes mention of this officer, *Mahāpīlupati.* This indicates beyond doubt that every limb of the army had its chief commandant and other officials, who helped their chief.

That there were similar commandants for the other arms of the army, viz., infantry and cavalry who were in charge of their establishments and looked to the welfare of both men and animals in their custody is evident from the term *Baṭa aśvapati.* This is a compound and can be split up into three words, *baṭa, aśva, pati. Baṭa* may mean the Infantry soldiers, who made up the rank and file of the army and whose services were of different kinds to the army. They were indeed innumerable. From the term *aśva* we

79. Excavations at Basarh. *Op. cit.*
80. Fleet: *Op. cit.* p. 145.
81. See D. C. Sircar: *Select Inscriptions,* Vol. I. p. 333 and 264n.

may safely infer that the cavalry force was meant and that it was active not only in the actual operations but in theatres of war as well. What therefore transpires is that there were separate commandants for both the infantry and cavalry. We may however add that the part played by chariots was more or less declining and they were falling into disuse. For in the period of Harṣa the use of war-chariots was completely extinct generally in wars. At least we have no inscriptional evidence relating to the Gupta period, especially the Imperial Guptas to show that the chariots were much pressed into service and were freely used in wars. The *Kāmandakīya* is the sole authority to say that chariots were also used in the wars. Whether this is true of the Imperial Guptas, we cannot say definitely, but we have accepted that the *Kāmandakīya* belonged to the period of Candragupta II Vikramāditya.

Section VIII

Conclusion

We have rapidly surveyed the position of the army and the army officials in the Gupta period. General conscription was not made in any war waged by any monarch. The fighting caste, viz., the Kṣatriyas formed the rank and file of the army, though the army officers were sometimes drawn from the other castes also. An emperor might advance or add country after country and be even the master of the colonial empire as the Imperial Guptas undoubtedly were. But still they were not militarists in the literal sense of the term. In other words though they were good and tried soldiers and made the foresters, the forest chiefs and the border monarchs obey them, still they were *Kavirājas*.[82] They were anxious for permanent peace and for the develop-

82. See in this connection the article by Dr. V. Raghavan on the Allahabad Pillar Inscription. verses 3 & 8 in *J.O.R.* Madras, March 1947, Vol. XVI, pt. iii: Also Dr. Chhabra's article in the *Indian Culture*, Vol. XIV, pp. 141-150.

ment of literature and religion for which their patronage was something extraordinary. It must be said to the credit of Samudragupta that his vast achievement in making a colossal empire was of no mean order: nor were the achievements of Candragupta II who added considerably to the empire and who perfectly carried out the work of consolidation a symbol of success. This conquest of the Guptas might in itself be termed *Digvijaya* in the fashion of the traditional monarchs of old, and Samudragupta may be specially mentioned as hugging his empire with his two hands. He was further so proud of it that he performed the *Aśvamedha* sacrifice which only an emperor of his standing and status could perform. This sacrifice was a symbol of his unparalleled victory achieved in so short a time. After him we find rarely kings, performing this sacrifice. For it should be done by one who is the emperor of All-India, not to say of Greater India as well.

CHAPTER VI

PROVINCIAL GOVERNMENT

Section I

Administrative Divisions

It has been shown earlier that the empire of the Guptas was one of the largest in the history of ancient India. But the extent of the Empire varied from reign to reign of the Gupta kings. Under Candragupta I the empire extended over Magadha, Allahabad and Oudh. The importance of his reign lies in the fact that it was then that the independent history of the Gupta kingdom commenced. Under Samudragupta the boundaries of the empire were extended on all sides, and by the closing years of his reign it covered the region from the Himālayas to the Vindhyas and the River Tapti and from the mouth of the River Ganges to the River Cambal. Besides, his overlordship was acknowledged by the rulers of Dakṣiṇāpatha, Samataṭa, Davāka, Kāmarūpa and Nēpāla as also by the republican tribes of the Punjab like the Mālavas, Ārjunāyanas, the Yaudheyas, Mādrakas and the Ābhiras. Distant rulers like the Shāhānuṣhāhi and the king of Ceylon were his allies. During the days of Candragupta II the empire was rounded off on the western side by the conquest of Western Mālva and Gujarat, and by the rule of the Western Kṣatrapas of Kathiawar being brought to an end. Probably on account of the exigencies of the administration, Ujjain was then made the second Capital of the empire.

The vast empire was intact even under Skandagupta one of the great galaxy of Gupta sovereigns and covered practically the whole of North India from Kathiawar to Bengal. But the death of Skandagupta was followed by a period of weak rule, and foreign invasions and the consequent prevalence of anarchy. The later Gupta kings therefore lost control over the distant provinces of Skandagupta's empire such as Gujarat, Mālva and Surāṣṭra. In the early decades of the sixth century Yaśodharman of Mālva carved out for himself an independent kingdom in Central India, and extended his empire in the east as far as the Lauhitya. And with the rise of the Maukharis to power in the middle of the century, the days of the Imperial Guptas became numbered. As our review of the Gupta polity is confined to the period of the Imperial Guptas, we shall now proceed to describe the provincial administration as it obtained in this period.

For purposes of efficient administration the Gupta empire was divided into a number of administrative units which themselves, in their turn, were sub-divided into small ones, which may, for purposes of convenience, be called provinces, districts and villages. With regard to the formation of such territorial divisions for administrative purposes, it must be pointed out, it was not based on any scientific principle such as linguistic affinity or geographical contiguity, but largely on historical and political accidents. Hence as regards their size, resources and importance there appear to have existed much variation from province to province and from time to time. Further in the formation of provinces no novel or original procedure was adopted. The older geographical and political units were accepted as such by the Guptas and allowed to continue in the frame-work of the territorial divisions under them. Thus the territorial divisions that obtained under the Mauryas and the Kuṣāns were also current in the Gupta empire. Further no attempt appears to have been made by the Gupta emperors to give even a uniform name to the different administrative units in the empire. Hence we find in existence during the period different types of divisions with different names in the several parts of the empire. Anyway the following details about them may be noted.

Dēśa. In the Gupta empire the largest administrative unit appears to have been the *dēśa.* The Sāñchi Stone inscription of Candragupta II of A.D. 412-13 makes reference to the town of Nasṭi in the Sukuli *dēśa.*[1] Again the Kapāleśvar grant of Mahābhava Gupta refers to the Yodha *viṣaya* as existing in the Kośala*dēśa.*[2] We get reference again to a Dabhāla *rājya.*[3] It is difficult to say anything definite about the size and importance of the *dēśa* during the period. The term which is a technical one ordinarily means a region, country, province etc., the exact meaning and bearing of which it is not possible to determine. But since according to the inscription referred to above, the Yodha *viṣaya* was part of the Kosala *dēśa,* the latter, must have been a larger territorial division bearing the relationship of a province to a district, particularly in the central portions of the Gupta empire. This can be seen from the provenance of epigraphs mentioning such a territorial division in that area.

It may be of some interest to note here that the names of these divisions continued even in later times, but they appear to have come to be used as synonymous terms. For instance in the Terdāl inscription of Cālukya Vikramāditya VI of A.D. 1123-24 the terms *dēśa* and *viṣaya* are applied to the division of India that is best known as Bharata Khaṇḍa or Bharata Kṣetra and also to the Kūṇḍi District in the Karnāṭaka country.[4] In the western parts of the empire the

1. Fleet, *Gupta Inscriptions,* No. 3, p. 32.
2. *Ind. Ant.* V., p. 55.
3. Fleet, *op. cit.,* pp. 113, 114.
4. *Ind. Ant.,* XIV. p. 16; Fleet, *Gupta Inscriptions,* p. 33' n.

The text of the Terdāl Inscription as translated reads "there where Bharata Khaṇḍa is situated, appears full of charms the great country of Kuntala; and in that land shines the great District called Kūṇḍi and in the heart of this District the Teridāla Twelve shines...... *Ind. Ant.,* XIV. p. 21.

province appears to have been known also as *āvanī*. The Surāṣṭra country is referred to as Surāṣṭra *āvanī* in an epigraph.[5]

Bhukti. An equally important but probably smaller division than the *dēśa* was the *bhukti* which obtained in some parts of the empire. In the Dāmodarpūr copper-plate grants of Kumāragupta, ascribed to the fifth century A.D., reference is made to the *Uparika* in the province (*bhukti*) of Puṇḍravardhana who appointed Kumārāmātya Vetravarman to the district (*viṣaya*) of Koṭivarṣa[6] situated in the modern Dinājpur District. Another inscription of the same king of A.D. 448-49 mentions again that Koṭivarṣa *viṣaya* formed part of the Puṇḍravardhana *bhukti*.[7] This division continued as an administrative unit even during the days of Harṣa which is indicated by the Madhuban plates of the Emperor which refer to the Somakuṇḍaka *grāma* which belonged to the Kuṇḍadhānī *viṣaya* in the Srāvastī *bhukti*.[8] It is difficult to say anything definite about the size and importance of the above territorial division. It cannot however be doubted that it was bigger than a *viṣaya* which was in all likelihood the ancient proto-type of a modern District.

Viṣaya. Another territorial division which was probably the most popular and stable administrative unit was the *viṣaya*, of which mention is made in many inscriptions of the Gupta period. Thus Koṭivarṣa was a *viṣaya* in the Puṇḍravardhana *bhukti*.[9] The importance of a *visaya* as an admi-

5. Fleet; *op. cit.*, p. 59.
6. *Ep. Ind.*, XV, No. 7, p. 130.
7. *Ibid*, p. 133: see for another reference *Ibid*, pp. 138-9
8. *Ibid.*, VII. no. 22. p. 159.
9. *Ibid.*, XV. pp. 130, 133, 138-39.

पुण्ड्रवर्धन भुक्तावुपरिक महाराज जय
दत्तस्य भोगेनानु (वहमा)
नक (को) टि (वर्ष) विषये च तन्नियुक्तके . . .
कोटिवर्षं समासाद्य नगरं देवपूजितं

nistrative unit was due evidently to its long historical antecedents. For instance Koṭivarṣa which was both a town and a *viṣaya* was an old unit of administration mentioned even in the *Vāyu Purāṇa*.[10] Though territorially it was a part of the *bhukti*, its exact size is not clearly known. From the Mandasor Stone Inscription of Kumāragupta and Bandhuvarman of A.D. 473-74, we learn that the whole Lāṭa country was called a *viṣaya* in which was situated the important town of Daśapura.[11] According to the Indor copper-plate grant of Skandagupta dated 465-66, the Antarvedi country lying between the Ganges and the Jamna was a *viṣaya* which was ruled by a *viṣayapati*.[12] Thus it appears to have covered a fair extent of territory. From the provenance of inscriptions referring to the *viṣaya* in different parts of the Empire it appears to have been in existence in all parts of it. In the latter half of the fifth century on account of the invasions of the Hūṇas and the rebellions of half-subdued tribes like the Puṣyamitras, it appears that the *viṣaya* was reorganised as an administrative unit of greater importance and probably of extent also. It is perhaps on account of that reason that the Deo-Baranark inscription of Jīvitagupta II refers to a village called Vāruṇikā as forming part of the Nagara *bhukti* which belonged to the Vālavi *viṣaya*.[13]

Khaṇḍa. Another sub-division of the *dēśa* was probably the *Khaṇḍa*.[14] For instance the unpublished grant of king Mahābhavagupta mentions a territorial division called the Tulumba Khaṇḍa as a part of the Kośala *dēśa*.[15] Another

10. Ch. XXIII, v. 209.
11. Fleet. *Op. cit.* p. 81.
12. *Ibid.*, p. 69.
13. *Ibid.*, p. 218.
14. *Ibid.*, p. 33 n. Fleet says that this is perhaps synonymous with Viṣaya.
15. *Ibid.*, 33 *n*.

territorial division mentioned in a few epigraphs of the period is the *vīthi*. In the Mallasarul copper-plate of Vijayasena there is reference to the Vākāṭaka *vīthi* representing a part of Vardhamāna *bhukti,* and extending over a strip of the country along the north bank of the River Damodar.[16] Another grant of the Gupta period from the Monghyr district of Bihar mentions a *Nanda vīthi* on the banks of the River Ganges.[17] This division appears to have continued even in later times. In ancient times the *vīthi* appears to have denoted a tract of land that was immediately bordering on a river.

Pura. The *Pura* was an urban administrative unit in some parts of the Empire. It was a town or even a large city. The Mandasor Inscription of Kumāragupta and Bandhuvarman of A.D. 473-74 mentions the town of Daśapura, now known as Daśor.[18] A city called Sarabhapura is said to have been the place wherefrom the Arang plates of Raja Mahājayarāja were issued.[19] It appears that the town was also called a *dranga,* the officer in charge of the administration of which was called *Drāngika.*[20] For instance, the Maliya copper-plate inscription (Fleet. *op. cit.*, p. 169) of the Mahārāja Dharasena II of A.D. 571-72 refers to the *Drāngika.*

Grāma. As in all periods of Indian history, in the Gupta period also, the *grāma* was the smallest administrative unit, and for which we get a good many references in the epigraphs of the period.[21] Probably parts of the village were known as *grāmaka.*[22] A territorial division and an administrative unit

16. *Ep. Ind.*, XXIII, p. 158.
17. *Ibid.*, p. 55.
18. Fleet, *op. cit.*, p. 81.
19. *Ibid.*, p. 192; see also *ibid.*, p. 70 for the mention of the town of Indrapura.
20. Dr. Buhler thinks that the term *dranga* means *township* and *drāngika* means 'head of a town'. (See *Ind. Ant.*, Vol. IV, p. 105, line 15, and p. 175. 1. 6. See also Fleet, *op. cit.*, p. 169 *n.*)
21 See Fleet, *op. cit.*, p. 50, 54, 67, 256, etc.
22. *Ibid.* p. 103.

called the *paṭṭa* of which the village formed a part is mentioned in some epigraphs. The Khoh copper-plate of Mahārāja Hastin dated 482-3 which refers to the *agrahāra* of Korparika in the northern *paṭṭa* is an instance in point.[23]

Another territorial division probably of the size of a *paṭṭa* was the *peṭha* to which we get a few references in the Gupta inscriptions. The Khoh plates of Mahārāja Samkṣobha dated A.D. 528-29 point to "half of the village of Opāṇi in the Manināga *peṭha*[24] while the Khoh copper-plate grant of Mahārāja Sarvanātha dated 533-34 which was issued from Ucchakalpa refers to the villages of Vyāghrā *Pallikā* and Kācara *pallikā* in the same *peṭha*.[25] It may be noted in passing that the term *peṭha* is represented in the modern term *Pēṭa* in Marāthi. Probably in later inscriptions it was called the *veṇṭheya*.[26] Anyway the fact that the *paṭṭa* was territorially smaller than the *viṣaya* is well borne out by the Valabhi grant of Dhruvasena III dated 653-54, which mentions the village of Paṭṭapadraka in the southern division (*dakṣiṇa paṭṭa*) of the district (*viṣaya*) of Sivabhāgapura (8).[27] Evidently on account of the comparatively large size of the *viṣaya* it was divided into two parts in the course of the reign of Skandagupta, when the provincial administration appears to have undergone some reorganization.[28]

23. *Ibid.*, p. 104.
24. *Ibid.* p. 116.
25. *Ibid.* p. 138.
26. See *Ibid.*, p. 116 and n., *J.B.B.R.A.S.*, XIII, 347; *Ind. Ant.*, Vol. IV, p. 332.
27. *E.I.*, No. I, p. 92.
28. His trouble with the Pusyamitras in spite of the reading Udyamitras by Vivekar in the *Annals of the Bhandarkar Institute*, his conquest of the Hūṇas and the *Mlecchas*, his military engagements with the Vākāṭakas and the troubles at home all led to the weakening of the Gupta empire in the days of Skandagupta. But the Kauham Inscription refers to Sāntavarsa of his regime. Nevertheless Skandagupta seems to have taken special pains to appoint capable viceroys and governors like Parṇadatta and Cakrapālita over the Saurāstra. Sarvanaga over the Doab and Bhimavarman over the Kosam region. His records seem to show that he was the overlord of the empire at least from Kathiawar to Bengal. (See also R. N. Dandekar, *History of the Guptas*, p. 114).

In the Vākāṭaka territories, however, these smaller units of administration appear to have been known by some other names. Below the *viṣaya* and analogous to the *paṭṭa* was the *bhāga* in those territories. The Siwaṇi copper-plate grant of the Vākāṭaka Mahārāja Pravarasena II states that in the Beṇṇākārpara *bhāga* were situated the villages of Brahmā *pūraka*, Kiṇihī *kheṭaka*, Pavarajjā *vāṭaka* and Kollā *pūraka*.[29] It is evident that the terms *pūraka, kheṭaka* and *vāṭaka* were the names of different grades of villages. In the western parts of the empire the smallest units of the administration were known as the *pallika*[30] the exact significance or connotation of which is not clearly known. It is difficult to say what territorial unit the term *bhoga* indicated. The Bhūmara Stone Pillar Inscription of the Mahārājās Hastin and Sarvanātha mentions the village of Āmbloda in the *bhoga* of Mahārāja Sarvanātha. By itself the term *bhōga* means "enjoyment, possession and government", and such an interpretation quite fits in here. But Fleet would interpret it as a technical territorial term "probably having much the same purport as a *bhukti*".[31] If that interpretation is accepted the term *bhogika*[32] would mean an officer in charge of a *bhoga* and the term *bhoga-bhāga* would mean a tax collected by the *bhogika*.[33]

Maṇḍala. In some parts of the empire some territorial divisions bore names not current in the other parts of the empire. In the eastern and western parts of it the largest territorial unit of administration was the *maṇḍala.* The Faridpur grant of king Dharmāditya of A.D. 531

29. Fleet, *op. cit.*, p. 248.

30. *Ibid.*, p. 138.

31. *Ibid.* p. 112 and n.

32. Fleet remarks that it is a technical official title possibly connected with the territorial terms *bhoga* and *bhukti*. Examining 1. 8 of the Kāvi grant of Jaya Bhata II it is assumed that the *Bhogikas* came in rank below the *Sāmantās* and above the *viṣayapatis*. (See also *Ind. Ant.*, V. p. 114.).

33. Fleet, *op. cit.*, p. 189, etc.

mentions the Vāraka *maṇḍala* in which were a number of districts.[34] But it is difficult to say as to how many districts made a *maṇḍala*. If not larger at least equivalent in size to the *maṇḍala* was the *rāṣṭra*, the existence of which territorial and administrative division in the western and eastern parts of the Gupta Empire is indicated by the provenance of inscriptions in those regions referring to them. The Surāṣṭra country is mentioned by the Junāgadh Rock Inscription of Skandagupta,[35] while the *Pūrvarāṣṭra* country is mentioned in the Ārang Copper-plate grant of Rāja Mahājayarāja.[36] The exact relationship that existed between a *maṇḍala* and a *rāṣṭra* is not clearly known. From the Junagadh inscription[37] which mentions *rāṣṭra* as a territorial division, it appears that it was an administrative unit of some importance in the early centuries of the Christian era. Probably in course of time it lost its significance as an administrative unit, but continued to be used in a loose way to denote a territorial division. In fact from the administrative point of view, the *maṇḍala* more than the *rāṣṭra* appears to have been recognised as a unit.

As in other parts of the empire here also the province or *maṇḍāla* was divided into a number of *viṣayas* or districts, each of which was in its turn divided into a number of villages or *grāmas*. But a Valabhi grant of Dharasena IV dated *Samvat* 330 (A.D. 650) mentions the *viṣaya, bhūmi* and *grāma* in a descending scale as the units of administration in the western parts of the empire.[38] Probably a group of

34. *Ind. Ant.* XXXIX, pp. 195, 197; See also p. 200.
35. Fleet, *op. cit.*, No. 14.
36. *Ibid.*, p. 193.
37. *E.I.* Vol. VIII. p. 43 l. 8.
38. *Ind. Ant.*, VII. p. 79.

शिवभागपुरविषये

घृतालय भूमी

पञ्चुल्लपल्लिकग्राम : ?

villages constituted a *bhūmi*. Evidently it was analogous to the *nāḍu* of the South Indian inscriptions which was an administrative unit which lay between the district (*Kōṭṭam*) and the village (*ūr*). Probably in this part of the country the *viṣaya* was also at times called the *bhukti*. This is suggested by the fact that the Nogawa plates of Dhruvasena II of A.D. 639-40 mention the Mālavaka *bhukti* which was also known as the Malavaka *Viṣaya*.[39]

Sthali. The administrative unit next to the *viṣaya* in the descending scale was the *sthali*, which term occurs in a number of inscriptions found in the western parts of the Gupta Empire. For instance, it finds mention in the Palitāna plates of Dhruvasena II of A.D. 571, as also in the Jhar grant of Dharasena II the latter of which refers to the village of *Vaṭagrāma* as existing in the Dipaṇaka *Peṭha* and the Bhilva Khāṭa *sthali*.[40] The word *sthali* has probably some phonetic relation with the word *sthala* (place), but its significance as a territorial or administrative unit cannot be properly made out. But one thing is evident from the inscription referred to above, namely, it was the territorial division which was larger than the *peṭha* and the *grāma*. Hence it is that in some inscriptions villages are said to have been situated in some *sthala*.[41]

Pathaka. Another important administrative division in the western parts of the Empire was the *Pathaka*. The grant of Dhruvasena II mentions that the Vasanta *grāma* was situated in the Kātapaka *pathaka* which latter formed part of the Surāṣtra country.[42] From the above inscription we are led to think that the *pathaka* was an administrative unit smaller than the *viṣaya*. Probably it was akin to the

39. See *E.I.*, VIII, 188 and 189.
40. *Ind. Ant.*, XV. p. 187.
41. *Ind. Ant.*, VI, p. 12.
42. *Ibid.*, p. 15.

paṭṭa, paṭi, paṭṭi and *paṭṭika* of the inscriptions, which appear to have been the same as a *peṭha*. The word *peṭha* means a market town, a place of sale or a long street of shops in a town according to Kittel.[43] If that be so, and the identification of the term *paṭhaka* with the term of *peṭha* is accepted, the former would also mean a market town. But it is rather strange that a village should be said to be a part of such a market town. Probably the market town was the centre or the nucleus of a group of adjoining village for purposes of the administration of local affairs. But one thing is clear. The *peṭha* whatever might have been its exact position as an administrative unit, territorially was smaller than the *sthali* and *viṣaya*.

Some other territorial divisions referred to in the inscriptions of the western parts of the Gupta empire are the *praveśa, prāpa, āhāra* and *grāma*.[44] The last one can easily be made out; it was the village, the smallest administrative unit. The *āhāra* was probably a bigger administrative unit. We do not know if the *āhāra* had anything to do with the *agrahāra*. If there was any close relationship between the two it is possible that the *āhāra* like the *agrahāra* was one for the rise of which the reason was partly religious, for the formation and grant of an *agrahāra* was considered to be an act of religious duty or charity. *Praveśa* and *prāpa* were likewise small territorial divisions, the exact significance of which however we are not able to make out at present. In fact, references to the last two are very few and far between. In a group of about eighty-five inscriptions belonging to the Valabhi rulers it is only in two that we find reference to the territorial divisions, *praveśa,* and *prāpa*.[45]

43. *Kannada Dictionary,* p. 1015. See also Fleet, *op. cit.,* p. 104 *n.*
44. See *E.I.,* XVII, pp. 106-07.
45. Dr. S. V. Suktankar remarks: "Hultzsch appears to me to be undoubtedly on the right track. He looks upon *Prāpiya* as a derivative of *Prāpa* which he takes to be a word denoting a territorial division smaller than an *āhāra*. Similarly the analogous term *Pravesya* should also be looked upon as a taddhita of *Prāvēsa*". (*Ibid.,* p. 106).

Section II

Provincial Organisations

The provincial organisation under the Guptas appears to have been of two kinds. One was the organisation of the administration of the territories which accepted the overlordship of the Guptas but which were not administered directly by the officers appointed by the Gupta kings for the purpose; the other was the organisation of the administration of the provinces which were directly under the control of the Gupta kings. With regard to the former type of provinces, the control exercised over them by the imperial government was only indirect and nominal. Such feudatories were those that were originally independent but, were, after having been defeated, permitted to rule over their respective territories on their accepting the overlordship of the imperial sovereign. But the autonomy enjoyed by a feudatory state appears to have varied with its size, geographical position and the financial resources. Thus we see that there were such feudatory states as those of the Parivrājakas,[46] the Ucchakalpas[47] and the kings of Mandasor[48] who, on account of their large size and great resources enjoyed autonomy within their respective territories to such a large extent that they enjoyed the right of making land grants without any reference to the imperial government. While the Parivrājakas and Varmans make passing reference to the imperial government in their grants, the Ucchakalpas do not do even that.[49] The local kingdom was known as *dēśa*.[50]

46. Fleet, Gupta Ins. Nos. 21-25.

47. *Ibid.*, Nos. 26-31.

48. *Ibid.*, Nos. 33-35.

49. The Bhūmra Pillar Inscription of the Mahārājas Hastin and Sarvanātha (No. 24) points out that the Parivrājaka Mahārājas and the Mahārājas of Uchchakalpa were contemporaries.

50. *Mandasor Inscription*, No. 35.

Some of these feudatory chieftains had sub-feudatories under them. Thus king Suraśmicandra who was a feudatory of Budhagupta had a subordinate in the person of king Mātṛ Viṣṇu of Erān.[51] Likewise the Parivrājakas had also their feudatories. At the same time there were also feudatory vassals, who probably on account of the nearness of their territories to the Imperial Capital and the limited resources that they had, were not allowed to enjoy any great internal autonomy. They did not enjoy the right to dispose of the revenues of their respective territories in any manner they pleased. We may refer to king Rudradatta[52] who was a feudatory of Vainyagupta who had to get the imperial sanction for making a grant of a portion of his revenues for some purpose. The feudal vassals of the Gupta Emperors were usually known as *nṛpa, nṛpati, pārthiva, mahārāja,*[53] etc. Probably if they were big and important they were known as *mahāsāmantas.*[54]

It is difficult to describe the exact relationship that existed between the imperial government and the feudal vassals. But it is possible that as a general rule they were required to pay regular tribute and pay visits to the imperial court to pay their homage during specified periods. They were expected to offer their daughters in marriage to the emperor. The foreign minister of the emperor, the *mahāsandhivigrahika*[55] and his staff appear to have exercised rigid control over the policy and activities of the feudatory princes. We do not know for certain if the feudal vassals kept their representatives at the imperial court on a permanent basis to serve as a hostage for their loyalty, or if the imperial government stationed their officers at the courts of these vassals to

51. *Ibid.*, p. 90.
52. See the Gunaighar Ins. *I.H.Q.* V, p. 53.
53. Fleet, *op. cit.* No. 18.
54. *Ibid.*, No. 80.
55. *Ibid.*, p. 109, etc.

ensure their loyalty. But spies were employed by the imperial court to keep watch over their activities. They were not allowed evidently to issue coins of their own, and hence we do not find the coins of the feudatories issued during the Gupta period. It appears that the feudatories were required to use the imperial era and hence it is we find the Gupta era being used by them.[56]

The territories directly under the control of the emperor, formed a regular part of the empire. They were divided into a number of provinces to ensure efficient administration and over each one of them was appointed a governor to administer the same. But we have no correct idea about the number of provinces in the Gupta Empire, particularly in view of the fact that the provincial organisation underwent changes from time to time to meet the exigencies of the administration. The Junagādh Rock Inscription of Skandagupta's time mentions the king's defeat of his enemies, the conquest of the whole earth and the appointment of many provincial governors particularly in the western parts of his empire which had suffered terribly at the hands of the Huns. The appointment of able men as governors of provinces appears to have given the emperor a sense of great relief.[57]

Any way the existence of the following provinces during the days of Skandagupta, the great Gupta ruler, is known from inscriptions. On the westernmost part of the empire was the Surāṣṭra province (Kathiawār) to which was appointed one Parṇadatta as governor by Skandagupta.[58] A little eastward was the Mālva kingdom the Governor of which was one Ghaṭotkaca Gupta during the

56. *Ibid.*, p. 118.

57. *Ibid.*, No. 14.

58. *Ibid.*

days of Kumāragupta.[59] It extended over all the region between the Jumna and the Narmadā. On the eastern side of the empire there was a province which was called the Puṇḍravardhana *bhukti,* the governor of which was one *Uparika* Citrādadatta during the days of Kumāragupta, one *Uparika* Mahārāja Jayadatta during the days of emperor Budhagupta, and one Uparika Mahārāja Rājaputra-deva Bhaṭṭāraka who was evidently the son of the king. It comprised the districts of Dinajpur, Bogra and Raj Shahi in northern Bengal. A little to the west of it lay the Magadha *bhukti* comprising the regions of Gayā, Rājagṛha and Pāṭaliputra. Above this was evidently the Tīra *bhukti* which appears to have been roughly of the size of the modern Darbhanga division. Besides these known provinces, there were a good number of others, of which, however, our knowledge is very meagre. These provinces appear to have differed very much from one another in their size, resources and importance. Probably the provinces in the western part of the empire were bigger than those on the eastern side, and were called *dēśas.* Probably the officer in charge of such a division of the empire was called *gopa.*[60]

The next administrative division was the *bhukti* which may be said to have corresponded to a Commissioner's division in the Government of India in British times. For the first time in the history of India we find this term used to denote a comparatively large administrative unit. We do not know if the *bhukti* as an administrative and political division obtained in the regions where there existed the division called the *dēśa.* It is difficult to say anything about

59. R. N. Dandekar, *A History of the Guptas,* p. 119. He refers to the newly discovered Tumanian inscription where Ghatotkaca is mentioned after Kumāragupta. It means that he did not ascend the throne but he gave up his loyalty to the emperor.

60. Fleet, *op. cit.,* p. 62.
The inscription reads *Sarveṣu dēśeṣu vidhāya goptrin.*

the relationship between the two so far as the administration of the respective units was concerned. One thing however may be surmised. From the point of view of its size the *bhukti*, was certainly smaller than the *dēśa*. But from the point of view of the administration, it was better knit and served well as a useful unit.

The officer in charge of the *bhukti* had the title *Uparika* prefixed to his name. We are told that during the days of Kumāragupta the head of the *bhukti* of Puṇḍravardhana was one *Uparika* Citrādadatta.[61] During the days of Budhagupta again, the governors of the *bhukti* were successively *Uparika mahārājas* Brahmadatta and Jayadatta.[62] In the days of Bhānugupta, the governor of the same province was one *Uparika-mahārāja-rājaputra-deva-bhaṭṭāraka*. The name of the officer is not given in the inscription, but the title shows that he was the king's son.[63] The title *Uparika* that is found prefixed to the names of the governors mentioned above shows that it was an honorific one held by them. Subsequent to the days of Kumāragupta it appears that the titles *mahārāja* and *bhogika* were also used by the provincial governors. The meaning or significance of the title *Uparika* is not clearly known.[64] According to A. A. Macdonell the term *Upari* means above, over, upwards, one above the other, always upwards etc. *Uparika* would mean one who is above others. It was evidently a title of distinction at times held by the governors of provinces in virtue of the high position which they held in the governmental machinery.

The assumption of the title *mahārāja* by these governors can easily be understood when we see that the inscriptions in

61. *Ep. Ind.* XV. p. 131, Pls. Nos. 1 and 2.
62. *Ibid.*, Pls. Nos. 3 and 4.
63. *Ibid.*, p. 115, Pl. No. 5.
64. See above.

which the governors are called *mahārājas* mention the emperors as *paramadaivata, Paramabhaṭṭāraka, mahārājādhirāja,* etc. When the emperor was a *mahārājādhirāja* there was nothing seriously objectionable in a governor being called a *mahārāja*. Further the taking of this title by the provincial governors can be justified by the fact that in the course of the reign of Skandagupta, the government appears to have been decentralised to a considerable extent which must have given a larger amount of autonomy for the provinces.

As regards the title *bhogika,*[65] it appears to have been taken by the officers in charge of territorial units bigger than a *viṣaya*. Thus his position was higher than that of a *Viṣayapati,* and lower than that of a *Sāmanta,* who was the minister in charge of the provinces. As said above the Dāmodarpūr copper-plate No. 5 of Bhānugupta mentions the king's son who was then the governor of the Puṇḍravardhana *bhukti* by his titles only, namely *Uparika mahārājarājaputra-deva-bhaṭṭāraka,* and not by his name.[66] One wonders why his name has not been mentioned here. Surely it was not due to the fact that the authors of the inscription did not know the name of the prince. But it was probably due to their deference to the person of the prince, though nothing prevented them from mentioning the name of the emperor evidently because he was far away from the scene, and did not have much to do with the administration of the local area.

In one of the Gupta inscriptions occurs the word *Rājasthānīya*. It is a technical official title which has been interpreted by Dr. Fleet as "one who belongs to a *Rājasthāna* or king's abode" or perhaps "one who occupies the position of a rājan".[67] Kṣemendra in his *Lokaprakāśa* IV explains the

65. Fleet, *op. cit.*, p. 100 and *n*.
66. *E.I.* XV. p. 115.
67. Fleet, *op. cit.*, p. 157.

term as follows: *Prajā pālanārtham Udvahati rakṣayati ca sa Rājasthānīyah* (i.e.) the officer who shoulders the burden of protecting and promoting the welfare of the subjects.[68] But in the Māliya grant of Dharasena II, the Deo-Baraṇārak inscription of Jīvita Gupta II, and the Bhagalpur grant of Nārāyaṇa Pāla[69] the term is used to denote a lower official. Evidently it can only mean a political agent or regent.[70] Whatever that may be, the study of these inscriptions shows that only senior officers of the government were appointed to such posts and in the selection of proper men for these places, great thought was spent. It is said that Skandagupta appointed Parṇadatta as governor of the Surāṣṭra Province after "deliberate consideration for nights and days".[71]

While referring to his choice, the inscription says, he cogitated in many ways,—"Among all my servants put together, who is there, who—suitable; endowed with intellect; modest; possessed of a disposition that is not destitute of wisdom and memory; endowed with truth, straightforwardness, nobility and prudent behaviour; and possessed of sweetness, civility and fame;—loyal; affectionate; endowed with manly characteristics and possessed of a mind that (*has been tried and*) is (*found to be*) pure by all the tests of honesty; possessed of an inner soul pervaded by (*the inclination for*) the acquittance of debts and obligations; occupied with the welfare of all mankind;—capable both in the lawful acquisition of wealth and also in the preservation of it, when acquired, and further in causing the increase of it, when protected, (*and able*) to dispense it on worthy objects, when it has been increased,—shall govern all my (countries of the) Surāṣṭras? I have it; (there is) just one man, Parṇadatta competent to bear this burden" After his appointment

68. *Ind. Ant.*, V, p. 207.
69. Fleet, *op. cit.*, Nos. 38 and 46 and *Ind. Ant.* XV, p. 306.
70. See Fleet, *op. cit.*, p. 157 and *n*.
71. *Ibid.*, pp. 59 and 63.

the king was relieved of his anxiety.[72] At times when men of ripe experience or dependable character were not available to be appointed as governors, some member of the royal family closely related to the ruling king was appointed to the office.

The provincial administrative system was largely a replica of the system of government at the centre. The Viceroy in the province was assisted in his government by a staff of officers who were also the Heads of Departments. Among them were the *Balādhi-karaṇika, Daṇḍapāśadhi-karaṇika, Raṇabhāṇḍārika, Mahādaṇḍānāyaka, Vinaya sti-thi sthāpaka, Bhaṭāśvapati* etc. The above names are indicative of the departments to which the officers belonged and the duties they discharged. The term *adhikaraṇa* means a department or a court. *Bala* means army, and *balādhika-raṇa*[73] would naturally mean the military department, and the *balādhikaraṇika* was one who was in charge of the military department. The *Daṇḍapāśādhikaraṇa* was evidently the same as the *Daṇḍapāśika*. The latter term means one who holds the fetters or the noose of punishment. He was evidently the officer who was in charge of the Police Department.[74] The *Raṇa bhāṇḍārika* was the officer in charge of the finances relating to the army.[75] He was probably the precursor of the military paymaster (*bhakshi*), of the Muslim period.

Generally speaking the term *daṇḍanāyaka* admits of two different interpretations. It may either be taken as a military title meaning 'leader of the forces' or 'administrator of punishments' or magistrate, for the word *daṇḍa* means both army and justice. But puzzlingly enough we get reference to three

72. *Ibid.*, pp. 62 and 63.
73. *A.S.R.*, 1903-04 p. 108.
74. *Ibid.*, p. 108.
75. *Ibid.*, p. 108.

different officers, the *balādhikaraṇa, daṇḍapāśādhikaraṇika* and the *mahādaṇḍanāyaka* whose exact functions are very much left to our guess. It has been said above that the *balādhikaraṇika* was the head of the Military Department and that the *daṇḍapāśādhikaraṇika* was probably the head of the Police Department. Though the word *daṇḍa* admits of two meanings, namely the army and justice, in view of the fact that there was an officer in charge of the Military Department who was called the *balādhikaraṇika,* it is reasonable to assume that the *daṇḍanāyaka* was the head of the department of justice. If he occupied a higher position than the other heads of departments in the provincial administration, he was probably called a *mahādaṇḍanāyaka.*

The *Vinaya stithi sthāpaka*[76] was evidently the minister in charge of Law and Order, while the *Bhaṭāśvapati* was the commandant of the infantry and the cavalry. The Gunaighar inscription of Vainya Gupta mentions an officer under his *Pīlupati* while the spurious Nālandā Copper-plate inscription of Samudragupta mentions a *Mahāpīlupati*, meaning the head of the elephant force.[77] If the *balādhikaraṇika* was a military officer (Field-Marshal) it is difficult to say anything about the position of either the *Bhaṭāśvapati* or the *Pīlupati* in relation to him. Probably they occupied only subordinate positions in the Military department, though by virtue of the distinctive nature of their departments they were also considered to be heads. But in matters of co-ordination and general management, the *Balādhikaraṇa* must have exercised great control and supervision. There appears to have been in the staff of Heads of Departments with the governor another officer who was

76. *Ibid.*, p. 109.

77. *Pīlu* (originally Persian) would mean elephant. Words like *Pīlu* were probably introduced into the Indian administration by the foreign invaders. See D. C. Sircar, *Select Inscriptions bearing on Indian History and civilization*, Vol. I, pp. 333 and 264 n.

called the *Pañcūdhi-karaṇoparika*.[78] It is not known what his functions were. Probably he was something like a Divisional Commissioner who controlled five districts as Dr. Radhakumud Mookerjee feels,[79] or more probably he supervised the work of five Departmental heads, in the office of the Governor. Among the other Heads of Departments who constituted the staff of the provincial governor were the *Mahāpratīhāra* the chief officer superintending the door-keepers of the royal palace, i.e., the palace guards and possibly also the royal body-guards.

The *Pāṭyuparika* was perhaps the chief officer of the Accounts Department. The *Sādhanika* appears to have been an officer who had to deal with debts and fines,[80] evidently a Special Officer attached to the Judicial Department. The *Vyāpārakūraṇaya*, was the officer to regulate trade?[81]

The Mallasarul copper-plate of Vijayasena[82] mentions a few other officers who were also probably members of the staff of the governor of the Province. Among them are *kārttākṛitika, chaurōddharaṇika, audrangika, āgrahārika aurṇasthānika, bhōgapatika. viṣayapati, tadāyuktaka, hiraṇya sāmudāyika, pattalaka, Āvasathika*, and *devadrōṇī*. These names are difficult of correct interpretation, but they appear to be certainly the names of officers, connected with the administration of the province. The term *Kārttakṛtika*[83] is probably derived from the word *kṛtākṛta* which means business done and to be done, and may possibly mean Superintendent or Manager of state affairs. In all likelihood he was the Chief Secretary to the Government, and therefore

78. Gunaighar Ins., l. 15.

79. *The Gupta Empire* p. 157.

80. See the Gunaighar Ins.. ll. 15 and 16; and the Faridpur Ins of Dharmāditya. *Ind. Ant.*, XXXIX. p. 200.

81. D. C. Sircar, *op. cit.*, pp. 333 and 334.

82. *Ep. Ind.*, XXIII. p. 159. l. 4.

83. *Ibid.*, l. 3.

the chief executive officer responsible for the day-to-day administration in the Province. The term *uddharaṇa* means removal, deliverance, and *uddharaṇika* would mean one who removes or delivers. *Corauddharaṇika*[84] would naturally mean therefore one who removes thieves, or delivers thieves. Evidently he was the Commissioner of Police in charge of the Police Department.

The *Audrangika*[85] was probably the collector of tax and was hence the revenue minister. *Udranga* was possibly a tax on permanent tenants. As is so well known an *agrahāra* is a gift village to a Brāhmana or sometimes a deity, and the *Āgrahārika*[86] of the inscription must have been an officer whose duty it was to exercise control over the *agrahāras*. The *Aurṇasthāniya*[87] could have been the controller of woollen textiles, *ūrṇa* meaning wool, and *Ūrṇasthāno* a woollen factory. There was another officer called *Bhogapatika*. *Bhoga*[88] admits of different meanings. It means a stable, a small territorial unit or a piece of land granted to individuals for enjoyment. Equally difficult it is to say much about the *bhogapati*, and his functions in the Gupta province. He could have been the Superintendent of the governor's stable or the officer-in-charge of the service and other grants made by the government and his duty was probably to see that the main objects of the grant made were not defeated. Or he could have been in charge of a division of the province which was larger than a *viṣaya*, and he could have been one of the members of the governor's staff of officers in the same manner and for the same reason as the *Viṣayapati* found his way into the governor's staff.

84. *Ibid.*, 1. 4.
85. *Ibid.*
86. *Ibid.*
87. *Ibid.*
88. *Ibid.*

The *Tadāyuktaka* was probably connected with the treasury department, and was the Chief Treasury Officer. The *Hiraṇya-Sāmudāyaka*[90] as distinct from the above was in all likelihood the chief officer-in-charge of the mint department, and was responsible for the issue of coins etc. The *āvasatika*[91] was possibly the Superintendent of the *avastas* or the *dharmaśālas*. He was evidently the Superintendent of charitable institutions. The *Devadroṇi samvadda*[92] appears to have been an officer having control over the general administration of the temple endowments and properties. It seems that the functions of the *devadroni samvadda* were different from those of the *āvasatika*. The term *devadronī* means procession in temples and probably refers to the properties of temples also.

The inscription under reference mentions also the *Viṣayapati.*[93] How it was that he was also on the staff of officers with the provincial governor is not easy to explain. Probably the headquarters of a *bhukti* over which a governor ruled must have been located in a *viṣaya* for the administration of which there must have been a *Viṣayapati*. He was perhaps from the administrative point of view a subordinate of the governor of the *bhukti*. It is not impossible that he could have been included in the list of officers working under the control of the governor. The relation between the two may be better grasped if we take a modern parallel, the relation between the governor of a state in India, and the Collector of the district in which the state headquarters are located.

89. *Ibid.*
90. *Ibid.*
91. *Ibid.*
92. *Ibid.*
93 *Ibid.*

Personal Secretaries

The Provincial governors were usually attended and assisted by a body of what may be called personal secretaries who served as the channel of communication between him and the administrative officers under him and conveyed to them his orders. These officers were called *dūtas, dūtakas* and *ājñādāpakas.* As the functions they discharged were of a very responsible nature it is possible that only men of ripe experience and great ability who had been in the service of the government for a good number of years and had risen to positions of importance like the *Rājasthānīya* and the *Uparika* were chosen as such officers. In fact it appears that the office of the *Dūtaka* was considered very superior. He was honoured with four official titles. According to the Gunaighar inscription of Vainyagupta, Vijayasena was a *Pañcādhikaraṇoparika, Pāṭyuparika, Purapāloparika* and *Mahāsāmanta.*[94] He had a scribe with him who was himself the holder of a distinguished office possibly connected with peace and war (*sandhi-vigraha*).

Kumārāmātyas

Though the above mentioned several officers were in charge of the different departments of the Provincial government, the day-to-day details of administration were gone through by a large body of officers who were usually known as the *Kumārāmātyas*[95] and their subordinates. The term *Kumārāmātya* appears (as has been said earlier) to have been usually used in the Gupta period to denote a class of officers who belonged to a particular cadre like the *mahāmātras* of the Mauryan period, or even of the Sātavāhana period[96] or the I.C.S. or I.A.S. men of modern times. Some of

94. *I.H.Q.*, VI, p. 55.
95. See *ante.*
96. *Ep. Ind.*, VIII, p. 93.

them were attached to the imperial government, and some were attached to the provincial government. A *Kumārāmātya* worked under the direction of a bigger officer like the *mahābalādhikṛta* or *mahādaṇḍanāyaka* to which positions they were also at times promoted.[97] If he was attached to the government of a province at the head of which was a prince of the royal blood, he was referred to as the *yuvarāja pādīya kumārāmātya,* and if he was attached to the office of the emperor himself, he was evidently referred to as *paramabhaṭṭāraka pādīya kumārāmātya.*

Our knowledge of the powers and responsibilities of the governors of the *bhuktis* or provinces is unfortunately very slender. They appear to have been in the enjoyment of complete autonomous powers with regard to the administration of their respective areas; but they were always answerable to the emperor. Much was expected of the governor in the protection of the people. He had control over the *viṣayas* and towns in the province. In fact it appears that at least from the days of Skandagupta the officers-in-charge of towns and cities were appointed by him. The Junagādh Rock inscription of Skandagupta, says that Parṇadatta the governor who ruled over the Surāṣṭra province, appointed his own son Cakrapālita as the ruler or mayor (*nagara rakṣaka*) of the city of Girinagara, which was also the headquarters of the provincial government of Surāṣṭra.[98] Likewise it is said that during the days of Budhagupta, *Uparika* Mahārāja Jayadatta who was ruling over Puṇḍravardhana *bhukti* appointed one Saṇḍaka as the officer-in-charge of the district of Koṭivarsa (*Koṭivarṣa viṣaya*).[99] These instances clearly point out that there was a large volume of devolution of powers to the provinces from the days of Skandagupta.

97. *Ibid.,* X, p. 72.
98. Fleet, *op. cit.,* No. 14.
99. *Ep. Ind.* XV. p. 140.

Section III

Frontier Kingdoms

Besides having direct control over the different parts of their empire the Gupta sovereigns enjoyed overlordship over certain territories on its borders by virtue of the fact that the rulers of such territories accepted their dependence on the Gupta kings. They were usually of two kinds, monarchical states, the rulers of which are referred to in the Allahabad Pillar Inscription as *pratyanta nṛpatis*[100], and republican states. It is not likely that the Gupta kings could have interfered in the internal administration of such states in any manner. But the governments of such states wished to enter into friendly relations with the Gupta monarchs by satisfying them in regard to their demands, which usually consisted of the payment of various taxes (*sarvakaradāna*). obeying the orders of the imperial authority (*ājñā karaṇa*) and attending the imperial Darbars for doing homage to the emperor in person (*praṇāmāgamana*).[101]

Among such frontier kingdoms five are known to have existed on the eastern side of the Gupta Empire in the days of Samudragupta. They were the kingdoms of Samataṭa, Davāka, Kāmarūpa, Nepal and Karttripura.[102] Samataṭa, has been identified with the region to the east of the Tāmralipti and bordering on the sea. Its capital was Karmmānta which is supposed to be the same as the modern Kamta in the Tipperah District. Davāka will very probably correspond to the valley of the Kapilī-Yamunā-Kolang rivers of Assam; and the chief city of the kingdom has been sought to be identified with modern Dabok in the Nowgong district of Assam. Kāmarūpa may be taken to be the Gauhati district

100. Fleet, *op. cit.*, p. 14.
101. *Ibid.*, p. 14.
102. *Ibid.*, p. 14.

of Assam. The position of Nepal is too well known to be described here. Karttripura was a Himalayan State, the territory of Katuriya or the Katyur kingdom of Kumaon, Garhwal and Rohilkhand.

We also get reference to a number of republican states during the period of Samudragupta and they were all found on the western and south-western parts of the Gupta Empire. Among such states were those of the Mālavas, Ārjunāyanas, Yaudheyas, Mādrakas, Ābhīras, Prārjunas, Sanakānikas, Kākas, Kharaparikas etc.[103] The Mālavas appear to have occupied the region of Mandasor in Mālva during the period under consideration. The Ārjunāyanas (called after Arjuna) may be assigned to the region lying west of Agra and Mathurā roughly corresponding to Bharatpur and Alwar. The Yaudheyas appear to have been in the occupation of northern Rajputāna and south-east Panjab besides the territory as far as Bhahawalpur. The Mādrakas were an old republican clan who occupied the region to the north of that of the Yaudheyas. The Ābhīras had their kingdom in northern Mahārāṣṭra and probably the western portions of Central India also. The Prārjunas were probably the same as the Prājjūnakas mentioned in the *Arthaśāstra* of Kauṭalya and they may be supposed to have been living in the Narasimhapur district in the Central Provinces. The Sanakānīkas who are mentioned in one of the Udayagiri inscriptions of Candragupta II seem to have ruled in the region near Bhilsa. The Kākas whom Dr. V. A. Smith connects with Kākanāda (Sāñcī) probably lived in that region and were the neighbours of the Sanakānīkas. The Kharaparikas have been sought to be identified with the Kharparas who lived in the Damoh district in the Central Provinces.

103. *Ibid.*, p. 14.

Section IV

District Administration

For purposes of efficient administration the Province in the Gupta Empire was subdivided into districts or *viṣayas*, each of which was ruled by a *Viṣayapati* or District Magistrate. In the Gupta inscriptions we get reference to a number of such districts. Thus in the Puṇḍravardhana *bhukti* which was an important Province in the days of Kumāragupta was situated the Koṭivarṣa *viṣaya*.[104] Probably it was in the same *bhukti* that the *viṣaya* of Khādā (ṭā) mentioned in the Dhānāidaha (Raj-Shahi District) grant of the year 128 (A.D. 447) was situated. It is possible also that the *viṣaya* which had for its headquarters a place called Pañcanagari and must have been called by the same name was also situated in the Puṇḍravardhana *bhukti* about the year 128 (A.D. 447).[105] Thus we may say that every Province in the Gupta period must have consisted of at least three or four districts. From the Mandasor inscription we learn that there was a district in the western part of the Empire called Lāṭa *viṣaya*.[106]

As said above the head of the district administration was the *viṣayapati*. From the inscriptions of the period we are able to gather some interesting details regarding the method of the appointment of the officer. The Baigram Charter of the year 128 referred to above says that Viṣayapati Kula Vṛddhi who ruled from his District office (*Viṣayādnikaraṇa*) located at the town of Pañcanagari paid his homage to the emperor. The words used in the inscription to denote it are *Bhaṭṭāraka pādānudhyāta* which literally means "one directly meditating on the feet of His

104. E.I., XXI, p. 79.
105. *Ibid*.
106. Fleet, *op. cit.*, No. 18, p. 84.

Majesty".[107] It must be noted here that the *Viṣayapati* under reference paid homage directly to the Emperor though there was just above him the *Uparika Mahārāja*, who was the governor of the *bhukti* of which the *viṣaya* was only an administrative division. This may lead us to the conclusion that the District Officer was directly controlled by the Emperor himself.

But the Damodarpur copper-plates to which reference has been made earlier, mention that *Viṣayapati* Kumārāmātya Vetravarman was appointed to his post (*tanniyuktaka*) by the *Uparika* Citrādadatta the Governor of the Puṇḍravardhana *bhukti*.[108] This would drive us to the conclusion that the District Officer was appointed by the Provincial Governor who was himself appointed by the Emperor. It is difficult to see how two different methods could have been adopted at the same period and almost in the same region with regard to the appointment of the District Official. In the light of the available evidence, however, it is reasonable to assume that the selection of the official was obviously made by the Provincial Governor while his appointment was made by the emperor himself. We do not know however if the practice of the appointment of the District Officer by the Emperor himself obtained throughout the period of the Gupta history. Obviously it was a change in the administrative practice that was made during the days of Kumāragupta to prevent any provincial intransigence.

Probably when the empire grew to large proportions and was divided into many provinces and districts, it was the natural anxiety of the Emperors to have contact with the districts which were in fact the real units of the empire. If the above administrative procedure was universal in the Gupta Empire in the period under survey, there could have

107. Ep. Ind. XXI, p. 80.
108. *Ibid.*, XV. p. 133.

been no difference in the constitutional position of Kula Vṛddhi and Vetravarman who were contemporary District Officers under the same sovereign in two separate *viṣayas* in North Bengal. The *Viṣayapati* enjoyed the distinction of the use of the title of *Kumārāmātya.* As said above in some cases the *viṣaya* was divided into smaller administrative units called the *vīthi* and the officer in charge of it was called the *Āyuktaka* as may be seen from the Kalaikuri inscription.[109]

The District Headquarters were known as *adhiṣṭhānas* while the office of the District Officer was known as the *Viṣaya adhikaraṇa.* From a Dāmodarpur copper-plate we get an idea of the administration of the District. The District Officer or Magistrate was helped in his administration by an Advisory Council consisting of non-officials who were the representatives of different interests that flourished in the locality. The first among them says that *Kumārāmātya* Vetravarman, the officer in charge of the district called Koṭivarṣa administered the government of the locality in the company of Dhṛtipāla the *nagaraśreṣṭhi,* Bandhumitra, the *Sārthavāha,* Dhṛtimitra, the *Prathamakulika* and Sāmbapāla, the *Prathamakāyastha.*[110] The *nagaraśreṣṭhi* was the President of the Chamber of Commerce and probably, the Mayor of the Town Corporation. The *Sārthavāha* was the representative of the Merchant Guild or Guilds. The *Prathamakulika* was very probably the Chief of the Guild of artisans.[111] The *Prathama Kāyastha* was the chief scribe or writer in the administrative office and was probably the Chief Secretary to the administrative Board. It is not improbable that the

109. R. K. Mookerjee, *The Gupta Empire,* p. 81.

110. See *E.I.*. XV, p. 130.

111. The word *Kulika* appears to be a variant of the word *Kulaka* (*Kulakah syāt Kulaśreṣṭhi—Amara,* II. 10.5). The word has been explained as the foremost person in a company of artisans by the commentator Bhānūji Dikshita. See *E.I.,* XV. p. 131 f.n. 6. But Dr. K. P. Jayaswal is of opinion that the *Prathamakulika* was the senior Town Judge (*Hindu Polity,* 2nd Edn, p. 397).

Prathama Kāyastha mentioned here was the same as the *Jyeṣṭha Kāyastha* mentioned in the Faridpur grants B and C and the Khalinpur plate of Dharmapāla.[112] Thus the *Viṣaya-pati* was assisted in his administration of the District by a Board of Advisers representative of different interests in the area concerned.

The details of the administration of the District were looked after by a body of officers each in charge of a Department and working under the control of the District Magistrate. All of them constituted the *viṣaya adhikaraṇa.* Among the Heads of Departments and officers who worked under the District Magistrate mention may be made of the *Śaulkika* (Superintendent of tolls or customs) (*Śulka*), *Āgrahārika* (an officer in special charge of *agrahāras*—settlements made in favour of Brahmanas and temples), *Gaulmika* (Superintendent of forests and woods),[113] *Dhruvādhikaraṇika* (Superintendent of the collection of the royal share of the produce in grain),[114] *Bhaṇḍā Kārādhikṛta* (Officer-in-charge of the treasury), *Utkheṭayita* (Collector of taxes)[115] and *Talāvāṭaka* (village accountant?).[116]

The Records section of the office of the District Magistrate was an important department. It was called the *akṣa-patala* and the Head of the Department was the *mahākṣa paṭa-lika.*[117] The department employed a good number of clerks called *Diviras,*[118] whose main duty appears to have been to write and copy down records. The documents were drafted by a special officer called the *Kartri* or *Sāsayitrī.*[119] Under

112. Dr. K. P. Jayaswal however interprets this term as the Senior City Registrar (*Hindu Polity*, 2nd Edn. p. 397).

113. Fleet, *op. cit.*, p. 52.

114. *Ibid.* p. 170.

115. *E.I.*, XII, p. 75.

116. Fleet, *op. cit.*, p. 217.

117. *Ibid.* p. 190.

118. *Ibid.* p. 123.

119. *E. I.* XII, 79.

these different heads of departments mentioned above, there were working many general Superintendents who were called *Sarvādhyakṣas.*

Among the different functions of the District Council matters relating to land formed an important one. As promoters of the religious and charitable institutions in the Empire, the Government were anxious to give every sort of help to private donors wishing to make gifts of land for such purposes. A set procedure was usually followed in such gifts. According to the practice that obtained during the period, the permission of the government was essential for the transfer or alienation of land by a private individual, and such permission was granted only if the Government were satisfied on two points. Firstly, the land in question must be a fallow one, from which no revenue was collected and had not been the subject of a gift previously. Such lands as were to be the subjects of gift should be therefore unoccupied and untilled ones. This was evidently to safeguard the land tenures that obtained in the empire and to see that no diminution was experienced in the total yield from land for the people.

Secondly, the government were not prepared to allow gifts of lands which were sought to be made without any provision for the continued maintenance of the gift or charity made by a party. The phrases used in the inscriptions to denote this aspect of the gift by private parties are *nīvi-dharmeṇa*[120] or *apradākṣaya nīvī*. *Nīvī* means *mūladhana* or capital or principal in the matter of sale. It means the fixed capital out of the interest from which the expenses were to be borne. *Prada* means gift and *aprada* naturally means, anything that cannot be settled away or given away. *Apradākṣaya nīvī*[121] would mean therefore the capital or the

120. *Ibid.* XV, p. 114.
121. *Ibid.* p. 134.

mūladhana which could not be spent in any way, but its interest alone was to be spent for meeting the expenses connected with the endowment. The government as the promoters of the charitable and religious purposes were anxious to see that the purpose of the endowment was not in any manner defeated by sale, transfer or any other method of disposal of the endowed property. Hence it is that the Government controlled the sale or transfer of land in the empire.

According to the Damodarpur Copper-plates[122] the procedure adopted with regard to the gift of land by a person for a charitable purpose was as follows. First the donor made an application to the government for the purchase of a specified piece of land. It was usually addressed to the *Pusta pālas* who were the Keepers of the Records of the Government, and constituted a body of three persons. In the course of his petition, the petitioner was expected to state that his gift was to be according to *nīvī dharma,* the land in question was *khila* as yet unploughed and not given to anyone, and was free of revenue, and that the price to be paid was according to the rates prevailing in the village. As soon as the petition was received, the *Pusta pālas*[123] placed the matter before four groups of people in the village concerned, namely the *mahattaras, aṣṭakulādhikaraṇas, grāmikas*[124] and the *kuṭumbins.*[125] The word *mahattara* is obviously derived from the word *mahat* meaning 'great'. *Mahattara* would mean "the head or the oldest men of a village" (i.e.) the village elders. *Adhikaraṇa* means usually administration, an officer in charge of the administration, the Board of administration, or even individually the members of the Board of Administration. *Aṣṭakulādhikaraṇa* would then mean the

122. *Ibid.* p. 113 ff.
123. *Ibid.* XV, p. 136.
124. *Ibid.* p. 139.
125. *I.H.Q.* XIX. p. 15.

Board consisting of the representatives from eight families, which were evidently prominent ones in the locality concerned; or probably he was an officer in charge of land measurement and survey in the village. The *grāmika* was probably an officer of the government who was in charge of the administration of the village as a whole. According to Manu among his duties were the collection of revenue and the administration of justice. The *Kuṭumbins* were in all likelihood the leading men in the village and which could have been due to their wealth or their social influence. We do not know however if these representative men in the village were elected or nominated. Very probably they received recognition as such and were co-opted and were not elected. Anyway when the matter was placed before them, these four groups of men, referred the petition to the leading Brahmanas, citizens and householders of the village concerned. The *Mahattaras,* householders and other officers of the locality inspected the lands in question and finally referred the matter back to the *Pusta pālas* for report. The *Pusta pālas* would carefully examine the question whether the request conformed to the rules and practices relating to sales, such as the application being a proper one, and in conformity with the customary rules for sales etc. If he was satisfied with every aspect of the question it was recommended that the land might be given. On the recommendation of the *Pusta pālas* then the land was sold.

We have another instance of a similar kind recorded in the Baigram copper-plate inscription dated Gupta year 128 (A.D. 447-48).[126] The Emperor Kumāragupta is referred to in the inscription simply as *Bhaṭṭārakapāda.*[127] According to the copper-plate the householders of a locality, Bhoyila and

126. Ep. Ind. XXI. pp. 78 ff.
127. *Ibid*. p. 83.

Bhāskara by name, both of them brothers, applied to *Kumārāmātya* Kula Vṛddhi the *Viṣayapati* who was ruling from Pañcanagari, the headquarters of the District.[128] The reason for the request was the creation of a provision for the repair of the temple and the supply of things required for worship such as scents, incense, light, flowers etc. The application was for the purchase of a specified measure of fallow land which was (1) not paying any rent or revenue to the state, (2) was an uncultivated waste land without any vegetation over it, and (3) was not enjoyed by any private individual to whom compensation would have to be paid if it was in his possession. As described in the previous case, the *Pusta pālas* or Record Keepers of the government in the local area examined the whole question and recommended the sale of the government lands, asked for, to the private parties for the following reasons:—

(a) the lands were lying fallow and without any vegetation;

(b) they were capable of yielding revenue to the king;

(c) there could be no objection to the sale on the ground that it would result in financial loss to the king;

(d) but the king was likely to gain materially from the sale besides spiritual gain in the shape of *dharma*; and

(e) that the lands were situated in areas which would not affect adversely the cultivation of the settled lands.

Accordingly the sale was made by the government to the two brothers who made the application for the same.

Vīthi Administration

Some Gupta inscriptions contain reference to the *vīthi*, an administrative division. The Kalaikuri copper-plate

128. *Ibid*. p. 81.

inscription[129] of the Gupta year 120 (A.D. 430) assignable to the reign of Kumāragupta mentions the Sṛngavera *vīthi* with its headquarters Pūrṇakauśikā, situated most probably in the Puṇḍravardhana *viṣaya.*[130] The Pāhāṛpūr Copper-plate inscription[131] of the Gupta year 159 (A.D. 479) mentions an administrative division called the Daksiṇāmśaka *vīthi* in the Nāgiratta maṇḍala.[132] The Nālanda grant of Devapāla mentions the Kumudasutra *vīthi* in the Gayā *viṣaya.*[133] The Nandāpūr incription refers to the Nandāpūr *vīthi.*[134] Thus instances can be multiplied. It is doubtful however if every *viṣaya* was subdivided into *vīthis* almost in the same way. Probably not. It is possible that only the big *viṣayas* difficult of being administered efficiently by *viṣayapatis* single-handed were divided in that manner. Obviously the *Āyuktaka* division was not universal.[135]

The officer in charge of the administration of the sub-division was the *āyuktaka* who was assisted in his work by a council of non-officials consisting of the *vīthi mahattaras* and the *Kuṭumbins.* The former of the two were the elders while the latter were the leading agricultural house-holders both residing in the same division. The staff of the Sub-Divisional officer, as of the District Magistrate, consisted of the *Pusta pālas* (Keepers of Records), *Kāyasthas* (scribes or clerks) and *Kulikas* or representative craftsmen whose duty appears to have been to deal with the interests of the local handicrafts.[136]

129. *I.H.Q.* XIX. pp. 12 ff.
130. *Ibid.* p. 24.
131. *E. I.* XX. pp. 59 ff.
132. *Ibid.*, XX. p. 61 f.
133. *Ibid.*. XVII. pp. 318 ff.
134. *Ibid.*. XXIII. p. 54.
135. It has been suggested by some that the term *Vīthi* indicated a district on the bank of a river.
136. *I.H.Q.* XIX. p. 16.

The functions of the *Āyuktaka* of the *vīthi* were almost similar to those of the *Viṣayapati*, and largely related to land transactions. The Kalaikuri copper-plate inscription to which reference has been made earlier gives us an idea about the nature of the work done by the *Āyuktaka*.[137] According to the plates under consideration one *Kulika* Bhīma and some other persons of the Śṛṇgavera *vīthi* who are described respectively as the *Kāyasthas* and *Pusta pālas* requested the *Āyuktaka* and a number of other persons described as the *vīthi mahattaras* and *kuṭumbins* to allow them to purchase specified pieces of uncultivated fallow land in these villages within the jurisdiction of the *vīthi* at the rates prevalent in the area. The purpose was to grant the same as an *akṣayanīvī* to three Brahmanas (named) who were well versed in the four Vedas and belonged to the Vājasaneya Caraṇa with a view to enable them to perform their *pañca mahāyajñas* without any interruption.[138]

As in the case mentioned earlier, the conditions necessary for the validity of an application were (a) the land applied for must be fallow and not settled so that its transfer was not subject to compensation payable to the possessor who was dispossessed; (b) it must be given as a perpetual grant and remain an *akṣayanīvī*; (c) it should be given for a religious or charitable purpose (such as the performance of the *pañca mahāyajñas* as in the present case); and (d) that the price must be at the customary rates obtaining in the locality. The application was as usual referred to the *Pusta pālas* for examination and report. When they reported that the application was in order and that the sale would not affect adversely the interests of the state, the *Āyuktaka* gave permission for the sale of the lands asked for.[139]

137. *Ibid.* pp. 21 ff.
138. *I.H.Q.* XIX, p. 17.
139. *Ibid.*

City Administration

The Gupta Empire contained a good number of cities each of which constituted an important unit of local administration. Among the important cities in the empire may be mentioned Pāṭlīputra, Ayodhyā, Ujjain, Daśapura, Girinagara etc. Each city was administered by a Council called the *Pariṣad* as for instance in the case of the city of Udānakūpa.[140] If the city was also the District Headquarters probably its administration was carried on by the District Magistrate himself with the help of his non-official District Council. But if it was one other than the District Headquarters, its administration was carried on by a separate Council. This is indicated by the Pāhārpūr copper-plate inscription[141] of the time of Budhagupta and dated G. E. 159 (A.D. 479) which refers to *Āyuktakas* as the executive officers of the District and the *Adhiṣṭhānādhikaraṇa* as the city municipality, at the head of which was the *Puroga* also called *Purara pāla* or *nagara-rakṣaka*. That officer was evidently the Mayor of the city,[142] and was called so after the name of the city itself. We may note that the Mayor of Daśapura is referred to *Daśapura pāla*.[143] Though a good measure of local autonomy was enjoyed by these urban units their administration was controlled by the Central Government through an officer called the *Pura-pāla Uparika*..

Mayor nominated?

The Mayor of the municipality was usually appointed by the Governor of the Province in which the municipal town was situated. This practice is indicated by the Junagādh Rock Inscription of Skandagupta which mentions that

140. *Arch. Sur. Report* 1903-4 P. 109.
141. *Ep. Ind.*, XX. pp. 61 ff.
142. D. C. Sircar, *op. cit.*, p. 333; Fleet *op. cit.*, No. 14.
143. Fleet, *op. cit.*, No. 18. P. 83.

Parṇadatta, the Governor of Surāṣṭra appointed his son Cakrapālita as the Mayor of the city of Girinagara which had passed through great difficulties. The inscription under reference catalogues the qualities which a Mayor should possess, and mentions with great satisfaction that Cakrapālita had the qualifications. The inscription says that a Mayor should be free from debt so that he might be able to rise above bribery, corruption and other financial temptations of his office. He must be one who could speak with eloquence so that he might be able to carry the members of the municipal council with him; he must be kind, courteous and always cheerful; he must be able to understand and respect the feelings of others; he must be able to get into close contact with the people by making social calls on them without any ceremony and win their popularity by holding receptions at his own residence to which the people in the town might be invited. Cakrapālita, the Mayor of Girinagara, is said to have been endowed with "patience, lordship, modesty, good behaviour, heroism without too great an estimation of his prowess, eloquence, self-control, liberality and high spiritedness, civility, the acquittance of debts, obligations, and freedom from empty-headedness, beauty, reprobation of things that are not right, absence of astonishment, firmness and generosity."[144]

The City Council

The City Council which worked under the leadership of the Mayor had onerous responsibilities, and duties, the main nature of its work being to provide amenities and convenience to the people living in the city. Even in those days it was felt that every city must be provided with water facilities both for irrigation and drinking purposes, with temples for the Gods that were worshipped, halls for holding public meetings

144. *Ibid.*, p. 63.

and other functions and pleasure gardens of different kinds, causeways, etc. It is evident from the Gangdhar stone inscription of Viśvavarman (A. D. 480) that both the officers of the government and the public tried to do much with a view to improve the civic amenities.[145]

In fact the anxiety of the ruling princes and the officers of the Government to provide and if necessary to restore and improve irrigation works is well borne out by the Junagādh inscription of Skandagupta. The inscription gives a graphic description as to how efficiently and effectively Cakrapālita, the Mayor of Girinagara, attended to the damming up of the great Sudarśana lake which suddenly burst on account of excessive rains.[146] As a result of the rains, the lake which was beautiful to look at was drained of its waters and it became veritably a *durdarśana* lake. When the people did not know what to do under the circumstances Cakrapālita came to their rescue anxious to provide for the welfare of the city and the surrounding region, and closed the breach and strengthened the enbankment at great cost within a short period of two months. The new embankment was 100 cubits long, 68 broad and 7 in height.[147] In A.D. 457-58 the same Cakrapālita constructed a temple for Viṣṇu on the banks of the lake.

Each city appears to have had a *dharmśāla* under a Superintendent (*āvasatika*).

145. *Ibid.*, p. 77-78.

146. Fleet. *op. cit.*, p. 64.

147. The Sudarśana lake has had an interesting history. About 310 B.C. during the reign of Candragupta Maurya, one Vaiśya Pusyagupta who was the governor of the Province of Girnar excavated the lake at the foot of the mountain Gujarat. During the days of Aśoka, Tuṣāspa the Yavana governor of the region made a number of canals from the lake for irrigation purposes. When Mahākṣatrapa Rudradāman was ruling over the region about A.D. 150 the lake was destroyed by storm, and, the water having escaped the lake lost all its charm and beauty. However the dams were soon rebuilt by Suviśāka, the Pahlava minister of the king. Again about three centuries later in August 455-56 once more the great lake burst its bunds and they were repaired by Cakrapālita.

Guilds

An important aspect of urban life in the Gupta period relates to guilds and their activities. During the period under survey there flourished many corporations of professionals who acted as a body in matters of common interest. Some of such corporations were also associated with the administration of the area in which they flourished. Of the 274 specimens of clay seals discovered by Bloch at Vaiśāli many bear the legend *śreṣṭhi sārthavāha kulika nigama* which has been translated into "the corporation of bankers, traders and merchants".[148] In the inscriptions the terms used to denote a guild were *nigama, śreṇi* and *nikāya,* and the place where they usually met was called the *nigama sabhā* which may be compared to guild-halls of modern Europe.[149]

Mention has been made earlier as to the way in which the *adhikaraṇa* of the Kōṭivarṣa *viṣaya* was carrying on the administration of his district during the days of Kumāragupta and Budhagupta with the help of an advisory council consisting of the representatives or heads of organisations like those of the Town Corporation, merchants, artisans and the writers or scribes. The *nagara śreṣṭhin* who may be called the President of the City Corporation was the prototype of the *Paṭṭaṇasvāmi* who figures very frequently in the mediæval inscriptions of South India.[150] The mercantile community was also represented in the advisory council of the *Viṣayapati* through its President. The artisans during the period appear to have organised themselves into a corporate body which was probably very influential, and hence it was also represented on the advisory council of the District Officer. It is difficult to see how the scribes, (*kāyasthas*) got representation in the advisory council of the officer of the

148. See the Excavations at Basrah *ASR,* 1903-1904. pp 112-118.
149. R. D. Banerji—*The Age of the Imperial Guptas,* pp. 83-85.
150. *E. I.,* XV, p. 131.

viṣaya. Probably the humbler sections of people who were employed in different establishments in the city, and belonged either to the government service or non-government service organised themselves into a corporation in order to be associated with the running of the local administration.

Besides the organisations referred to above, there were a good number of other corporations which played a great part in the areas in which they flourished. One among them was the guild of the silk-cloth weavers,[151] that flourished in the city of Daśapura identified with Mandasor in modern Gwalior. This guild of weavers were originally living in the Lāṭa *viṣaya* to the west of Mālva, but migrated to Daśapura because of the virtues of those that carried on the administration in that region. The weavers soon after their settlement in the region constructed a temple for the Sun God in A.D. 436 at their own expense. But about A.D. 472 part of the temple fell into repair. The guild of the silk-cloth weavers who were responsible for the construction of the Sun temple, now came forward and reconstructed the temple. During that period the country of Mālva is said to have been ruled by *pārthivas*[152] or local kings, which shows that the hold which the Central government exercised over that region was weak. Probably it was a period of political confusion in the Mālva country and naturally therefore a well organised and flourishing corporation of the type that prospered at Daśapura took upon itself the responsibility for the beautification of the city by the reconstruction of the temple.[153]

From the Indore copper-plate inscription of Skandagupta of G.E. 146 (A.D. 465) we learn of the existence of a guild of oilmen (*tailika śreṇi*) in the city of Indrapura,[154] which

151. Fleet, *op. cit.*, No. 18, pp. 80-85.
152. *Ibid.*, p. 81 l. 3.
153. See *ibid.*, pp. 86, 87.
154. *Ibid.*, pp. 70 ff.

had a leader, (*Pravara*). The guild appears to have been in such a prosperous condition that people in and around the locality began to have great confidence in it. It undertook the work of a modern bank, namely the receipt of deposit, its investment and the payment of interest on the same. Mention may be made of the fact that it received from a Brahmana the donation of a sum of money which was to be held in perpetuity (*ājasrikam*), as the capital, (*mūlya*) from the interest of which the guild according to its agreement with the Brahmana was to provide two *palas* by weight of oil for burning a lamp in the Sun temple at the place. Probably the interest was got by the investment of the money in some remunerative undertaking. The violation of the agreement was considered a great sin.

This shows that the guild had high integrity in the local region, and that it undertook not only functions of an economic nature like the receiving of deposits, but also of a religious kind like the keeping of an endowment for the maintenance of a lamp in the Sun temple at the place. Similarly the Bihar Stone Inscription also of Skandagupta records the gift of a permanent religious endowment as an *akṣayanīvī* created in the town of Ajapuraka. But unfortunately the name of the corporation to whom the donation was entrusted could not be traced in the inscription.[155] Likewise we get reference to the existence of a guild of painters.[156]

Some other contemporary sources suggest the existence of corporate organisations like those of traders, artisans and bankers, largely for commercial purposes. One of the Gupta seals bears the following inscription, namely *śreṣṭhi sārthavāha kulika nigama* or *nigamā* representing the corporation of bankers, traders and merchants. In fact the seals very often refer to guilds of bankers.[157] Commenting on the

155. *Ibid.*, p. 49 ff.
156. Meyer, *Hindu Tales*. p. 174.
157. *An. Rep. of Arch. Sur. of India*, 1913-14, p. 122.

seals D. B. Spooner remarked: "Banking was evidently as prominent in Vaiśāli as we should have expected it to be, judging from the notice in Manu to the effect that the people in Magadha were bards and traders".[158] The existence of the *śreṣṭhi* at Pāṭalīputra is referred to in the *Mudrārākṣasa* of Viśākhadatta.[159] The *śreṣṭhins* had a chief appointed by the king; and he controlled the affairs of the guild. From the Damodarpur Copper-plate Grant we learn that the *nagara śreṣṭhin* had a seat in the non-official council of the *adhikaraṇa* of the district.

Our attention is drawn to another seal at Bhita. The legend here is as interesting as that of Vaiśāli or Tīra bhukti. Here the term *Kulika,* according to Spooner, stands for the expression "bankers".[160] Whatever this may be, the Bhita finds testify to the existence of a separate guild of *Kulikas.* Sometimes personal seal impressions like *Prathama Kulikas* in Bengal were also discovered at Vaiśāli. There were the seals also of ordinary *Kulikas.* From an examination of various seals we are made to infer with others that there were three separate guilds, of bankers, merchants and traders besides a number of other guilds pertaining to their profession. One must say that these various guilds participated in the administration of the town and went a long way to make it a success.

Village Administration

The village was the lowest unit of the administrative system under the Guptas. It appears to have enjoyed a considerable amount of autonomy with regard to its administration which was carried on by a body of local officers and an assembly of the villagers.

158. *Ibid.*
159. Act VII, p. 540 (Ed. by Saradaranjan Ray), Calcutta, 1918.
160. *An. Rep. of Arch. Sur. of India,* 1913-14, p. 108.

One of the most important officers of the village was the *grāmika*,[161] who appears to have been its headman. The word is evidently derived from the word *grāma*, meaning village. It is difficult to state categorically what his functions were, but an important duty attached to his office was to guard the boundaries of his village by erecting boundary pillars wherever necessary, and maintaining them. He appears to have had also something to do with the administration of lands. One of the Damodarpur Copper-plates of the time of Budhagupta mentions that when one Nābhaka, a resident of the village, applied for the purchase of some uncultivated and unsettled land in his village called Caṇḍagrāma, the chief inhabitants of the place were informed of it by the *mahattaras*, *aṣṭakulādhikaraṇas* the *grāmikas* and others.[162] According to Manu they were in the enjoyment of several privileges such as the use for themselves of the king's dues received from the villages, and the referring of criminal cases to the head of ten villages and so on.[163]

Another important officer in the village was the *aṣṭa-kulādhikaraṇa* who finds mention in some of the Gupta inscriptions of the fifth century. The Damodarpur Copper-plate inscription mentions the *aṣṭakulādhikaraṇas* along with the *mahattaras* and the *grāmikas* and says that all of them informed the chief Brahmanas about certain particulars of a plot of land.[164] Again the Dhanaidaha inscription of the

161. Fleet, *op. cit.*, p. 112.
162. *Ep. Ind.* XV. p. 137.
163. *Ibid.* p. 137 *n.* 3.

ग्रामदोषान्समुत्पन्नान् ग्रामिकः शनकैः स्वयम् ।
शंसेद्ग्रामदशेशाय दशेशो विंशतीशिने ॥
यानि राजप्रदेयानि प्रत्यहं ग्रामवासिभिः ।
अन्नपानेन्धनादीनि ग्रामिकस्तान्यवाप्नुयात् (*Mann*, VII, 116. 118.

164. *Ep. Ind.* XV. P. 137.

reign of Kumāragupta and issued in A.D. 432-33 says that an officer called Viṣṇu mentioned some details about a plot of land to the ryots, Brahmanas, the *mahattaras,* the *aṣṭakulādhikaraṇas* and a few others.[165] These references are indicative of the fact that the *aṣṭakulādhikaraṇas* were important village officials like the *grāmikas, mahattaras* etc. and had a voice in matters relating to the purchase, disposal and administration of lands in the villages.

But it is not easy to offer a satisfactory explanation for the term either etymologically or otherwise. Different writers have offered different explanations for the term. One writer explains the term as a "local officer who exercised authority over eight villages".[166] But the explanation is not convincing for there is nothing in the term to suggest that authority was exercised by the officer over eight villages. There is no evidence to show that in the Gupta period eight villages were clubbed together into an administrative unit. Further the word *kula* does not lend itself to the meaning 'village' being given to it. Then again N. N. Das Gupta thinks that it means the *adhikaraṇa* or judicial court in the village composed of (more or less) eight judges. He further says that the term is analogous to the phrase *jyeṣṭhādhikaraṇaka-dāmuka-Pramukamadhikaraṇam* which occurs in the Gugrahati grant of Samācaradeva.[167] The above explanation also is difficult of acceptance for the following reasons. There is no evidence to show that the *aṣṭakulādhikaraṇa* was an officer entrusted with judicial functions. In the *adhikaraṇas* of the districts and the provinces we do not hear of the *aṣṭakulādhikaraṇa* as a member. From the two inscriptions referred to above and relating to the administration of the villages, he is mentioned as holding an office on a par with

165. *Ibid.* XVII. p. 346.
166. R. D. Bandoypādhyaya, J.A.S.B., (N.S.). V, pp. 460-1 l. 6.
167. *Indian Culture,* V, pp. 110-11.

the *mahattaras* and the *grāmikas* and discharging functions which were similar to those that were discharged by them. Thus the interpretation of the term as a judicial court is not acceptable.

Dr. R. G. Basak says that the term means "an officer in the village having supervising authority over eight *kulas*".[168] The term *kula* may mean a family, in which case the term *aṣṭakulādhikaraṇa* would mean an officer having control over eight families. The word *kula* also means an inhabited country (as much ground as can be ploughed by two ploughs each drawn by six bulls *vide* Kullūka's commentary on *Manu,* VII. v. 119).[169] Since the officers of the village were closely associated with the land transactions in the village it is possible there might have been appointed a person to have supervisory control over small land units in the village, each of which could be ploughed by sixteen ploughs. Even this explanation is not quite convincing. But it is interesting that the term *aṭṭhakulaka* is used to mean a Council of Justice in Buddhagosha's commentary on *Mahāparinibbana Suttānta.* It would seem that it functioned as a Court of Justice in the heydey of the Licchavi Republic. It might have perhaps continued its duties even in the Gupta period.

Mention has been made earlier to the *mahattaras.* They constituted another important group of officers who are referred to frequently in the inscriptions of the period. Sometimes they were also called *mahattamas.* A record of Dharasena II dated A.D. 571-72 mentions them along with the policemen and the soldiers or the *caṭa bhaṭa* corps.[170] The Damodarpur Copper-plates also mention them.[171] They

168. *Ep. Ind.* XVII P. 348 *n.*
169. *Ibid.* XV, p. 137.
170. Fleet, *op. cit.,* p. 169, *n* 7.
171. *E.I.,* XV, p. 137.

are often referred to as being associated with land transactions. According to Monier Williams the word means "the head or the oldest man in a village". Probably they were the leading men in the village either on account of their age or their wealth, social position and ability.

Talāvāṭaka

A fourth official in the village administration was the *Talāvāṭaka* mentioned in the Deo-Baranark inscription of Jīvita Gupta II. Probably it was the same as the *Talavārika* of the South Indian inscriptions, and indicated the office of the village watchman though it was once suggested that it indicated the office of the village accountant.[172]

Valat Kauṣan

Another official connected with the village administration was the *Valat kauṣan* who was very possibly a land revenue official primarily concerned with the recovery of income like the *Uparikara* and was also one who was the custodian of the privileges of the village. We gather these details from the Gaya copper-plate grant of Samudragupta in the course of which the following occurs: "Be it known to you (Valat kauṣans and others). For the sake of increasing the religious merit of (my) parents and of myself, this village is granted by me, as an *agrahāra,* with the assignment of the *uparikara* to the religious student, the Brahmana Gopasvāmin, of the Bhāradvāja gotra and the Bahvṛicha śākhā. Therefore attention should be paid to him, by you; and his commands should be obeyed; and all the customary tributes of the village, consisting of that which is to be measured, gold etc. should be given. And, from this time forth the tax-paying cultivators, artisans etc. of other villages should not

172. Fleet, *op. cit.*, p. 217.

be introduced by the *Agrahārika* of this (village) (for the purpose of settling in it and carrying on their occupations); (for) otherwise there would certainly be a violation of (the privileges of an *agrahāra*)".[173] Thus the *Valat kauṣaṇ* appears to have had varied duties, which were connected with the guarding of the interests of the village.

Akṣapaṭalika

Another important officer associated with the adminis tration of the village was the *Akṣapaṭalika.* According to Monier Williams the term *Akṣapaṭala* means a "court of law", "a depository of legal documents". The *Arthaśāstra* of Kauṭalya mentions the *Akṣapaṭala.* According to Monahan the *akṣapaṭala* of the *Kauṭalīya* was the Accounts Office as also the general Record room.[174] Probably in the Gupta period copics of the records of the government relating to title deeds, royal grants etc. were kept in the Records office of the village concerned. In the Mauryan period these *Akṣapaṭalas* were imperial officers connected with revenue. By the time of the Guptas the *Akṣapaṭalas* are designated as lower officials mostly connected with the village accounts. The explanation given above may be tentative. But the fact remains that the designations of one period need not be the same in another period.

The designation *akṣapaṭala* is an instance in point. It may be pointed out that ancient Indian polity was never stagnant but was progressive in character. Probably the *akṣapaṭalika* was the custodian of the legal documents in the local area and his superior was the *Mahākṣapaṭalika* who had his office probably at the capital.[175]

173. *Ibid.*, p. 257.

174. Early *History of Bengal*, p. 45. See also V. R. R. Dikshitar: *Mauryan Polity*. p. 157.

175. Fleet, *op. cit.*, p. 190.

In the Gaya copper-plate inscription of Samudragupta it is said that one *dūta* Gopasvāmin was the *Akṣapaṭalādhikṛta* of another village.[176] This points to the fact that in the Gupta period a local officer could hold two distinct posts. It is difficult to fix the place of this officer in the hierarchy of local officials then prevailing. Still if a guess could be made the offices of the *dūta* and the *akṣapaṭalādhikṛta* must have been of co-equal status or rank but certainly superior to that of the *agrahārika* who was probably an officer in special charge of an *agrahāra*.[177]

Other Officials

The Deo-Baranark inscription of Jīvita Gupta mentions an officer of the village called *Sīmakarmakāra* who was probably an official in charge of the maintenance of the boundary marks in the village.[178] It is not known if he was the same as the *Sīmā pradāta* who was also the fixer of the boundaries.[179] Among the other minor officers in the local areas were the *Pramātri* (the surveyor and measurer).[180] *Nyāya karaṇika* (an officer in charge of the settlement of disputes and cases especially arising out of the fixation of land boundaries),[181] *Dhruvādhikaraṇa* (probably a revenue superintendent).[182] *Karaṇika* (a records officer)[183] and the *Haṭṭika* very probably the collector of market dues.[184]

These numerous petty village officials carried on the administration of the village with the help of an assembly or

176. *Ibid.*, p. 257.
177. *Ibid.*, p. 52 and *n*.
178. *Ibid.*, p. 217 and *n*.
179. *E.I.* XII. p. 75.
180. *Ibid.*, XVII. p. 325.
181. *Ibid.*, XII. p. 79.
182. Fleet, *op. cit.*, pp. 169-170 and *n*.
183. See for instance *Ep. Ind.*, Vol. IV, pp. 105-106.
184. *Ibid.*, p. 254.

Pariṣad which must have been representative in character. It was evidently a counterpart of the District Council or *adhikaraṇa.* One of the Basārh seals refers to the Udana-kūpa *Pariṣad* which means probably the assembly of Udana-kūpa.[185] We have no clear idea of the strength of the *Pariṣad* or its functions. If any inference may be drawn from a similar institution that administered the affairs of the Buddhist vihāra at Sāñci, then it may be said that the *Pariṣad* was a committee which consisted of five persons. The Sāñci stone inscription of Candragupta II of A.D. 412-13 says that one Amrākārdava, a dependant of the Emperor having prostrated himself in an assembly of five persons (*pañca maṇḍalyām praṇipatya*) granted them the village or allotment of Iśvaravāsaka.[186] The five persons were monks and probably *Sthaviras*, and the chief officials in charge of the administration of the monastery of Kākanādaboṭa. If the *Pariṣad* discharged similar functions it may be said that it decided matters pertaining to the administration, and it was with its approval and sanction, that the village officials carried on the administration of the village.

---

185. *ASIR*. 1903-04, p. 109.
186. Fleet, *op. cit.*, p. 31.

CHAPTER VII

RELIGION

Section I

Conception of a Secular State

On 15th August, 1947, the dawn of freedom greeted entire India with all its charm and beauty. The charm of a bloodless revolution and the beauty of the achievement of independence were widely marked. The Indian State is built upon a secular basis. If we understand rightly the position of a secular state it is one in which what is called a state religion does not find a place. If a state is bound by a religion then the beliefs and doctrines of that religion would be fostered more as against those of other religions. In a secular state as we conceive it to-day there will be absolute freedom of conscience for its citizens. Such a state of freedom is to profess any faith and even to propagate it. But the government rightly reserves to itself the right to introduce social reform by law and interfere with religious and educational institutions if they go wrong. But it would be in the interest of religion and its followers to observe religious neutrality to which the British Government in India pledged itself as early as 1840. It was at this time the British authority gave up the exercise of surveillance and control over Hindu religious endowments. To interfere actively with these endowments by a secular democratic state is to say the least anomalous. The history of any country is partly influenced by its religious beliefs. A state would become absolutely materialistic if it would completely ignore the force of religion and the moral conduct of the people. But some of the religious beliefs and customs might have become obsolete and may be deemed anachronisms. A new view of social and moral welfare might be taken in conformity with enlightened public opinion. Such customs might be regulated by law even in a secular state. The introduction of such healthy reforms would not detract from the spirit of a secular state in general.

The most fundamental implication of the secular state should be the non-recognition of communalism in any form. It has been unequivocally said that the modern government in India would fight relentlessly this demon of communalism and root it out not only in the public services but also in the educational institutions. He alone is a true citizen who is not swayed by religious motives in public life. Here community or caste should have no place but merit and efficiency should alone count. But in adumbrating this view one should guard against the danger of the outlook becoming essentially materialistic. A secular state must therefore be based on the ethical and moral considerations of the people committed to its charge. In any sphere of activity fanaticism of any kind should not be tolerated but on the other hand a secular state must be based on liberal and democratic principles calculated to preserve the freedom of not only individuals but also groups. Such a state would be really constitutional and its citizens law-abiding. It has been well said recently 'A liberal democratic state, actively promoting the well-being of all its citizens without distinction, under conditions that will secure the freedom of individuals and groups of all kinds to pursue their legitimate activities without undue interference from their neighbours or from the state —that should be our ideal'.[1]

Dharma and the State

Let us now turn our attention to the Gupta state in relation to Dharma. Dharma is a mysterious expression

1. K. A. N. Sastri: 'The Concept of a Secular State', p. 32.

denoting various things, political, economic, social and religious. Any definition of Dharma will not be very satisfactory but Dharma Śāstras promulgate rules and regulations of what they understand to be the correct definition of the word Dharma. The Gupta age was in particular a thriving epoch in the field of Dharma Sāstra literature. As we have pointed out at the outset in dealing with the sources of information, several Dharma Śāstras from which we still draw our material, were reduced to writing or were composed in this epoch. Not only this class of literature but also the literature which we call the Purāṇas to-day, underwent also final redaction during this period. The Purāṇas which contain old material in other respects added considerably to the Vamśānucarita portion and were brought up-to-date in the time of the early Gupta Kings. Besides containing the names of kings of the various dynasties which ruled in India at that time, the Purāṇas throw a flood of light on the social and religious conditions. They form a mine of information for a student of sociology. So far as we are able to gather both the Dharma Śāstras and the Purānic texts do not seem to preach any differences in the religious beliefs and customs; much less can they be dubbed as sectarian in character and considered as preaching sectarianism or separatism in religion. A careful student of Gupta history will at once testify to the cosmopolitan character and the catholicity with which they deal with questions, social and religious. In short the sectarian rancour and spirit which disfigure this wonderful land, which has always striven for the fundamental unity, were absent in Gupta times. Not even in the time of Harsavardhana can we speak of sectarianism with any certainty. The imperial age of the Guptas was marked by a rational and sensible cosmopolitanism in which no rancour or jealousy was present.

The Dharma Śāstras and for the matter of that even the Purānas of the time gave vent to the lay elements as distinguished from the religious. But in the time we are speaking of, there was no lay element as such; for even politics to them was based upon Dharma or religion. It was religion that permeated the life of not only the ancient citizen but of the state as well. In this connection a word may be said about the nature and character of the Gupta states. We have already said that in ancient India in general and in the Gupta epoch in particular, there was nothing purely secular for everything was rooted in Dharma, whatever that term may connote. Speaking about the constitution of the state, reference has already been made that there was no legislature as such in Gupta India. The State could not make new laws and amendments to law. There was already the Law which had been established by the ancient seers and sages and the state had only to administer that Law. In other words the judges could interpret the Law according to their ingenuity and it was for the king to accept or reject the judgement offered by these judges, if ever an appeal was preferred to him. So the Dharma *śāstras* of the time were accepted both by the state and the common man to be the Law code, and any infringement was considered libellous The Dharma śāstras which embodied the code of Law divided their subject into two broad classifications, the *Rāja Dharma*[2] and the *Prajā Dharma.* The *Prajā Dharma*[3] consisted in its turn of *Svadharma* or doing one's own duties ordained and observing what is called *Sanātana Dharma, i.e.,* duties expected of every individual in the accomplishment of the moral and material welfare of the community at large. This system was healthy to the extent that each one was expected to discharge his or her functions and each contributed thereby not to the clash of ideologies but to the sum total of the

2. See the *Rāja Dharma* by Prof. K. V. Rangaswami Ayyangar, Adyar, 1946.

3. See Chapter LX of the *Rāja-Dharma* portion of the *Mahābhārata.*

society in which he or she was a member. A feeling of brotherliness was naturally created and the prayer was for the *yoga-kṣema* of the state and its citizens. The *Rāja-dharma* helped in so far as every member of the society did his work without any clash and every member of the community, whether orthodox or heterodox, pursued his ideas and ideals. The *Rāja Dharma* came in handy to prevent malpractices among the peoples not only in religion but also in social and economic matters so that no confusion would arise in the rank and file of society and state.

Institutions pertaining to a State are secular, if we have to judge by modern notions of polity, but political institutions devoid of moral and ethical considerations were considered an impediment to human welfare and progress. This was abundantly realised in Gupta India and positive steps were taken to infuse the spirit of religion in everything secular. It did not mean and need not mean that religion largely guided and controlled the state policy and administration. It however meant that Law and Morality had a large place in politics and it was Dharma that exerted a moderate influence even in the day-to-day administration of the Imperial Guptas. The old conception was that Dharma was eternal and everlasting and the ancients had therefore no faith in man-made law which would be changing according to the whims and fancies of the legislature. If a state had the welfare of the society at its heart and if it worked for the common good of that society, that state could not escape easily from its function of absolutely preserving the social order. With this end in view even secular things were founded on the bed-rock of Dharma and this prevented an arbitrary monarch or a tyrannical ruler to transgress this Dharma and to let in what he thought was best for his people. If he indulged in the transgression of laws and rules, which had been already established, it would be disturbing the tranquillity and peace of the people who would then be swayed by notions of revolt, revolution and anarchy.

So the Gupta monarchs in conformity with the monarchs of old looked upon Dharma as something sacerdotal and endeavoured according to their best to protect the people according to the *Rāja dharma* prescribed. Viewed from every aspect it was Dharma that was responsible for the well-being of both state and society. In the words of the Upaniṣad (*Bṛahadāraṇyakopaniṣad*) 'Dharma is the king of kings'.[4] It could not be supposed that the king who presided over so many secular institutions in the state was at the very top of the administration and that he could prove in the nature of things an arbitrary monarch. It was not so. Above the king the ancients cleverly devised an impersonal institution, which was called in popular parlance Dharma. This put spokes in the wheel of administration. If the administrative machinery went wrong, it was Dharma which came to the aid of both the king and the people. The king therefore respected the conventions of a certain group or guild, pursued their rules and regulations and ultimately pronounced judgment. Even with regard to every territorial division, whether it be a village or a district or even a town, the king would not ignore the rules peculiar to it and always showed a tendency to abide by them rather than press his own point of view. Therefore by skilfully weaving the web of Dharma and by providing cleverly checks and balances on the otherwise arbitrary nature of a king, the ancients imposed the beliefs and customs of their religion which made even secular things appear in the garb of religion. This was of course possible because the state consisted of one society and community though it was split into different sects whose material differences were not much but whose activities pointed to the

4. 1-4. 14 (Sri Ramakrishna Math. 1945).

direction of unity, not only cultural but even administrative. This we call the Smārta dharma or the Dharma incumbent upon the common people who were not affected by sectarian spirit but who were all working in unison with one belief in one common God.

Section II

Personal religion of the Guptas

It has been taken for granted by all scholars, European and Indian, who have written on the history of the Imperial Guptas that they belonged to Vaiṣṇavism by religion and that they were followers of the Vaiṣṇava school. This view has been largely based upon certain terms and expressions which are found not only in their inscriptions but also in their coins. Unfortunately for us, there are no literary evidences even of doubtful value to settle this question of their religion. Therefore we have to depend mostly upon inscriptions which have been handed down to us and also on the numismatic evidence furnished to us by the large find of coins of different denominations. One should accept that inscriptions and coins are of primary value and there could be no controversy about these evidences which have to be believed more or less implicitly. While considering the question of the religion of the Imperial Guptas, the scholars who have already tackled the subject have reached the unanimous conclusion that the Guptas of the Imperial age were the followers of the Vaiṣṇava school and had implicit faith in Vaiṣṇavism.

It is undoubtedly true that the swing of the pendulum pointed more towards the revival of Vedic religion, tradition and tenets from the time of the Śungas if not earlier, which may be attributed to the reactionary doctrines and principles which were enunciated by the two monastic schools which developed into two religions, Buddhism and Jainism long afterwards. Both these schools of thought laid more stress on the doctrine of *Ahimsā* (which by the way is one of the tenets of Sanātana Dharma) and consequently questioned the Vedic sacrifices which involve injury to living beings like the *paśumedha* in *yajña*. Reason and Logic exercised the minds of people at large and they found their rationale in the tenets of the new schools of thought. Hence the two monastic schools which became soon converted to two different cults attracted a large number of people and claimed a number of adherents to their religions. In the course of centuries when the great Upaniṣads were composed and following which these two monastic sects were in vogue, it is but natural that the new religions found a greater fillip and there was a tendency to bypass the established Vedic religion and its ritual. But the Vedic *yajñas* died hard and there was a follower here and there who still clung to the old ideals with faith and belief, and who still continued to perform the Vedic sacrifice as enjoined by the Śrauta texts.

Apart from the Brahmana community, the Kṣatriya community, from whose ranks monarchs were selected to wield the rod of punishment impartially and justly, had its own obligations not only towards itself but also towards its subjects and country. Though we do not hear either in literature or inscriptions of the revival of the ancient rite of Rājasūya, still it is made very explicit that the Aśvamedha or horse-sacrifice enjoined upon righteous Kṣatriya monarchs, was performed by more than one monarch of the Imperial Guptas, and this sacrifice seems to have been performed by other monarchs such as the Vākāṭakas during the time of the Guptas and earlier in the historical period by Puṣyamitra Śunga.

The Aśvamedha[5] is an old sacrifice attributed to some very ancient kings like Rāma and Yudhiṣṭhira. The idea was

5. See the author's *Hindu Administrative Institutions*, p. 93.

that when once the Kṣatriya felt that he was an emperor and overlord of all-India (the old conception of all-India was the territory between the Cape Comorin and the Himālayas) he could assert his suzerainty effectively and visibly by letting loose the horse to be sacrificed; and when once it returned to the capital unmolested by any prince then he resorted to this Vedic rite which was known as Aśvamedha. We know that the Imperial Gupta emperor, Samudragupta and his grandson Kumāragupta indulged in this rite after the completion of their *digvijaya* which amounted to the conquest of all-India. The principle underlying this *digvijaya* concept was to find a secure place in Heaven which the performance of this rite, Aśvamedha, ensured.

Our conviction has always been that history was coloured by the religious beliefs and customs of the times and the Gupta history was no exception to the rule. During this time it was abundantly believed that the enjoyment in Heaven and the attainment thereof were the goal of the ruling monarchs who had full faith in such things. Therefore it is no matter for surprise that Samudragupta or his grandson was carried away by the passions of the times and both are known as Aśvamedha-kartas. We are at some length on this subject just to indicate to the common reader that the sectarian rancour was still absent in the horizon of Gupta religion, that we are still in the last days of Vedic injunctions and prescriptions and that institutions like the Aśvamedha were still live-institutions full of vigour and energy. In a period when the Vedic injunctions were the law of the land, the religion of that land cannot be narrowed down to one particular form; and it is therefore not correct on the part of scholars to import new ideas in a place where even imagination has no place to play a significant part; for it is wrong to conceive of any sectarian spirit in religious matters, especially when the Vedic religion was rooted in the minds of both the kings and the people to such an extent that it could not be shaken. It is therefore legitimate to conclude that we are still living in the Gupta period in the Vedic age which knew no separate deity and which realised that every separate deity was a manifestation of the one God who pervaded the universe with all His attributes.

This idea viz., that the Gupta period enunciated beliefs and principles of the Vedic age gains further support if we carefully study and analyse the inscriptions, especially the Bilsad stone pillar inscription of Kumāragupta.[6] Samudragupta is known as *Dhanada varuṇendrāntaka samasya kṛtāntaparaśoh,* an epithet which has almost become standardised as we see from the later inscriptions of Skandagupta. The epithet at once suggests itself that the Vedic religion is too much with us. Here the comparison of the king and his exploits is not to the minor deities of Hinduism as we understand today. We are too familiar with deities like Śiva and Viṣṇu, Kārttikeya and Vināyaka. But these deities are not found mentioned in the inscriptions before us. The Gupta inscriptions under discussion elect to glorify the monarch as compared with the deities mentioned in the Vedic texts like Yama, Varuṇa and others, the dikpālas of Hindu literature. Dhanada with whom Samudragupta is compared is no less than Kubera. This comparison with a Vedic deity like Kubera demonstrates beyond doubt that the king's riches could be compared only with the wealth of the Vedic deity.

The next comparison is with Varuṇa the god of the waters. Varuṇa is a powerful deity who wanders at his will both in the atmosphere and the waters and is invoked generally when persons are stricken with difficulties relating to air and water. It may be remarked in passing that one of

6. Fleet, *op. cit.* No. 10. p. 43.

the early Tamil god was Varuṇa mentioned in the extant Śangam literature.[7] Another god equally great and equally honoured was Indra, king of the Devas. Indra holds a considerable position in the Vedic pantheon as the lord of the gods and as signifying strength and awe. In invoking this god of gods the Vedic seers always prayed for safety and to endow them with courage and strength. It is believed that Indra was able to remove the weeds and thorns on the path of love and kindness. Very nearly till the Gupta times the ancient Tamils instituted a festival in honour of Indra and if the *Śilappadikāram*, a Tamil classic of about 150 A.D. could be believed, Tamil India instituted a festival in honour of Indra and which nearly lasted for a month.[8] What we wish to drive at is that Indra is predominantly a very old deity.

The king is also compared to Antaka the god of death. The god of death would invoke fear in the minds of common people who fear death. The god of death is primarily concerned with justice meting it out impartially by his *daṇḍa* or the rod of punishment. In the case of Samudragupta it may be interpreted in both ways. From the evidence of the coins we understand that he possessed unequalled prowess and it may be interpreted that this prowess was only second to that of god Yama. But a strong man like Samudragupta could act justly, and could award punishment according to the gravity of the offence. In other words Samudragupta was not a mere militarist but an acute thinker and a shrewd judge. He knew when and against whom arms should be used. He knew how to conquer a territory and overcome its people and to act at the same time gently. The very fact that Samudragupta had these honorifics shows that the Gupta age had not yet

7. *Tolkāppiyam*, Porul. 1.5.
8. See *Silappadikāram* Canto V.

witnessed the birth of neo Hinduism by which we understand that religion to-day.

Reference is also made frequently in the inscriptions to Agnihotras[9] and Mahāyajñas.[10] The frequent occurrence of these expressions shows the hold of Vedic religion on the common people. The Agnihotra, it need not be told, was a Vedic rite enjoined especially on the Brahmanas. So also the Mahāyajñas. The Pañcamahāyajñas or the five sacrifices are duties incumbent on a true householder who is known as the Gṛhastha. They are in honour of Gods, Pitṛs, etc. If we compare the foregoing details mentioned both in the inscriptions and coins of the Gupta emperors we do not feel that the Gupta age was rent by separatist movement, which disfigured the pages of history in later years. It was then felt also that Sanskrit which was the vehicle of Vedic practices was indispensable, and patronage was given not only to men learned in Sanskrit and the Vidyās relating to it, but sufficient encouragement was shown to authors whether the subjects dealt with were of a religious or quasi-religious nature. Even technical sciences were shown due consideration; in fact the Gupta age produced a vast literature on humanities and sciences, part of which is extant even to-day. What we want to show is that Sanskrit was the language of the literate and it was perhaps the state language as we can gather from the various Sanskrit inscriptions.

Section III

Case for Vaiṣṇavism

The foregoing survey must make it abundantly clear to students of Gupta history that the Vedic religion still persisted in that age almost as a live-religion and to read into it any other meaning may not prove entirely based on facts.

9. Fleet. *op. cit.* p. 71.
10. *Ibid.* pp. 170 & 190.

Scholars are not wanting to say that the Imperial Guptas belonged to the school of Vaiṣṇavism and were Vaiṣṇavas in religion; but this seems to be not the whole truth. If one goes into the question with caution and care, which it deserves, it is patent that a separate school or a separate sect of Vaiṣṇavism was still to be born. It was in this age that people looked upon different deities as the manifestation of one God in whom they had implicit faith. Those who believe in Vaiṣṇavism as distinct from Śaivism hold the view that the early Guptas were its followers. In support of this they point out the following which occur repeatedly both in inscriptions and the coins:—

(1) The Gupta monarchs style themselves Paramabhāgavatas and this is sufficient to show that they clung to the Vaiṣṇava religion and they were themselves Vaiṣṇavas.

(2) Lakṣmī, the goddess of wealth who is supposed to be the consort of Viṣṇu, figures in several of the coins of the period.

(3) Garuḍa taken to be the vehicle (*vāhana*) of Viṣṇu is portrayed in the seals of the period.

(4) Viṣṇudhvaja or the Flag-staff of Viṣṇu is mentioned by name in the last inscription of Budhagupta.

(5) The Junagāḍh inscription of Skandagupta opens with an invocation to Viṣṇu forcing upon us the inference that the king was an ardent worshipper of Viṣṇu.

These are facts of great importance and must be pondered over seriously and cautiously by a student of history. Let us take up for examination every one of them and point out that the views of the adherents of this theory of Vaiṣṇavism are not supported by facts.[11]

11. *Ibid.*, Nos. 7, 8, 9, etc.

(1) The Imperial Guptas are generally known as *Paramabhāgavatas*. This term is of paramount importance to a student of Hindu religion. The great seal of Kumāragupta which was discovered at Bitāri contains also the significant term *Paramabhāgavata*. By the term *Paramabhāgavata* one can understand to-day that one is a devotee of Lord Viṣṇu but was it so meant in the time of the Guptas is a question that cannot be answered with any definiteness. The term consists of two words, *Parama* and *Bhāgavata*. The word *Bhāgavata* means and should mean that which pertains to Bhagavān. The question is who is this Bhagavān? According to the conception which prevailed in the days of the Guptas, the term Bhagavān should connote the one god who is a Sāḍguṇya-paripūrṇa. In other words this Bhagavān must have the six attributes which are (1) Aiśvarya, (2) Vīrya, (3) Yaśas, (4) Tiru (Śrī), (5) Jñāna, and (6) Vairāgya. These six attributes find mention in the foot-note of the celebrated commentator Parimelalagar in the opening portion of the *Kural* where occurs the term Bhagavān.[12] The attributes mentioned are not peculiar to any one deity but peculiar to the one deity whom we call God. Bhagavān is a term which is applied to all gods of different sects prevailing in the land. For example we speak of Bhagavān Buddha. In our own time we speak of the late Maharṣi at Tiruvaṇṇāmalai as a Bhagavān. Therefore the term Bhagavān need not be applicable to any one deity. It is a general term connoting the greatness of the Lord who is said to permeate the Universe, with all His attributes. Nearly two or three centuries before the Guptas, the author of the *Tirukkural* flourished and spoke of Ādi Bhagavān as the first of all the world. We cannot say that the author of the *Tirukkural* referred by this expression to God Viṣṇu. He might have referred to Jaina god or to

12. *Tirukkural* with the commentary of Parimelalagar: Note to verse 1.

Śiva or any other deity. What we wish to point out is that the term did not stand in the Gupta days only for God Viṣṇu.

In a comparatively recent work *Bhagavatbhajanotsava Paddhati* which is full of Dhyāna ślokas and which is essentially religious there is a popular stanza which refers to Prahlāda, Parāśara, Nārada, Puṇḍarīka, Vyāsa, Rukmāngada, Śuka and Śaunaka as Parama Bhāgavatas. One may say at once that these great personages were celebrated devotees of Hari; but this did not prevent them from being equally devoted to other deities as such. For instance, Parāśara and Śaunaka need not be marked out as particularly devoted to Lord Viṣṇu. They were equally devoted to other gods and to them there was what is known as *abheda-buddhi*. In other words they believed in one Universal God who is himself the Creator, the Protector and the Destroyer. The division of functions assigned differently to the Gods viz., Creation, Protection and Destruction and the conception of the triple deities, manifesting the one Lord are much later than the Gupta age. And therefore by using this expression, the imperial monarchs of the Gupta age styled themselves devotees of the one God who pervades the Universe and they did not mean any one particular deity.

The word *Parama* which is attached to the expression Bhāgavata means simply that these kings were very much devoted to the great God. This means broadly that in the discharge of their administrative duties they would not be carried away by the materialistic outlook but would ever have a thought of God in the background. They were anxious to execute their duties religiously and conscientiously so that it would be pleasing to their subjects. A few critics may associate the term Bhāgavata with the *Bhāgavata Purāṇa* which goes today by the name of *Śrīmad Bhāgavatam*. Though tradition avers that the *Śrīmad Bhāgavatam* is a major purāṇa and must be included in the eighteen purāṇas doubts have been raised as to the antiquity of it. Though literally Vyāsa is the compiler of all Purāṇas, still some would attribute its authorship to Śrī Śuka or Śuka Brahmam as he is known while others would regard Bopadeva who is the author of the *Muktāphala,* a work dependent on the *Bhāgavata,* as its author. If so, this Purāṇa could not have originated before the 13th century: but this view is not tenable.

The *Bhāgavata* is largely based upon the *Viṣṇu Purāṇa* and repeats the materials contained there in some portions and amplifies them in other portions. It is of course significant to note that Rāmānuja, who was perhaps the contemporary of Kulōttunga Cōla II had not mentioned the *Bhāgavata* as an authority but from this it is not proper to conclude that the great Vaiṣṇava reformer was not aware of this work. But we do not want to enter into this controversial question of the date of the *Śrīmad Bhāgavatam* but suffice it to say that it could have been an inspiration and a guide to the Imperial Guptas, as we take this Purāṇa as a pre-Gupta production.[13]

It may be pertinently asked then if the term *'Bhāgavata'* in the *Dēvi Bhāgavata Purāṇa* has any special significance. *Devī Bhāgavatam* means a purāṇa dealing entirely with the Devī or Goddess and also in Her honour. Devotees of Devī read it a number of times during the Navarātri festival even to-day, and attach a certain amount of sacredness to it. From this one can understand that the term *Bhāgavata* has been used broadly to mean one fully absorbed in the glories of the Lord and also in the glories of the Devī. This does not mean that there was inferiority or superiority of deities but it means definitely one deity manifesting itself in different ways. At least the Gupta inscriptions do not mean any sectarian deity but certainly refer to Bhagavān whoever he may be.

13. See the author's paper on the date of the *Bhāgavata Purāṇa.* Journal of the Madras University, January and July 1949, pp. 85-95.

The usage of referring to Bhagavān is always present with us from very ancient times. Even to-day in difficulties or worries we speak of *Bhagavat-Samkalpam*. In the Gupta days, however, it should mean comprehensively as denoting personal gods who, to repeat once again, are the manifestation of one great deity, wonderfully set forth in the Upaniṣadic lore.

(2) Another plank in support of the theory is that the figure of Lakṣmī is made use of largely in the Gupta coins.[14] The explanation that she is the consort of Lord Viṣṇu is not satisfactory though not wrong. With the revival of faith in absolute Vedic monotheism and the definition and purpose of each and every manifestation, Lakṣmī has to be taken as embodying the wealth and riches of the land. The Gupta monarchs who had amassed wealth by different ways hankered after more riches to be spent on worthy causes. Lakṣmī is considered as the Goddess presiding over immeasurable wealth and they made it a point to worship her and honour her by striking coins with Her image. One need not be surprised at this knowing full well the financial stability of the huge Gupta Empire from the days of Samudragupta onwards. If we further probe into the subject and find out the true interpretation that could be placed upon this curious phenomenon indulged in largely by the Guptas, we are much more strengthened in our belief that the Gupta monarchs were out to preserve pure democracy not incompatible with a constitutional monarchy and this they exhibited by carving an image of Lakṣmī on their coins. This image, it can be said without fear of contradiction, represents the Rājyaśrī, that is, the wealth of the kingdom of the ancient Hindu monarchs. The feeling was that everything depended upon finance and the Gupta monarchs who knew it invoked the Goddess of Wealth to shower them with plenty so as to enable them to

14. Fleet, *op. cit.*, p. 61. Allan: *Gupta coins*, p. 116.

realise the ends of the State. On Rājyaśrī depended the sovereignty of the kingdom.

A sovereign depended much upon the Śrī or the wealth of the state. In fact the treasury of a state has been regarded as the barometer on which depended the security and prosperity of its subjects. To say that a state is prosperous and flourishing is to say that in that state Śrī always puts on a smiling appearance. To realise the well-meaning ends of a state, *Kośa* or the treasury was the safety-valve and by honouring the Śrī, the Gupta monarchs honoured themselves. They were free from all wants and were ready to spend money on laudable objects. This explains why the image of Lakṣmī has figured so widely in the Gupta coins. No doubt the conception of Lakṣmī as the consort of Viṣṇu was there. To all intents and purposes they did not magnify it but they did glorify the goddess of riches.

(3) Another argument in favour of Vaiṣṇavism has been put forth, namely, the Guptas paid particular attention to Garuḍa, the vāhana of Viṣṇu.[15] After all the vāhana is only a paraphernalia and this cannot be trotted out as an argument in favour of their religion. If Garuḍa is the vāhana of Viṣṇu, Ṛṣabha or the bull is equally the vehicle of Lord Śiva. In the inscriptions of the Guptas one meets with Nandi or the bull to which equal importance is attached. To say in the same breath that the Gupta monarchs who were Vaiṣṇavas, paid a great tribute to Nandi is meaningless. It would be meaningful if we take the Gupta monarchs were cosmopolitan in outlook and realised that they were Hindu monarchs first and foremost.

(4) The same argument will hold good in respect of the Viṣṇudhvaja or the Flag-staff of Viṣṇu which is recorded in the inscription of Budhagupta and which was raised by one

15. *Ibid.*, pp. 52, 90.

Māṭri-Viṣṇu and his brother.[16] It may be said in passing that the monuments which have been left to us by the Gupta monarchs of old have to be treated as a source of information so far as their religion goes. The monuments discovered so far are temples and vihāras. The latter pertained to the cults of the Buddha and Vardhamāna which were also flourishing, as we shall soon see in the sequel, side by side with the Hindu religion. In all Hindu temples not only of this period but also of the later period, a *dhvaja* is another paraphernalia of a temple institution. Every Hindu temple possesses its flag-staff and it is no wonder that mention is made of the particular flag-staff of a Vaiṣṇava temple. Hinduism was in transition, the Vedic religion giving way slowly and surely to Purāṇic Hinduism. Hindu Gods and Goddesses began to be enshrined in temples and worshipped. That was the one sure way of indicating one's piety or predilection to certain Gods or Goddesses. It is therefore not surprising that the Gupta monarchs erected huge edifices for different gods accepted in popular religious tradition. This accounts largely for the existence of the *dhvajasthamba* in each and every temple either erected by these monarchs or by devotees.

(5) It is said that Skandagupta has explicitly invoked Lord Viṣṇu which is vouchsafed to us from a Rock Inscription from Junāgaḍh.[17] From this inscription we are told that the Gupta monarch Skandagupta was a particular devotee of Lord Viṣṇu and must have been a Vaiṣṇava in religion. At the outset one must clear his mind of all doubts concerning the true condition of religion at this period. Then there were no developed sectarian gods like Śiva or Viṣṇu, Devī or Mother Goddess. Each God or Goddess manifested Himself or Herself to fulfil a certain definite purpose or measure and it was natural that He or She was honoured by being built a

16. *Ibid.* p. 90.
17. *Ibid.* No. 14.

temple or with the celebration of a festival in His or Her honour. The Gupta monarchs were Smārtas by religion by which term we mean that they would worship Śiva or Viṣṇu, Devī or Kārttikeya without any difference and who would invoke a particular deity for a particular purpose. This does not mean that they were devotees of only one deity to the neglect of other deities.

The celebrated author of the Tamil classic *Śilappadikāram* has in his invocatory stanzas praised first the Moon, then the Sun and then the rains, the presiding god of which was Indra.[18] He was the brother of the monarch Cēran-Śenguṭṭuvan who was equally devoted to Śiva and Viṣṇu He had himself renounced worldly life and become a Sannyāsin. Therefore for all intents and purposes he was a Hindu. But he invoked the Moon and the Sun. By this it cannot mean that he was the follower of the Sun cult or the Moon cult. All that might be said of him is that he was a pious and good Hindu, who believed in the different manifestations of one Supreme God. In the same way we must treat the Gupta monarchs who would invoke this god or the other accepted by the Hindu pantheon at that time.

Section IV

Were they Śaivas?

The protagonists of the theory of Vaisṇavism as the religion of the Imperial Guptas are oblivious of the fact that Śaivism was also the accepted religion of both royalty and the common folk and effectively left its impress on the people in the Gupta times. The fact was that there was no sectarian spirit among the followers of orthodox religion who looked upon the different cults, which were peculiar to Hinduism, with favour and approval. That Śaivism was a force is

18. See the opening Canto of the Epic.

seen from three facts which cannot be controverted. There is first the evidence of architecture. Secondly the coins of the period warrant this assumption. Above all, there is the evidence of inscriptions, which throw abundant light on this question.

Speaking on the evidence furnished by the monuments of the period we have both Śiva and Viṣṇu temples side by side erected by devotees of the Gupta period. We can mention three of the surviving Gupta temples:—

(1) The Śiva temple at Bhumra in Nagod, (2) Pārvatī temple at Nachna-Kuṭhāra in Ajaigarh, (3) a temple of Śiva at Khoh in Nagaudh. A study of these monuments reveals that the Gupta monarchs were worshippers of Śiva in His different manifestations. They were not only devotees of this god but were equally devoted to the consort of Śiva, Pārvatī and Kārttikeya, the son of Śiva and also of the Saptamātṛkas all connected with Śiva worship. These monuments devoted to the various gods and goddesses of the Śaiva pantheon are enough to demonstrate the fact fully that they were worshippers both in Viṣṇu and Śiva temples as the practice was then as it is now with the persons of the Smārta Sect. There are other monuments also which belong to this period and which are devoted to the cult of Śiva. For example, the monuments of the Valabhi Senāpatis who were Śaiva devotees and followers may be quoted.

Secondly, there is the evidence of coins minted during this period. It is a fact of utmost importance that the Gupta emperors issued coins of different denominations, some in gold, some in silver and some in base metal. The coins contain figures of Garuḍa, Lakṣmī, Nandi and so on.[19] If we examine the silver coins of Skandagupta, we would find that they are valuable not only for determining the limits

19. Allan, *Coins of the Gupta dynasty*, pp. 119 ff.

of his empire, but also his religion. There are three different types on the obverse. They are Garuḍa, Nandi and Altar. The first reaction on the examination of these different types is that his religion was catholic in outlook. It was not a narrow religion of this sect or that. It was broad-based. All that is known is that he was a follower of the orthodox Hindu religion.[20]

Examining particularly the bull-type of coins of Skandagupta one has to presume that he had Śaiva leanings but the fact was he like his predecessors had no special leanings and he looked upon all the sects of the orthodox fold with impartiality and sagacity. From the fact that Śiva's bull, Nandi largely figures on the obverse of the coins of this Gupta monarch, the suggestion has been made that these coins were probably struck at Valabhi, for the bull is the badge of the later Senāpatis of Valabhi. But this suggestion is far-fetched and cannot stand the test of reason. We are not concerned here with the question as to which territory this set of coins belonged; but we want to show that his coins contained the figures of Śiva's vāhana, Nandi, and the existence of such types shows clearly that there was no partisan feeling in matters religious.

We now come upon a very important evidence, which is furnished by the inscriptions of this period. There is, first the significant epithet *Kṛtāntaparaśaḥ* which occurs in almost all the inscriptions of the Imperial Guptas. It means the "destroyer of Yama" and this destroyer of Yama was none else than Śiva. Therefore the inscriptions compare the Gupta monarchs generally with god Śiva. In this respect they do not show any sectarian bias. Next is the Mathurā Pillar inscription of Candragupta II dated in the Gupta year 61. The object of this inscription is to record that one Uditācārya who was living at that time installed two

20. *Ibid.* pp. 121-22.

images known as Kapileśvara and Upamiteśvara in the Gurvvāyatana. The inscription under reference clearly shows that the images installed were *lingas*. These *lingas* were named after his two teachers in the shrine intended for the perpetuation of the memory of his gurus. It was a practice in those days to erect memorials for gurus or teachers and this was done by Uditācārya who according to tradition was fourth in succession from Parāśara and tenth from Kuśika. It is said that this teacher, Uditācārya was a Maheśvara. While he is designated an ārya meaning 'respectable', the other teachers like Upamitra and Kapila are called Bhāgavatas i.e. persons who attained the rank of divinity. It is interesting to note here that the term Bhagavan was applied in Gupta times to eminent preceptors who could be ranked with divine beings. The term Bhāgavata therefore was a general name and could not be applied to a particular sect or religion.

This inscription, Śaiva in character raises an important issue whether there were Maheśvaras as such at this time. The one simple meaning that we can at once give to the word Maheśvara found in this inscription is that he was a follower of Śiva since He is also known as Maheśvara in important religious books. Dr. D. R. Bhandarkar who has edited this inscription[21] takes occasion to examine the Maheśvara doctrine, its origin and development from its early times. He contends that Lakulīśa Pāśupata mentioned in the *Vāyu Purāṇa* was perhaps the originator of this sect. We have examined this question at some length in our '*Some Aspects of the Vāyu Purāṇa*'. We do not agree with the view that there was one Lakulīśa sect among the Śaivas. But yogic practices were attributed to Śivayogins and one of them was the Pāśupata yoga, Paśupati being another name of God Śiva. The Pāśupata Yoga was quite different from

21. *Ep. Ind.*, Vol. XXI No. 1.

what the Pāśupata sect of later times followed. At the most the teachers mentioned in these inscriptions belong to the special school devoted to the Pāśupata Yoga. We do not see any reason for taking that our religion branched off into sects in the Gupta period or before. At the most we can regard this Maheśvara movement as a school of Yoga to which a few brilliant men belonged. One can say that it signified an aspect of Śaivism in the country.[22]

Again, there is the undated Udayagiri Cave inscription of Candragupta II. Dr. Fleet who has edited the Gupta inscriptions has remarked that it is a Śaiva inscription.[23] There is no doubt that the inscription belongs to the time of Candragupta Vikramāditya. The purpose of this inscription is to record the consecration of the Cave temple to God Śambhu which is one of the appellations of God Śiva. The excavation of this temple was at Udayagiri which was done by a hereditary minister of Candragupta, Śāba by name. This minister is also known by the family appellation, Vīrasena, and was a respected citizen of Pāṭalīputra and minister of Candragupta II. He must have sought the permission and assent of the king to excavate a temple in honour of God Śambhu. The most interesting fact is that Candragupta II himself came to Udayagiri in his company and perhaps saw the temple himself.

There is again the celebrated inscription which belongs to the reign of Kumāragupta dated in the Gupta year 117 and known as Karamdaṇḍa inscription in general. The peculiarity of this inscription is that it is incised on a *linga* which is of stone and is found in a site called Bharādhi Dīh which is near the village of Karamdaṇḍa in Faizabad (U.P.).[24] The interesting portion of the inscription is the

22. *Ibid.*, Vol. XXI. pp. 1-9.
23. Fleet, *op. cit.* p. 35.
24. *Ep. Ind.*, X, pp. 70 ff.

opening line which says, "Namo Mahādevāya". The inscription registers a gift made by Pṛthivīsena, the son of Śikharasvāmin who was a notable minister of Candragupta II. Pṛthivīsena himself was a distinguished son of Śikharasvāmin and is said to have been the *mantrin* of Kumāragupta and later on designated as *Kumārāmātya* and *Mahābalādhikṛta*. Pṛthivīsena's gift consisted of rightful offerings for the worship of the Mahādeva known as Pṛthivīsena. It has been surmised correctly that the donees of this temple were some Brahmanas from Ayodhyā of different gotras and cāraṇas.[25] It would appear from the term *Devadroṇi* that these Brahmanas were proficient in different branches of study especially in the Mantras and Sūtras and participated in the function got up in honour of God Śiva in their own place at Bārāthi. The Devadroṇi function was to take out in procession the image of Śiva. It would appear that even in those days the worship of Śiva did not merely consist in prayers offered to the *linga* but also in that the authorities of the temple took real part in the procession here of God Śiva on specified days. This evidence is enough to show that image worship was prevalent in ancient Gupta India, the images themselves being cast in metals. Therefore the knowledge of Indian iconography can be traced to Gupta India and perhaps even before that.[26]

It is further interesting to note that one of the feudatories of king Kumāragupta, Bandhuvarman by name who was ruling from Daśapura and who was a devotee of the Sun God is mentioned in the Mandaśor stone inscription. In this document mention is made of the season when God Śiva destroyed the body of Kāmadeva. This reference in 1.21 is interesting in as much as it is a reference to the legend

25. *Ibid.*

26. *Ibid.*, X pp. 70-72. Prof. Sten Konow has edited this inscription.

that God Śiva burnt the body of Manmatha in honour of which a festival was instituted and is conducted even today.[27] It transpires from this therefore that we almost live in modern India in the Gupta times. The Guptas were becoming more and more familiar with the Purāṇa legends which sing the glory of Śiva and Viṣṇu. What we wish to point out is that Śaivism as a religion was popular with the Gupta monarchs and they paid as much attention to this form of religion as they did to Vaiṣnavism.

We now come upon another inscription belonging to the year 156 of the Gupta era, which is known as the Khoh copper-plate inscription of the Mahārāja Hastin. The village of Khoh is in the Baghalkhand division in Central India. It must not be mistaken that Mahārāja Hastin who is known as Parivrājaka Mahārāja Hastin is one of the Gupta kings though his kingdom which was independent was subordinate to the Gupta empire. The inscription opens with the verse 'Namo Mahādevāya,' which at once shows the prevalence of Śaivism as a religion in Gupta times. Dr. Fleet who has edited the inscription says that it is non-sectarian. But in our opinion all the inscriptions of this period are generally non-sectarian. This Khoh inscription of Mahārāja Hastin, is indeed valuable for its opening invocation to God Śiva though the object of the document is to record the grant of a village by name Vasuntaraṣaṇḍika to some Brahmanas.[28]

The next inscription which has been edited by Dr. Fleet is also called the Khoh inscription of the Mahārāja Hastin. It is dated in the Gupta year 163. The object of the inscription is to register a gift by Mahārāja Hastin to certain Brahmanas; but what interests us is the opening invocation

27. Fleet, *op. cit.*, No. 18.
28. *Ibid.*, No. 21.

to God Śiva, 'Namo Mahādevāya'.[29] Though these inscriptions just mentioned before are not inscriptions of the Gupta monarchs as such still, they are of value in as much as these grants are made by a feudatory of the Imperial Guptas mentioning the Gupta year from which the grants took effect. In the respect that these inscriptions belong to the period of Imperial Guptas they are of value by indicating to us the trends in their religion. From these four documents we have to gather that the Guptas were followers of both Śaivism and Vaiṣṇavism which were as it were the twin established religions of the land. In the inscriptions of the period we can gather several names being appellations of Lord Śiva like Hara. Kokhāmukhasvāmin, Paśupati, Śūlapāṇi, Sthāṇu and others. These appellations point out that the common people in Gupta times were quite familiar with the Śaiva religion as much as the Vaiṣṇava religion. The phallic worship or the worship of Linga as god Śiva which has been with us for millenniums together was developed on a large scale. So we find the existence of Ekalingas prominently and predominantly in the Gupta period. There is much evidence to show that while this form of worship was fairly common in this period, examples of the figure of Śiva standing are not uncommon. There are some rare varieties of Caturmukhalinga but the most popular was only the Ekamukhalinga. These evidences and surviving Śaiva monuments of the period point out explicitly the fact that Śaivism was as much a popular religion as Vaiṣṇavism.

In this connection mention must be made of the Ardhanārīśvara form of Śiva in the Brahmanical iconography at Mathurā.[30] Mention has already been made of the iconographic wealth in the Gupta period and the spirit of religious tolerance that then prevailed. This form of

29. *Ibid.*, No. 22.

30. *Ibid.*, p. 224.

Śiva worship is very ancient and need not be treated as a legacy from the Buddhists. The Ardhanārīśvara form is nothing but that of Umāmaheśvara. This means that the Śakta becomes inactive without the Śakti. Umā is Śakti and Maheśvara is Śakta. If a child among the Tamils goes wrong even today we say *'Ummācci aḍikkum'* just to inculcate some religious fear in the mind of the child. It is an old saying among the Tamils and Ummācci stands for Umāmaheśvara. This speaks volumes about the ancientness of the Ardhanārīśvara cult. We have to take it that it was popular in Gupta India also.

We may further mention the forms of the Gaṅgā and the Yamunā, the two divine rivers of much importance for a student of ancient Indian history. These two rivers have been assigned the status of Goddesses and in the period of the Guptas they appear to have attained sufficient importance in the scheme of temple architecture. Dr. Agrawala seems to find in their mention a connection with Kālidāsa's *Kumārasambhava.* Though it is difficult to attribute that this special motif has anything to do with Kālidāsa's writings, a detached view may be taken of the artistic work done, for example, on the doorway of the Devagarh temple where the goddesses Gaṅgā and Yamunā are treated as attendants of the great god Śiva.[31] Whatever this may be, we have to take it that Śaivism was as important as Vaiṣṇavism in the Gupta period and virtually there was no distinction as we would have it.

To add to these hosts of evidence we may mention that the Imperial Gupta monarchs were given names which would testify that they were neither Śaivas nor Vaiṣṇavas in their religion. We mean by this that among these monarchs there are names like Kumāragupta and Skandagupta. The

31. *Journal of the U.P. Historical Society,* Vol. XVIII p. 108.

first reaction is that these names could not be claimed to have anything to do with the Vaiṣṇava religion. Among the Hindus considerable significance is attached to naming the new born child, male or female. It is believed generally that the naming of persons after their chosen deities will be to honour those deities and remember them for ever. It is said that even in one's death-bed one calling the name of the Lord will be absolved of all his sins, which he had committed in his life and which would surely take him to the world of heavenly bliss. Some such idea must have dominated the minds of the Gupta monarchs when they gave different names to their sons and grandsons. If we believe in the ceremony of *nāmakaraṇa*, which is still with us, it may be at once asserted that the Gupta monarchs of old were simply following the tradition by naming their sons after the deities near and dear to them. Thus if we examine the names of Gupta monarchs there is very little evidence in support of the theory that they were by religion Vaiṣṇavas pure and simple.

Section V

Śāktism

We have already mentioned that among the surviving Gupta temples there is a Pārvati temple at Nachna Kuṭhāra in Ajaigarh. In its friezes are figures carved which are full of vigour and energy. The temple of Śiva at Bhumra seems to be the earliest so far as the Gupta sculptures go. Here is a huge Ekamukhalinga of which mention has already been made. But what interests us are the various images in the Sanakānīka cave at Udayagiri near Bhilsa which was probably excavated early in the fifth century. Next to the image of Viṣṇu there is the figure of Mahiṣāsuramardanī.[32]

32. For details see *Mārkaṇḍeya Purāṇa*, chh. 82-87.

The figure possesses four arms.[33] There is no doubt that this figure of Mahisāsuramardanī is another form of Durgā who is well known in this period. The Udayagiri cave contains also the images of the seven divine Mothers.

If we turn our attention to the coins of Candragupta I and II, not to speak of the coins issued in the reign of Kumāragupta, there are undoubtedly several varieties and distinct types with legends on the obverse. Whatever the attributes held by the goddess may represent, the presence of the lion in these legends strongly suggests that the goddess is Durgā who is usually represented as riding on a lion. The goddess represented on the coins should therefore be identified with Ambikā, generally taken to be the consort of Śiva. Ambikā in traditional literature is called Simharathā or Simhavāhinī. Besides, a Devī trampling under foot Mahiṣāsura, the Demon in the form of a buffalo, sets at rest this polemic of polemics and the lion-slayer type of coins may be taken to represent Durgā for success in battle. This type of lion-slayer coins is one of the common varieties attributed to several kings of the Gupta dynasty. Therefore we have to take it that the goddess is Durgā and her cult was popular with the Gupta monarchs.[34]

This leads us to the examination of one aspect of Śāktism viz., the Durgā cult. The Purāṇas like the *Brahmāṇḍa*, the *Devī Bhāgavata* and the *Mārkaṇḍeya* deal with this cult in extenso. But Durgā mantras are held to be Vedic mantras, which, if uttered, in the proper way will be very effective in dealing with an enemy. That is why the Pāṇḍavas offered this prayer for their success and this is found in the *Mahābhārata*. The hymns to Durgā are not only found in the

33. *Memoirs of the Archaeological Survey of India* No. 16. p. 13.

34. *Catalogue of Coins of Gupta Dynasties* by John Allan, Intro., pp. 42-43.

Virāṭa Parvan[35] but also in the *Bhīṣma Parvan.*[36] In the latter she is invoked as Umā Śankarī, mother of Skanda, the embodiment of the Vedas, Śāstras etc.

Apart from this, the cult seems to be very ancient and it is usual with South Indians especially with the people of Malabar to regard her as Bhagavatī or Kālī. Perhaps she was worshipped in this form from primitive times and she is held in reverence even to-day in that form. The Tamil epic would attribute to this deity the power to confer on them success in their undertakings. Durgā may be said to be a pre-historic deity conceived specially to destroy Mahiṣa and Asuras generally. The *Devī Bhāgavatam* describes her, and also the war with Mahiṣa in some chapters.[37] What is significant for us is that it is put in the mouth of Hari, (Bk. VI) who says that neither He, nor Brahmā nor Śiva could measure her superb powers and her three guṇas. In one aspect the early Gupta kings worshipped Lakṣmī for plenty of riches to place the kingdom on a sound basis. In another aspect they worshipped Durgā to remove their difficulties and offer them success in battles which they often undertook. There is nothing strange in this because the kings were fired with the ambition to conquer a huge empire and consolidate it well.

To achieve this end the Durgā cult came in very handy and by offering their prayers to this goddess they were able to win a large empire. That is why we find that they engaged themselves in the worship of Śakti; for they realised that Śāktism as an aspect of religion was rooted in Vedic literature, and without Śakti the Puruṣa becomes an inactive principle. The very fact that the worship of Śakti was a fundamental concept in their religion indicates beyond a

35. Chapter VIII—21.
36. Chapter 23.
37. Bk. V, Chapters VIII—XX.

shadow of doubt that the Gupta monarchs were to some extent Śākta worshippers also.[38]

There is another aspect of Mother-worship which is found from the Gupta inscriptions. Though the monuments support and strengthen this theory that the Imperial Guptas were given to the worship of the Divine Mothers the term Sapta Mātṛkā frequently occurs in their inscriptions. The Seven Mothers to which reference is often made are Brāhmī, Māheśvarī, Kaumārī, Vaiṣṇavī, Vārāhi, Māhendrī and Cāmuṇḍī. The worship of the Seven Mothers persists with us and several temples in South India especially contain their images. To them worship is offered and it forms part and parcel of our popular religion.

The *Devīmāhātmya* in the *Mārkaṇḍeya Purāṇa*[39] contains a clue to the genesis of the worship of the Seven Mothers. This section of the *Mārkaṇḍeya Purāṇa* gives us a glimpse of the condition of the Śakti cult as prevailing in the early centuries of the Christian era before and after. The story goes that there were two demons, Śumbha and Niśumbha by name. They were found to be disturbers of peace to people of the earth who prayed to various gods but in vain. At last Durgā offered to vanquish the Asuras in a contest and restore the tranquillity of the world. In the course of this battle the various deities commencing with Brāhmī, encouraged the Devī in her legitimate mission. Brāhmī is the Śakti of Brahmā, Vaishṇavī is the Śakti of Visṇu, while Māheśvarī is the Śakti of Śiva. In this way[40] the Śaktis of different gods came forward to aid and fulfil their mission. When the enemy found the seven Śaktis offering battle, he remarked that it was *adharmic* warfare, one against

38. See *Lalithā Cult* by V. R. R. Dikshitar, pp. 58-70.

39. Chh. 88, 89, 90.

40. See *Mārkaṇḍeya Purāṇa*, ch. 88.

seven. Thereupon the Devī who was none else than Mahāmāyā and who could easily absorb these Śaktis in Her form, fought against the Asuras, vanquished them and became successful. This removed the stumbling block to the peace of the world which was much disturbed by them. This indicates that the worship of the Seven Mothers who offered their services to put down the atrocities of the Asuras, must have commenced with this incident.

It is but appropriate that the Gupta emperors who showed tenderness and toleration to the popular orthodox religion took to the worship of Divine Mothers also. If we proceed to examine the Bihar Stone Pillar Inscription of Skandagupta we find that the inscription records that a Yūpa or sacrificial post was erected apparently by some minister whose sister had become Kumāragupta's wife.[41] What is significant to us is that in line 9 occurs the expression 'mātṛibhis-ca', which seems to have belonged to the Śaiva form of worship in its Śākta development. If we compare this record[42] with the inscription of the same period, Gangadhar inscription of Viśvavarman, the Mātaraḥ stand for the personified energies of the principal deities.[43] Fleet seems to think that they represented the Pleiades, the Seven nurses of Kārttikeya, the son of Śiva. Afterwards the number was increased to eight, nine, sixteen and various other figures. They were the objects of worship with the early Kadambas[44] and the early Cālukyas.[45] If we turn to inscription No. XVII (Fleet: Gupta Inscriptions) we are surprised to come across an independent data which points to the prevalence of the cult of Divine Mothers. The inscription is by

41. Fleet, *op. cit.*, No. 12.
42. *Ibid.* No. 17.
43. *Ibid.*, p. 48.
44. *Ind. Ant.* Vol. VI, p. 27 *n*.
45. *Ibid.*, Vol. VIII, pp. 16 & 27.

one Viśvavarman, whose son was Bandhuvarman. He was a contemporary of Kumāragupta. His minister Mayūrākṣaka is said to have built a temple for the Divine Mothers. This again demonstrates that there was no difference between Vaiṣṇavism and Śaivism in the Gupta period. A king like Viśvavarman is equally Vaiṣṇava and Śaiva in outlook. His minister, the illustrious Mayūrākṣaka, built a shrine to the Divine God, Viṣṇu and erected for the sake of religious merit, an abode for the divine Mothers.[46] These evidences are enough to show the prevalence and popularity of the worship of the divine Mothers. By permitting and patronising such forms of divine worship the Imperial Gupta monarchs endeared themselves to their subjects who were keenly interested in the promotion and development of popular religion.

Section VI

The Skanda Cult.

Intimately connected with Śaivism is the cult known as Skanda cult. It is mysterious how the two important cults, one of Gaṇeśa and the other of Muruga or Kanda attained so much popularity in all-India especially South India. A Vedic student would not fail to note that these cults are not rooted in Vedic literature. If we proceed to examine the Vedic Samhitās neither of these gods is mentioned anywhere. It seems to an impartial student of history that the Gaṇapati cult is much later than the Skanda cult. The Vedic *mantras,* 'Subrahmaṇyom Subrahmaṇyom' have to be explained and interpreted in a way, quite different from the cult, now known as the Skanda cult. To a student of very early Tamil literature the Muruga cult is well known and according to the testimony of the Śangam literature of the Tamils, there were more than half-a-dozen important shrines,

46. ll. 35 and 36.

scattered throughout the length and breadth of the Tamil land. Muruga is always associated with his war-weapon, the spear (*Vēl*). He is a mountain-god and a war-god. His mighty influence has been felt probably by the authors of Sanskrit culture and efforts were made to give him a fitting place as the son of Śiva. The Kārttikeya stories were then current and were probably coalesced with the Muruga cult of the South. The result was far-reaching. By peaceful methods the Tamil Muruga was absorbed in the Kārttikeya legend and people believed in the significance of the cult.

In the later inscriptions edited by Dr. Fleet, for example, in Inscription No. 42 Kārttikeya is the son of Hara, and his riding animal is the peacock.[47] There is also a reference in another inscription to the banner of a peacock which is associated with the god Kārttikeya.[48] Prakaṭāditya is compared to God Kārttikeya both in virtue and prowess. From these various inscriptions it is explicit that in the Gupta times and after, the cult of Skanda as riding on a peacock and as a war-god, which have been elaborately treated in the Purāṇas like the *Skānda Purāṇa*, was known to the people of the Gupta days.[49] It is not surprising therefore to find a number of temples dedicated to Kārttikeya, or Svāmi Mahāsena as he is known during the Gupta days. The popularity of this cult which is unknown to the Vedas and which has been incorporated in the Hindu Purānas is to a great extent due to the prince of poets, Kālidāsa, who speaks highly of the temple of the war-god in his time.

In accordance with the popular sentiment, the Guptas were generally the followers of this cult as they were followers of other cults. This fact finds mention in a record during the reign of Kumāragupta in the Gupta year 96. This is

47. See Aphsad Stone Inscription of Adityasena 1 5.

48. Alina copper-plate inscription of Silāditya VII. Fleet, *op. cit.*, No. 79.

49. *Ibid.*, pp. 43-44.

known as the Bilsad stone pillar inscription.[50] The object of this record is to improve the temple of Svāmi Mahāsena which was apparently in Bilsad. One Dhruvaśarman undertook certain works in connection with this temple. (1) He wanted to build a *pratoli,* i.e. a gateway with a flight of steps. The flight of steps represented the svarga-sopāna as the ladder leading to heaven. (2) He wanted to establish a *Sattra* as a charitable alms-house apparently for feeding the devotees and mendicants who came on a pilgrimage to worship the lord enshrined. (3) He was animated with a passion to erect a column on which was inscribed the acts which he did for the improvement of the temple.[51] There is one expression in line 7 Brahmaṇyadeva translated as the god Brahmaṇya and hence the popular name in use to-day as Subrahmaṇya. This Brahmaṇya is a common term applied to high divinities as we have in the opening stanża of the *Vishnu Sahasranāma, Brahmaṇyam Sarvadharmajñam.* This means that the god mentioned with this attribute is simply a great god like Brahmā. It is interesting to note that this war-god Mahāsena, as he is called, has attained the status of Brahmaṇya if we can believe the inscription.

Not long after this period we have the Bihar Stone Pillar inscription of Skandagupta.[52] In 1. 9 of the inscription occurs the significant expression Skandapradānaiḥ, which means that Skaṇda has been accepted as a god and has become popular with the Hindus generally and the Gupta monarchs in particular. There is no doubt that the royalty took to this form of worship. It is seen from the fact that the imperial kings of this dynasty were known as Kumāragupta and Skandagupta, Kumara and Skanda being the names of one and the same god Kārttikeya. There is no doubt, therefore.

50. *Ibid.*, No. 10.
51. *Ibid.*
52 *Ibid.*, No. 12.

that the Imperial Guptas sent their prayers to god Muruga and this shows their wide outlook in matters religious.

Section VII

Gaṇeśa.

A word about the Ganeśa cult. It centres round the image of Gaṇeśa found among the coins of the Bhumra cave. This image is in such a dilapidated condition that it is very difficult to identify it with Gaṇeśa. But we will accept that it is the image of Gaṇeśa. Among the terra-cottas of this period there is a huge figure of Pārvatī seated with her two sons, Gaṇeśa and Kārttikeya. This is from Kasia.[53] Apart from the fact that it is a tribute to the Gupta clay modeller, what interests us is that the figure of Gaṇeśa was slowly coming into prominence.

Alice Getty who has devoted much attention for a study of this cult has put forth a proposition that Gaṇeśa must be regarded as a primitive deity. Though reference is made to the group of Vināyakas in the Yājñavalkya smṛti, yet the earliest reference invoking Gaṇeśa as an elephant-headed deity is found in the opening stanza of the *Mālatīmādhava* which can be attributed possibly to the 8th century A.D.[54] For one thing we find the absence of the term denoting this god even in any of the ancient Indian literature whether it be in Sanskrit language or Tamil. The cult called in popular parlance in South India as the *Pillaiyār* cult is much later in age than the twin epics the *Śilappadikāram* and the *Maṇimēkhalai* in Tamil.[55] In our opinion this Gaṇeśa cult was at first a Mahārāshtrian cult which migrated to several parts of South India. It caught peoples' imagination and became a popular religion with the Tamils. To say that it existed

53. Gaṇesa (O. U. P. 1936), Ch. 1.
54. See Bhandarkar: *Vaiṣṇavism*, etc. p. 149.
55. We have assigned roughly second century A.D. as the date of their compositions. Vide V. R. R. Dikshitar: *Silappadikaram*, Intro. 10.

in the time of the Guptas one needs more evidence. It would not be far wrong to say that while Skanda is a Tamilian deity identified later on with Kārttikeya, Ganeśa must have been imported from Western India. At any rate the cult of Gaṇeśa as an elephant-headed deity may be post-Gupta in date, say 6th century A.D. while the cult of Skanda is very ancient at least separated by six to eight centuries.

Section VIII

The Cult of Sūrya.

This cult which finds elaborate mention in the Gupta times and after, seems to be Vedic in origin. The group of deities which went by the name of Ādityas and about whom the Śatapatha Brāhmana speaks so eloquently has been invoked from immemorial times by the Vedic and post-Vedic followers. The Ādityas are evidently sons of Aditi and are solar deities. The Sun has been worshipped not only in India but also by the Magas of Persia who were devoted to the Sun God. About the worship of the Sun God much valuable information is given in the Archaeological Survey Reports of Mayurbanj. This has been edited by Nagendranath Vasu who appears to think that the Māgas are Scythian Brahmaṇas, who must have introduced the Sun worship into India. This does not seem to be the correct position.

If at all there is anything which is characteristically Sanskrit culture it is the Fire-worship and the worship of the Sun. Even to-day every Hindu has to perform his Sandhyā and offer his prayers principally to Sūrya for the increase of his earthly prosperity and for good physique. So the cult is Indian, continuous and without any break. The story in the Zend Avesta may be indebted to what had happened in Āryāvarta. At least there is no definite evidence that the cult has been introduced into India. Being the god of Light and also a Pratyakṣa Devatā, Sūrya worship has been recommended through the ages. There is evidence of solar worship even among the Neolithic peoples, especially of South India. To make an image of him and worship him in temples must have been evolved towards the beginning of the Christian era. Even in the Rāmāyana of Vālmiki, where Agastya instructs the *Āditya Hṛdayam* to Rāma to vanquish Rāvaṇa, we do not find any mention of the deity installed in a temple.[56]

The one peculiarity about this god is that it can be identified with the Vaiṣṇava cult as the inscription like the Khoh copper-plate of Mahārāja Sarvanātha does[57] or the Śiva cult as the Nirmand copper-plate of the Mahāsāmanta and Mahārāja Samudrasena informs us.[58] Here the name of the Sun is Mihira and the name of Śiva Mihiresvara would indicate some form or other of Solar worship combined with Śaiva rites.[59] In South India there is a temple called Sūryanārkoyil perhaps tracing its origin to the Cōla sovereigns. There are thus images of Sūrya which are definitely North Indian and South Indian. Minor differences between these images, in the North and South need not deter us.[60]

Generally, the Sūrya cult is common to all sects and creeds among the Hindus. If the Gupta monarchs had patronised this cult of Sūrya it does not show that the Persian influence is sufficiently marked in the images of this time. Nothing prevents the Hindus of the Gupta epoch to develop independently a cult though the inter-relation between India and Persia was intimate and frequent. There is nothing wrong if the Gupta artist has taken the Persian

56. See *Rāmāyana Yuddhakhāṇḍa* Ch. 107.
57. *Op. cit.*, No. 28.
58. *Ibid.*, No. 80.
59. Fleet, p. 288.
60. T. A. Gopinatha Rao: *Elements of Hindu Iconography*, Vol. 1, pt. ii, Ādityas and Navagrahas, pp. 299-317.

Like the Surya Cult, there was also a cult for the Moon but later on these cults seem to have been absorbed in the pūja that is daily offered to the Navagrahas. (See also my article on the *Lunar Cult in India* in the *Ind. Ant.*, LXII, pp. 173-74.

or Sassanian forms as a model but to contend that our images were prototypes of Persian ones is to say the least untenable.

Proceeding to examine one or two inscriptions[61] which belong to the Gupta period, we find in the Indore copper-plate of Skandagupta dated in the Gupta Era 146 "May that Sun, the rich source of rays that pierce (the darkness which is) the envelope of the earth, protect you—whom the Brahmans, of enlightened minds (have recourse to) according to due rite, (and thus become) the utterers of praises in meditation which are directed solely to him; whose limit, either vertically or from side to side, neither the gods nor the demons could ascertain; (and) by having recourse to whom, mankind, when they have lost control of themselves through much disease and agitation of the mind acquire consciousness (again)".[62] The inscription records further that one Brahmana Devavishṇu endowed a lamp for the Divine Sun, consecrated in a temple by the Kṣatriyas and merchants of the town of Indrāpura. The temple of the Sun at Indrāpura seems to have been the property of the guild of oilmen. The endowment furnished by the Brahmaṇa Devavishṇu became the perpetual property of the guild which was therefore held responsible for the maintenance of a lamp and for the proper maintenance of the endowment.

Further, in inscription No. 17[63] which, there is reason to believe, is that of the reign of Kumāragupta, there is the legend of the Sun being praised in chorus by the saints possessed of super-human power, riding on his chariot-horses.[64] This shows the Purāṇic influence exerted in the Gupta times. It is described in the *Viśvakarma Śilpa,* that the chariot of the Sun has only one wheel but is drawn by seven horses

61. Fleet, *op. cit.,* No. 16.
62. *Ibid.,* p. 71.
63. Gangadhar Stone inscription of Viśvavarman.
64. Fleet, *op. cit.,* p. 75.

surrounded by a halo of light. This is an evidence to show that the people of the Gupta times were familiar with the tradition relating to the Sun.

Proceeding to examine the inscriptions[65] of this period, the Mandasor Stone inscription of Kumāragupta and Bandhuvarman contains an interesting datum about the solar form of worship. The opening lines of this inscription begin thus: 'May that Sun protect you, who is worshipped by the hosts of Gods for the sake of existence and by the Siddhas who wish for super natural powers, (and) by ascetics, entirely given over to abstract meditation, (and) having worldly attractions well under control, who wish for the final liberation of the soul, and, with devotion by saints, practising strict penances, (who wish to become) able to counteract curses; and who is the cause of destruction and commencing again of the Universe.'

The inscription proceeds thus: "Reverence to that Sun, —whom (even) the Brahmanical sages, though they knew the knowledge of the truth (and) exerted themselves, failed to comprehend, and who nourished the whole of the three worlds with his rays diffused in all directions; who, when he is risen is praised by Gandharvas, Devas, Siddhas, Kinnaras and Naras; and who grants (their) desires to those who worship him! May that Sun decorated with glorious beams protect you." From this invocation it is clear that the *Āditya Hṛdayam* of the *Rāmāyaṇa* had a good deal of influence over the minds of the Gupta people. It seems to echo what is contained in this invocation, which says

Nāśayatyeṣa Vai Bhūtaṁ Tadeva Sṛjati Prabhuḥ |
Enam āpatsu kṛtsneṣu kāntāreṣu bhayeṣu ca
kīrtayan puruṣaḥ kaścit na avasīdati Rāghava ||
Sarva devātmako hyeṣa tejasvī raśmi bhāvanaḥ
eṣa devāsuragaṇān lokān pāti gabhastibhiḥ ||

65. *Ibid.*, p. 84.

Here the Sun is taken to represent the principal deities like Brahmā, Viṣṇu, Śiva, Skanda and Prajāpati. The following line makes this distinct:

eṣa Brahmāsca Viṣṇuśca Śiva Skanda Prajāpatiḥ[66].

A little later the Sun God is dubbed as Brahmeśāna acyuta. A close study of this important invocation which has benefited millions of mankind shows that the Sun God is neither Viṣṇu nor Śiva in character, but he is the embodiment of all gods including the Vedic gods and whose worship is eclectic. The object of this record issued during the reign of the feudatory Bandhuvarman who was reigning as the Governor of Daśapura is that a flourishing guild of silk-cloth weavers built a temple in honour of the Sun with lofty spires Sometime after there were certain repairs in the temple and in order to increase their religious merit this temple was repaired by it. An examination of the above inscriptions shows that even the Corporations and guilds took keen interest in the propagation of this cult.[67]

In the inscriptions collected by Dr. Fleet, there is epigraphical evidence to show that the Sun worship continued to thrive in later years also. For instance in No. 28 Khoh copper-plate of the Mahārāja Sarvanātha we have the interesting term Āditya bhaṭṭāraka, the name given to the local Sun God. The term Bhaṭṭāraka means simply a Divine personage. We find also traces of Sun worship under Mihirakula, the son of Toramāna.[68] It is recorded that one Mātricheṭa constructed a stone temple for the Sun in the Gwalior fortress. Even the seals of the period point out the wide prevalence of the Sun worship. For instance, the Asirgadh copper-seal grant of Śarvavarman has a wheel or

66. Rāmāyana Yuddha, Ch. 107.
67. Fleet, *op. cit.*, p. 71.
68. *Ibid.* No. 37.

a Sun emblem on the top of it, though the king himself was a devotee of Maheśvara.[69]

A close study of the various inscriptions, seals and the literature connected with the period reveals the astounding fact that he is a common deity who does not belong to this sect or other and who is rightly called the Prajāpati. Even the powers of creation and destruction are vested in him. The Vedic hymns and the epic poems, not to speak of the Purāṇas, have special hymns, by chanting which, one would fulfil his desire in this earth and even would get eternal liberation. The Gupta kings and people to whom the established religion of the land gave a welcome message found, in the worship of the Sun side by side with the Śaiva and Vaiṣṇava gods, comforting solace both to satisfy their material and spiritual aspirations. It is in this spirit that we students of history should approach this difficult problem which is complex in character.

Section IX

Hinduism

So far we have been examining the different aspects of the orthodox system of religion that obtained in the days of the Imperial Guptas. A close examination of the different aspects has demonstrated beyond shadow of a doubt that the Imperial Guptas were close followers of the orthodox system, which now goes by the name Hinduism. And it was too early to expect something of a sectarian spirit albeit Vaiṣṇava or Śaiva or even Śākta in those times. The Sūrya worship, which was largely prevalent in the Gupta period is again a standing testimony to the fact that the Guptas could be neither Vaiṣṇavas nor Śaivas, because in the worship of Sūrya which was a common god, they showed themselves followers of orthodox Hinduism. In the following pages we

69. *Ibid.*, p. 219.

should like to travel once more the hazardous path of the early Gupta inscriptions to conclude, what has been previously said, that the Gupta monarchs as a whole were actuated by the ideas and ideals which inspired a devout Hindu of those days.

First, if we take the Allahabad Pillar inscription into account we find that the emperor, Samudragupta was influenced much by the Bhakti movement, which was just coming into prominence. Though the emperor believed implicitly in the Bhakti cult, still the Karma-mārga appealed to him as equally important. Long ago the *Bhagavadgīta* has shown the inevitability of *karma* and the need of *karma* for *lokasangraha.*[70] According to the Digvijaya principle, which he cherished he built up a huge empire and engaged himself in the Aśvamedha sacrifices. Besides, the expressions of the early Gupta records comparing the emperor with Dhanada, Varuṇa, Indra and Antaka show that they were still under Vedic influence. Further, Samudragupta's devout minister and favourite Hariṣena, who was responsible for this inscription must have been an acknowledged Śaiva, if there was any Śaivism at all at that time.

Proceeding to examine the Eran stone inscription we unfortunately meet with lacunae which leaves us without any clue as to what form of religion the emperor embraced. Cunningham who had occasion to examine it, has pronounced as his opinion that it may be Vaiṣṇavism.[71] It may be that it was with reference to Viṣṇu, as Cunningham surmises, or it may not be. The Western scholars in general have known the Hindus partly as followers of Viṣṇu and partly as followers of Śiva. That inscription which would glorify God Viṣṇu, they would not hesitate to call a Vaiṣṇava one. That

70. A. S. P. Aiyar: A layman's Bhagavadgita, General Intro. p. LXXX.

71. Fleet: *Gupta Inscriptions*, p. 20, *Arch. Survey of India*, Vol. X, p. 89.

inscription which is an invocation to Lord Śiva, they would pronounce to be a Śaiva one. As they do not possess the necessary background and as several of them do not know that the different cults developed in India little by little, they cannot visualise a period when the Hindu looked upon the different manifestations as of one supreme God pervading the Universe. Whatever this may be the Eran Stone inscription is eloquent in showing that the Gupta kings were wedded to Hinduism.

Coming to the Udayagiri Cave inscription No. 3 of Candragupta II it is said by Fleet[72] "the cave appears to be a Vaiṣṇava cave and this must therefore be a Vaiṣṇava inscription." Here again we are in a world of guess. Dr. Fleet is not positive about the Cave itself and he says 'If the cave could be Vaiṣṇava, why not the inscription too'.[73] This is certainly the blind leading the blind. What occurs in the inscription is simple. The expression in the inscription is 'Deya dharma'. This itself suggests that it was a fit day for *dānam* i.e. a religious gift. It is said that the 11th Lunar day of the bright fortnight of the month of Āsāḍha was appropriate enough for this *dāna* ceremony, and this was made by one Sanakānika. The conclusion is therefore irresistible that there is nothing particular here to dub either the donor or his master as a follower of a particular cult or religion. The inscription after all records a gift made by Sanakānīka, a feudatory of Candragupta II. No doubt, every one will agree that the inscription accords well with the tenets of the Hindu principle of Dāna dharma also called Deya dharma.[74]

If we analyse another inscription of the same king, Candragupta II, viz., the Udayagiri Cave inscription No. 6,

72. Fleet, *op. cit.*, p. 23.
73. *Ibid.*, p. 25, etc.
74. See also *Arch. Survey of W. India.* Vol. IV. p. 83.

it is amusing to read what Dr. Fleet has written by way of introduction. He says "It is a Śaiva inscription; and the object of it is to record the excavation of the cave as a temple of the God Śiva under the name of Śambhu by the order of a certain Virasēna."[75] The first inscription cannot be Vaiṣṇava; nor this inscription a Śaiva one. It is to confound the real issue. The same monarch like Candragupta II cannot be said to be Vaiṣṇava at one stroke and Śaiva at another. The absurdity of this position is palpable enough to show that the inscription relating to the same king now as Vaiṣṇava and now as Śaiva denoted the mind of the donor and demonstrates clearly that the king was not perturbed by one donor leaning towards Vaiṣṇavism or another donor leaning towards Śaivism. This also demonstrates that the king was a pious Hindu, a Hindu in outlook and spirit.

The same fact faces us if we go to the Gadhwa Stone inscription of Candragupta II.[76] Here is a gift of ten *dinaras* as a contribution to the perpetual maintenance of a *sattara,* probably an alms house. Here again we cannot determine the form of religion to which the king belonged. But we know there was no form of religion in Hinduism at this time. The inscription mentions the Brahmana community in general. That itself is a clue to the view that the community was never guilty of belonging to this form of religion or that form in the days of the Guptas. We are met by the same fact if we further proceed in our examination of the inscriptions of this period. For instance we can point out from the Gadhwa stone inscription of Kumāragupta that two gifts in *dinaras* are made for the perpetual maintenance of a *sattara.* Here again the form of religion which was followed by the king is conspicuously absent. Even an impartial observer cannot determine the form of religion to

75. Fleet, *op. cit.,* p. 35.
76. *Ibid.,* No. 7.

which Kumāragupta belonged. Evidently this early Gupta king was a true Hindu in character. He never bothered himself with this or that god. He wanted to perpetuate the dharma of his religion and this is explicit from the records.[77]

If we continue our examination, we see in the Bilsad Stone Pillar[78] inscription of this king Kumāragupta that it belongs to the Śaiva form of worship. Here it is recorded that one Dhruvaśarman repaired and effected some improvements to the temple of God Kārttikeya. We have already said that God Kārttikeya according to Hindu mythology is the son of God Śiva. This confirms our theory, originally propounded, that the Gupta monarchs looked upon all forms of Hinduism as their religion. And it is difficult in the case of specific rulers to determine their form of religion as there was no preference to any particular form.

Again if we go through an inscription of another Gupta king, viz. Skandagupta, the Indore copper-plate inscription, we find this inscription is spoken of as indicating solar worship. The record says that a Brahmana Devaviṣṇu by name made an endowment to the local temple dedicated to the Sun to maintain a lamp.[79] If these inscriptions have a lesson to impart then we are driven to the conclusion that the form of religion the Imperial Guptas followed was only one form, going by the name of Hinduism today and was marked by tolerance and catholicity in outlook. The inscriptions bear the indelible mark that the Guptas were followers of orthodox Hinduism, were at home with the solar or Kārttikeya worship and could at the same time practise the ancient forms of rituals and indulge in Aśvamedha sacrifices.

The five sins and the ten sins mentioned now and then in these records betray their abundant faith in public trusts

77. *Ibid.*, Nos. 8 and 9.
78. *Ibid.* No. 10.
79. *Ibid.* pp. 70, 71.

and the necessity to encourage such trusts. They dared not interfere with these trusts as they were afraid of the various sins and their repercussions. They had faith in Dāna, and absolutely took their stand in Dharma; the Dāna for the deserving is commended and that too profusely. But it must be admitted that the Karmayoga of Hinduism was slowly giving way to the Bhakti movement which later on played a wonderful part in the propagation and spread of the religion.

If we proceed to examine the Damodarpur copper-plate inscriptions, further light is thrown on this question. In the very first plate, the sovereign Kumāragupta is named Parama Daivata.[80] The record is concerned with the purchase of land measuring one *kulyavāpa* made by a Brahmana named Kārpaṭika for the purpose of his *Agnihotra* rites. If we turn to the next plate the object of that again is to record the purchase of land evidently by a Brahmana for the purpose of performing the *Pañcamahāyajñas,* the five daily sacrifices. Both plates bear witness to the fact that in the 5th and 6th centuries A.D. there were orthodox Brahmanas in Bengal who were given to performing *Agnihotra* and *Pañcamahāyajñas* which are the Vedic rites incumbent upon the Brahmanas.

Plate No. III[81] which belongs to the reign of Budhagupta mentions that the state was anxious to provide lands for Brahmanas for the conduct of their five daily sacrifices and gifts of land to their community were considered to enhance the religious merit of the donors. The plate concludes with two verses evidently from the *Mahābhārata* addressed to Yudhiṣṭhira on the importance of the preservation of land grants.

80. Ep. Ind. XV. p. 130.

81. *Ibid.* p. 135.

Further, it is interesting to read in plate No. 4 of the erection[82] of two temples for the two gods Kokāmukhasvāmin and Śvetavarāhasvāmin. Kokāmukhasvāmin must have been a representative of God Śiva, for it has been well-assumed by scholars that Kokāmukhā is one of the epithets of Durgā. The mention of the two gods Kokāmukhasvāmin and Śvetavarāhasvāmin, the latter undoubtedly a Vaiṣṇava god and the details contained in plate No. 5[83] about the provisions for the daily worship of these gods such as the *bali, caru, sattara* have gathered momentum, and the Imperial Guptas made no secret of their worship of Śiva or Viṣṇu so long as they were satisfied with the tenets of the Hindu religion. The Damodarpur inscriptions corroborate the statement made at the commencement of this chapter that the Imperial Guptas were Smārtas in their concept and practice of religion.

Section X

Buddhism

We have so far seen that the early Guptas were the followers of the established religion and each of them patronised this religion and its institutions according to his lights. One was a devotee of Viṣṇu, a second was a devotee of Śiva, and a third of Muruga and a fourth of the Sun-God. But this did not preclude any of them from tolerating other religions in the land allowing every one of their subjects complete freedom of conscience and worship. I-tsing the Chinese traveller records a tradition that the temple of Mṛgaśikhāvanam was built by one Śrīgupta exclusively for worship by people from China. There is much discussion about the identification of this Śrīgupta who does not appear to be the Śrīgupta who was the founder of the Gupta dynasty.

82. *Ibid.* p. 140.
83. *Ibid.* p. 144.

But whoever be the founder, this temple of Mṛgaśikhāvana was in a flourishing condition even in the seventh century as is borne out by a record of Hwui Lun, another Chinese pilgrim.

It would appear that it was a Buddhist shrine which was tolerated by the early Gupta monarchs. It can be said without fear of contradiction that Buddhism flourished in the days of the early Imperial Guptas as also the established religion of the land; but the followers of this religion were dwindling in numbers with the result that Buddhism did not occupy the prominent place it occupied once upon a time. During the time of Samudragupta, we are told that the Ceylon Buddhists enjoyed the privilege of being votaries of the Buddha in the land of his birth. The story[84] has been already told that king Meghavarṇa of Ceylon despatched certain monks to the Gupta monarch, to seek permission to erect a monastery at Bodhgayā, sacred to the memory of the Buddha. It is said that these monks were not properly treated and they preferred a complaint to their king in Ceylon. Upon this, Meghavarṇa gave gifts to Samudragupta and obtained perpetual sanction for the Ceylonese pilgrims to reside at Bodhgayā.[85] This tradition would show that the Gupta monarch was tolerant and treated other religions of the land with courtesy.

Proceeding to the reign of Candragupta II we find on the evidence of the Sāñci Pillar inscription that Sāñci continued to be a centre of attraction for Buddhists not only in India but also from abroad. If one reads the Sāñci stone inscription correctly,[86] then, an official of the emperor by name Amrakādava endowed a Buddhist vihāra at the place known as Kākanādaboṭa (now Sāñci) for maintaining not

84. See ante ch. 6.
85. Sylvain Levi: JA. 1900 pp. 406-11.
86. Fleet. *op. cit.* No. 5.

only Bhiksus but also for the burning of a lamp. The reign of Candragupta II is important for the visit of the Chinese pilgrim Fa-hien.[87] According to the account left by him, there was the Hināyāna institution at Gāndhara. He came across hundreds of monks at Peshawar. The Buddhist faith was prevalent in all important towns and cities. For example, he observed at Sankāsi a thousand monks and nuns belonging to both schools of Hināyāna and Mahāyāna. Followers of Hināyāna were largely found in the monasteries at Kanyākubja while a few monks were seen at Rāmagrāma and at Kuśinagara. In the capital, Pāṭaliputra, the Chinese pilgrim found two monasteries one belonging to the Mahāyāna school and the other to the Hināyāna. But in some important centres like Kapilavāstu the pilgrim found the vihāras and stūpas neglected and in ruins. Such were the impressions of the Chinese pilgrim who visited India in the time of Candragupta Vikramāditya. Though the head of the state was not a Buddhist by faith, he had a firm belief in the Law prescribed by that faith. Hence he and his followers were tolerant of this faith.

In the days of Kumāragupta we have inscriptional evidence[88] supplied by the Mankuwar stone image inscription how one Bhiksu, Buddhamitra by name, installed an image of the Buddha. Sāñci which was an influential centre of the Buddhist faith in the reign of Candragupta II continued to flourish during the time of Kumāragupta and even of Skandagupta, for, in the reign of the latter it is said that one woman Harisvāminī made an endowment to the Buddhist community residing at the vihāra of Kākanādaboṭa. We hear of the feeding of the Bhikṣus in the vihāra.

It cannot be said that Buddhism died a natural death in the period of the early Guptas. On the other hand,

87. Giles: *Travels of Fa-hien*, p. 30 ff.
88. Fleet: *Ibid*. No. 11.

there is evidence to show that the images of the Buddha were installed here and there and the old vihāras continued to prosper. If we turn our attention to the Mathurā stone inscription which may possibly belong to the reign of Skandagupta we hear that one Vihārasvāminī gifted a statue of the Buddha to this place.[89] Another gift of the statue of the Sākyamuni is made mention of in the Deoriya stone inscription.[90] Yet another epigraph not different in age from the preceding one, the Kasia stone inscription, records another gift of the same nature. Here the gift was made by Mahāvihārasvāmin Haribala. Yet again the undated Sāñci stone inscription refers to one Vihārasvāmin who presented a pillar to the shrine at the place.[91] It was again a custom then to make gifts in honour of one's preceptor and parents. This we meet with in the Sārnāth stone inscription where one Bhiksu named Harigupta made an image in their memory.[92]

The history of Buddhism in the period of the early Guptas would not be complete if we make no mention of it as it flourished early in the 6th century. In the Mathurā stone image inscription[93] dated about A.D. 550 there is mention of a monastery called Yaśovihāra to which was presented a standing figure of the Buddha by a Śākya lady by name Jayabhaṭṭā[94] Thus we have the testimony of monuments and epigraphs to show that Buddhism continued to flourish during the days of the early Guptas who did not interfere with the faith or its tenets. Also many epigraphs furnish information about the gift of an image of the Buddha or an endowment to the Buddhist shrine made by its votaries, the State not meddling with them. In the history of Buddhism

89. Fleet, *op. cit.*, p. 263.
90. *Ibid.*, p. 27.
91. *Ibid.*, pp. 279 and 280.
92. *Ibid.*, No. 75.
93. *Ibid.* No. 70.
94. *Ibid.* p. 274.

during this period Bodhgayā, Sāñci, Mathurā and Sārnāth seem to have been flourishing centres of Buddhism.[95]

Section XI

Jainism

With the advent of the Guptas and with the revival of Brahmanism, Buddhism and Jainism could not be said to have been in a prosperous condition. We have seen already how Buddhism flourished and how it had its own important centres. But in this period the other religion Jainism was not so prominent as was Buddhism. If inscriptional evidence is a test we have only two or three inscriptions in which mention is made of Jaina images installed by the pious benefactions of private individuals. There is no inscription either of the period of the early king Samudragupta or even Candragupta II which may be called Jaina. The absolute silence of any activity on the part of Jaina enthusiasts is well marked in this period. Even a foreigner like Fa-hien has nothing to say about the Jains and their activities. The Śramaṇas are however mentioned by him but it is not possible to make out that the reference is to the Jaina ascetics in particular. In our opinion the reference may also be to the ascetics of the Hindu fold.

Until we come to the time of Kumāragupta we meet with no Jaina inscription. But when Kumāragupta was ruling, we come across an inscription at Mathurā underneath a large Jaina image dated in the Gupta era 113 which would correspond to A.D. 432. It states that a lady by name Sāmādhyā, daughter of Bhaṭṭibhāva made an image of the Jaina and obtaining permission from Dattilācārya who belonged to the Koṭṭiyagaṇa and the Vidhyādari Śāka, set it up at Mathurā. This record is interesting in that images of

95. See for more details Saletore: *Life in the Gupta Age*, pp. 514-520.

the Jaina Tirthankaras were set up only after the necessary permission was obtained from their ācārya or preceptor. This ācārya had the power to sanction such dedication. In this inscription[96] not only the name of the ācārya is given but also his gaṇa and Śāka are mentioned.

There is yet another inscription which is of equal value to a student of Jainism. The Udayagiri Cave Inscription of Kumāragupta I[97] records how a devotee by name Śankara installed the image of the Jaina which represented the Tīrthankara Pārśvanātha near the cave. It is further recorded that Śankara who is said to be a son of Aśvapati Sanghila was a student of Ācārya Gośarman. Further it is stated that this shrine had rich endowments in the shape of ornaments and other images. It transpires therefore that in the period of the early Guptas Jainism was also prevalent though not in a prosperous condition.

If we proceed further and examine the inscriptions of his successor, Skandagupta, the Kahaum stone pillar inscription which is dated A.D. 460-61, it is interesting for the information it contains about Jainism. It records among others that one Madra was responsible for installing five images of the Jīna in a column in the village of Kahaum to increase his religious merit and augment the welfare of all.[98] In the reign of his successors we do not hear much about the state of the Jaina faith until we come to the period of Harṣavardhana of Kanauj. It would thus appear that Jainism was not much in favour during the time when the early Guptas occupied Northern India. The Kahaum inscription[99] of Skandagupta gives us a real insight into the conditions of various religions which prevailed then. Even Madra who installed five stone

96. E.I., II. pp. 210-11.
97. Fleet, *op. cit.*, pp. 259-60.
98. *Ibid.*, pp. 67-68.
99. *Ibid.*

images of *arhats* was alive to the fact that great changes were rapidly taking place in the field of religion. With the state and its presiding chiefs favouring a particular form of religion, viz., the reviving Hinduism, other sects and creeds like Buddhism and Jainism had few followers though the Buddhist rule of life was not non-existent. Along with the Hindu reaction and the revival of the Brahmanical religion, the diffusion of Sanskrit and especially classical Sanskrit was wide in extent. But whatever we may say of the Gupta emperors of the fourth and fifth centuries A.D., one thing is certain that they were perfectly tolerant towards Buddhism and Jainism.[100]

---

100. V. A. Smith: *Early History of India*, 4th Edn. p. 320.

APPENDIX

The following inscriptions cited in the book together with translations have been reproduced from *Corpus Inscriptionum Indicarum*, Vol. III, edited by J. F. Fleet.

THE GUPTA INSCRIPTIONS

No. 1

1. [Yaḥ] Kulyaiḥ svai...... ātasa................

2. ya (?) sya (?) .... [||] [!]

3. Pu(?)mv ....
tra ....

4. sphā(?)ra-dva(?) .... kshaḥ spuṭōddhva(m)sita...... pravitata...... [||] [2]

5. Yasya prajñ-ānushaṅg-ōchita-sukha-manasaḥ śāstra-tattv-ārtha-bharttuḥ (— —)
stabdh-ō (— — —)ni(— — —)n-ōchchhṛi(— —)

6. [sa] t-kāvya-śrī-virōdhān=budha-guṇita-guṇ-ājñ-āhatān=ēva kritvā v[i]dval-lōkē vi[— —]sphuṭa-bahu-kavi-tā-kīrtti-rājyam bhunakti [||*] 3

7. [Ā] ryyō h=īty=upaguhya bhāva-piśunair=utkarṇ-ṇitai rōmabhiḥ sabhyēsh=ūchchhuvasitēshu tulyakulaja-mlān-ānan-ōdvīkshi [ta]ḥ

8. sn[ē]ha-vyālulitēna bāshpa-guruṇā tattv-ēkshiṇā chakshushā yaḥ pitr=ābhihitō ni[r]īksh[y]a nikhi[lām pāhy=ēva]m=[u]rv[v]īm=iti [||*] 4

9. [Dṛi]shṭvā karmmāṇy=anēkāny-amanuja-sadṛisāny =adbhut-ōdbhinna-harshā bh[ā*]vair=āsvādaya [— — — — — — —] [kē]chit

10. Vīryy-ōttaptāś-cha kēchich=chharaṇam-upagatā yasya vrittē praṇāmē=py=art[t] ē (?) [— — —] 5

11. Samgrāmēshu sva-bhuja-vijitā nityam=uchch-āpakārāḥ śvaḥ-śvō mānapra [..........]

12. tōsh-ōttuṅgaiḥ sphuṭa-bahu-rasa-snēha-phullair=mmanōbhiḥ paśchāttāpam va [. . . .]ma[m(?)] sy[ā]d=vasa(?)nta[m(?)]

13. Udvēl - ōdita - bāhu - vīryya - rabhasād=ēkēna yēna kshaṇād=unmūly=Āchyuta Nāgasēna-g[. . . .]

14. daṇḍair=grāhayat=aiva Kōta-kula-jam Pushpāhvayē krīḍatā sūryyēn ē [— — — —] tata [— — — — — — — —] [||*] [7]

15. Dharmma - prāchīra - bandhaḥ śaśi - kara -śuchayaḥ kīrttayaḥ sa-pratānā vaidushyam tattva-bhēdi praśama [— — — —] uku[—]y k[—]mu(?)t[—u] tārttham(?)

16. Addhyeyaḥ sūkta-mārggaḥ kavi-mati-vibhav-ōtsāraṇam ch=āpi kāvyam kō nu syād=yō=sya na syād=guṇa-mati-v[i] dushām dhyāna-pātram ya ēkaḥ [||*] 8

17. Tasya vividha-samara-śat-āvataraṇa-dakshasya sva-bhuja-bala-parākkram-aika-bandhōḥ parākkrām-ānkasya paraśu--śara-śanku-śakti-prās-āsi-tōmara-

18. bhindipāla-n[ā]rācha - vaitastik-ādy-anēka-praharaṇa - virūḍh - ākula - vraṇa - śat - āṇka - śobhā - samuday-ōpachita-kāntatara-varshmaṇaḥ

19. Kausalaka - Mahēndra - Mah[ā*]kāntāraka-Vyāgra-rāja-Kaurālaka - Manṭarāja - Paishṭapuraka - Mahēndra - giri Kauṭṭūraka - Svāmidatt - Airaṇḍapallaka - Damana - Kāñcheyaka Vishṇugōp-Āvamuktaka-

20. Nīlarāja - Vaingēyaka - Hastivarma - Pālakkak-Ōgrasēna - Daivarāshtraka - Kubēra - Kausthalapuraka-Dhanañjaya - prabhriti - sarvva - dakshiṇāpatha - rāja-grahana - mōksh - āanguraha - janita - pratāp - ōnmiśra-mahābhāgyasya

21. Rudradēva - Matila - Nāgadatta - Chandravarmma-Gaṇapatināga - Nāgaśen - Āchyuta - Nandi - Balavarmm-ādy - anēk - Āryyāvartta - rāja - prasabh - ōddharaṇ - ōdvṛitta - prabhāva - mahataḥ - parichārakīkrita - sarvv - āṭavika-rājasya

22. Samataṭa - Davāka - Kāmarūpa - Nēpāla - Karttṛipur - ādipratyanta - nṛipatibhir=Mmālav - Ārjunāyana-Yaudhēya - Mādrak - Ābhīra - Prārjuna - Sanakānīka - Kāka-Kharaparik - ādibhiś=cha - sarvvakaradān - ājñākaraṇa-prāṇāmā - gamana-

23. paritōshita - prachaṇḍa - śāsanasya anēka - bhrashṭa-rājyotsanna - rājavamśa - pratishthā - pan -ōdbhūta - nikhila-bh[uva]na - vicha[ra]ṇa - śānta - yāśasaḥ Daivaputra - Shāhi-Shāhānushāhi - Saka - Muruṇḍaih Saimhalak - ādibhiś=cha

24. sarvva - dvīpa.vāsibhir=ātmanivedana - kanyōpā-yanadāna - garutmadaṅka - svavishayabhukti - śāsana[y] āchan - ādy - upāya - sēvā - kṛita - bāhu - vīryya - prasara-dharaṇi - bandhasya pri(pṛi)thivyām=a - pratirathasya

25. sucharita - śat - ālaṅkrit - ānēka - guṇa - gaṇ-otisiktibhiś=charaṇa - tala - pramrisht - ānya - narapati-kīrtteḥ sāddhv - asādh - ūdaya - pralaya - hētu - purushasy=ā - chintyasya bhakty - avanati - mātra - grāhya - mṛidu-hṛidayasy=anukampāvato=nēka - gō - śata - sahasra - pra-dāyinaḥ

26. kṛipaṇa - dīn - ānāth - ātura - jan - ōdharaṇa-sa(ma)ntradīksh - ādy - upagata - manasaḥ samiddhasya vigrahavatō - lōk - ānugrahasya Dhanada - Varuṇ - Endr-Āntaka - samasya - sva - bhuja - bala - vijit - ānēka - narapati-vibhava - pratyarppaṇā - nitya - vyāpṛt - āyuktapurushasya

27. niśita - vidagdha - mati - gāndharvva - lal itair=vrīḍita - tridaśapatiguru - Tumburu - Nāradāder=vvidvaj-jan - ōpajīvy - ānēka - kāvya - kkriyābhiḥ pratishṭhita - kavi-rāja - śabdasya suchira - stōtavy - ānēk - ādbhut - ōdāra-charitasya

28. lōka - samaya - kkriy - ānuvidhāna - mātra - mānushasya - lōka - dhāmnō - dēvasya mahārāja - śri - Gupta-prapautrasya mahārāja - śri Ghaṭoṭkacha - pautrasya mahārājādhirāja - śri - Chandragupta - putrasya

29. Lichchavi - dauhitrasya mahādēvyām Kumāradevyām=utpha(tpa)nnasya mahārājadhi rāja - śri - Samudraguptasya sarvva - pṛithivī - vijaya - janit - ōdaya - vyāptanikhil - āvanitalām kīrttim=itas=tridaśapati-

30. bhavana - gaman - Avāpta - lalita - sukha - vicharaṇām - āchakshāṇa iva bhuvō bāhur - ayam=uchchritaḥ stambhah [||] yasya | pradāna - bhujavikkrama - praśamaśāstravāky - ōdayair - uparyupari - sañchay - ōchchhritam= anēka - mārggam yaśah

31. punāti bhuvana - trayam Paśupater=jjaṭ - āntarguhā - nirōdha - parimōksha - śighram=iva pāṇḍu Gāngam p [ayaḥ] [||] Ētach=cha kāvyam—ēshām=ēve bhaṭṭārakapādāṇām dasasya samīpa - parisarppāṇ - ānugrah - onmīlitamatēḥ

32. Khādyatapākikasya mahādaṇḍanāyaka - Dhruvabhūti - putrasya sāndhivigrahika - kumārāmātya - ma [hādaṇḍanāya] ka - Harishēṇasya sarvva - bhūta - hita - sukhāy= āstu | (||)

33. Anushṭhitam cha paramabhaṭṭāraka - pād - anudhyātēna mahādaṇḍanāyaka Tilabhaṭṭakēna

TRANSLATION

(Line 29.)—This lofty column (is) as it were an arm of the earth proclaiming the fame,—which, having pervaded the entire surface of the earth with (its) development that was caused by (his) conquest of the whole world, (has departed) hence (and now) experiences the sweet happiness attained by (his) having gone to the abode of (Indra) the lord of the gods—of the Mahārājādhirāja, the glorious Samudragupta,—

(Line 1.)—(Who) . . . . by his own kinsmen. . . . . ;—whose. . . . . ;—

(Line 3.—(Who). . . . . .twanging of the bow-string). . . . . .burst open and scattered. . . . . .dishevelled. . . . .,—

(Line 5.)—whose happy mind was accustomed to associate with learned people;—who was the supporter of the real truth of the scriptures;. . . . . .firmly fixed. . . . . .; —who, having overwhelmed, with the (force of the) commands of the collective merits of (his) learned men, those things which obstruct the beauty of excellent poetry, (still) enjoys, in the world of the wise, the sovereignty of the fame (produced) by much poetry,. . . . . .and of clear meaning;—

(Line 7.)—who, being looked at (with envy) by the faces, melancholy (through the rejection of themselves), of others of equal birth, while the attendants of the court breathed forth deep sighs (of happiness), was bidden by (his) father,—who, exclaiming "verily (he is) worthy," embraced (him) with the hairs of (his) body standing erect (through pleasure) (and thus) indicative of (his) sentiments, and scanned (him) with an eye turning round and round in affection, (and) laden with tears (of joy), (and) perceptive of (his noble) nature,—(to govern of a surety) the whole world;—

(Line 9.)—Whose. . . . . .some people (were accustomed to) taste with affection displaying exceeding great joy when they beheld (his) many actions that resembled nothing of a mortal nature; (and) whose protection other people, afflicted by (his) prowess, sought, performing obeisance,. . . . . . . ;—

(Line 11.)—(Whose). . . . . .doers of great wrong, always conquered by his arm in battle,. . . . . .to-morrow and to-morrow. . . . . . .pride. . . . . . .repentance, with minds filled with contentment (and) expanding with much clearly displayed pleasure and affection,. . . . . .the spring(?) ;—

(Line 13.)—By whom,—having, unassisted, with the force of the prowess of (his) arm that rose up so as to pass all bounds, uprooted Achyuta and Nāgasēna..........;—(by whom), causing him who was born in the family of the Kōtas to be captured by (his) armies, (and) taking his pleasure at (the city) that had the name of Pushpa, while the sun......the banks......;—

(Line 15.)—(Of whom it used to be said),—"The building of the pale of religion; fame as white as the rays of the moon, (and) spreading far and wide; wisdom that pierced the essential nature of things;........calmness......; the path of the sacred hymns, that is worthy to be studied; and even poetry, which gives free vent to the power of the mind of poets; (all these are his); (in short) what (virtue) is there that does not belong to him, who alone is a worthy subject of contemplation for those who can recognise merit and intellect?;"—

(Line 17.)—who was skilful in engaging in a hundred battles of various kinds;—whose only ally was the prowess of the strength of his own arm;—who was noted for prowess;—whose most charming body was covered over with all the beauty of the marks of a hundred confused wounds, caused by the blows of battle-axes, arrows, spears, pikes, barbed darts, swords, lances, javelins for throwing, iron arrows, *vaitastikas*, and many other (weapons);—

(Line 19.)—Whose great good fortune was mixed with, so as to be increased by (his) glory produced by the favour shewn in capturing and then liberating Mahēndra of Kōsala, Vyāghrarāja of Mahākāntāra, Maṇṭarāja of Kērala, Mahēndra of Pishṭapura, Svāmidatta of Koṭṭūra on the hill, Damana of Ēraṇḍapalla, Vishṇugōpa of Kāñchī, Nīlarāja of Avamukta, Hastivarman of Vengī, Ugrasēna of Palakka, Kubēra of Dēvarāshṭra, Dhanamjaya of Kusthalapura, and all the other kings of the region of the south;—

(Line 21.)—Who abounded in majesty that had been increased by violently exterminating Rudradēva, Matila, Nāgadatta, Chandravarman, Gaṇapatināga, Nāgasēna, Achyuta, Nandin, Balavarman, and many other kings of (the land of) Āryāvarta;—who made all the kings of the forest countries to become (his) servants;—

(Line 22.)—Whose imperious commands were fully gratified, by giving all (kinds of) taxes and obeying (his) orders and coming to perform obeisance, by the frontier kings of Samatata, Davāka, Kāmarūpa, Nēpāla, Kartṛipura, and other (countries), and by the Mālavas, Ārjunāyanas, Yaudhēyas, Mādrakas, Ābhīras, Prārjunas, Sanakānikas, Kākas, Kharaparikas, and other (tribes);—

(Line 23.)—Whose tranquil fame, pervading the whole world was generated by establishing (again) many royal families, fallen and deprived of sovereignty;—whose binding together of the (whole) world, by means of the amplitude of the vigour of (his) arm, was effected by the acts of respectful service, such as offering themselves as sacrifices, bringing presents of maidens, (giving) Garuḍa-tokens, (surrendering) the enjoyment of their own territories, soliciting (his) commands, &c., (rendered) by the Daivaputrās, Shāhis, Shāhānushāhis, Sakas, and Muruṇḍās, and by the people of Siṁhala and all (other) dwellers in islands;—who had no antagonist (of equal power) in the world;—who, by the overflow of the multitude of (his) various virtues adorned by a hundred good actions, rubbed out the fame of other kings with the soles of (his) feet;—who, being incomprehensible, was the spirit that was the cause of the production of good and the destruction of evil;—who, being full of compassion, had a tender heart that could be won over simply by devotion and obeisance;—who was the giver of many hundreds of thousands of cows;—

(Line 26.)—whose mind busied itself with the support and the initiation, &c., of the miserable, the poor, the helpless, and the afflicted;—who was the glorified personification of kindness to mankind;—who was equal to (the gods) Dhanada and Varuṇa and Indra and Antaka;—whose officers were always employed in restoring the wealth of the various kings who had been conquered by the strength of his arms;—

(Line 27.)—Who put to shame (Kaśyapa) the preceptor of (Indra) the lord of the gods, and Tumburu, and Nārada, and others, by (his) sharp and polished intellect and choral skill and musical accomplishments;—who established (his) title of 'King of poets' by various poetical compositions that were fit to be the means of subsistence of learned people;—whose many wonderful and noble deeds are worthy to be praised for a very long time;—

(Line 28.)—Who was a mortal only in celebrating the rites of the observances of mankind, (but was otherwise) a god, dwelling on the earth;—who was the son of the son's son of the Mahārāja, the illustrious Gupta;—who was the son's son of the Mahārāja, the illustrious Ghaṭōṭkacha;—who was the son of the Mahārājādhirāja, the glorious Chandragupta (I), (and) the daughter's son of Lichchavi, begotten on the Mahādēvī Kumāradēvī;—

(Line 30.)—(And) whose fame,—ever heaped up higher and higher by the development of (his) liberality and prowess of arm and composure and (study of) the precepts of the scriptures,—travelling by many paths, purifies the three worlds, as if it were the pale yellow water of (the river) Gaṅgā, flowing quickly on being liberated from confinement in the thickests of the matted hair of (the god) Paśupati.

(Line 31.)—And this poetical composition,—(the work) of the Khādyaṭapākika, the son of the Mahādaṇḍanāyaka Dhruvabhūti, the Sāmdhivigrahika and Kumārāmātya, the Mahādaṇḍanāyaka Harishēna, who is the slave of these same feet of the Bhaṭṭāraka, (and) whose mind is expanded by the favour of constantly walking about in (his) presence,—let it be for the welfare and happiness of all existing beings!

(Line 33.)—And the accomplishment of the matter has been effected by the Mahādaṇḍanāyaka Tilabhaṭṭaka, who meditates on the feet of the Paramabhaṭṭāraka.

No. 2.

ERAN STONE INSCRIPTION OF SAMUDRAGUPTA.

Text.

(Lines 1 to 6 containing the whole of the first verse and the first half of the second, are entirely broken away and lost.)

7. .... suvarṇṇa-dānē

8. .... ritā nṛipatayah prithu-Rāghav-ādyāḥ 2

9. ...... babhūva Dhanad-Āntaka-tushṭi-kōpa-tulyaḥ

10. ma-nayena Samudraguptah

11. .. .. ..pya pārtthiva-gaṇas-sakalaḥ prithivyām

12. sta(?sva)-rājya-vibhava-ddhrutam-āsthito-bhūt 3

13. ....na.. ...bhakti-naya-vikkrama-tōshitēna

14. [yo] . . .rāja-sabda-vibhavair=abhishēchan-ādyaiḥ [|*]

15. .. ..nitah.. .. parama-tushṭi-puraskritēna

16... ..vo ....nṛipatir= aprativāryya-vīryyaḥ 4

17. .. .. sya paurusha-parākkrama-datta-śulkā

18. [hasty-a]śva - ratna - dhana - dhānya - samṛiddhi-yuktā [1*]

19. ṅ=gṛihēshu . . muditā . . bahu-putra-pautra-

20. [sa]nkrāmiṇī kula-vadhuḥ vratinī nivishṭā [11*] 5

21. [Yas] y= ōrjjitam samara-karmma parākkram-ēddham

22. . . . yaśaḥ su-vipulam=paribambhramīti [|*]

23. .. .. ṇi.. yasya.. ripavaś=cha raṇ-ōrjjitāni

24. [svȧ]pn-āntarēshv=api vichintya paritrasanti [11*] 6

25. pta(?)ḥ sva-bhōga-nagar-
Airikiṇa-pradēśe [|*]

26. .. ..[sam]sthāpitas=sva-yaśasaḥ
paribrinhan(ṇ)-ārttham [||*] 7

27. .. ..vō nṛipatir=āha yadā

(The rest of the inscription is entirely broken away and lost).

TRANSLATION.

(Lines 1 to 6, containing the whole of the first verse and the first half of the second, are entirely broken away and lost).

(Line 7.)—.......in giving gold........(by whom) Pṛithu and Rāghava and other kings (were outshone.)

(Line 9.)—......, there was Samudragupta, equal to (the gods) Dhanada and Antaka in (respectively) pleasure and anger;......by policy; (and) (by whom) the whole tribe of kings upon the earth was (overthrown) and reduced to the loss of the wealth of their sovereignty;—

(Line 13.)—(who), by......satisfied by devotion and policy and valour,—by the glories, consisting of the consecration by besprinkling, &c., that belong to the title of 'king', —(and) by........combined with supreme satisfaction,— ......(was) a king whose vigour could not be resisted;—

(Line 17.)—(By whom) there was married a virtuous and faithful wife, whose dower was provided by (his) manliness and prowess; who was possessed of an abundance of (elephants) and horses and money and grain; who delighted in the houses of......; (and) who went about in the company of many sons and sons' sons;—

(Line 21.)—Whose deeds in battle (are) kindled with prowess; (whose)......very mighty fame is always circling round about; and whose enemies are terrified, when they think, even in the intervals of dreaming, of (his)......that are vigorous in war;—

(Line 25.)—......in a place in Airikiṇa, the city of his own enjoyment......has been set up, for the sake of augmenting his own fame.

(Line 27.)—......when the king said......

(The rest of the inscription is entirely broken away and lost).

No. 3.

UDAYAGIRI CAVE INSCRIPTION OF CHANDRAGUPTA II.

THE YEAR 82.

Text.

1. Siddham || Saṃvatsarē 80 2 Āshāḍha-māsa-sūkl-ē(ai) kādaśyām | paramabhaṭṭāraka-mahārājādhi-śri-Chandra [g]upta-pād-ānuddhyātasya |

2. mahārāja-Chhagalaga-pautrasya mahārāja-Vishṇu-dāsa-putrasya Sanakānikasya mahār [aja].... dha (?)lasy= āyam dēya-dharmmaḥ ||

TRANSLATION.

Perfection has been attained! In the year 80 (and) 2, on the eleventh lunar day of the bright fortnight of the month Āshāḍha,—this (is) the appropriate religious gift of the Sanakānika, the Mahārāja......dhala(?),—the son's son of the Mahārāja Chhagalaga; (and) the son of the Mahārāja Vishṇudāsa,—who meditates on the feet of the Paramabhaṭṭāraka and Mahārājādhirāja, the glorious Chandragupta (II.).

No. 4.

MATHURA STONE INSCRIPTION OF CHANDRAGUPTA II.

Text.

1\. . . . . . . [Sarvva-rāj-ōchhēttuḥ pṛithiv] y [ām=apratiratha]

2\. [sya. . chatur-udadhi-sali] l-āsvādita-ya[śaśo Dha-]

3\. [nada-varuṇ-Ēndr-Antaka-sa] masya Kṛitānta-[paraśoḥ]

4\. [nyāy - āgat - ānēka - gō] - hiraṇya - kōṭi - prada[sya chir-ō] -

5\. [tsann-aśvamēdh-āharttur= mma] hārājā-śrī-Gupta-prapau[t] r[asya]

6\. [mahārāja-śrī-Ghaṭōtka]cha-pautrasya mahārāja-dhir[āja]-

7\. [śri-Chandragupta-pu] trasya Lichchhavi-dauhitrasya mahā[dē]

8\. [vyām] [Kumāra] d [ē]vyām= utpannasya mahā-rājādhirā-

9\. [ja-śrī-Sa mudraguptasya putrēṇa tat-parigṛi-]

10\. [hi] t [ē]na mahādēv[y]ām Dat [t]adēv[y]am= ut[p]an[n]ē-

11\. [ṇa paramabhāgavatēna mahārājādhirāja-śrī -

12\. [Chandraguptēna] . . . .

(The rest of the inscription is entirely broken away and lost).

TRANSLATION.

(Line 8.)—By him who is the son,—accepted by him, (and) begotten on the Mahādēvī Dattadēvī,—of the Mahārājādhirāja, (the glorious) Samudragupta,—

(Line 1.)—(Who was the exterminator of all kings; who had no antagonist (of equal power) in the world; (whose fame was) tasted (by the waters of the four oceans); who was equal to (the gods) (Dhanada and Varuṇa and Indra and Antaka); who was (the very axe) of (the god) Kṛitānta; who was the giver of (many) millions of (lawfully acquired cows) and gold; (who was the restorer of the aśvamēdha—sacrifice, that had been long in abeyance),—

(Line 5.)—Who was the son of the son's son of the Mahārāja, the illustrious Gupta; the son's son of (the Mahārāja, the illustrious) Ghaṭōṭkacha; (and) the son of the Mahārājādhirāja (the glorious Chandragupta (I)., (and) the daughter's son of Lichhavi, begotten on the Mahādēvī Kumāradēvī;—

(Line 11.)—(By him, the most devout worshipper of the Divine one, the Mahārājādhirāja, the glorious Chandragupta (II),........

(The rest of the inscription is entirely broken away and lost).

No. 5.

SANCHI STONE INSCRIPTION OF CHANDRAGUPTA II. THE YEAR 93.

Text.

1. Siddham[||*] Kā [Kanā] dabōṭa-śrī-mahā-vihārē-śīla-Samādhi prajñā-guṇa-bhāvit-ēndriyāya parama-puṇya-

2. kri...... tāya chatur-ddig-abhyāgatāya śramaṇa-puṅgav-āvasathāy=āryya-saṅghāya mahā rājādhi-

3. rā [ja-ś]r[ī]- Chandragupta-pāda-prasād-āpyāyita-jīvita=sādhanaḥ anujīvi-satpurushasadbhāva-

4. vṛi ttim(?) jagati prakhyāpayan anēka-samar-āvāpta-vijaya-yaśas-patākaḥ Sukuli-dēśa-Na-

5. shṭī......vāstavya Undāna-putr-Āmrakārddavō Maja-Sarabhang-Āmrarāta-rājakula-mūlya-krī-

6. tam(?)......ya.... Īśvaravāsakam pañcha-maṇḍalayā(m*) praṇipatya dadāti pañcha-vimśatiś(ñ)=cha dīnā-

7. rān[||*]Ta [d-da] tta...... yād-arddhēna mahārājādhirāja-śrī-Chandraguptasya Dēvarāja iti pri-

8. ya-nām......y . tasya sarvva-guṇa-sampattayē yāvach=chandr-ādityau tāvat=pañcha bhikshavō bhumja-

9. tām ratna-gṛihē [cha dī]pakō jvalatu [|*]mama ch=āpar-āraddhāt=pañch=aiva bhikshavō bhumjatām ratna-grihē cha

10. dīpaka iti [||*]Tad=ētat-pravṛittam ya uchchhindyāt=sa gō-brahma-hatyaya samyuktō bhavēt=pancha-bhiś=ch=āna-

11. ntaryyair=iti [||*] Sam 90 3 Bhādrapada di 4 [||*]

TRANSLATION.

Perfection has been attained! To the community of the faithful in the holy great vihara of Kākanādabōṭa,—in which the organs of sense (of the members of it) have been subdued by the virtues of (good) character, religious meditation, and wisdom; which......deeds of the very highest religious merit; which has come together from the four quarters of the world; (and) which is the abode of most excellent Sramaṇas, —having prostrated himself in an assembly of five persons, Amrakārdava, the son of Undāna,—whose means of subsistence have been made comfortable by the favour of the feet of the Mahārājādhirāja, the glorious Chandragupta (II); who is publishing in the world the amiable behaviour of the virtuous people who are the dependents (of the king); who has acquired banners of victory and fame in many battles; (and) who is an inhabitant of (the town of) Nashti...... in the Sukuli dēśa,—gives (the village or allotment of) Īśvaravāsaka,......purchased with the endowment of Maja and Sarabhaṅga and Amrarāta of the royal household, and (also gives) twenty-five *dīnāras*.

(Line 7.)—From (the interest of the *Dīnāras*) given by him,—with half, as long as the moon and the sun (endure), let five *Bhikshus* be fed, and let a lamp burn in the jewel house, for the perfection of all the virtues of......the familiar name of Dēvarāja).......of the Mahārājādhirāja, the glorious Chandragupta (II); and with the other half, which is mine, let the same number of five *Bhikshus* be fed, and (let) a lamp (burn) in the jewel-house.

(Line 10.)—Whosoever shall interfere with this his arrangement,—he shall become invested with (the guilt of) the slaughter of a cow or of a Brāhman, and with (the guilt of) the five sins that entail immediate retribution.

(Line 11.)—The year 90 (and) 3; (the month) Bhādrapada; the day 4.

No. 6.

UDAYAGIRI CAVE INSCRIPTION OF CHANDRAGUPTA II.

Text.

1. Siddham [||*] Yad=a[m]tarjjyōtir-arkk-ābham= urvvyām .. ..vyāpi Chandragupt-ākhyam=adbhutam [||*] .

2. Vikram - āvakraya - krītā dāsya - nyagbhūta - pārttiv [ā].. .. .. māna-samraktā dharmma ......[||*] 2

3. Tasya rājādhirāj-arshēr=achinty-ō [.. ..] rmmanaḥ anvaya-prāpta-sāchivyō vyā[pṛita-san] dh [i]-v[i]grahaḥ 3

4. Kautsaś=Sāba iti khyātō Vīrasenaḥ kul-ākhyayā śabdārttha-nyāya - lōka - jñah=kaviḥ=Pāṭalīputrakaḥ [||*] 4

5. Kṛitsna-pṛithvī-jay-ārtthēna rājñ=aiv=ēha sah=āgatah bhaktyā bhagavataś=Sambhōr=gguhām=ētām-akārayat [||*] 5

TRANSLATION.

Perfection has been attained!........which shines like the sun, radiant with internal light,........upon the earth ....,pervades.........(and) has the appellation of Chandragupta (II), (and is) wonderful;—

(Line 2.)—Bought by the purchase-money of (whose) prowess, (the earth) in which (all other) princes are humiliated by the slavery (imposed on them by him),......gratified by......religion.

(Line 3.)—He who holds the position, acquired by hereditary descent, of being a minister of that same saintly sovereign, possessed of inconceivable......., (and) (has been appointed to) (the office of arranging) peace and war; (viz).—

(Line 4.)—He who, belonging to the Kautsa (gōtra) is well-known under the name of Sāba, (but is called) Vīraśēna by (his) family-appellation;—who knows the meanings of words, and logic, and (the ways of) mankind;—who is a poet;—and who belongs to (the city of) Pātaliputra.

(Line 5.)—He came here, accompanied by the king in person, who was seeking to conquer the whole world; and, through devotion towards the divine (god) Sambhu, he caused this cave to be made.

No. 7.

GADHWA STONE INSCRIPTION OF CHANDRAGUPTA II.

THE YEAR 88.

Text.

FIRST PART.

1. Paramabhāgavata - mahārājādhirāja - śrī - Chandragupta - rājya-
2. samvvatsarē ....asyām
3. divasa-pūrvvāyām.... .. ..
4. ka-Mātṛidāsa-pra[mukha].. .. .. ..[puny-ā]-
5. pyāyan-ārttham rachi[ta].... .. .. [sa]-
6. dā-sat[t*]ra-sāmānya(nya)-brāhma[ṇa].. .. .. ..
7. dīnārair=ddaśabhiḥ 10.. .. ..[||]
8. Yaś=ch=ainam dharmma-skanda(ndha)m vyuchchhindyāt=sa pañcha-mahāpātakaiḥ [sam]-
9. yyukta[h*]syād-iti ¦ (||)

SECOND PART.

10. Paramabhāgavata - mahā[rājādhirāja - śri - Chandragupta - rā]-
11. jya-samvvatsarē 80 8.... .. ..[asyām] [divasa]-
12. pūrvvāyam Pātā(ṭa)liput(t)ra.. .. .. ..[gri]-
13. hasthasya bhāryyā y.... .. ..
14 .=ātma-uny-ōpachay-[ārttham].. .. ..
15. sadā-sattra-sāmānya-b[rāhmaṇa].... .. ..
16. dīnārāḥ daśa 10.. .. ..[||] [Yaś=ch=ainam]
17. dharmma-skanda(ndha)m vyuchchhindyā[t=sa pañcha-mahāpātakaiḥ saṃyuktah syād=iti [||]

TRANSLATION.

FIRST PART.

(In the reign of the most devout worshipper of the Divine One, the Mahārājādhirāja the glorious Chandragupta (II); in the year)........................On this (lunar day), (specified) as above by the day (&c.) :—

(Line 3).—.......headed by Mātṛidāsa.......for the purpose of increasing (the religious merit).......fashioned ......the Brāhmaṇs of the community of a perpetual almshouse......by ten *dīnāras,* (or in figures) 10

(Line 8.)—And whosoever (shall interfere with) this branch of religion,—(he) shall become invested with (the guilt of) the five great sins!

SECOND PART.

(Line 10.)—In the reign of the most devout worshipper of the Divine One, the Mahārājādhirāja the glorious Chandragupta (II); in the year 80 (and) 8;..........(on this) (lunar day,) (specified) as above by the day, (&c.) :—

(Line 12.)—......Pātaliputra......the wife of the householder........(for the purpose) of adding to (her) own religious merit......the Brāhmaṇs of the community of a perpetual almshouse......ten *dīnāras,* (or in figures) 10.

(Line 16.)—(And whosoever) shall interfere with (this) branch of religion,—(he shall become invested with (the guilt) of five great sins)!

No. 8.

GADHWA STONE INSCRIPTION OF KUMARAGUPTA.

Text.

1. [Jitam bhagavatā Pa] ramabhāgavata-mahārājādhirāja
2. śrī-Kumāragupta-rājya-[Samvatsarē] .. ..

3. divasē 10 [asyām divasa-pūrvvāyam]........ ....
4. ....
5. ....sadā-sat [t*]ra-sā[mānya]........
6. [da]ttā dīnārāḥ 10 ṭa(?) ....
7. ti sattrē cha dīnārās=tray.. .. .. [||]
Yaś=ch=ainam dharmma-skandham vyuchchhi]-
8. ndyāt=sa pañcha-mahāpa[tākaiḥ] samyuktaḥ syād =iti [||]
9. Gōyiṇḍā Lakshmā.. .. ..

TRANSLATION.

Victory has been achieved by the Divine One! In the reign of (the most devout worshipper of the Divine One, the Mahārājādhirāja), the glorious Kumāragupta; (in the year) ......; on the day 10; on this (lunar day), (specified) as above by the day (&c.) :—

(Line 3.)—......(the community of) a perpetual almshouse......there were given ten *dīnāras*........and in the almshouse......three *dīnāras*......

(Line 7.)—(and whosoever shall interfere with this branch of religion),—he (shall become invested) with (the guilt of) the five great sins!

(Line 9.)—Gōyindā, Lakshmā,......

No. 9.

GADHWA STONE INSCRIPTION OF KUMARAGUPTA.

THE YEAR 98.

1. [Jitam bhagavatā || Para]mabh[ā]gavata - mahārājādhi-
2. rāja-śrī-Kumāragupta-rājya-sambasta]re 90 8....
3. ......asyām divasa-pūrvvāyām paṭṭa.. ....

4. ......ne(?)n=ātma-puṇy-ōpa[cha]-
5. [y-ārttham]..............kāliyam sadā-sat [t]ra-
6. .... kasya talakanivansē (?)...........
7. .... tya (?)m dīnārāh dvādaśa
8. ....sy=āmkur-ōdbha(?)sta-chchha........
9. ......[sam]yukta[ḥ*] syād=iti | (||)

TRANSLATION.

(Victory has been achieved by the Divine One! (In the reign) of the most devout worshipper of the Divine One, (the Mahārājādhirāja, the glorious Kumāragupta); in the year 90 (and) 8;......(on this) (lunar day), (specified) as above by the day (&c);—

(Line 3.)—......(for the purpose) of adding to (his) own religious merit......(to endure) for the same time with ......a perpetual almshouse......twelve *dīnāras*........

(Line 9.)—......shall become invested with......

No. 10.

BILSAD STONE PILLAR INSCRIPTION OF KUMARAGUPTA.

THE YEAR 96.

Text.

1. ......[Sarvva-rāj-ōchchhēttuḥ pṛithivyām=a-pratirathasya chatur-uda] dhi-salil-āsvādita-yaśasō

2. [Dhanada-Varuṇ-Ēndr-Āntaka-samasya Kṛitānta-paraśoh nyāy-āgat-ānēka-gō-hi]raṇya-kōṭipradasya chir-ōtsann-āśvamēdh-āharttuḥ

3. mahārāja-śrī-Gupta-prapauttrasya mahārāja-śrī Ghaṭōtkacha - pauttrasya ma]hārājādhirāja - śrī - Chandragupta-puttrasya

4. Lichchhavi-dauhi(t)r(asya mahādevyām Kumāradēvyām=utpannasya mahārā]jādhirāja-śrī-Samudragupta-puttrasya

5. mahādēvyām Dattadēvyām=utpannasya svaya[m=a-pratira-thasya] [parama]- bhāgavatasya mahārājādhirāja-śrī-Chandragupta-puttrasya

6. mahādēvyām Dhruvadēvyām=utpannasya mahā rājadhirāja - śrī - Kumāraguptasy=ābhivarddhamāna-vijaya-rājya-samvatsarē shaṇ-navatē [| *]

7. Asyān=divasa-pūrvvāyyām bhagavatas=trailōkya-tējas-sambhāra - samtat - ādbhuta - mūrtter=Brahmaṇya-dēvasya

8. ......nivāsinaḥ Svāmi - Mahāsenasy=āyatanē=smin=Kārttayug -āchāra - saddharmma - vartın - ānuyāyinā

9. āta......[pa]rshadā mānitēna Dhruvaśarmmanā karmma mahat=kṛit=ēdam

10. Kṛit[v]ā [— —ā]-bhirāmām muni-vasati [—] svargga-sōpāna-r[ū]pām kauberachchhanda-bimbām sphaṭika-maṇi-dal-ābhāsa-gaurām pratōlīm

11. prāsād-āgr-āḥhirūpam guṇa-vara-bhavanam dharmma-sa(?)ttram yathāvat |
punyēshv=ēv=ābhirāmam vrajati śubha-matis=tāta Śarmmā dhruvō=stu! (||)

12. [-] ā [-] i [-] sya [-]śubh-āmrita-vara-prakhyāta-labdhā bhuvi | [-] ē [-] ē bhaktir-ahīna-sat[t*] va-samatā kas=tam na sampūjayēt |

13. yēn=āpūrvva-vibhūti-sañchya-chayaiḥ [-] ai [-] i ....h | tēn=ayam Dhruvaśar-mmaṇā sthira-varas =(st) ambh-ōch [chhr] yaḥ kāritaḥ (||

TRANSLATION.

(Line 6.)—In the ninety-sixth year, (and) in the augmenting victorious reign of the Mahārājādhirāja, the glorious Kumāragupta,—

(Line 5.)—Who is the son, begotten on the Mahādēvī Dhruvadēvī, of the Mahārājādhirāja, the glorious Chandragupta (II), who was himself without an antagonist (of equal power); who was a most devout worshipper of the Divine One; (and)

(Line 4.)—Who was the son, begotten on the Mahādēvī Dattadēvī, of the Mahārājādhirāja, the glorious Samudragupta,—

(Line 1.)—(who was the exterminator of all kings; who had no antagonist (of equal power) in the world); whose fame was tasted by the waters (of the four oceans); (who was equal to (the gods) Dhanada and Varuṇa and Indra and Antaka; who was the very axe of (the god) Kṛitānta); who was the giver of (many) millions of (lawfully acquired cows and) gold; who was the restorer of the aśvamēdha-sacrifice, that had been long in abeyance; (and)

(Line 3.)—(who was the son of the son's son of the Mahārāja, the illustrious Gupta;—the son's son of the Mahāraja, the illustrious Ghatōtkacha);—(and) the son of the Mahārājādhirāja, the glorious Chandragupta (I), (and) the daughter's son of Lichchavi, begotten on the Mahādēvī Kumāradēvī;—

(Line 7.)—On this (lunar day), (specified) as above by the day (&c.).—at this temple of the divine (god) Svāmi-Mahāsēna, whose wondrous form is covered over with the accumulation of the lustre of the three worlds; who is the god Brahmaṇya; (and) who resides at............,—this great work has been accomplished by Dhruvaśarman, who follows the path of the customs of the Kṛita age, and of the true religion, (and) who is honoured by the assembly......

(Line 10.)—Having made a gateway, charming, (and) ......the abode of saints, (and) having the form of a staircase leading to heaven, (and) resembling a (pearl)-necklace of the kind called Kaubērachchhanda, (and) white with the radiance of pieces of crystalline gems;—(and having made), in a very proper manner, a (religious) almshouse (?), the abode of those who are eminent in respect of virtuous qualities; resembling in form the top part of a temple;—he, the virtuous-minded one, roams in a charming manner among the items of religious merit (that he has thus accumulated); may the venerable Śarman endure for a long time!

(Line 12.)—This lofty pillar, firm and excellent, has been caused to be made by that same Dhruvaśarman, whose piety, having acquired the excellent reputation of nectar.... ....on the earth, is so highly esteemed by all perfect beings that there is no one who would fail to worship him; (and) by whom......by means of the abundance of (his) unprecedented accumulation of superhuman power.

No. 11.

MANKUWAR STONE IMAGE INSCRIPTION OF KUMARAGUPTA.

THE YEAR 129.

Text.

1. Ōm Namō Bhudhāna Bhagavatō samyak-sambuddhasya sva-mat-āviruddhasya iyam pratimā pratishthāpitā bhikshu-Buddhamitrēṇa

2. Samvat 100 20 9 mahārāja-śrī-Kumāraguptasya rājyē Jeshṭha-māsa di 10 8 sarvva-duhkkha-prahān (ṅ)-ārttham

TRANSLATION.

Ōm! Reverence to the Buddhas! This image of the Divine One, who thoroughly attained perfect knowledge, (and) who was never refuted in respect of his tenets, has been installed by the Bhikshu Buddhamitra,—(in) the year 100 (and) 20(and) 9; in the reign of the Mahārāja, the glorious Kumāragupta; (in) the month Jyēshṭha; (on) the day 10 (and) 8—with the object of averting all unhappiness,

No. 12.

BIHAR STONE PILLAR INSCRIPTION OF SKANDAGUPTA.

Text.

FIRST PART

1. [— —]ḥ nṛi-chandra Indrānuja-tulya-vīryyō guṇair =a-tulyaḥ

2. [— —] [ta]sy-āpi sūnur=bhuvi svāmi-nēyaḥ khyātaḥ svakīrttyā

3. [— —] [sva] s=aiva yasy=ātula-vikramēṇa Kumāragup[t] ē[na]

4. [— —] p[i]tri(tṛī)mś=cha dēvāmś=cha hi havyakavyaiḥ sadā nṛiśamsy-ādi [......] [||]

5. [— —] [a]chīkarad-dēvanikēta-maṇḍalam kshitāv=an-aupamya- [........]

6. ......ba(?)tē(?) kila stambha-var-ōchchhri (chchhra)ya-prabhāsē tu maṇḍa......[||]

7. .... bhir=vṛikshāṇām kusuma-bhar-ānat-āgraśum(?)ga(?)-vyālambhastavak.. .. ..

8. [— —] Bhadrāryyayā bhāti griham navābhra-nirmmōka-nirmu[kta...] [||]

9. [— —] Skanda-pradhānair=bhuvi mātṛibhiś=cha lōkān=sa su(?)shya(?) [...] [||]

10. [— —] yūp-ōchchhrayam=ēva chakkrē [||*] Bhadrāryy-ādi-................

11. ..... [Ska](?)ndaguptabaṭē anśāni 30 5 tā(?) mrakaṭāku(?)h kala.. ....

12. ..... pituḥ sva-mātur=yyady=asti hi dushkṛitam bhajatu tanē ....

13. ..... k-āgrahārē anśāni 3 Anantasēnēn=ōpa..

SECOND PART.

14. . . . [Sarvva-rāj-ōchchhē]ttuḥ pri(pṛi) thivyām=a-pratirathasya

15. [chatur-udahi-salil-āsvādita-yaśaso Dhanada-Varuṇ-Ē]ndr-Āntaka-samasya Kṛitānta-

16. [paraśōḥ nyāy-āgat-ānēka-gō-hiraṇya-kōṭi-pradasya chir-ō]tsann-āśvamēdh-āharttuḥ

17. mahārāja-śrī-Gupta-prapauttrasya mahārāja-śrī- Ghatō]tkacha-pauttrasya mahārāja-

18. dhirāja - śrī - Chandragupta - puttrasya Lichchhavi-dauhittrasya ma] hā-dēvyām Kumāradēvyām=utpannasya

19. mahārājādhirāja-śrī-Samudraguptasya puttra] s=tat-parigṛihitō mahādēvyām

20. [Dattadēvyām=utpannaḥ svayam= a- pratirathaḥ para] ma-bhāgavatō mahārājā-

21. [dhirāja-śrī-Chandraguptas=tasya puttras=tat-pād-ānuddhyā]tō mahādēvyām Dhruvadēvyām=

22. [utpannaḥ paramabhāgavatō mahārājādhirāja-śrī-Kumāraguptas-tasya] puttras=tat-pād-ānuddhyātaḥ

23. [paramabhāgavatō mahārājādhi rāja-śrī-Ska]nda-guptaḥ

24. . . . . parama-bhāgavatō

25. [mahārājadhirāja-śrī-Skandaguptah] . . . . . . [vai]shayik-Ājapuraka-Sā(?)mai(?)-

26. . . . . .grā . . .ka . . . . .[āk] shaya-nīvī grāma-kshēttram

27. . . . .Kri. . . .uparika-Kumārāmātya-

28. . . . . .ṅgikula(?)ḥ(?) vaṇi[ja*]ka-pādit-ārika-

29. . . . . . . [ā]grahārika-śaulkika-gaulmik-āsanyām śra(?)-

30. . , , . . , . vās[i]k-ādīn=asmat-prāsād-ōpajīvinaḥ

31. [samājñapāyāmi] . . . . Varrmmaṇā vijñāpitō-smi mama pitāmahēna

32. . . . . . . .namē bhaṭṭa-Guhilasvāminā Bhadrā[r] yyakā

33. . . . . . m. g. p[r]ati. . . . ā . āgrōkaya. . . . . nākaya. .

(The rest of the inscription had been broken away and lost, before the time when it was discovered.)

TRANSLATION.

FIRST PART.

. . . . a very moon of a man; equal in prowess to (the god Vishṇu) the younger brother of Indra; unequalled in respect of virtuous qualities;—. . . . . .

(Line 2.)—. . . . . moreover, his son, docile towards (his) master on the earth, renowned;. . . . . . by his own fame.

(Line 3.)—. . . . whose sister, indeed, (was espoused) by Kumāragupta, of unequalled prowess.

(Line 4.)—. . . . . . . both the deceased ancestors and the gods, with the oblations proper for each of them;. . . . . always . . . . things that are injurious to man &c.

(Line 5.)—. . . . . . caused to be made a group of temples, not (rivalled by) anything else that could be compared with it in the world.

(Line 6.)—. . . . . assuredly in. . . . . which is beautiful with the erection of (this) best of columns.

(Line 7.)— . . . . . of the trees . . . . the groups of fig-trees and castor oil plants, the tops of which are bent down by the weight of (their) flowers.

(Line 8.)— . . . . . by (the presence of) Bhadrāryā, the house shines . . . , the sky laden with fresh clouds.

(Line 9.)—. . . . . headed by (the god) Skanda, and by the divine Mothers, on the earth,. . . . mankind. . . .

(Line 10)—. . . . he made, indeed, the erection of (this) sacrificial post. . . . Bhadrāryā and others. . . . in (the village (?) called) Skandaguptabaṭa (?), 30(and) 5 shares. . . . . . .

(Line 12.)—. . . . if there be any misdeed on the part of (his) father (or) his mother, let him share. . . . .

(Line 13.)—. . . . . in the *agrahāra* of. . . . . . 3 shares. . . . . by Anantasēna. . . . . . .

SECOND PART.

(Line 14.)—. . . . The son of the Mahārājādhirāja, the glorious Samudragupta,—who was the exterminator of all kings; who had no antagonist (of equal power) in the world; whose fame was tasted by the waters of the four oceans; who was equal to (the gods) Dhanada and Varuṇa and Indra and Antaka; (who was the very axe) of (the god) Kṛitānta, (who was the giver of many millions of lawfully acquired cows and gold); who was the restorer of the aśvamēdha-sacrifice, that had been (long) in abeyance; (who was the son of the son's son of the Mahārāja, the illustrious Gupta); who was the son's son of (the Māhāraja, the illustrious) Ghaṭōtkacha; (and) who was (the son) of the Mahārājādhirāja, (the glorious Chandragupta (I), (and) the daughter's son of Lichchhavi), begotten on the Mahādēvī Kumāradēvī,—

(Line 19.)—(was) the most devout worshipper of the Divine One, the Mahārājādhirāja, (the glorious Chandragupta (II)),—who was accepted by him; (who was begotten on) the Mahādēvī (Dattadēvī); (and) (who was himself without an antagonist (of equal power.))

(Line 21.)—(His son), who meditated on (his feet), (and) (who was begotten) on the Mahādēvī Dhruvadēvī, (was) (the most devout worshipper of the Divine One), (the Mahārājādhirāja, the glorious Kumāragupta).

(Line 22.)—(His) son, who meditated on his feet, (is) (the most devout worshipper of the Divine One, the Mahārājādhirāja, the glorious Skandagupta).

(Line 24.)—I, the most devout worshipper of the Divine One, (the Mahārājādhirāja, the glorious Skandagupta, issue a command) . . . . . . of the town of Ajapura in the . . . . . . Vishaya. . . . . . a perpetual endowment. . . . . a village-field. . . . . the Uparika, the Kumārāmātya. . . . acquired by the merchant. . . . . . in the seat (of office) (?) of the Agrahārika, the Saulkika, and the Gaulmika. . . . . and others who subsist on Our favour;—

(Line 31.)—"I have been requested by . . . varman,—'By my father's father,. . . . by the *Bhaṭṭa* Guhilasvāmin, ... belonging to Bhadrārya. . . . .

No. 13.

BHITARI STONE PILLAR INSCRIPTION OF SKANDAGUPTA.

Text.

1. [Siddham] [||*] [Sar]vva-rāj[ō]chchh[ē]ttuḥ prithivyām=a-pratirathasya chatur-udadhi-salil-[ā]svādita-yaśaśo Dhanada-Varuṇ-Ēndr-[Ā]ntaka-sa[masya]

2. Kṛitānta-paraśōḥ nyāy-āgat-[ā]nēka-gō-hiraṇya-k[ō]ṭi-pradasya chir-ō[t]sannāśvamēdh-āharattur=mahārāja-śrī-Gupta-prapautra[sya]

3. mahārāja-śrī-Ghaṭōtkacha-pauttrasya mahārājādhirāja-śrīChandragupta-putrasya Lichchhivi-dauhitrasya mahādēvyām Kum[ā]rad[ē]vyā-

4. m=utpannasya mahārājādhirāja-śrī-Samudraguptasya putras = tat-parigṛihītō mahādēvyām = Dattadēvyām=utpannaḥ svayam=a-pratirathaḥ

5. paramabhāgavatō mahārājadhirāja-śrī-Chandraguptas =tasya putras=tat-pādānuddhyātō mahādēvyām Ḍhruvadēvyām=utpannaḥ parama-

6 bhāgavatō mahārājādhir[ā]ja-śrī-Kumāraguptas=Tasya[|*] Prathita-pṛithu-mati-svabhāva-śaktēḥ prithu-yaśasaḥ prithīvīpatēh prithu-śrīh

7. pi[tri]-pa[r]igata-pādapadma-vartti prathita-yaśāḥ prithīvipatiḥ sutō=yam [||*]
Jagati bhu[ja]-bal-āḍyō(dhyō) Gupta-vaṅś-aika-vīraḥ prathita-vipula-

8. dhāmā nāmataḥ Skandaguptaḥ sucharita-charitānām yēna vṛittēna vrittam na vihatam=amal-ātmā tāna-dhidā(?)-vinītaḥ [||*] Vinaya-

9. bala-sunītair=vvikkramēṇa kkramēṇa pratidinam=abhiyōgād-īpsitam yēna la[b]dhvā svabhimata-vijigishā prōdyatānām parēshām praṇi-

10. hita iva lē (bhē sa)mvidhān-ōpadēśaḥ [||*] Vichalita-kula-lakshmī-stambhanāy=ōdyatēna kshititala-śayanīyē yēna nītā triyāmā samu-

11. dita-ba[la]-kōshān=Pushyamitrāmś=cha [j] itvā kshitipa-charaṇa-pīthē sthāpitō vāma-pādaḥ[||*] Prasabham-anupam[ai]r=vvidhvasta-śāstra-pratāpai[r]=vina[. .] mu-

12. [— —]kshānti-śaury[ai]r=nnirūḍhām charitam=amala-kīrttēr=ggīyatē yasya śubhram diśi-diśi paritushṭair=ā-kumāram manushyaiḥ [||*] Pitari divam=upē[tē]

13. viputām vaṅśa-lakshmīm bhuja-bala-vijit-ārir=yyah pratishṭhāpya bhūyaḥjitam=iti paritōshān =mātaram sāsra-nēttrām hata-ripur=iva Kṛishṇō Dēvakīm=abhyupē-

14. [ta]ḥ [||*] Sv [aijr=ddaṇḍ[aiḥ] [. . .] ra(?)tyu [. . .] t-prachalitam vaṅśam pratishṭhāpya yō bāhubhyām=avanīm vijitya hi jitēshv=ārttēshu kritvā dayām n=ōtsiktō [na] cha vismitaḥ pratidinam

15. Samvarddhamāna-dyutiḥ gītaiś=cha stutibhiś=cha vandaka-ja(?)nō(?) yam prā(?)payaty=āryyatām [||*] Hūṇair=yyasya samāgatasya samarē dōrbhyām dharā kampitā bhīm-āvartta-karasya

16. Satrushu śarā [— — — — — — — — —] — vira(?)chi(?)tam prakhyāpitō [—]i [—] na dyō(?)ti [—] nabhī(?)shu lakshyata iva śrōtrēshu Gāṅga-dhvaniḥ [||*]

17. S[v]a-pituḥ kīrtti [— — — — — — — — — — — — — — — — — — — —] [||*]— — — * [Karttavyā] pratimā kāchit=pratimām tasya Sārṅgiṇaḥ

18. s[u]-pratitaś=chakār=ēmām y[āvad=ā-chandra-tārakam [||*] Iha ch=ainam pratishthāpya su-pratishṭhita-śāsanaḥ gramam=ēnam sa vidadh[ē] pituḥ pu[ṇ]y-ābhivriddhayē [||*]

19. Atō bhagavatō mūrttir=iyam yaś=ch=ātra samsthi(?)-ta(?)ḥ ubhayam nirddidēś=āsau pituḥ puṇyāya puṇya-dhīr=iti [||*]

TRANSLATION.

(Perfection has been attained! The son of the Mahārājādhirāja, the glorious Samudragupta,—who was the exterminator of all kings; who had no antagonist (of equal power) in the world; whose fame was tasted by the waters of the four oceans; who was equal to (the gods) Dhanada and Varuṇa and Indra and Antaka; who was the very axe of (the god) Kṛitānta; who was the giver of many millions of lawfully acquired cows and gold; who was the restorer of the aśvamēdha-sacrifice, that had been long in abeyance; who was the son of the son's son of the Mahārāja, the illustrious

Gupta; who was the son's son of the Mahārāja, the illustrious Ghaṭōṭkacha; (and) who was the son of the Mahārājādhirāja, the glorious Chandragupta (I.), (and) the daughter's son of Lichchhivi, begotten on the Mahādēvī Kumāradēvi,--

(Line 4.)—(was) the most devout worshipper of the Divine One, the Mahārājādhirāja, the glorious Chandragupta (II.), who was accepted by him; who was begotten on the Mahādēvī Dattadēvī; (and) who was himself without an antagonist (of equal power).

(Line 5.)—His son (was) the most devout worshipper of the Divine One, the Mahārājādhirāja, the glorious Kumāragupta, who meditated on his feet, (and) who was begotten on the Mahādēvī Dhruvadēvī.

(Line 6.)—The son of him, the king, who was renowned for the innate power of (his) mighty intellect (and) whose fame was great, (is) this (Present) king, by name Skandagupta, who possesses great glory; who subsisted (Like a bee) on the wide-spreading waterlilies which were the feet of (his) father; whose fame is spread far and wide;—who is amply endowed with strength of arm in the world; who is the most eminent hero in the lineage of the Guptas; whose great splendour is spread far and wide; by whom, practising (good) behaviour, the conduct of those who perform good actions is not obstructed; who is of spotless soul; (and) who is well-disciplined in the understanding of musical keys(?);—

(Line 8.)—By whom,—having, with daily intense application, step by step attained his object by means of good behaviour and strength and politic conduct,—instruction in the art of disposition (of resources) was acquired, (and) was employed as the means of (subduing his) enemies who had put themselves forward in the desire for conquest that was so highly welcome (to them):—

(Line 10.)—By whom, when he prepared himself to restore the fallen fortunes of (his) family, a (whole) night was spent on a couch that was the bare earth; and then, having conquered the Pushyamitras, who had developed great power and wealth, he placed (his) left foot on a foot-stool which was the king (of that tribe himself):—

(Line 11.)—The resplendent behaviour of whom, possessed of spotless fame,—inherent, (but increased) by. . . . and patience and heroism which are emphatically unequalled, (and) which destroy the efficacy of the weapons (of his enemies),—is sung in every region by happy men, even down to the children:—

(Line 12.)—Who, when (his) father had attained the skies, conquered (his) enemies by the strength of (his) arm, and established again the ruined fortunes of (his) lineage; and then, crying "the victory has been achieved," betook himself to (his) mother, whose eyes were full of tears from joy, just as Kṛishna, when he had slain (his) enemies, betook himself to (his mother) Dēvakī;—

(Line 14.) —Who, with his own armies, established (again) (this) lineage that had been made to totter. . . ., (and) with his two arms subjugated the earth, (and) shewed mercy to the conquered peoples in distress, (but) has become neither proud nor arrogant, though his glory is increasing day by day; (and) whom the bards raise to distinction with (their) songs and praises:—

(Line 15.)—By whose two arms the earth was shaken, when he, the creator (of a disturbance like that) of a terrible whirlpool, joined in close conflict with the Hūṇās.— — — among enemies. . . . arrows. . . . . .proclaimed. . . . just as if it were the roaring of (the river) Gaṅgā, making itself noticed in (their) ears.

(Line 17.). . . .the fame of his father. . . . . . . (saying to himself that) an image of some kind or other (should be made), he, the very celebrated one, made this image of that (famous) (god) Sārṅgin, (to endure as long as the moon and stars may last). And, having here installed this (god), he, whose commands are well-established, has allotted this village (to the idol), in order to increase the religious merit of (his) father.

(Line 19.)—Accordingly, this image of the Divine One, and (this village) which has been here agreed to,—both of these, he, the pious-minded one, has assigned for (the increase of) the religious merit of (his) father.

No. 14.

JUNAGADH ROCK INSCRIPTION OF SKANDAGUPTA.

THE YEARS 136, 137 and 138.

Text.

FIRST PART.

1. Siddham[||*] Sriyam=abhimata-bhōgyām naika-kāl-āpanītām tridaśapati-sukh-ārttham yō Balēr=ājahāra kamala-nilayanāyāḥ sāsvatam dhāma Lakshmyāḥ

2. sa jayati vijit-ārttir=vvishnur=atyanta-jishṇuh Tad =anu jayati Sāśvat śrī-parikshipta-vakshāḥ svabhuja-janita-vīryō rājarājādhirājaḥ | narapati-

3. bhujagānām mana-darpp-ōtphaṇānām pratikṛiti-Garuḍ-ājñā[m] nirvvishī[m] ch=āvakarttā || Nripati-guna-nikētaḥ Skandaguptaḥ pṛithu-śrīh chaturudadhi-ja(?)l(?)-āntām sphīta-paryanta-dēsām |

4. avanīm=avanat-ārir=yaḥ chakār=ātma-samsthām pitari sura-sakhitvam prāptavaty=ātma-śaktyā || Api cha jitam =[ē]va tēna prathayamti yaśāmsi yasya ripavō=pi āmūla-bhagna-darpā niva. . . . Mlechchha-dēśeshu ||

5. Kramēṇa buddhyā nipuṇam pradhārya dhyātva cha kṛitsnān=guṇa-dōsha-hētūn | vyapētya sarvān=manujēndra-putrām=llakshmīḥ svayam yam varayām=chakāra || Tasmin

=nripē śāsati n=aiva kaśchid=dharmmād=apētō manujaḥ prajāsu |

6. ārttō daridrō vyasanī kadaryō daṇḍ[yō*] na vā yō bhṛiśa-pīḍitaḥ syāt || Evam sa jitvā pṛithivīm samagrām bhagn-āgra-darpā[n] dvishataś=cha kṛitvā | sarvvēshu dēśēshu vidhāya gōptṛi(ptṛi)n samchintayā[m-ā]sa bahu-prakāram || Syāt=kō=nurūpō

7. matimān=vini(nī)tō mēdhā-smṛitibhyām=anapēta-bhāvaḥ | saty-ārjav-audārya-nay-ōpapannō mādhuryadākshiṇya-yaśō-nvitaś=cha || Bhaktō=nuraktō nṛiv[i] ś[ē]sha-yuktaḥ sarvv-ōpadhābhiś=cha viśuddha-buddhiḥ | ānṛiṇya-bhāv-ōpa-gat-āntarātmāḥ sarvvasya lōkasya hitē pravṛittaḥ ||

8. Nyāy-ārjanē=rthasya cha kaḥ samarthaḥ syād=arjitasy=āpy=athā rakshanē cha| gōpāyitasy=āpi[cha] vṛid-dhi-hētau vṛiddhasya pātra-pratipādanāya || Sarvvēshu bhrityēshv=api samhatēshu yō mē praśishyān=nikilān=Surāshṭrān | ām jñātam=ēkaḥ khalu Parṇadattō bhārasya tasy=ōdvahanē samarthaḥ ||

9. Evam viniśchitya nṛip-ādhipēna naikān=ahō-rātra-gaṇañ=sva-matyā | yaḥ samniyuktō=rthanayā kathamchit samyak=Surāshṭr-āvani-pālanāya || Niyujya dēvā Varuṇam pratīchyām svasthā yathā n=ōnmanasō babhūvu[ḥ] (|) pūrv-vetarasyam diśi Parṇadaṭṭam niyujya rājādhṛitimāms=tath=ābhūt | (||)

10. Tasy=ātmajō hy=ātmaja-bhāva-yuktō dvidh=ēva ch=ātm=ātma-vaśēna nītaḥ | sarvvātman=ātm=ēva cha rakshaṇīyō nity-ātmavān=ātmaja-kāntarūpah ! (||) Rūp-ānurūpair=lalitair=vichitraiḥ nitya-pramōd-ānvita-sarva-bhā-vaḥ | prabhuddha-padmākara-padmavaktrō nṛiṇām śaraṇyah śaraṇāgatānām | (||)

11. Abhavad=bhuvi Chakrapālitō=sāv=iti nāmnā pra-thitah priyō janasya | sva-guṇair=an-upaskritair=udātti [ai]ḥ pitaram yaś=cha viśēshayām=chakāra ! (||) Kshamā pra-bhutvam vinayō nayaś=cha śauryam vinā śaurya-mah-[ā?]

rchchanam cha | vā(?)kya(?)m damō dānam=adīnatā cha dākshiṇyam=ānṛiṇyam=aś(ū) nyatā cha | (||) Saumdaryam =āryētara-nigrahaś=cha a-vismayō dhairyam=udīrnatā cha |

12. ity=ēvam=ētē= tiśayēna yasminn=a - vipravāsēna guṇā vasanti | (||) Na vidyatē=sau sakalē=pi lokē yatr= ōpamā tasya guṇaiḥ kriyēta | sa ēva kārtsnyēna guṇ-ānvitanām babhūva nṛi(nrī)ṇām=upamāna-bhūtaḥ | (||) Ity= ēvam = ētān = adhikān = atō = nyān = guṇān = par[ī] kshya svayam=ēva pitrā | yaḥ samniyuktō nagarasyā rakshām viśishya pūrvān=prachakāra samyak | (||)

13. Āśritya vi(vī)ryam su(?)-bhu(?)ja(?)-dvayasya svasy=aiva n=ānyasya narasya darpam | n=ōdvējayām-āsa cha kamchid=ēvam=asmin=purē ch=aiva śa śāsa dushtaḥ(n) | (||) Visrambham=alpē na śa śāma yō=smin kālē na lōkēshu sa-nāgarēshu | yō lālayām=āsa cha paura-vargān [— —] putrān=su-parīkshya dōshān | (||) Samramjayām cha prakṛitīr=babhūva pūrvasmitābhāshaṇa-māna-dānaiḥ |

14. niryantraṇ - ānyōnya - gṛiha - pravēsai[h*] samvarddhita-prīti-gṛih-ōpachāraiḥ | (||) Brahmaṇya-bhāvēna parēṇa yuktaḥ śaklaḥ śuchir=dana-parō yathāvat | prāpyān=Sa kālē vishayān=sishēvē dharm-ārthayōś=ch=ā [py=a*]-virōdhanēna | (||) Yō [— — —] Parṇadattāt=sa nyāyavān=atra kim=asti chitram | (||)muktākalāp- āmbujapadma-śītāch=chandrāt=kim=ushṇam bhavitā kadāchit | (||)

15. Athā kramēn=āmbuda-kāla Āgat(ē) n(i)dāghakālam pravidārya tōyadaiḥ | va varsha tōyam bahu samtatam chiram Sudarśanam yēna bibhēda ch=ātvarāt | (||) Samvatsarāṇām=adhikē śatē tu trimśadbhir=anyair=api shadbhir= ēva | rātrau dinē Praushṭhapadasya shashthē Gupta-prakālē gaṇanām vidhāya | (||)

16. Imās=cha yā Raivatakād=vinirgatā[ḥ*] Palāśin= īyam sikatā-vilāsinī |samudra-kāntāḥ chira-bandhan-ōshitāḥ punaḥ patim śāstra-yathōchitam yayuḥ | (||) Avēkshya varsh-

āgama-jam mah-ōbhramam mah-ōdadhēr=Ūrjayatā priyēpsunā | anēka-tīrantaja-pushpa-śōbhitō

17. Nadīmayō hasta iva praśāritaḥ | (||) Vishādya [mānāḥ]khalu sarvatō ja]nāḥ katham-katham kāryam=iti pravādinaḥ | mithō hi purv-āpara-rātram=utthitā vichintayām ch=āpi babhūvur=utsukāḥ | (||) Ap=īha lōkē sakalē Sudarśanam pumām(n) hi durdarśanatām gatam kshaṇāt |

18. bhavēn=nu s-āmbhō nidhi-tulya-darśanam su-darśanam [— — — — — — — — ——] vanē sa bhūtvā pituḥ parām bhaktim=api pradarsya dharmam purō-dhāya śubh-ānubandham rājñō hit-ārtham nagarasya ch=aiva | (||) Samvatsarāṇām=adhikē śatē tu

19. trimśadbhir=anyair=api saptabhiś=cha pra[. . .] śāstra-chēttā vi(?)svō(?)=py=anu jñāta-mahā-prabhāvaḥ | (||) Ājya-pranamaīh vibudhān=ath=ēshṭvā dhanair=dvijātīn=api tarpayitvā | paurāms=tath=ābhyarchya yathārha-mānaiḥ bhrityāmś=cha pūjyan=suhṛidaś=cha dānaiḥ | (||)

20. Graishmasya māsasya tu pūrva-pa kshē [. . . . . . . pra] thamē=hni samyak | māsa-dvayēn=ādaravān=sa bhūtvā dhanasya kritvā vyayam=a-pramēyam | (||) Āyāmatō hasta-śatam samagram vistārataḥ shashṭir=ath=āpi ch=āshṭau |

21. utsēdhatō=nyat purushāni sa(?)pta(?) [. . . .ha] sta-śata-dvayasya | (||) Babandha yatanān=mahatā ṇridēvān =[abhyarchya(?)] samyag-ghaṭitōpalēna | a-jāti-dushtam=prathitam taṭākam Sudarśanam śaśvata-kalpa-kālam | (||)

22. Api cha sudṛiḍha-sētu-prānta(?)-vinyasta-śobha-rathacharaṇa-samāhva-kraumcha-hamś-āsa-dhūtam | vimala-salila [— — — — — — — — —] bhuvi ta-

[—— —]da [-a]rkaḥ śaśicha | (||)

23. Nagaram=api cha bhūyād=vṛiddhimat=paura-jushtam dvija-bahu-śata-gīta-brahma-nirnashṭa-pāpam | śatam=api cha samānām=īti-durbhikhsa [— —— — —— —— — — — ———] [||] [Iti Suda]rśana-taṭāka-samskāra-gramtha-rachanā [sa]māptā ||

SECOND PART.

24. Dript-āri-darpa-praṇudaḥ pṛithu-śriyaḥ sva-vanśa-kētōḥ sakal-āvani-patēḥ | rājādhirājy- ādbhuta-puṇya-[karmaṇaḥ] [— — —— — — — —— ——] [—— —— — — — — —] [||]dvīpasya gōptā mahatām cha nētā daṇḍa-dvi(?) [-—]nām

25. dvishatām damāya | (||)Tasy=ātmajēn=ātma-guṇānvitēna Gōvinda-pād-ārpita-jīvitēna [— —— — —] [||] [-- — — — — —] gdham Vishṇōś=cha pāda-kamalē samvāpya tatra | artha-vyayēna

26. mahatā mahatā cha kalēn=ātma=-prabhāva-nata-paura-janēna tēna | (||) Chakram bibharti ripu [—— — — —] tasya sva-tamtra-vidhi-kāraṇa-mānushashya | (||)

27. Kāritam=avakra-matinā Chakrabhṛitaḥ Chakrapalitēna griham | varsha śatē=shṭā- trimśe Guptānām kāla. . . [||] [—— — — —— — — —— — — — — — — ——. ā]rtham=utthitam=iv=Ōrjayatō=chalasya

28. kurvat=prabhutvam=iva bhāti purasya mūrdhni || Anyach=cha mūrddhani su [— — — —— — —- —]

29. ruddha-vihamga-mārgam vibhrājatō [. . .] [||]

TRANSLATION.

FIRST PART.

Perfection has been attained! Victorious is he, (the god) Vishṇu,—the perpetual abode of the (goddess) Lakshmī, whose dwelling is the waterlily; the conqueror of distress; the completely victorious one,—who, for the sake of the happiness of (Indra) the Lord of the gods, seized back from (the demon) Bali the goddess of wealth and splendour, who is admitted to be worthy of enjoyment, (and) who had been kept away from him for a very long time.

(Line 2.)—And next, victorious for ever is the supreme king of kings over kings, whose breast is embraced by the goddess of wealth and splendour; who has developed heroism by (the strength of his) arms; and who plucked (and utilised) the authority of (his local) representatives, who were so many Garuḍās, (and used it as) an antidote against the (hostile) kings, who were so many serpents, lifting up their hoods in pride and arrogance;—

Skandagupta, of great glory, the abode of kingly qualities, who, when (his) father by his own power had attained the position of being a friend of the gods, bowed down his enemies, and made subject to himself the (whole) earth, bounded by the waters of the four oceans, (and) full of thriving countries round the borders of it;—whose fame, moreover, even (his) enemies, in the countries of the Mlechchhas. . . . . having (their) pride broken down to the very root, announce with the words—"verily the victory has been achieved by him;"—(and) whom the goddess of fortune and splendour of her own accord selected as her husband, having in succession (and) with judgment skilfully taken into consideration and thought over all the causes of virtues and faults, (and) having discarded all (the other) sons of kings (as not coming up to her standard).

(Line 5.)—While he, the king, is reigning, verily no man among his subjects falls away from religion; (and) there is no one who is distressed, (or) in poverty, (or) in misery, (or) avaricious, or who, worthy of punishment, is over-much put to torture.

(Line 6.)—Thus having conquered the whole earth, (and) having destroyed the height of the pride of (his) enemies, (and) having appointed protectors in all the countries, he cogitated in many ways,—"Among all my servants put together, who is there, who—suitable; endowed with intellect; modest; possessed of a disposition that is not destitute of wisdom and memory; endowed with truth, straightforwardness, nobility, and prudent behaviour; and possessed of sweetness, civility, and fame;—loyal; affectionate; endowed with manly characteristics; and possessed of a mind that (has been tried and) is (found to be) pure by all the tests of honesty; possessed of an inner soul pervaded by (the inclination for) the acquittance of debts and obligations; occupied with the welfare of all mankind;—capable both in the lawful acquisition of wealth, and also in the preservation of it, when acquired, and further in causing the increase of it, when protected, (and able) to dispense it on worthy objects, when it has been increased,—shall govern all my (countries of the) Surâshṭrâs? I have it; (there is) just one man, Parṇadatta, competent to bear this burden."

(Line 9.)—(And it was this same Parṇadatta) who, with pressing (and) with difficulty, was appointed by the lord of kings, who had thus deliberated in his mind for many days and nights, to protect in a proper manner the land of the Surâshṭras. (And) just as the gods became comfortable, (and) not disturbed in mind, when they had appointed Varuṇa to the Western point of the compass, so the king was easy at heart, when he had appointed Parṇadatta over the region of the west.

(Line 10.)—His son,—possessed of a filial disposition; his own self, as it were, reduplicated; well trained by self-control; worthy to be protected, as if it were his own self, by the all-pervading spirit always self-possessed; endowed with a naturally beautiful form; having a disposition the whole of which was always pervaded with joy through a variety of charming actions that were in accordance with (his) beauty; having a waterlily of a face that resembled a bed of waterlilies in full bloom; the refuge of men who came to him for protection,—was this same one who is renowned on the earth under the name of Chakrapālita; who is beloved of the people; and who confers distinction upon (his) father by his own noble qualities which are everything except unpolished:—

(Line 11.)—In whom all these qualities dwell to a marked degree, (and) without ever wandering away (from him)—viz. patience; lordship; modesty; and good behaviour; and heroism without (too) great an estimation of prowess; eloquence (?); self-control; liberality; and high-spiritedness; civility; the acquittance of debts and obligations; and freedom from empty-headedness; beauty; and reprobation of things that are not right; absence of astonishment; firmness; and generosity. Even in the whole world there is no one to be found, in whom a comparison with his virtues may be made; verily he has become, in all entireness, the standard of comparison for men who are endowed with virtuous qualities.

(Line 12.)—(And it was he) who was appointed by (his) father, after testing in person (the existence in him of) these same qualities mentioned above, and higher ones even than them; and who then accomplished the protection of (this) city in a way that quite distinguished him above his predecessors. Relying upon the process of his own two excellent arms(?), not on the pride of any other man, he subjected no one in this city to any anxiety; and he punished wicked people. Even in this time which is a mean one, he failed not to maintain confidence in the people, together with the inhabitants of the city; and, by carefully inquiring into faults, he has charmed all the citizens, together with. . . . .and children. And he has made (his) subjects happy by conversations addressed with smiles, and marks of honour, and presents; by free and reciprocal entering into (each other's) houses; (and) by carefully nourishing the family ceremonies of affection. Endowed with the highest piety, affable, pure, (and) in a suitable manner devoted to charity, he has, even without any conflict between religion and wealth, applied himself to such pleasures as may be attained at the proper time. What wonder is there in the fact that he, (born) from Parnadatta, is possessed of such proper behaviour?; can heat ever be produced from the moon, which is cold like a string of pearls or like a waterlily?

(Line 15.)—Then, in due course of time, there came the season of clouds, bursting asunder with (its) clouds the season of heat, when much water rained down unceasingly for a long time; by reason of which (the lake) Sudarśana suddenly burst,—making the calculation in the reckoning of the Guptas, in a century of years, increased by thirty and also six more, at night, on the sixth day of (the month) Praushṭhapada. And these (other rivers) which take their source from (the mountain) Raivataka, (and also) this Palāśinī, beautiful with (its) sandy stretches,—(all of them) the mistresses of the ocean,—having dwelt so long in captivity,—went again, in due accordance with the scriptures, to their lord (the sea). (And) having noticed the great bewilderment, caused by the excess of rain, (the mountain) Ūrjayat, desirous of appropriating the wives of the mighty ocean, stretched forth as it were a hand, consisting of the river (Palāśini), decorated with the numerous flowers that grew on the edges of (its) banks.

(Line 17.)—(Then on all sides) the people fell into despair, discussing how they should act; and, spending the whole night awake in vain, in great anxiety they reflected,—"Here in a moment, (the lake) Sudarśana has (by the overflowing of its waters) assumed an unpleasing appearance towards all the people, (as if it were) a man (?); having the appearance of the ocean, quite full of water, can it ever (again) become pleasing of aspect,. . . . . . ?"

(Line 18.)—. . . .he having become. . . . .and displaying the height of devotion towards his father, (and) holding in full view, for the welfare of the king and of the city also, religion, which has such auspicious results,—in a century of years, increased by thirty and seven others also, ... attentive to the sacred writings. . . . whose majesty is well known. Then having sacrificed to the gods with oblations of clarified butter and with obeisances; and having gratified the twice-born with (presents of) riches; and having paid respect to the citizens with such honours as they deserved, and to such of (his) servants as were worthy of notice, and to (his) friends with presents,—in the first fortnight of the month. . . . belonging to the hot season, on the first day, he, having practised (all the above) respectful observances for two months, made an immeasurable expenditure of wealth, and, (built an embankment) a hundred cubits in all in length, and sixty-eight in breadth, and seven (?) men's height in elevation,. . . . . of two hundred cubits. (Thus), having done honour to the kings, he laboriously built up, with a great masonry work, properly constructed, the lake Sudarśana, which is renowned as not being evil by nature, so that it should last for all eternity,—agitated by the defiances of the ruddy-geese which display (their) beauty along the edges of the firmly-built embankment, and by the settling down (in its waters) of the herons and the swans . . . . . pure waters; on the earth. . . . . the sun and the moon.

(Line 23.)—And may the city become prosperous; full of inhabitants; cleansed from sin by prayers sung by many hundreds of Brāhmaṇs; (and free from) drought and famine for a hundred years. . . . . . (Thus) ends the composition of the description of the restoration of (the lake) Sudarśana.

SECOND PART.

(Line 24.)—. . . : . of him (Skandagupta), who destroyed the pride of (his) haughty enemies; who is of great glory; who is the banner of his lineage; who is the lord of the whole earth; whose pious deeds are even more wonderful than his supreme sovereignty over kings;. . . . .

(Line 24.)—. . . . . (Parṇadatta), the protector of the island, and the leader of great. . . .of armies for the subjugation of (his) enemies.

(Line 25.)—By his son, who is endowed with his own good qualities, (and) whose life is devoted to (the worship of) the feet of (the god) Gōvinda—. . . . . by him, who causes, the citizens to bow down by his own prowess, having there attained. . . . . and the feet, which are like waterlilies, of (the god) Vishṇu, with a great expenditure of wealth and time (there was built a temple) of that famous (god Vishṇu) who carries the discus. . . . enemies, (and) who became (incarnate and) human by the exercise of his own free will. (Thus) by Chakrapālita, who is of a straightforward mind, there has been caused to be built a temple of (the god) Chakṛabhrit, in a century of years, together with the thirty-eighth (year) . . . . . the time of the Guptas.

(Line 27.)— . . . . . . uprisen, as it were, of the mountain Ūrjayat, shines as if displaying (its) lordship on the forehead of the city.

(Line 28.)—And another . . . . . on the forehead . . . . obstructing the path of the birds, is resplendent . . . .

No. 15.

KAHAUM STONE PILLAR INSCRIPTION OF SKANDAGUPTA. THE YEAR 141.

Text.

1. Siddham [||*] Yasy=Ōpasthāna-bhūmir=nṛipati-śata-śiraḥpāta-vāt-āvadhūtā

2. Guptānām vaṅsà-jasya pravisṛiṭa-yaśasas = tasya sarvv-ōttam-arddhēḥ

3. rājyē Sakr-ōpamasya kshitipa-śata-patēh Skanda-guptasya śāntē

4. varshē ttrinśad-das-aik-ōttaraka-śātatamē Jyeshṭha-māśi prapannē | (||)

5. khyātē=smin=grāma-ratnē Kakubha iti janais=sādhu-samsarga-pūtē |

6. puttrō yas=Sōmilasya prachura-guṇa-nidher=Bhattisōmō mahāt [m] ā

7. tat-sūnū Rudrasōma (ḥ*) pṛithula-mati-yaśā Vyāghra ity=anya-samjñō |

8. Madras=tasy=ātmajō=bhūd=dvija — guru-yatishu prāyasaḥ prītimān=yah | (||)

9. Puṇya-skandham sa chakkrē jagad=idam=akkilam samsarad=vīkshya bhītō

10. śrēyō-rttham bhūta-bhūtyai pathi niyamavatām=arhatām=ādikarttṛīn

11. pañch=ēndrām(n) sthāpayitvā dharaṇidharamayān=sannikhātas=tatō=yam

12. śaila-stambhaḥ su-chārur-giri-vara-sikhar-āgr-ōmpamaḥ kīrtti-karttā [||*]

TRANSLATION.

Perfection has been attained! In the tranquil reign of Skandagupta, whose hall of audience is shaken by the wind caused by the falling down (in the act of performing obeisance) of the heads of a hundred kings; who is born in the lineage of the Guptas; whose fame is spread far and wide; who excels all others in prosperity; who resembles (the god) Śakra; (and) who is the lord of a hundred kings;—in the one hundredth year, increased by thirty and ten and one; the month Jyēshṭha having arrived;—

(Line 5.)—In this jewel of a village, which is known by people under the name of Kakubha, (and) which is pure from association with holy men,—(there was) the high-minded Bhaṭṭisōma, who (was) the son of Somila, that receptacle of many good qualities. His son (was) Rudrasōma, of great intellect and fame, who had the other appellation of Vyāghra. His son was Madra who (was) especially full of affection for Brāhmaṇs and religious preceptors and ascetics.

(Line 9.)—He, being alarmed when he observed the whole of this world (to be ever) passing through a succession of changes, acquired for himself a large mass of religious merit. (And by him),—having set up, for the sake of final beatitude (and) for the welfare of (all) existing beings, five excellent (images), made of stone, (of) those who led the way in the path of the *Arhats* who practise religious observances,—there was then planted in the ground this most beautiful pillar of stone, which resembles the tip of the summit of the best of mountains, (and) which confers fame (upon him).

No. 16.

INDOR COPPER-PLATE INSCRIPTION OF SKANDAGUPTA.

THE YEAR 146.

Text.

1. Siddham[||*]Yam viprā vidhi-vat = prabuddha-manasō dhyān-aika-tānā(na)-stuvaḥ yasy=āntam tridaś-āsurā na vividur=nn=ōrdhvam na tirya—

2. g-gatiḥ(m) yam lōkō bahu-rōga-vēga-vivaśaḥ samśritya chētō-labhaḥ pāyād=vaḥ sa jagat-pidhāna-puṭa-bhid-raśmy-ā

3. karō bhāskaraḥ || Paramabhattāraka-mahārājādhi-raja - śrī - Skandaguptasy = ābhivarddhamāna - vijaya - rājya-samvatsara-śate shach(ṭ)-chatvā—

4. [ri*]ṅśad-uttaratamē Phālguna-māsē tat-p[ā*] da-parigṛihītasya vishayapati-Sarvvanāgasy = Antarvvēdyām bhōg-ābhivriddhayē vartta—

5. mānē [*] Chandrāpuraka - Padmā - chāturvvidya-sāmānya-brāhmana-Dēva-Vishṇur = Ddēva-putrō Haritrāta-pauttraḥ Duḍika-prapauttraḥ satat-āgnihō—

6. tra-[ch*]chhandōgō Rāṇāyanī(ni)yō Varshagaṇa-sagōttra Indrāpuraka-vaṇig-bhyām kshattriy-Āchalavarma-Bhri(bhru) kuṇṭhasinhābhyām=adhishṭā (shthā)—

7. nasya prāchyām diś=Indrapur-ādhishthāna-mādā-syāta-lagnam=ēva pratishṭhāpitaka-bhagavatē savitrē dīp-ōpa-yōjyam=ātma-yaśō—

8. bhivṛiddhayē mūlyam prayachchhatiḥ [||*] Indra-pura-nivāsinyās=tailika-śrēṇyā Jīvanta-pravarāyā itō=dhish-ṭhānād=apakkrama—

9. ṇa-sampravēśa-yathāsthirāyāḥ ājasrikam grahapatēr=dvija=mūlya-dattam-Anayātu śrēṇyā yad=abhagna-yōgam

10. prattha(tha)m-ārh - āvya[va*] chchhinna-samstham dēyam tailasya tulyēna paladvayam tu 2 chandr-ārkka-samakā-līyam (||*)

11. Yo vyakkramēd=dāyam=imam nibaddham gō-ghnō guru-ghnō dvija-ghātakaḥ sah taih pātakai(h*)

12. pañchabhir = anvitō = dhar = gachchhēn=naraḥ s-ōpanipāta-kaiś=ch=ēti ||

TRANSLATION.

Perfection has been attained! May that Sun, the rich source of rays that pierce (the darkness which is) the envelope of the earth, protect you,—whom Brāhmaṇs, of enlightened minds, (have recourse to) according to due rite, (and thus become) the utterers of praises in meditation, which are directed solely to him; whose limit, either vertically or from side to side, neither the gods nor the demons could ascertain; (and) by having recourse to whom, mankind, when they have lost control of themselves through such disease and agitation of the mind, acquire consciousness (again)!

(Line 3.)—In the augmenting victorious reign of the Paramabhattāraka and Mahārājādhirāja, the glorious Skandagupta; in the year one hundred, increased by forty-six; (and) while the month Phālguṇa is current for the increase of the enjoyment, in (the land of) Antarvēdī, of the *Vishayapati* Sarvanāga, who has been accepted (with favour) by his feet;—

(Line 5.)—The Brāhmaṇ Dēvavishṇu, who belongs to the community of Chaturvēdins of Padmā of the town of Chandrāpura,—who is the son of Dēva, (and) the son's son of Haritrāta, (and) the son of the son's son of Duḍika; who always recited the hymns of the agnihōtra-sacrifice; who belongs to the Rāṇāyanīya (śākhā); (and) who is of the Varshagaṇa gōtra,—for the increase of his own fame gives an endowment, (of which the interest is) to be applied to (the maintenance of) a lamp for the divine Sun, which has been established (in a temple) by the Kshatriyas Achalavarman and Bhrukuṇṭhasiṁha, merchants of the town of Indrapura, on the east of the settlement, (and) actually touching . . . . of the settlement of the town of Indrapura.

(Line 8.)—This gift of a Brāhmaṇ's endowment of (the temple of) the Sun, (is) the perpetual property of the guild of oil-men, of which Jīvanta is the head, residing at the town of Indrapura, as long as it continues in complete unity, (even) in moving away from this settlement. But there should be given by this guild, for the same time as the moon and the sun endure, two *palas* of oil by weight, (or in figures) by weight 2, uninterrupted in use, (and) continuing without any diminution from the original value.

(Line 11.)—Whosoever shall transgress this grant that has been assigned,--that man, (becoming as guilty as) the slayer of a cow, (or) the slayer of a spiritual preceptor, (or) the slayer of a Brāhmaṇ, shall go down (into hell), invested with (the guilt of) those (well-known) five sins, together with the minor sins.

* * * *

BUDHAGUPTA AND BHANUGUPTA.

No. 19.

ERAN STONE PILLAR INSCRIPTION OF BUDHAGUPTA.

THE YEAR 165.

Text.

1. Jayati vibhuś = chatur - bhujas = chatur = arṇṇava-vipula-salila-paryyankaḥ jagataḥ sthity-utpatti-nya[y-ādi]—

2. hētur=Ggaruḍa-kētuḥ [||*] Sate pañcha-shashty-adhikē varshāṇām bhūpatau cha Budhaguptē Āshāḍha-māsa-ś(ukla)—

3. dvādaśyām Suragurōr=ddivasē | (||) Sam 100 60 5 [|| *] Kālindī-Narmmadayōr=mmadhyam pālayati lōkapāla-gunair=jjagati mahār [āja]—

4. Srīyam=anubhavati Suraśmichandrē cha(||)Asyām samvatsara-māsa-divasa-pūrvvāyām sva-karmm-ābhiratasya kratu-yāji [naḥ]

5. adhita-svādhyāyasya vipr-arshēr = Mnaitrāyanīya vṛishabhasy=Endravishṇōḥ prapauttrēṇa pitru=gun-ānukār-iṇō Varuṇav(i)sh(nōḥ)

6. pauttrēṇa pitaram=anu-jātasya sva-vamśa-vṛiddhi-hētōr = Harivishnōḥ puttrēṇ = ātyanta - bhagavd - bhaktena Vidhātur=ichchhayā svayamvary=ēva r(ā) ja—

7. lakshmy = ādhigatēna chatuh - samudra-paryyanta-prathita-yaśaśa akshīṇa-māna-dhanēn = ānēka- śattru-samara-jishnuṇā mahārāja-Mātrivishnuṇ(ā)

8. tasy=aiv=ānujēna tad-anuvidhāyin(ā) tat-prasāda-parigri(hī)tēna Dhanyavishṇunā cha | mātri(tā)pittroḥ puṇy-apyāyan-ārtham=esha bhagavataḥ |

9. puṇyajan-ārddanasya Janārddanasya dhvaja-stambhō =bhyuchchhritaḥ [||*]

Svasty=astu gō-brahmaṇa-p(u)rōgābhyah sarvva-prajābhya iti (||)

TRANSLATION.

Victorious is the lord, the four-armed (god Vishṇu)—whose couch is the broad waters of the four oceans; who is the cause of the continuance, the production, and the destruction, etc., of the universe; (and) whose ensign is Garuḍa!

(Line 2.)—In a century of years, increased by sixty-five; and while Budhagupta (is) king; on the twelfth lunar day of the bright fortnight of the month Āshāḍha; on the day of Suraguru; (or in figures) the year 100 (and) 60 (and) 5:—

(Line 3.)—And while Suraśmichandra is governing, with the qualities of a regent of one of the quarters of the world, (the country that lies) between the (rivers) Kālinḍi and Narmadā, (and) is enjoying in the world the glory of (being) a Mahārāja;—

(Line 4.)—On this (lunar day), (specified) as above by the year and month and day;—by the Mahārāja Māṭṛivishṇu, who is excessively devoted to the Divine One, who, by the will of (the god) Vidhāṭṛi, was approached (in marriage-choice) by the goddess of sovereignty, as if by a maiden choosing (him) of her own accord (to be her husband); whose fame extends up to the borders of the four oceans; who is possessed of unimpaired honour and wealth; (and) who has been victorious in battle against many enemies;—who is the son of the son's son Indravishṇu, who was attentive to his duties; who celebrated sacrifices; who practised private study (of the scriptures); who was a Brāhmaṇ saint; (and) who was the most excellent (of the followers) of the Maitrāyaṇīya (Śākha);—who is the son's son of Varuṇavishṇu, who imitated the virtuous qualities of (his) father;—(and) who is the son of Harivishṇu, who was the counterpart of (his) father in meritorious qualities, (and) was the cause of the advancement of his race;—

(Line 8.)—(By him) and by his younger brother Dhanya-vishṇu, who is obedient to him, (and) has been accepted with favour by him,—this flag-staff of the divine (god) Janārdhana, the troubler of the demons, has been erected, for the purpose of increasing the religious merit of (their) parents.

(Line 9.)—Let prosperity attend all the subjects, headed by the cows and the Brāhmaṇs!

No. 20.

ERAN POSTHUMOUS STONE PILLAR INSCRIPTION OF GOPARAJA.

THE YEAR 191.

Text.

1. Ōm Samvatsara-śatē ēka-navaty-uttarē Srāvaṇa-bahula-paksha-sap(t)amy(ām)

2. saṁvat 100 90 1 śrāvaṇa ba di 7 || (-)la(?)ksha-vaṅśād=utpannō (- -)

3. Rāj-ēti-viśrutaḥ tasya puttrō=ti-vikkrāntō nāmnā rāj=ātha=Mādhavaḥ || Gōparāja(ḥ)

4. sutas=tasya śrīmān=vikhyāta-paurushah Sarabha-rāja-dauhittraḥ sva-vaṅśa-tilakō=dhu(?)nā(?) [||]

5. Srī-Bhānuguptō jagati pravīrō rājā mahān=Pārtha-samō=ti-śūraḥ tēn=ātha sārddhan=tv=iha Gōpar(ā)j(ō)

6. Mittrān = uva(?)tyā(?)ra(?) kil = ānuyātaḥ || Kṛitvā (cha) y(u)ddham sumahat-prak(ā)śam svarggam gatō divya-narē(?)(ndra-kalpaḥ)

7. bhakt=ānuraktā cha priyā cha kāntā bh(a)r(y)=ā(va)lag(n)=ānugat-āg(n) i-r(ā) śim ||

TRANSLATION.

Ōm! In a century of years, increased by ninety-one; on the seventh lunar day of the dark fortnight of (the month)

Srāvaṇa; (or in figures) the year 100 (and) 90 (and) 1; (the month) Srāvaṇa; the dark fortnight; the day 7:—

(Line 2.)—(There was) a king, renowned under the name of . . . . rāja, sprung from the . . . . . laksha (?) lineage; and his son (was) that very valorous king (who was known) by the name (of) Mādhava.

(Line 3.)—His son was the illustrious Gōparāja renowned for manliness; the daughter's son of the Sarabha king; who is (even) now (?) the ornament of (his) lineage.

(Line 5.)—(There is) the glorious Bhānugupta, the bravest man on the earth, a mighty king, equal to Pārtha, exceedingly heroic; and, along with him, Gōparāja followed . . . . . (his) friends (and came) here. (And*) having fought a very famous battle, he (who was but little short of being equal to) the celestial (king (Indra)), (died and) went to heaven; and (his) devoted, attached, beloved, and beautious wife, in close companionship, accompanied (him) on to the funeral pyre.

No. 21.

KHOH COPPER-PLATE INSCRIPTION OF THE MAHARAJA HASTIN.

THE YEAR 156.

Text.

FIRST PLATE.

1. Namō Mahādēvāya || Svasti Shatpañchās-ōttarē= bda-śatē Gupta-nṛipa-rājya-bhuktau Mahā-Vaisākha-Sāmbatsarē Kārttika-māsa-śukla-paksha-tritīyā—

3. yām=asyān=divasa-pūrvvāyām nṛipatiparivrājaka-kul-ōtpannēna mahā—

4. rāja-Dēvādhya-pranaptrā mā(ma)hārāja-Prabhanjaña-naptranā mahārāja-Dāmōdara-sutēna

5. gō - sahasra - hasty - aśva - hiraṇy - ānēka - bhūmi-pradēna guru - pitri - mātri - pūjā - tatpare—

6. ṇ=ātyanta-dēva-brāhmaṇa-bhaktēna || naika-samara-satata-vijayinā sva-vans-ā—

7. Mōdakarēṇa mahārāja Śrī-Hastinā sva-puṇy-āpyān-ārtham=ātmānam sva-

8. rgga-sōpāna-panktibhir=ārōha(pa)yatā brāhmaṇa-Vājisinēya Mādhya—

9. ndina-Kautsasagōttra-Gōpasvāmi Bhavasvāmī Sandh-yāputtra | Divākara—

10. dattaḥ Bhāskaradatta | Sūryyadattasya Vasuntara-shaṇḍika-grāmō—

11. tisrishtaḥ || Samantād=garttā uttarē paśchimō(mē) na

SECOND PLATE.

12. pūrvva-bhuktā mā(ma) ryyādāḥ Samndhyāputtra-pramukhānām s-ōdraṅgaḥ s-ōparikaraḥ

13. a - chāṭa - bhaṭa - prāvēśyaḥ chōra - varjjam[||*] Tad=asmat-kul-ōtthaiḥ matpādapiṇḍ-ōpajī—

14. vibhir=vvā kālāntarēshv=api na vyāghātaḥ kāryaḥ [|*] ēvam=ājñāpta yō=nyathā ku—

15. ryāt=tam=aham dēhāntara-gatō=pi mahat=āvad-dhyānēna nirdahēd=Uktam cha bhagavatā pa—

16. ram-arshiṇā vēda-vyāśēna | Pūrvva-dattām dvijāti-bhyō yatnād=rakshya(ksha) Yudhishthiraḥ

17. mahi(hī)m mahimatām śrēshṭha dānāch=chhrēyō=nupālanamm [||*] Bahubhir=vvasudhā bhuktā rā—

18. jabhiḥ Sagar-ādibhiḥ yasya yasya yadā bhūmis=tasya tasya tadā phalam [||*]

19. Shashṭim = ba(va)rsha-sahasrāṇi svarggē mōdati bhūmi-daḥ āchchhēttā ch=ānuma—

20. ntā cha tāny=ēva narakē vasēd=iti || Likhitañ=cha Vakkr-āmātya—

21. (pra*)naptrā bhōgik-āmātya - Naradatta - naptrā bhōgika-Ravidatta-puttr(ēṇa*) Sūryya—

22. dattēn=ēti [|*] Dūtakō Bhāgrahaḥ [||*]

TRANSLATION.

Reverence to (the god) Mahādeva! Hail! In a century of years, increased by the fifty-sixth (year); in the enjoyment of sovereignty by the Gupta kings; in the Mahāvaiśākha samvatsara; on the third lunar day of the bright fortnight of the month Kārttika,—on this (lunar day), (specified) as above by the day (etc.).—

(Line 3.)—By the Mahārāja, the illustrious Hastin,—who is born in the family of a kingly ascetic;—who is the great-grandson of the Mahārāja Dēvāḍhya;—who is the grandson of the Mahārāja Prabhañjana;—who is the son of the Mahārāja Dāmodara;who is the giver of thousands of cows, and elephants, and horses, and gold and many lands;—who is earnest in paying respect to (his) spiritual preceptor and (his) father and mother;—who is extremely devoted to the gods and Brāhmans;—who has been victorious in many hundreds of battles;—(and) who causes the happiness of his own race,—

(Line 7.)—(*By him*),—for the purpose of increasing his own religious merit, (*and*) in order to cause (*himself*) to ascend by the steps of the ladder that leads to heaven,—the village of Vasuntarashaṇḍika is granted to the Brāhmaṇ Gōpasvāmin, of the Vājasanēya—Mādhyamdina (*śākhā*) and the Kautsa *gōtra,* and to Bhavasvāmin, Sandhyāputra, Divākaradatta, Bhāskaradatta, and Sūryadatta.

(Line 11.)—On all sides (there are) trenches (of demarcation); (and) on the north by the west, the boundaries are those that have been previously enjoyed. (This village is made the property) of Sandhyāputra and the others, with the udraṅga and the uparikara, (and with the privilege that it is) not to be entered by the irregular or regular troops, (but) with the exception of (the right to fines imposed on) thieves.

(Line 13.)—Therefore, even in future times, no obstacle (to the enjoyment of this grant) is to be caused by those who are born in Our family, or by my feudatories. This injunction having been given, he who behaves otherwise,—him I will consume with a great contempt, even when I have passed into another body.

(Line 15.)—And it has been said by the venerable supreme sage, the arranger of the Vēdas,—"O Yudhishṭhira, best of kings, carefully preserve land that has previously been given to the twice-born; (verily) the preservation (of a grant) (is) more meritorious than making a grant! The earth has been enjoyed by many kings, commencing with Sagara; whosoever at any time possesses the earth, to him belongs, at that time, the reward (of this grant that is now made, if he continue it)! The giver of land enjoys happiness in heaven for sixty thousand years; (but) the confiscator (of a grant), and he who assents (to an act of confiscation), shall dwell for the same number of years in hell!"

(Line 20.)—And (this charter) has been written by Sūryadatta, the (great*)-grand-son of the Amātya Vakra; the grandson of the Bhōgika and Amātya Naradatta; (and) the son of the Bhōgika Ravidatta. The Dūttaka (is) Bhāgraha.

No. 22.

KHOH COPPER-PLATE INSCRIPTION OF THE MAHARAJA HASTIN.

THE YEAR 163.

1. Namō Mahādēvāya || Svasti Ttṛi-shashyṭy-uttarē= bda=śatē Gupta-nṛipa-rājya-bhuktau

2. Mah-Āśvayuja-sāmvatyarē Chaittra-māsa-śukla-paksha-dvitīy(ā*)yām=asy(ȧ*)n=divasa-

3. pūrvv(ā*)yā(m*) nṛipatiparivrājaka-kul-ōtpannēna mahārāja-Dēvāḍhya-pranapt(r*)ȧ

4. mahārāja-śrī-Prabhañjana-naptrā mahārāja-Dāmōdara-sutēna-gōsahasra-

5. hasty-aśva-hiraṇy-anēka-bhūmi-pradēna guru-pitṛi-mātṛi pūja-tanatparēn=ā-

6. tyanta-dēva-brāhmaṇa-bhaktēna naika-samara-śata-vijayinā sva-vans-āmōdaka-

7. rēṇa mahārāja - śrī - Hastinā sva-puṇy -āpyāyan-ārtham=Agnisv(ā*)miputtra-Bharadvāja-

8. Sagōttra-Vāji(ja)sanēyasabrahmacharuiṇē Dēvasvāminē Sarvvasvāminē cha

9. Gōrisvāminē (Vāji(ja)sanēya - sabrahmachāriṇē Kautsa-sagōttrāya-Di-

10. vākarasvāminē cha Sv(a*)tisvāminē Vājasanēya-sabrā(bra)hmachāriṇē Bhārgga-

11. va-sagōttrāya Varuṇaśarmmaṇaḥ Bappasvāminē Vāsula-sagōttr(ā*)ya

12. Kaṭha-sabrahmachāriṇē Kumāradēvarēva Vāji(ja) sanēya-sabrahmachāri-

13. na (Māt(ṛi*)śarmmah Nāgaśa(r*)mma Rukharadēvaḥ Kaudravadēvaḥ Vishṇ(u*) dēvaḥ

SECOND PLATE.

14. Dēvanāga Kumārasēna Rudraśamma Dēvadā(?) ṅgarā(?) Lamvō(mbō)shṭha Dēdamita

15. Mahadēva Gunṭḥaka ity-ēvam-ādibhyō brāhmaṇēbhy =ōttare paṭṭē Kōrppari

16. k-āgrāharaḥ s-ōdraṅgaḥ s-ōparikaraḥ a-chāṭa-bhaṭa-prāvēśyō=tisristaḥ

17. s=Tasy=āghāṭāḥ pūrvvēṇa Kōrpparagarttā | Uttarēn=Ānimuktakakōṇakaḥ

18. Vaṅgara-grāmakasya dakshiṇa-p(ā*)rsvē Valakamaddhyēma vṛikah amvrāta-samtāra-

19. kaḥ (*) paśchimēna Nāgasarī | dakshiṇēna Balavarmma-parichchhēdaḥ [||*]

20. (t*) - kul - ōtthair=mmat - pādam(pi)ṇḍ - ōpajīvibhir=vvā kālāntareshv=api na vyāghātaḥ kāryy(ḥ)

21. ēvam=ājñapta yō=nyathā kuryyān(t)=tam=aham dēhāntara-gatō=pi mahat=āvadhyānē-

22. na nirddahed=Uktañ=cha bhagavatā param-arshiṇā vēda-vyāsēna (|*) Pūrvva-dattām(m*)

23. dvijātibhyō yatnād=rakshya(ksha) Yudhishṭhraḥ mahī(m*) mah(i*)matām śrēshṭha dānāch=chhrē-

24. yō=nupālanam | (||) Bahubhir=vvasudhā bhuktā rājabhiḥ Sagar-ādibhiḥ sa(ya)sya ya-

25. yasya yadā bhūmis=tasya (tasya*) tadā phalan(m) [||*] Svadattā(m*) para-dattām vā yo harē-

26. ta vasundharāḥ(m) sa vishṭh(ā*)yā(m*) kṛimirbhūtvā pitrabhi saha pachyatē (|| *)

THIRD PLATE.

27. Sh(a)shṭ(im) v(ar)vva(sha) - sahasrāṇi svarggē mōdati bhu(bhū)mi-daḥ āchchhēt(t*)ā

28. ch=ānumant(ā*) ma(cha) t(ā*)ny=ēva narakē vasē(t*) [||*] (*) Likhitañ=cha Vakkr-ām(ā*)tya-prana-

29. ptranatrā bhōgika - Naradatta - napt(r*)ā bhōgika-Ravidatta-putrēna (ṇa) mahā

30. sāndhivigahika-Suryadatēnaḥ* (*) Bhagrahō dūtaka (ḥ*) [||*]

TRANSLATION.

Reverence to (the god) Mahādēva! Hail! In a century of years, increased by sixty-three; in the enjoyment of sovereignty by the Gupta kings; in the mahā-Āśvayuja saṁvatsara; on the second lunar day of the bright fortnight of the month of Chaitra,—on this (lunar day), (specified) as above by the day (&c.),—

(Line 3.)—By the Mahārāja, the illustrious Hastin,—who is born in the family of a kingly ascetic;—who is the great grandson of the Mahārāja Dēvāḍhya;—who is the grandson of the Mahārāja, the illustrious Prabhañjana; —who is the son of the Mahārāja Dāmōdara;—who is the giver of thousands of cows, and elephants, and horses, and gold, and many lands;—who is earnest in paying respect to (his) spiritual preceptor and (his) father and mother;—who is extremely devoted to the gods and Brāhmaṇs;—who has been victorious in many hundreds of battles;—(and) who causes the happiness of his own race,—

(Line 7.)—(By him),—for the purpose of increasing his own religious merit,—the agrahāra of Kōrpārika, in the northern paṭṭa, is granted, with the udraṅga and the uparikara, and (with the privilege that it is) not to be entered by the irregular or regular troops, to (certain) Brāhmaṇs, commencing with Dēvasvāmin, the son of Agnisvāmin, of the Bhāradvāja gōtra (and) a student of the Vājasanēya (śākhā), and Sarvasvāmin, (and) Gōrisvāmin,—Divākarasvāmin, of the Kautsa gōtra, a student of the Vājasanēya (śākhā), (and) svātisvāmin,— Varuṇaśarman, of the Bhārgava gōtra, a student of the Vājasanēya (śākhā), (and) Bappasvāmin-Kumāradēva, of the Vāsula gōtra, a student of the Katha śākhā—(and) Mātriśarman, a student of the Vājasanēya, (śākhā), (and) Nāgaśarman, Rukharadēva, Kaudravadēva, Vishṇudēva, Dēvanāga, Kumārasēna, Rudraśarman, Devadāṅgiras (?), Lamboshṭha, Dēvamitra(?) Mahādēva, (and) Guṇṭhaka.

(Line 17.)—The boundaries of it (are),—on the east, (the boundary-trench or village called) Kōrparagartā; on the north, Animuktakakōṇaka, (and) a vṛika-tree in the centre of Valaka on the south side of the village of Vaṅgara, (and) a clump of amrāta-trees; on the west, (the tank or village called) Nāgasarī; (and) on the south, the Parichheda of Balavarman.

(Line 19.)—Therefore, even in future times, no obstacle (to the enjoyment of this grant) is to be caused by those who are born in Our family, or by my feudatories. This injunction having been given, he who behaves otherwise,—him I will consume with a great contempt, even when I have passed into another body.

(Line 22.)—And it has been said by the venerable supreme sage, the arranger of the Vēdas,—"O Yudhishṭhira, best of kings, carefully preserve land that has previously been given to the twice-born; (verily) the preservation (of a grant) (is) more meritorious than making a grant! The earth has been enjoyed by many kings, commencing with Sagara; whosoever at any time possesses the earth, to him belongs, at that time, the reward (of this grant that is now made, if he continues it)! He becomes a worm in ordure, and is tormented together with his ancestors, who confiscates land that has been given, whether by himself or by another! The giver of land enjoys happiness in heaven for sixty thousand years; (but) the confiscator (of a grant), and he who assents (to an act of confiscation), shall dwell for the same number of years in hell!"

(Line 28.)—And (this charter) has been written by the Mahāsamdhivigrahika Sūryadatta; the great-grandson of the Amātya Vakra; the grandson of Bhōgika Naradatta; (and) the son of the Bhōgika Ravidatta. Bhagraha (is) the Dūtaka.

* * *

No. 32.

MEHARAULI POSTHUMOUS IRON PILLAR INSCRIPTION OF CHANDRA.

Text.

1. Yasy=ōdvarttayataḥ pratīpam=urasā śattrūn=samēty = āgatān = Vaṅgeshv = āhava - varittinō = bhilikhitā khaḍgēna kīrttir=bhujē

2. tīrtvā sapta mukhāni yēna samarē Sindhōr=jjitā Vāhlikā yasy=ādyāpy=adhivāsyatē jalanidhir=vvīryy-ānilair=ddakshiṇaḥ (|| *)

3. Khinnasy=ēva visṛijya gām narapatēr=ggām=āsritasy=ētarām mūrt(t*)yā karmma-jit-āvanim gatavataḥ kīrt(t*)yā sthitasya kshitau

4. śāntasy=ēva mahā-vanē hutabhujō yasya pratāpō mahān=n=ādyāpy=utsṛijati praṇāśita-ripōr-yyatnasya śēshaḥ kshitim (|| *)

5. Prāptēna sva-bhuj-ārjjitān=cha suchirañ=ch=aikādhi-rājyam kshitau Chandrāhvēna samagra-chandra-sadriśīm vaktra-śriyam bibhratā

6. tēn=āyam praṇidhāya bhūmipatinā dhāvēna Vishṇō (shṇau) maṭim prānśur=Vvishṇupadē girau bhagavatō vishṇor=dhvajaḥ sthāpitaḥ [|| *]

TRANSLATION.

He, on whose arm fame was inscribed by the sword, when, in battle in the Vaṅga countries, he kneaded (and turned) back with (his) breast the enemies, who, uniting together, came against (him);—he, by whom, having crossed in warfare the seven mouths of (the river) Sindhu, the Vāhlikas were conquered;—he, by the breezes of whose prowess the southern ocean is even still perfumed;—

(Line 3.)—He, the remnant of the great zeal of whose energy, which utterly destroyed (his) enemies like (the remnant of the great glowing heat) of a burned-out fire in a great forest, even now leaves not the earth; though he, the king, as if wearied, has quilted this earth, and has gone to the other world, moving in (bodily) form to the land (of paradise) won by (the merit of his) actions, (but) remaining on (this) earth by (the memory of his) fame;—

(Line 5.)—By him, the king,—who attained sole supreme sovereignty in the world, acquired by his own arm and (enjoyed) for a very long time; (and) who, having the name of Chandra, carried a beauty of countenance like (the beauty of) the full-moon,—having in faith fixed his mind upon (the god) Vishṇu, this lofty standard of the divine Vishṇu was set up on the hill (called) Vishnupada.

* * *

No. 60.

SPURIOUS GAYA COPPER-PLATE INSCRIPTION OF SAMUDRAGUPTA.

THE YEAR 9.

Text.

1. Ōm Svasti Mahā-nau-hasty-aśva-jayaskandhāvārāj (d)=Ā(a)yōddhyā-vāsakāt=sarvva-rāj-ōchchhēttu(ḥ*) pri-

2. thivyām=a-pratirathasya chatur-udadhi-salil-āsvādita-yaśa(sō*) Dhanada-Varuṇ-Ēndr-Ā

3. ntaka-samasya Kṛitānta-paraśōr=nyāya-āgat-ānēka gō-hiraṇya-kōti-pradasya chir-ōchhha-

4. nn-āśvamēdh-āharttu(h*) mahārāja-śrī-Gupta-prapauttrasya mahārāja-śrī-Ghaṭotkacha-pauttrasya

5. mahārājadhirāja-śrī-Chandragupta-puttrasya Lichhvi-dauhittrasya mahādevyā(m*) Ku-

6. māradēvyām=utpanna(ḥ*) paramabhāgavatō mahārājādhirāja-śrī-Samudra-

7. guptaḥ Gayā-vaishaika-Rēvatikā-grāmē vrā(bra) hmaṇa-purōga-grāma-vala-

8. tkaushabhyām=āha | Ēva ch=ārtha(m*) viditam=bō(vō) bhavatv=ēśa(sha) grāmō mayā māttāpittrōr=ā-

9. tmanaś=cha puṇy-ābhivṛiddhayē Bhāradvāja-sagōttrāya Va(ba) hvṛichāya sav(r)a(bra)hmachā-

10. riṇē vrā(brā)hmaṇa-Gōpadēvasvāminē s-ōparikar-ōddēśēn=āgrahāratvēn=āti-

11. sṛishṭaḥ (|*) tad-yushmābhir=asya śrōtavyam-ājñā cha karttavyā sarvvē cha samuchitā grāma-pra-

12. tyayā mēya-hiraṇy-ādayō dēyāḥ (|*) na ch=ē(ai) tat-prabhṛity=ētad-āgrahārikēṇ=(ā*)nyad-grā-

13. m-ādi-karada-kuṭumbi-kāruk-ādayaḥ pravēsayitavyā ma(a)nyathā niyatam=ā(a)gra-

14. hār-ākshēpa(ḥ*) syād=iti (||*) Samba(mva)t 9 Vaiśākha di 10 (||*)

15. Anya - grām - ākshapatalādhikṛita - Dyūta - Gōpa-svāmy-ādēśa-likhitaḥ (||*)

TRANSLATION.

Ōm! Hail! From the victorious camp, full of great ships and elephants, and horses, situated at (the city of) Ayōdhyā,—the most devout worshipper of the Divine One, the Mahārājādhirāja, the glorious Samudragupta,—who is the exterminator of all kings; who has no antagonist (of equal power) in the world; whose fame is tasted by the waters of the four oceans; who is equal to (the gods) Dhanada and Varuṇa and Indra and Antaka; who is the very axe of (the god) Kritānta; who is the giver of many millions of lawfully acquired cows and gold; who is the restorer of the aśvamēdha-sacrifice, that has been long in abeyance; who is the son of the son's son of the Mahārāja, the illustrious Gupta; who is the son's of the Mahārāja, the illustrious Ghaṭōṭkacha; (and) who is the son of the Mahārājādhirāja, the glorious Chandragupta (I.), (and) the daughter's son of

Lichchhavi, begotten on the Mahādēvī Kumāradēvī,—says to the two village Valatkaushans, together with the Brāhmans, at the village of Rēvatikā belonging to Gayā *vishaya*;—

(Line 8.)—"Be it known to you! For the sake of increasing the religious merit of (my) parents and of myself, this village is granted by me, as an agrahāra, with the assignment of the uparikara, to the religious student, the Brāhmaṇ Gōpasvāmin, of the Bhāradvāja gōtra (and) the Bahvricha (śākhā)—

(Line 11.)—"Therefore attention should be paid to him by you; and (his) commands should be obeyed; and all the customary tributes of the village, consisting of that which is to be measured; gold, &c., should be given. And, from this time forth, the tax-paying cultivators, artizans, &c., of other villages, &c., should not be introduced by the Āgrahārika of this (village) (for the purpose of settling in it and carrying on their occupations); (for) otherwise there would certainly be a violation of (the privileges of) an agrahāra." The year 9; (the month) Vaiśākha; the day 10.

(Line 15.)—(This deed) has been written by the order of Dyūta-Gōpasvāmin, the Akshapaṭalādhikrita of another village.

No. 61.
UDAYAGIRI CAVE INSCRIPTION.
THE YEAR 106.
Text.

1. Namaḥ siddhebhyāḥ (||*) Srī-samyutānām guna-tōyadhīnām Guptā-anvayānām nripa-sattamānām

2. Rajyē kulasy=ābhivivardhamānē shaḍbhir=yyutē varsha-śatē=tha māśe (||*) Su-Kārttikē bahula-dinē=tha-pamchamē

3. guhā-mukhē sphaṭavikaṭ-ōrkaṭām=imām jita-dvishō Jina-vara-Pārśva-samjñikām Jin-ākṛitim śama-damavān=a-

4. chīkarat (||*) Āchāryya-Bhadr-ānvaya-bhūshaṇasya śishyō hy=asāv=āryyā-kul-ōdgatasya āchāryya-Gōśa-

5. rmma-munēs-sutas-tu Padmāvatāv=aśvapatēr=bbhaṭasya (||*) Parair=a-jēyasya Ripughna-māninas=sa Saṅghi-

6. lasy=ēty=abhiviśrutō bhuvi sva-samjñayā Saṅkara-nāma-śabditō vidhāna-yuktam yati-mā-

7. rggam=āśthitaḥ (||*) Sa uttarāṇām sadṛiśē Kurūṇām udag-diśā-dēśa-varē prasūtaḥ

8. kshayāya karmm-āri-gaṇasya dhīmān yad=atra puṇyam tad=apasasarjja (||*)

TRANSLATION.

Reverence to the Perfect Ones! In the augmenting reign of the family of the best of kings, belonging to the Gupta lineage, who are endowed with glory (and) are oceans of virtuous qualities;—in a century of years, coupled with six; and in the excellent month of Kārttika; and on the fifth day of the dark fortnight;—

(Line 3.)—He who has conquered the enemies (of religion), (and) is possessed of tranquillity and self-command, caused to be made (and set up) in the mouth of (this) cave, this image of a Jina, richly endowed with (the embellishments of) the expanded hoods of a snake and an attendant female divinity, (and) having the name of Pārśva, the best of the Jinas.

(Line 4.)—He is, indeed, the disciple of the saint, the Āchārya Gōśarman, who was the ornament of the lineage of the Āchārya Bhadra (and) sprang from a noble family; but he is more widely renowned on the earth (as being) the son, (begotten) on Padmāvatī of the Aśvapati, the soldier Saṅghila, who unconquerable by (his) enemies, took himself to be a very Ripughna;—by his own appellation, he is spoken of under the name of Samkara;—(and) he has adhered to the path of ascetics, conformable to the sacred precepts.

(Line 7.)—Born in the region of the north, the best of countries, which resembles (in beatitude) the land of the Northern Kurus,—he, the wise one, has set aside whatever religious merit (there is) in this (act), for the purpose of destroying the band of the enemies of religious actions.

No. 62.
SANCHI STONE INSCRIPTION.
THE YEAR 131.

Text.

1. S(iddha)m (||*) Upāsaka-Sanasiddha-bhāryyayā upāsik (ā*)-Harisvāminyā mātā-

2. pitaram=uddiśya Kākanādabōṭa-śrī-mahā-vihārē chāturddiśāy=āryya-sam-

3. ghāya akshaya-nīvī dattādīnārā dvādaśa (|*) ēshām dīnārāṇām yā vṛiddhi-

4. r=upajāyatē tayā divasē-divasē samgha-madhya-pravishṭaka-bhikshur=ēkaḥ bhōja-

5. yitavyaḥ (||*) Ratna-gṛihē=pi dīnāra-trayam dattam (|*) (ta)d-dīnāra-trayasya vri(d*)dhyā ratna-gṛihē

6. bhagavatō Buddhasya divasē-divasē dīpa-trayam prajvālayitavyam (||*) Chatur-Buddh-āsa-

7. nē=pi dattaḥ dīnāra ēkaḥ (|*) tasya vṛiddhyā chatur-Buddh-āsanē bhagavatō Buddhasya

8. divasē-divasē dīpaḥ prajvālayitavyaḥ (||*) Ēvam=ēsh=ākshaya=nīvī

9. ā-chandr-ārkka-śilā-lēkhya svāminī-Sanasiddha-bhāryyayā

10. upāsik(ā*)-Harisvāminyā pravarttitā iti (||*)

11. Samvvat 100 30 1 Aśvayug=di 5 ||

TRANSLATION.

Perfection has been attained! By the Upâsika Harisvâminī, the wife of the Upāsaka Sanasiddha, for the sake of (her) parents, twelve *dīnāras* are given, (as) a permanent endowment, to the community of the faithful, collected from the four quarters of the world, at the holy great vihāra of Kākanādaboṭa. With the interest that accrues of these *dīnāras,* day by day one Bhikshu, who has been introduced into the community, should be fed.

(Line 5.)—Also three *dīnāras* are given in the jewel-house. With the interest of these three dīnāras, day by day three lamps of the divine Buddha should be lit in the jewel-house.

(Line 6.)—Also, one *dīnāra* is given in the place where (the images of) the four Buddhas are seated. With the interest of this, day by day a lamp of the divine Buddha should be lit in the place where (the images) of the four Buddhas are seated.

(Line 8.)—Thus this permanent endowment,—written upon stone (so as to endure) for the same time with the moon and the sun,—has been accomplished by the Upâsikā Harisvâminī, the noble lady, the wife of Sanasiddha.

(Line 11.)—The year 100 (and) 30 (and) 1; (the month) Aśvayuj; the day 5.

No. 63.

MATHURA STONE IMAGE INSCRIPTION THE YEAR 135.

Text.

1. Samvvatsara-śatē pamcha-striś-ōttaratamē 100 30 5 Pushya-māśe divasē vi(m)s(ē) di 20 (|*) Dēya-dham(ō)=yam vihārasvāminy(ā)

2. Dēvtāyā (||*) Yad=atra puṇyam tad=bhavatu mātāpitrōḥ sarvva-sat(t*)vānāñ=ch anuttara-jñān-āptayē ||

3. Saubhāgyam pratiru(rū) patā guṇavatī kīrttis= sapatna-kshayaḥ śrīman(t)ō vibhavā bhavā(ḥ*) sukha-phalā nirvvāṇam=amte śivam

4. a-stabdhā(?)ni bhavanti dāna-niratau chittam niyōji =aikadā (-)ī(- - - -) vachā(?tā)raṇa (. . .)dhiyām(. . . . .)i(-)yām (||*)

TRANSLATION.

In a century of years, increased by the thirty-fifth (year), (or in figures) 100 (and) 30 (and) 5; in the month Pushya; on the twentieth day, (or in figures) the day 20;—this is the appropriate religious gift of the Vihārasvāminī Dēvatā. Whatever religious merit (there is) in this (act),—let it be for the acquisition of supreme knowledge by (her) parents and by all sentient beings!

(Line 3.)—Good fortune; the condition of being a model (worthy of imitation), abounding in virtuous qualities; fame; the destruction of the enemies (of religion); riches abounding in prosperity, births that result in happiness; (and) finally, an auspicious nirvāṇa;—(all these) are not permanent (?), having once fixed the thoughts upon the happiness of making gifts,..............

BOOKS CONSULTED

1. Original Sources

Abhinavabhārati. Abhinavagupta.

Agni Purāṇā.

Aitreya Brāhmaṇa.

Artha Śāstra. Kauṭalya.

Aucitya Vicāra.

Buddha Carita. Edited by E. B. Cowell. Oxford. 1893.

Baudhāyana Sūtras.

Bhagavad Gita.

Bhāgavata Purāṇa.

Bhāvaśatakṃ. Kāvyamālā Series.

Bṛahmāṇḍa Purāṇa.

Bṛhaspati Samhitā.

Bṛhaspati Smrti. Edited by Prof. K. V. Rangaswami Aiyangar.

Bṛhaspati Smṛti. Edited by Jolly (S. B. E. Vol. 33).

Dathavamśa. Edited by B. C. Law.

Daśakumāracarita. Dandin.

Devīcandraguptam.

Fo-Kuo-Ki. Travels of Fa-hien. Giles. Cambridge 1923.

Fo-Kuo-Ki. Travels of Fa-hien. Legge. Oxford 1886.

Fo-Kuo-Ki. Travels of Fa-hien. Beal.

Harṣacarita. Bāna. Washington. 1933.

Kālakācārya Katha Edited by Norman Brown.

Kātyāyana Smṛti.

Kaumudi Mahotsava. Edited by Ramakrishna Kavi and S. K. Ramanatha Sastri. Dakṣina Bharati Series, Madras.

Mahābhārata.

Mahāvaṁśa. Geiger.

Mālatīmādhava.

Mālavikāgnimitra.

Mānavadharma Śāstra

Maṇimekhalai.

Manusmṛti.

Mārkaṇḍeya Purāṇa.

Matsya Purāṇa.

Meghadūta.

Mṛcchakaṭika.

Mudrārākṣasa. Edited by Saradaranjan Ray, Calcutta 1918.

Mudrārākṣasa. Edited by K. T. Telang.

Mudrārākṣasa. Edited by M. R. Kale, Bombay.

Nārada Smṛti.

Nāradiya Manu Saṁhitā. Edited by Mm. T. Ganapati Sastri. Trivandrum.

Nāṭakalakṣana Ratnakośa. Sagara Nadin. Edited by Myles Dillon, London, 1937.

Nāṭyadarpaṇa. Ramacandra. (Gaekwad Oriental Series).

Pañcatantra.

Rāja dharma. Edited by K. V. Rangaswami Aiyangar.

Rājatarangīnī. Kalhana.

Raghuvaṁśa. Edited by Nandajikar, Poona. 3rd Edition.

Rāmāyaṇa.

Sākuntala.

Saptaśati. Hāla Sātavāhana.

Saundarānanda.

Śilappadikāram. Translated by Prof. V. R. R. Dikshitar.

Smṛti Candrikā.

Śṛngāraprakāśa. Bhoja.

Setubanda Kāvya Kāvyamālā Series, also Nirnayasagar Edition.

Tirukkural. Translated by V. R. R. Dikshitar.

Tolkāppiyam. Porulatikāram.

Vāyu Purāṇa.

Vāyu Purāna. Translated by Wilson.

Viṣṇu Purāṇa.

Vyāsa Smṛti.

Yājñavalkya Smṛti.

2. Journals Etc.

Annual Reports on Archaeological Survey.

Annual Reports on South Indian Epigraphy.

Corpus Inscriptionum Indicarum. Vol. III, Ed. J. F. Fleet.

Epigraphia Indica.

Allahabad University Studies. Vol. II.

Annals of the Bhandarkar Oriental Research Institute, Poona.

Annals of Oriental Research. Madras.

Archaeological Survey. Cunningham.

Archaeological Survey Report of Mayurbhanj.

Indian Antiquary (London).

Indian Culture. Calcutta.

Indian Historical Quarterly.

Journal of the Gangānāth Jha Research Institute.

Journal of the Asiatic Society of Bengal.

Journal of the University of Bombay.

Journal of the Bihar and Orissa Research Society, Patna.

Journal of the United Provinces Historical Research Society.

Journal of the Benares Hindu University.

Journal Asiatic.

Journal of the Madras University.

Journal of the Nagpur University.

Journal of Oriental Research, Madras.

Journal of the Royal Asiatic Society.

Journal of Indian History.

Proceedings of the Second Oriental Conference.

Proceedings of the Tenth Indian History Congress, Bombay.

Quarterly Journal of the Mythic Society, Bangalore.

3. Modern Works

Aiyangar, K. V. Rangaswami. *Some Aspects of Ancient Indian Polity* (Madras 1916).

Aiyar, A. S. P. *A Layman's Bhagavad Gita.*

Allan, J. C. *A Catalogue of the Gupta Coins in the British Museum.*

Apte, V. S. *Sanskrit—English Dictionary.*

Banerjee. *The Age of the Imperial Guptas.*

Banerjee, *Public Administration in Ancient India.*

Bhandarkar, Sir R. G. *Vaiṣṇavism, Śaivism and Minor Religious Systems.*

Bhandarkar Commemoration Volume.

Beal, S. *Buddhist Records of the Western World.*

Cambridge History of India, Vol. I.

Chavannes, *Memoirs sur les Religious Eminents*, 1894.

Coomaraswami, Ananda, K.

(1) *History of Fine Art in India and Ceylon.*

(2) *Spiritual Authority and Temporal power in the Indian theory of Government.*

Dandekar, R. N. *History of the Guptas.*

Dikshitar, Prof. V. R. R.,

(1) *Hindu Administrative Institutions.*

(2) *Lalitā Cult.*

(3) *Some Aspects of the Vāyu Purāṇa.*

(4) *Mauryan Polity.*

(5) *Southern India and China.*

Elliot and Dowson. *History of India as told by her own Historians.* Vol. I.

Gait. *History of Assam.*

Gerini. *Ptolemy's Geography.*

Ghoshal. Dr. U. N. *Hindu Revenue Systems.*

Gopinatha Rao, T. A. *Elements of Hindu Iconography*, 4 Vols.

Jayaswal, *History of India*, 150 A.D.—350 A.D.

Jouveau Dubreuil. *Ancient History of the Deccan.*

Kane P. V. *History of the Dharmaśāstras.*

Keith, A. B. *A History of Sanskrit Literature.*

Kielhorn. *List of Inscriptions in Northern India.*

King, Major K. S. *History of the Bāhmani Dynasty.*

Kittel. *English-Kannada Dictionary.*

Dr. S. Krishnaswami Aiyangar Commemoration Volume.

Majumdar, Dr. R. C (1) *Champa.*
(2) *Suvarṇadvīpa.*

Mālaviya Commemoration Volume.

Mayer. *Hindu Tales.*

Monahan, F. J. *Early History of Bengal.*

Moraes, G. M. *The Kadambakula.*

Mukherjee, Radhakumud. *Gupta Empire.*

New History of the Indian People, Vol. VI, Lahore.

Pandey, Raj Bali, *Vikramāditya of Ujjayinī* (Banaras).

Pargitar, F. E. *Dynasties of the Kali Age.*

Ramaswami Sastri, K. S. *Kālidāsa.*

Raychaudhuri, H. C. *Political History of Ancient India.*

Rothenstein, *Ancient India.*

Ruthnasamy, M. *Some influences that made the British Administration.*

Saletore, R. N. *Life in the Gupta Age.*

Sarkar, D. C. *Select Inscriptions.*

Sastri, Prof. K. A. N.
(1) *Concept of a Secular State.*
(2) *Foreign Notices of South India.*

Sinha, H. N. *Sovereignty in Ancient Indian Polity.*

Smith, V. A. *Early History of India.*

INDEX

C

E

F

G

H

L

M

R

S

T

U

V

W

Y